Progress
in
Communication
Sciences

Volume II

edited by

Brenda Dervin
University of Washington

Melvin J. Voigt
University of California, San Diego

ABLEX Publishing Corporation
Norwood, New Jersey 07648

ISBN 0-89391-060-0   ISSN 0163-5689

ABLEX Publishing Corporation
355 Chestnut Street
Norwood, New Jersey 07648

Contents

Contributors

CHARLES R. BERGER (1), Department of Communication Studies, Northwestern University, Evanston, Illinois.

JOHN E. BOWES (51), School of Communications, University of Washington, Seattle, Washington.

BRENDA DERVIN (73), School of Communications, University of Washington, Seattle, Washington.

MILDRED H. DOWNING (299), School of Library Science, University of North Carolina, Chapel Hill, North Carolina.

JAMES E. GRUNIG (167), College of Journalism, University of Maryland, College Park, Maryland.

ROBERT LaROSE (275), Annenberg School of Communications, University of Southern California, Los Angeles, California.

KAREN B. LEVITAN (241), Division of Information Science and Technology, National Science Foundation, Washington, D.C.

WILLIAM PAISLEY (113), Institute for Communication Research, Stanford University, Stanford, California.

RONALD E. RICE (215), Institute for Communication Research, Stanford University, Stanford, California.

MICHAEL E. ROLOFF (1), Department of Communication Studies, Northwestern University, Evanston, Illinois.

Preface

The purpose of this volume—the second in an annual series—is to provide the reader with high quality state of the art reviews of thought and research, with each review focusing on one or more of the following areas of emphasis: (1) information, information transfer, and information systems; (2) the uses and effects of communications; and (3) the control and regulating of communications and information.

Since these foci receive attention from scholars and thinkers in myriad fields (information science, political science, library science, communications, psychology, sociology, anthropology, economics, national planning and development, international relations, and so on), this annual reaches out to tap work by individuals in a wide variety of disciplines using a wide variety of perspectives and epistemological approaches. While in one respect this provides a volume with great diversity and a seeming lack of central focus, in a second sense this diversity and apparent lack of focus is also a fitting and appropriate description of the state of the art, as well as a useful vehicle for cross-fertilization among individuals traveling apparently divergent roads but heading toward a common focus—an understanding of information-communication processes.

In the most general sense, then, this is the purpose of this annual series—to provide the reader in one yearly volume a continuing series of high quality reviews that represent the full diversity of attentions that are being brought to bear to study and understand information-communication processes. The intent is to locate and publish reviews by individuals whose own work falls at the cutting edge of some specific area and whose state of the art review provides the reader with not only documentation of what is and what has been, but insight into what will come as well.

In such a format, there is no doubt that the reader will frequently find contradictions and anomalies between chapters. One author may support quantitative methods while another condemns them; another may cite evidence from one perspective supporting a proposition while another cites evidence from a different perspective contradicting the same proposition. At the same time, two other authors starting from seemingly divergent positions may show convergence.

It is natural to find a rigidifying of camps and perspectives occuring whenever the literatures in related areas become too large and too eclectic to be handled well by the individual scholar. In the past decade, we have seen a proliferation of specialized publications reporting research and thought relevant to communication and information processes. While such specialization has obvious advantages, the disadvantage is that it draws attention away from the search for fundamentals, from the belief that whatever is being studied in a variety of camps under a variety of rubrics relating to information and communication science is fundamentally related despite the surface appearance of eclectism.

In a more specific sense, then, another purpose of this series is to provide a context within which the reader can, not only find up-to-the-minute reviews of a variety of areas that fall within the broad rubrics of information and communication science, but can also, if he or she chooses, search for the divergences and convergences that can only appear when literature is brought together in a manner amenable to synthesis and interpretation.

Our current volume is a case in point. We have chapters focusing on interpersonal communication, others on mass communication; some focusing on technology; others focusing on people; some tied closely to empirical evidence; others taking conceptual journeys. At the concrete level, they look like a diverse group, at best an interesting collection; at worst, strange bedfellows. An overview of each chapter shows the apparent disparity:

I: Berger and Roloff's "Social Cognition, Self Awareness, and Interpersonal Communication" reviews in-depth the research on whether and how people think and pay attention while communicating interpersonally.

II: Bowes' "Mind vs Matter: Mass Utilization of Information Technology" reviews literature dealing with the question of the extent and nature of mass use of the new information technologies, a literature commonly referred to as addressing the "human factors" of technology.

III: Dervin's review, "Communication Gaps and Inequities: Moving Toward a Reconceptualization" studies the literature that has resulted in the formulation of the commonly accepted idea that information technology and knowledge expansion result in some people becoming information poor. This review goes on to show how recent theoretic trends are challenging these long-accepted findings and leading to changes in the very way in which information use is studied.

IV: Paisley's "Information and Work" demonstrates how, in much less than a century, information work has grown from a small set of specialized activities to a dominant economic factor in society and how the complex flow of information now determines the "productivity of industry and even the vigor of science."

V: Grunig's "Communication of Scientific Information to Nonscientists" focuses generally on what is known about the flow of scientific information within and between sectors—science writers, editors, audiences, scientists.

VI: Rice's chapter on "Computer Conferencing" details the present state and future potential of one of the new technologies—computer conferencing, a technology that is now beginning "to take its place alongside established data processing and newer word processing technologies."

VII: Levitan's "Applying a Holistic Framework to Synthesize Information Science Research" provides a description of how information is commonly observed and integrates the literature on information and systems theory into a holistic approach suggesting the application of this approach to science generally.

VIII: La Rose's chapter, "Formative Evaluation of Children's Television" characterizes the state of the art in formative evaluation research as applied to children's television programming from the perspective of mass communications theory and research.

IX: Downing's chapter on "American Television Drama" reviews studies that have focused on the nature of reality that television has presented to the American public in terms of portrayals of men, women, sex, and love in the 1970s.

As one overviews such diversity, the question becomes: what are the intersections amidst this disparity, what does one have to do with the other? The answer requires that one step back to fundamentals. Take, for example, one possible pragmatic concern—a wish to learn as much as possible about how new communication technologies can be used for the betterment of mankind. Taking this question as a starting point, each of the chapters can be viewed in terms of how it might speak to a reader.

Some chapters speak to the question directly: Rice's review of computer conferencing; Bowes' review of human use of information technologies generally. Other chapters provide context. Paisley's chapter sets a broad stage in portraying a society in which information work has become primary work and information technologies do and will play a major role. Grunig's chapter focuses on a specific context—the flow of scientific information in society, a context within which the new technologies play a bigger and bigger role.

Applications of these four chapters are obvious; others are less closely related. Two chapters (Levitan and Dervin) focus specifically on ways of thinking about information and its uses. They summarize literature which will impact the use of new technologies because, in essence, these literatures slowly are changing the nature of the questions which the technologies will be used to answer, the problems which the technologies will be asked to solve.

Other chapters portray some possible features for the new technologies.

Bowes speaks to this issue as does Dervin. The intersection of their reviews suggests that the introduction of new information technologies without improved communication systems will not necessarily better human conditions. Indirectly, other chapters speak to possible futures for the new technologies. Television was once labelled the "new" information technology, the medium that would yield an informed populace. Reviews by LaRose and Downing suggest the extent to which that dream was and was not realized and some dimensions of concern for the unexpected impacts of technological growth.

Throughout almost all of the chapters runs a concern for humans and how they can effectively use messages they receive by various means—via other people, via media, via new technologies. It is a focus that binds the chapters together. Even the Berger and Roloff chapter, which on the surface may appear most disparate, plays an important role in this context. They are concerned with how people attend to and process the communicating that they and others do interpersonally. Attending and information processing are fundamental processes, common to all message processing whether it be interpersonal, media, or new technology message processing. The insights from Berger and Roloff tell us something fundamental about how people use information. When intersected with insights from other chapters (Bowes, Dervin, and Grunig, in particular), we begin to get a picture of how the new technologies are used by people, how messages (transmitted by whatever means) are used by people to create their own betterments, and, thus, how systems can be designed which will allow meaningful use of the new technologies.

This has been one possible cut through these chapters. It is an attempt at a synthesizing approach to an eclectic set of "state of the art" reviews. Since convergences in the fields of communication and information science are currently few and far between, each interested reader will, no doubt, bring a unique perspective to bear and arrive at a different synthesis. This particular example is offered as an illustration of how the reader may use this volume for a variety of purposes. The most common will, no doubt, be for coverage—what's being done, where, by whom? Less common but necessary for the development of fundamental understandings will be the synthesizing function—what's being done in this area that has something to do with what's being done in that area?

This volume has been designed with both functions in mind—the search for coverage and the search for convergence. Each year, *Progress in Communication Sciences* will present 9 to 12 in-depth state of the art reviews as trends in communication and information science indicate a need.

BRENDA DERVIN
MELVIN J. VOIGT

1 Social Cognition, Self-Awareness, and Interpersonal Communication

Charles R. Berger
and
Michael E. Roloff
Department of Communication Studies
Northwestern University

I. INTRODUCTION

Recent theoretical statements concerning the explanation of social behavior in general and interpersonal communication in particular have argued that as communicators, persons are most accurately viewed as active agents who strive to achieve particular goals in social interaction situations. In addition, these theories assert that person's behaviors in many interpersonal communication contexts are not law governed or determined by environmental contingencies as the behaviorists would have it, but are the product of rule following and reasoned choice (Cushman and Pearce, 1977; Harré and Secord, 1973; Pearce, 1976). For example, Cushman and Pearce (1977, p. 351) argued that the *practical syllogism* of the following form is a useful way of explaining why some kinds of interpersonal communication routines or episodes are initiated:

> A intends to bring about C.
> A considers that in order to bring about C he must do B.
> Therefore, A sets himself to do B.

Subscribing to the practical syllogism as a means for explaining communicative conduct carries with it the assumption that in most interpersonal communication transactions persons engage in considerable conscious thought regarding the content and form of their conversations.

The perspectives mentioned above are not the only ones which contain the assumption that persons consciously plan and calculate while they are in social interaction situations. Attribution theories like those of Jones and Davis (1965) and Kelley (1967, 1972) are based upon the general view, initially proposed by Heider (1958), that persons attempt to make sense out of the social environments in which they find themselves. Not only do persons attribute particular characteristics to both themselves and others; they also seek to *explain* their own as well as other's actions by developing *causal attributions* for behavior. Heider noted, for example, that the behavior of another could be attributed to internal attributes of the person being observed, e.g., personality dispositions, or to external factors such as role demands or pressure from others. The theoretical work of both Jones and Davis and Kelley has been directed toward explicating the conditions under which persons are likely to make confident causal attributions and the extent to which overt behavior is considered by observers to be representative of underlying personality dispositions.

All of the positions outlined above are based on the proposition that when persons engage in interpersonal communication with others, they strive for an understanding of the situation and the other persons in it and plan and execute communicative responses in accordance with this understanding.

While the sheer number of activities outlined above suggests that considerable cognitive energy is expended in most interpersonal communication situations, consider the following observations from a number of social commentators:

> They always talk who never think, and who have the least to say.
>
> *Matthew Prior*

> They think too little who talk too much.
>
> *John Dryden*

> As it is characteristic of great wits to say much in few words, so it is of small wits to talk much and say nothing.
>
> *Duc Francois de La Rochefoucauld*

> Brisk talkers are usually slow thinkers. There is, indeed, no wild beast more to be dreaded than a communicative man having nothing to communicate.
>
> *Jonathan Swift*

Clearly, these commentators posit an inverse relationship between loquacity and thinking; those who talk the most are least likely to think about what they are saying.

While the inverse relationship between verbosity and thinking suggested by the above social commentators may be extreme, there have been those who have questioned the degree to which persons consciously control their actions in social interaction situations. For example, Cooley (1922, p. 209) asserted:

> It is true, however, that the attempt to describe the social self and to analyze the mental processes that enter into it almost unavoidably makes it appear more reflective and "self-conscious" than it usually is... Many people whose behavior shows that their idea of themselves is largely caught from the persons they are with, are yet quite innocent of any intentional posing; it is a matter of subconscious impulse or mere suggestion.

Clearly, in this statement Cooley allowed for the possibility that person's behaviors in social interaction situations might be influenced by factors outside of their conscious awareness and that social conduct might not spring from a set of well articulated goals and intentions.

More recently, Turk (1974) argued that within the context of family communication, it may be difficult for both family members and observers of their behavior to specify particular interaction goals. Turk's assertation is based upon his review of the literature concerned with communication and power in the family. Typically, family power is defined as the ability of one family member to influence other family members to come to a particular decision. In view of the rather consistent *inability* of process indices of power, based upon communication measures, to predict decision outcome measures of power, Turk concluded that the "power as achievement of ends" approach to the study of family power is not productive. Turk attributed the lack of consistency in research findings to the diffuseness of goals in family relationships. Turk further pointed out that psychoanalytic theory generally takes the position that persons may be motivated by goals which are outside of their conscious awareness.

Turk's position suggests that persons may not have a clear goal or set of goals in mind before they enter certain family interaction situations. Cooley's observations are relevant to the process of interaction itself; that is, when persons are actually engaged in social intercourse, they may not be aware of the attributes of themselves or the environment which are impacting upon their behavior. Taken together these two positions call into question theories which either explicitly or implicitly propose that when persons interact with others, they engage in high levels of conscious cognitive activity about their interaction most of the time. Moreover, these statements cast doubt upon theoretical positions which contain narratives concerning how persons *consciously reason* during interpersonal communication transactions.

We should make it clear that we are not proposing that persons always enact communication episodes in a totally thoughtless fashion. Also, we are not advocating a return to a behavioristic perspective which carries with it the view that persons are automatons at the mercy of reinforcement contingencies in their environments. What we are advocating is a position which recognizes that under certain circumstances certain kinds of persons do engage in considerable thinking activity prior to, during, and after social interactions with others. However, our position also assumes that in numerous social interaction situations, persons may deploy minimal perceptual and cognitive resources in the direction of monitoring the course of the interaction. In fact, persons may want *to automate* certain interaction sequences so that they can attend to other things while they are enacting these sequences. Furthermore, we assume that persons have finite attentional and cognitive resources which prevent them from engaging in complex, conscious thought processes in all of their daily encounters with others. Persons can and do become too *tired* to think and may reserve their resources for a limited number of significant interactions with others. In short, we cannot assume that persons are uniformly highly attentive and aware of their own as well as the behavior of others in social interaction situations.

Of course, one might respond to the above assertions by saying that much of what is communicated *nonverbally* in interpersonal communication situations is done so outside of conscious awareness and that this idea has been a generally accepted tenet for a considerable period of time. While we would certainly agree with this view, we would go on to assert that even in the domain of *verbal behavior* the degree of cognitive control of speech can be minimal. Persons are able to speak while thinking of something which is outside of their immediate environment and irrelevant to the conversation. These speech performances can be perceived as highly "attentive" by auditors. Moreover, persons are certainly capable of speaking to others while monitoring regions of the immediate environment totally unrelated to their present interaction. Many interactions at communication conventions are carried out in this manner. Interaction participants look past each other while talking to see whether potential interaction partners have appeared on the scene, e.g., a hotel lobby or a cocktail party.

In this chapter we explore situational and individual attributes which are related to cognitive activity during social interaction situations. In the first section we examine the concept of *scripts* and how it relates to the processing of social interactions. We also consider research in the areas of mindlessness, verbal access to mental processes and salience phenomena. The second section explores determinants of objective self-awareness and their impact upon social behavior. The next two sections deal with personality approaches to self-awareness and social interaction and review theory and research on self-consciousness and self-monitoring. Finally, we trace the implications of these research traditions for theory development in communication and consider potential applications of these various approaches in everyday communication situations.

II. SCRIPTS AND AWARENESS OF HIGHER MENTAL PROCESSES

This section examines the concept of scripts and its relationship to the operation of higher order mental processes in ongoing interaction situations. The material has been drawn from a variety of research traditions; some of which have not been linked previously. The general question to be considered is how and to what extent higher order mental processes impinge in a conscious way on encoding and decoding processes in social interaction situations.

A. Scripts and Understanding

While the focus of this section is on the concept of scripts and its relationship with higher order mental processes, it should be noted that there are similar terms which have been employed by various theorists to describe similar phenomena. For example, Minsky (1975) coined the term "frames" to describe knowledge structures which organize generic experience about objects or situations, and Rumelhart (1976) employed the term "schemata" to describe knowledge structures necessary for the understanding of textual passages. We have chosen to employ the concept of scripts in this discussion because it has exerted the most influence on those who are interested in the study of awareness processes in social interaction situations.

Abelson (1976, p. 33) defined the concept of cognitive script as *"a coherent sequence of events expected by the individual, involving him either as a participant or as an observer."* According to Abelson, scripts are learned throughout one's lifetime through both direct participation in event sequences or through vicarious observation. Although each individual has a unique learning history, many scripts are so overlearned by members of a culture that they become almost universal. The basic unit of a script is a *vignette.* Vignettes are events of short duration, which are encoded into memory, that include both an image and a conceptual representation of the event. Vignettes are much like the individual panels of a cartoon strip; that is, picture plus caption, and scripts are collections of vignettes which tell a story. Both scripts and vignettes can vary in terms of their level of abstraction. Features can be abstracted from specific scripts to form more general ones. For example, a child may realize that sneaking a cookie will result in a parent becoming angry and perhaps punishing the child. Over time, similar features of such concrete sequences may be abstracted to form a more generalized crime and punishment script.

Scripts are necessary for understanding certain domains of experience. Schank and Abelson (1977) point out that scripts do not constitute the only knowledge structures that are used to understand the world in which we find ourselves, but scripts are vital for understanding that portion of the world which is represented *verbally.* Most of their research involves the development of scripts which will make verbal stories understandable. Schank and Abelson have developed several computer programs which represent scripts which can demonstrate a kind of "understanding" of event sequences which are given to them as input.

Two studies demonstrate the importance of well formulated scripts for the understanding of event sequences. First, Chiesi et al. (1979) found that persons with high levels of knowledge about baseball terms and principles were better able to recognize informational changes in verbal descriptions of action sequences of baseball games, especially when the changes in the descriptions were of major importance to the outcome of the game. Moreover, persons with high knowledge levels recognized changes in event sequence descriptions faster than their low knowledge counterparts. High knowledge persons were also superior at recalling event sequences which followed a normal order. The differences observed between the high and low knowledge groups were attributed to the superior ability of high knowledge persons to relate successive game actions and changes in the state of the game to the game's goal structure.

In a related study, Spilich et al. (1979) reported that when high and low baseball knowledge subjects were presented with a narrative of one-half of an inning of a baseball game, persons with high knowledge levels were better able than their low knowledge counterparts to: (1) recall information that was related to the goals of the game (winning, scoring runs, etc.), (2) integrate sequences of goal-related actions, and (3) recall more information in an appropriate order. According to these researchers, the recall of the low knowledge persons showed little evidence of organization. By contrast, the recall of the high knowledge group was more coherent with respect to both organization and fineness of description of important events in the game. The superior performance of the high knowledge persons was attributed to their ability to relate the actions of the game to the goal structure of the game and their ability to process sequences of game actions. In general, both of these studies indicate that the existence of a well developed knowledge structure or script facilitates the acquisition, recall, and understanding of a sequence of events.

Schank and Abelson (1977) also introduced the "script pointer + tag" hypothesis which asserted that persons construct a specific memory representation for every activity that is read or enacted. The specific memory representation contains a "script pointer" to the generic script which best fits the activity. In addition, it contains "tagged" actions which are unrelated or inconsistent with the script. Graesser et al. (1979) tested two predictions from this hypothesis. First, discriminative memory for actions that are unrelated or inconsistent with the script will be better than discriminative accuracy for typical script actions. Second, memory discrimination for very typical scripted actions should be zero. These hypotheses were tested by having subjects listen to tape recorded stories containing appropriate typical and atypical actions for such scripted sequences as getting ready for school, going to a restaurant for dinner, and going to a laundromat. Recognition measures supported the two predictions of the study.

There is additional evidence that action sequences which contain unpredictable actions have an impact upon information processing. Newtson (1973) and Wilder (1978) found that when subjects were asked to unitize sequences of actions they observed on videotapes by indicating the beginning and end of each meaningful action, persons who saw sequences in which there were unpredictable actions used finer-unit perception (more units) than did persons who viewed predictable behavior sequences. Unpredictable actions inserted into an otherwise normal actional sequence apparently induce perceivers of that sequence to monitor it more carefully. This shift might account for the superior memory discriminations of the atypical actions reported in the study by Graesser et al. Newtson (1973) suggests that the employment of fine-unit perceptions may be an attempt by observers to restore the predictability of the sequence. Newtson (1976) also reported that still pictures which represented points at which most or all observers indicated the end of one meaningful action and the beginning of another (consensus break points) contained more information than still pictures extracted from nonbreak points. Persons who had not seen original action sequences could correctly arrange still pictures of break points in the proper sequence more frequently than they could correctly sequence pictures taken from nonbreak points. Newtson (1976) argued that persons segment the ongoing behavior sequences they observe by monitoring changes in criterial features from break point to break point. In addition, he pointed out that observers of behavior sequences usually begin their monitoring of the behavior stream with fine-unit perception and if nothing unpredictable happens, they move to gross units of perception with fewer break points.

In view of script theory, the movement of perceptual processing from fine to gross units may be an indication of the employment of scripts for comprehension of the action sequence. At the beginning of the sequence, more attention is necessary to determine what script is appropriate for understanding the actional sequence. Once the most plausible candidate is selected and engaged, *and* the actional sequence continues to unfold in a manner consistent with the script, the comprehender can afford to move to more gross unit processing. Unpredictable actions which subsequently occur may call into question the appropriateness of a script and force the comprehender to look carefully for cues which may lead to the selection of another script or some plausible variant of the present one. While Newtson's work has not dealt with verbal descriptions of actional sequences, the parallels between his research and the scripts research seem obvious and potentially fruitful to pursue.

Abelson (1976) pointed out that *cognitively mediated* social behavior is dependent upon two joint processes. First, a particular script must be selected to represent a social situation. Second, the person must take a *participant role* within that script. Furthermore, Schank and Abelson (1977, p. 67) asserted that, "A human understander comes equipped with thousands of scripts. He uses these scripts almost without thinking." Thus, as regularized social interaction sequences are enacted repeatedly, the social actor *overlearns* the script to such a degree that it can be employed for both understanding and enactment with a minimum of thought. Since a great majority of everyday social interaction situations are highly repetitive, the operation of the script-based understanding is pervasive. This position implies, in turn, that during such repetitive interaction sequences, persons with well formed scripts enact these communicative routines with little thought. The research considered in the next section bears directly on this issue.

B. Mindlessness

Langer (1978) has employed the concept of scripts to support the general proposition that much social interaction is carried out in an automatic and mindless fashion. She asserts:

A continuum of awareness varies directly with the degree of repeated experience that we have with the activity. The more often we have engaged in the activity the more likely it is that we will rely on scripts for the completion of the activity and the less likely it is that there will be any correspondence between our actions and those thoughts of ours that occur simultaneously (Langer, 1978, p. 39).

She further suggests that thinking about the behavior being enacted will frequently destroy the continuity of that action, e.g., thinking of every word we will utter before we actually utter it will disrupt the flow of speech.

Langer and her colleagues have carried out a number of studies designed to demonstrate that persons engage in minimal thought when they perform activities in which they have participated numerous times. These studies are reviewed in Langer (1978). In one of them of particular interest to communication researchers, Langer et al. (1978) reported the results of several experiments involving manipulations of communication content. In one of these experiments, subjects who were using a copying machine were approached by an experimenter who requested that the subject using the machine do him/her the favor of stopping and letting the experimenter make some copies. The experimenter told half the subjects that he/she wanted to make 5 copies (small favor), while the experimenter told the other half of the subjects that he/she wanted to make 20 copies (big favor). In addition, the experiment involved three information conditions. Some subjects were given no information in addition to the request. A second group of subjects were given placebic information, that is, "May I use the xerox machine, because I have to make copies." A third group was given sufficient information, which indicated that the experimenter wanted to use the machine because he/she was in a rush. The dependent variable of this study was the number of persons in each condition who complied with the request.

The results of the study revealed that in the small favor condition (5 copies) there was *no difference* in the proportions of persons complying with the request between the placebic and the sufficient information conditions (.93 and .94 respectively). Both of these conditions elicited higher compliance rates than the request only condition (.60). However, in the big favor condition (20 copies), the proportions of compliance for the request only and the placebic information conditions were identical (.24), while the proportion of compliance in the sufficient information condition was significantly greater than both (.42). These findings were interpreted as an indication that in the small favor condition, in which the subject took a placebic or totally redundant piece of information as equivalent to a reasonable justification (being in a hurry) subjects were relatively mindless. However, in the big favor condition, where subjects had to expend some effort, they became thoughtful enough to discriminate between a reasonable justification and a placebic one. Thus, the placebic justification produced no more compliance than no justification.

In another experiment in this series, secretaries' trash cans were searched for memos to determine whether the structure and content of memos received by secretaries were of any one form. This survey revealed that memos sent to secretaries were generally requests rather than demands. The memos were generally *not signed* by the person sending the memo. It was reasoned that messages conforming to the unsigned-request structure would provoke less thoughtful activity than would memos which did not conform to this pattern, for example, signed demands. Four types of memos were constructed to represent the four possible combinations of the request-demand and the signed-unsigned variables. Each message asked that the recipient return the piece of paper on which the memo was written to a nonexistant room. This message was obviously pointless, that is, why send out a piece of paper if one needed the piece of paper.

The results of this study revealed that 90 percent of those secretaries who received the memo in the usual form, an unsigned request, returned it through the mail, while only 60 percent of those secretaries who received the most structurally deviant message, signed demand, returned the memo. This findings were interpreted as support for the proposition that communications which are *structurally dissimilar* to those which are expected are likely to prompt mindfulness and closer attention to the semantics of the communication. Thus, those secretaries who received the communication which violated their expectations realized the absurd nature of the content of the message, while those who received the congruent message acted in a mindless fashion and returned the memo.

Langer and Newman (1979) found that persons who could recall fewer details about a stimulus person were more influenced by the communication style of the stimulus person than those subjects who recalled more details about the stimulus person. These researchers suggest that the typical social psychological experiment involves the planting of strong stimuli by the experimenter. Subjects who pay attention to these cues and to little else are *more likely* to be less mindful and more subject to direct influence by the stimulus. By contrast, subjects who monitor and process more cues are likely to be more mindful but less influenced by the experimental manipulations. Langer and Newman suggest that *mindful subjects* are likely to contribute more experimental error. In another series of experiments, Langer and Imber (1979) were able to demonstrate that the mindlessness which results from overlearning a task makes persons more susceptible to the debilitating effects of negative labels like "subordinate." This series of experiments also showed that it is possible to ameliorate the debilitating effects of negative labeling by making components of the overlearned task salient to the individual.

Langer (1978) summarized additional studies which provide indirect support for her mindlessness hypothesis. It should be noted, however, that Langer et al. (1978) caution that their use of the concept of mindlessness is somewhat different from Abelson's (1976) and Schank and Abelson's (1977) concept of scripts. They point out that the term mindlessness implies a minimum of cognitive activity, while the concept of scripts allows for a range of cognitive activities. Thus, while script processing of ongoing social interaction might proceed with a minimum of thought as Schank and Abelson (1977) suggest, it is also the case that specific actions which do not fit with the script must be tagged and some degree of attention must be paid early in the sequence to determine what, if any, script is appropriate for understanding a particular behavioral sequence. These processes require thoughtful activity.

After reviewing evidence supportive of the mindlessness hypothesis, Langer (1978) indicated the following five conditions that are likely to produce thoughtfulness in social interaction: (1) When one encounters a novel situation; (2) when the enactment of scripted behavior becomes effortful; (3) when the enactment of scripted behavior is interrupted by external factors which prevent its completion; (4) when one experiences consequences which are discrepant with the consequences of prior enactments of the same behavioral sequence; and (5) when the situation does not permit sufficient involvement.

C. Verbal Access to Higher Order Mental Processes

Another line of research related to the mindlessness studies Langer and her colleagues has been reported by a group of researchers led by Nisbett (Nisbett and Bellows, 1977; Nisbett and Wilson, 1977a,b; Wilson, 1979). Nisbett and Wilson (1977a) reviewed studies from such areas as subliminal perception, complex problem solving, cognitive dissonance, and attribution theory which demonstrated that when subjects are asked for verbal explanations for their behavior, they give answers which indicate that they are not aware of the stimuli which actually caused their responses. Moreover, they summarized evidence which indicates that subjects in attitude change studies will show attitude change on questionnaires but will insist that their attitudes have not changed. From their review of literature they drew three conclusions. First, persons are frequently unable to report accurately on the effects of stimuli on higher order, inference-based responses. Secondly, when persons report on the effects of stimuli, they tend to employ *a priori* causal theories which link stimuli to responses rather than to interrogate a memory of what cognitive processes operated on the stimuli. Third, sometimes subjective reports about higher order mental processes can be correct, but even in these cases they may not be correct because of direct introspective awareness. Rather, when such subjective reports are correct it may be due to a fortuitous congruity between *a priori* causal theories and the actual processes. Thus, when persons are asked why they behaved in a particular way or why they like or dislike something, the responses they give are likely to be based upon culturally accepted causal theories rather than accurate representations of why they behave or feel as they do. Obviously, Nisbett and Wilson's argument seriously calls into question the value of subjects' verbal reports about their mental processes. In general, Nisbett and Wilson (1977a) argue that persons are aware of the *products* of mental processes but are *not* generally aware of the processes themselves.

In research supportive of the above position, Nisbett and Wilson (1977b) demonstrated that subjects were unaware of the effect their global evaluation of a person had upon their evaluations of particular attributes he or she possessed. While the data of this study clearly demonstrated the operation of the halo effect, subjects denied that the effect operated. In fact, in one condition of the study subjects argued that it was particular attributes which influenced their global rating. In another study, Nisbett and Bellows (1977) gave subjects different kinds and amounts of background information about a prospective candidate for a job. After reading the information provided, subjects indicated how sympathetic, intelligent, and flexible they felt the person was and how much they liked the person. Subjects then indicated how much the specific types of information with which they were provided influenced their judgments on the above four factors. Analyses showed that for all judgments but intelligence, there was a low degree of correspondence between the actual impact the information exerted on the judgment and the subjective reports of the amount of influence. In the case of intelligence, those provided with information indicating high levels of academic achievement judged the applicant to be highly intelligent *and* indicated that the academic achievement information influenced their intelligence judgments. Judgments of intelligence and reports of effects for those who received no information about academic achievement also corresponded. While these results might be interpreted as support for the proposition that at least under some conditions persons can accurately report the effects of stimuli upon their responses, the study also revealed that an additional sample of "observer" subjects *who were given an impoverished description of the stimulus factors* rather than a set of detailed information about the target person responded *very similarily* to the subjects given the detailed background information. The investigators interpreted these findings as indicating that the correspondence between actual effects of information and subject reports about effects was due to the operation of an *a priori* causal theory linking academic achievement to intelligence. They justified this interpretation on the grounds that "observer" subjects were not provided with enough information to do any more than operate on such a theory. Most recently, Wilson (1979), employing a modified dichotic-listening procedure, demonstrated that persons who were exposed to repetitions of tones in an unattended channel found the tones to be more attractive than tones that were not repeated. Moreover, persons displayed low to chance recognitions of the critical stimuli. Thus, the affect enhancing effects of repeated exposure to a stimulus were *not* mediated by conscious knowledge about the stimulus or perceiving its familiarity.

Although the findings of the above studies generally lend support to the propositions advanced by Nisbett and Wilson (1977a), there has been at least one critique of both their theoretical stance and their research. Smith and Miller (1978) argue that Nisbett and Wilson have presented too extreme a position regarding the limitations of persons to report accurately upon the causes of their behavior. They contend that several of the experiments cited by Nisbett and Wilson involve between-subjects designs which place subjects in the impossible position of ascertaining the full range of causes for their responses. They argue that in these experiments it is only the experimenter, as an outside observer, who has access to all of the relevant information. Moreover, they present a reanalysis of the Nisbett and Bellows (1977) study which reports *within condition* correlations between individual subject reports about influences and the actual judgment data. This reanalysis indicates that there were reasonably consistent relationships between subjective reports and actual judgments with some correlations in excess of .50. Smith and Miller conclude that rather than asking the question of whether self-reports are ever based upon awareness of higher mental processes, the more interesting question is *when* self-reports will be veridical representations of such processes. At this point, it seems safe to assert that persons can be influenced by stimuli which are outside of their awareness and that even when persons are aware of stimuli which have exerted an influence on them they may deny any such impact and employ some kind of *a priori* causal theory to explain their responses. However, verbal access to higher mental processes may not be as limited as Nisbitt and Wilson (1977a) initially suggested.

D. Top of the Head Phenomena

The final line of research to be considered in this section explores the position that persons frequently form or change attributions, opinions, and impressions on the basis of the most *salient* stimulus or stimuli in their immediate environments with relatively little thought; that is, they respond "off the top of their heads." Taylor and Fiske (1978) have pointed out that experimental social psychology has been criticized on the grounds that experimental situations frequently expose subjects to an intense stimulus and little else. What is made salient determines the subjects' responses. It has been further argued that this kind of situation does not mirror everyday social reality and is somehow unreal. In response to this critique of social psychological experimentation, Taylor and Fiske maintain that the conditions in which subjects are placed in experiments, in which they respond to salient stimuli with relatively little thought, actually are a reasonable construction of social reality. Obviously, this position is similar to those of Langer and Nisbett.

Taylor and Fiske (1978) have reviewed a number of studies which provide evidence for what they label the "psychology of salience." For example, Taylor and Fiske (1975) had six observers watch a dialogue. The observers were seated in such a way that only one of the conversational participants was perceptually salient for them. Observers' ratings of the influence of each of the conversational partners revealed that the conversational partner who was made perceptually salient was judged to be more influential, even though the other informational aspects of the conversation were the same for all observers. In another variation of the same procedure, persons who viewed conversational participants on a split-screen presentation attributed more causality to the conversational partner to whom they were told to pay greater attention. In addition, Taylor et al. (1977) found that "solo" persons within a group, for example, a lone female in a group of males or a lone black person in a group of white persons, were perceived to be more causally prominent in the group discussion than when they were placed in groups with persons like themselves.

McArthur and Post (1977) varied several characteristics of persons and situations to highlight one member of a conversational dyad. In one situation, one dyad member was seated in *bright light,* while the other person was not; in another situation *movement* was manipulated by having one conversational participant rocking in a rocking chair. In both of these studies, it was found that the person who was highlighted was judged by observers to be more causally prominent and less situational than the person who was not highlighted by brightness or movement. Other experiments reported in this study did not produce consistent effects, but the general conclusion drawn from these experiments was that causal explanations for behavior tend to be dispositional when attentional focus is upon the actor; however, when the attributes of the situation are made salient, causality is attributed to situational factors.

Taylor and Fiske (1978) review a number of studies which have examined the relationship between attentional focus and both volume and availability of recall. Their review suggests differential attention may affect the amount of information taken in by the perceiver, such that more attention leads to more intake; however, some studies show no relationship between attention and volume of recall. There appears to be a reliable relationship between differential attention and availability of recall. For example, Pryor and Kriss (1977) demonstrated that stimuli with greater salience were more quickly identified in a reaction time task. It appears that more salient stimuli are more easily accessed than less salient stimuli. In a replication and extension of the Pryor and Kriss (1977) study, Smith and Miller (1979) were unable to eliminate salience effects by encouraging subjects to think about alternative causal attributions for behavior. In fact, subjects who were encouraged to think of alternative explanations demonstrated increased salience effects. Their results also indicated, however, that attribution processes as well as salience effects may operate when verbal material is encoded into memory. The pervasiveness of salience effects does not necessarily indicate that persons are thoughtless information processors who ignore alternative explanations for behavior.

Taylor and Fiske (1978) recognize that their salience hypotheses characterize persons as relatively unthinking information processors who utilize only the most salient cues in their immediate environments to form attributions, impressions and opinions; a picture quite at variance with the notion that persons are rational decision-makers who *seek* a variety of information upon which to make the "best" decision. They attempt to reconcile these two points of view by referring to the work of Schneider and Shiffrin (1977) which suggests a distinction between automatic and controlled information processing. These researchers argue that in the automatic processing mode, appropriate inputs activate a learned sequence of elements in long term memory which proceeds automatically and without the necessity of attention. By contrast, controlled processing is the activation of a sequence of elements which can be set up easily but requires attention and is controlled by the person. Taylor and Fiske (1978) suggest that salience effects are the result of automatic processing, while the more complex attribution processes posited by Heider (1958), Jones and Davis (1965), and Kelley (1967, 1972) are those which take place in the controlled mode. Taylor and Fiske (1978) also observe that reaction time, recall, and scanning measures might be appropriate for the study of automatic processes and open-ended subjective reports more appropriate for the study of controlled processing.

E. Summary

In this section we have reviewed several positions which all call into question the view that most of the time persons in face-to-face interactions communicate with each other on the basis of conscious thought processes which involve definition of interaction goals, choices of a general communication strategy, selection of particular messages, and the presentation of these messages in a style which is likely to maximize goal achievement. Rather, we would argue that the weight of evidence suggests that persons conduct a great majority of their everyday social interactions in a kind of automatic pilot mode, and it is only when the usual sequence is disrupted that they become highly conscious of the ways in which they are communicating with others. In fact, the conscious monitoring of overlearned interaction sequences may actually prove to be debilitating to performance and conscious monitoring requires considerable energy. For these reasons, persons may actually prefer to interact with low levels of conscious awareness.

III.   OBJECTIVE SELF-AWARENESS

Some theorists have focused on the situations that prompt the individual to vary his/her self-focus. Argyle (1969) argues that an individual is forced to focus upon self in the following situations: when being observed by an audience, when feeling that he/she is being assessed or evaluated, when presented with his/her image, when one becomes individuated from one's environment, and when one penetrates another's territory. While Argyle's analysis is insightful, it did not provide an in-depth analysis of what happens when self-focus is created. In this section, we examine the research stemming from the Theory of Objective Self-Awareness. The focus is on the theoretical statements and related research of the original version of Objective Self-Awareness Theory (Duval and Wicklund, 1972), a revision (Wicklund 1975b) and three alternative explanations (Carver, 1979; Diener and Srull, 1979; Hull and Levy, 1979).

A. The Theory of Objective Self Awareness: Version 1

Duval and Wicklund (1972) assume that an individual is limited as to the number of things on which he/she may focus attention. They argue that a person's attention oscillates between two states: objective self-awareness (OSA) and subjective self-awareness (SSA). OSA is "consciousness... focused exclusively upon the self and consequently the individual attends to his conscious state, his personal history, his body, or any other personal aspects of himself" (p. 2). SSA is a "state of consciousness in which attention is focused on events external to the individual's consciousness, personality history, or body..." (p. 2). Anything that causes an individual to focus his/her attention to some aspect of self should create OSA. Listening to an audio tape of one's voice, seeing a reflection of oneself in a mirror, watching a videotape of oneself, or the presence of an audience tends to promote OSA. Focusing attention on a task directs attention away from self and SSA is stimulated.

In addition, OSA and SSA are theorized to create different mediating processes. An individual in the OSA state is more likely to become aware of personal deficiencies and consequently, becomes more self-critical. The self-evaluation process is thought to involve self-perception of one's real self as reflected in attitudes and behaviors, a standard of correctness (ideal self) and a comparison between the real and ideal self. A person focusing on his/her reflection is prompted to think about his/her behavior and attitudes and compare them with their standard of correctness. A person focusing on the completion of a task is distracted from engaging in such thought and comparison processes and consequently, engages in less self-evaluation.

As a result, Duval and Wicklund (1972) predict that people confronting the OSA state should be motivated to (1) avoid the conditions that stimulate OSA, or (2) attempt to reduce a perceived discrepancy between real and ideal self. As originally conceived, OSA is a strictly aversive state to the individual experiencing it.

Duval and Wicklund also focus on the development of processes involved in OSA. Just as symbolic interactionists (Mead, 1934) assume that the self-concept is developed rather than innate, the ability to experience OSA is also assumed to develop through time. As children interact with significant others (particularly parents), they become aware of their own attitudes and behaviors toward an object, the attitudes and behaviors of others toward that object and the difference between themselves and others toward that object. As children become increasingly aware of differences between themselves and others, they become able to view themselves as objects or experience OSA. In addition, Duval and Wicklund argue that with increasing OSA experience, children learn to focus on a variety of dimensions of self. Thus, observing one's image in a mirror may prompt one to evaluate not only immediate physical appearance but a variety of other factors that may be salient in the situation including an opinion, ability, or way of thinking.

B. The Theory of Objective Self-Awareness: Version 2

Wicklund's (1975b) revision of the theory was based upon research findings which invalidate some of the initial assumptions of the theory. Wicklund begins with the same assumption as version 1: a person's attention is dichotomous and may be focused on either self or the environment. However, the reaction to OSA is different: Version 1 predicted that OSA would universally lead to negative self-affect because of the inherent self-evaluation processes. Version 2 predicts that OSA will lead to either positive or negative self-affect depending upon whether the state focuses attention on a positive or negative aspect of self. While Wicklund still assumes that the initial reaction to OSA is self-evaluation, he does suggest that if the evaluation process results in the awareness of a positive discrepancy between real and ideal self, then positive self-affect should result. However, he still maintains that all natural occurring discrepancies are negative and are only made positive by a recent success. In addition, this positive discrepancy is only temporary as the ideal self will increase beyond the real self (e.g., Scheier and Wicklund reported in Wicklund, 1975b, pp. 242–243).

Wicklund suggests that magnitude of self-affect associated with OSA is a joint function of the proportion of time spent focusing on a discrepancy between ideal and real self and the size of the discrepancy.

Version 2 suggests that OSA should prompt two behavioral consequences. First, OSA should create an approach or avoidance response. If the person is prompted to perceive a negative discrepancy between ideal and real self, he or she should actively seek to avoid the cues that create OSA including seeking distraction from focusing on the cues. If the perceived discrepancy is positive, the person will not only welcome OSA but will seek it out. Second, Wicklund argues that only in the case of a perceived negative discrepancy will the person be motivated to reduce the size of the discrepancy.

Finally, Wicklund addresses three theory relevant methodological issues. First, version 2 indicates a move away from the OSA properties associated with being observed by a group or audience. Due to the potential for demand characteristics inherent in group observation, Wicklund has chosen to avoid this stimulus for OSA. Second, version 2 recognizes the research problem of performing manipulation checks on OSA. Asking people if they are self-aware could well prompt the state even in a low OSA condition. Finally, version 2 does not deal with individual differences in self-awareness. Processes involved in self-consciousness (Fenigstein et al., 1975) are not included within version 2.

While version 1 and version 2 of the theory differ, the research stimulated by each is very similar. As such we will focus on the research issues investigated by both.

C. The Relationship Between OSA and Self-Perception

A critical assumption of both versions of the theory is that an individual in the OSA state should be more aware of him or herself. A variety of studies have validated this assumption. Using a mirror and camera to induce OSA, Geller and Shaver (1976) found that subjects in the OSA state took longer to identify the color of ink a self-relevant word was printed in than subjects not in the OSA State. The assumption being that subjects focusing on self had difficulty shifting their attention away from the meaning of the self-relevant word to the color of ink. Fenigstein and Carver (1978) replicated this finding employing perceived own heartbeat as a means of inducing OSA. Pryor et al. (1977), observed that OSA increased the validity of self-reports about various aspects of self including sociability, SAT scores, and task performance.

Research has also related OSA to perception of one's emotional or arousal states. Gibbons et al. (1979) report that subjects in the OSA state were less likely to report being influenced by a "placebo" drug than subjects not in the OSA state. Similarly, Scheier et al. (1979) found that OSA subjects were less influenced by the false expectations about their arousal levels created by experimenters than subjects not in the OSA state. In essence, these two studies suggest that OSA creates greater awareness of one's internal state. However, it should be noted that the OSA state can also increase a person's emotional reactions to stimuli when changes actually occur. Scheier and

Carver (1977) report that subjects in the OSA state rated slides of nude models as being more attractive than subjects viewing the same slides but not in the OSA state; in addition, subjects in the OSA state reported feeling more elated or depressed as, a result of a mood induction procedure than sujects not in the OSA state. Similarly, Fenigstein (1979) observed that subjects in the OSA state were more critical of negative feedback about themselves than non-OSA subjects. OSA subjects tended to respond more positively to positive feedback about themselves then non-OSA subjects; although the difference was not statistically significant. Thus, inducing OSA tends to prompt greater self-perception of attributes such as attitudes, previous behaviors or emotions. In addition, OSA may increase one's reaction to stimuli about self.

D. The Aversive Nature of OSA

Both versions of the theory argue that OSA is normally an aversive state. Initial research by Duval et al. (1972) found that subjects given negative information about their relative creativity tended to avoid OSA. However, other research has provided mixed results about the aversive nature of OSA.

Research by Lefcourt et al. (1975) reports that only some subjects seem to find OSA aversive; subjects who were high in internal locus of control engaged in more nonverbal anxiety behaviors (adapters) while experiencing OSA than when not. Subjects high in external locus of control did not differ between states in their use of adapters although they made more adapters than internals when SSA.

Paulus et al. (1978) suggest that different modes of inducing OSA may prompt different types of anxiety. Subjects performing a task before a mirror tended to experience a reduction in palmar sweat measures indicating increased arousal. Although speculative, they suggest that previous findings indicating increased palmar sweating from audience presence contrasted with reduced palmar sweating from mirror presence, may reflect anxiety due to focus on a stressful environment (audience presence) rather than anxiety due to focus on self (mirror presence).

While people may differ as to the amount or type of anxiety produced by OSA, the central cause of anxiety, loss of self-esteem has not been universally found. Ickes et al. (1973) report that OSA subjects tended to reduce their self-esteem on a series of measures more so than low OSA subjects; although this effect dissipated after the first few items were completed. In another experiment, OSA subjects who had received negative feedback about self tended to lower their self-esteem, while positive feedback about self tended to increase self-esteem.

The type of feedback received by the individual has been a critical predictor of the aversiveness of OSA. Davis and Brock (1975) found that OSA subjects receiving positive feedback about self tended to increase the number of personal pronouns in a task; whereas, OSA subjects receiving negative feedback tended to avoid them. Similarly, Gibbons and Wicklund (1976) report that subjects receiving positive feedback about self preferred listening to their own voice to a greater extent than subjects recieving negative feedback. Recently, Carver and Scheier (1978) observed that the presence of a mirror or an audience tends to increase the number of self-focused sentence completions but does not increase the number of negative self-affect statements.

As indicated earlier, version 2 of the theory has recognized this research and modified the prediction: only the reception of negative feedback tends to make OSA aversive. However, Steenbarger and Aderman (1979) suggest that this generalization may be too broad. Their research indicates that only when subjects receive negative information about self which is beyond their control do they avoid OSA. OSA subjects who receive negative feedback which they believe to be correctable, find OSA no more aversive than subjects not experiencing OSA. Thus, the aversiveness of OSA continues to be a cloudy issue. Under some conditions, OSA appears to be either aversive or rewarding.

E. OSA and Persuasion

The effect of OSA on persuasion processes has been examined in great detail elsewhere (Kleinke, 1978; Roloff, 1980). Consequently, this section will cover basic findings. OSA seems to enhance many of the processes suggested by theories normally used by persuasion researchers.

A critical factor in the persuasion process involves the receptivity to new information. People who selectively expose themselves to information consistent with their current attitudes and beliefs may never be changed. Wicklund and Ickes (1972) suggest that subjects experiencing OSA seek out more predecisional information than subjects not in the OSA state. In addition, there was a nonsignificant tendency for subjects in the OSA state to be more certain that the decisions they rendered would be correct than subjects not in the OSA state. Similarly, Mayer et al. (1975) report that subjects presented with their image prior to making a decision were less willing to change their decision than low OSA subjects. In other words, OSA may prompt information seeking but also may commit a person to his or her decisions.

Since OSA creates greater awareness of internal states, it is possible that the state may enhance the effect of persuasive messages. Duval and Wicklund (1972) pointed out that OSA may be a necessary condition for a person to be aware of internal inconsistency and be motivated to reduce it as suggested by cognitive consistency theories. Indeed, Gibbons (1978) found that OSA subjects showed more consistency between their attitudes and behaviors than low OSA subjects. Wicklund and Duval (1971) observed that subjects in a counterattitudinal adovacy condition were more likely to change their attitude to be consistent with their stated position when objectively self-aware. In addition, Insko et al. (1973) observed that OSA subjects in a forced compliance situation in which they chose to be inconsistent and engaged in significant effort were more likely to change their attitude to be consistent with their advocated position.

Two studies have attempted to predict increased psychological reactance from OSA. Carver (1977) reported that OSA subjects reported greater feelings of demand from threats and tended to change their attitudes in opposite direction of a threat more so than non-OSA subjects. However, Swart, et al. (1978) report greater compliance due to restriction of decisional freedom by OSA subjects than low OSA subjects.

Several studies report that conformity to group pressure tends to increase with OSA (Wicklund and Duval, 1971; Duval, 1976). It seems that feelings of being in the minority and attributing one's minority position to error of judgment is enhanced by focusing on self. Froming (1978) reports that this conformity effect is produced by an interaction between the person's stage of moral judgment, the degree of deviancy and OSA.

In summary, OSA may mediate some persuasive processes by focusing attention on self.

F. OSA and Causal Attribution

Duval and Hensley (1976) focused on the relationship between OSA and attribution of causality to self, others or the environment. In essence, OSA prompts the self to become a focal object rather than a nonfocal object; thereby increasing the likelihood of a causal attribution of self. In addition, by increasing the amount of time and intensity of focus on self, OSA increases the likelihood that the self will be chosen as the causal object relative to other competing focal objects.

Duval and Wicklund (1973) reported that OSA subjects engage in greater self-attributions that non-OSA subjects regardless of whether the situations involved positive or negative outcomes. Fenigstein and Carver (1978) found that subjects who heard a sound described as their own heartbeat tended to attribute more causality to self than subjects who were not self-aware. In addition, OSA subjects who heard a constant heartbeat or an increasing one made more self-attributions. Arkin et al. (1979) observed that the self-attributions of OSA subjects were influenced by both their degree of self-monitoring and the success or failure related to the situation. OSA influenced high self-monitors such that it prompted them to attribute more responsibility to self for successful outcomes than failures. Low self-monitors were not influenced by OSA but when not experiencing OSA they tended to attribute more responsibility to self for successful outcomes than failures. Thus, OSA creates a self-focus which prompts self-attribution but only for certain people in certain situations.

OSA also affects the degree of responsibility attributed to both self and another in a situation. Federoff and Harvey (1976) observed that OSA subjects attribute greater self responsibility when successful outcomes occur rather than failures; whereas OSA subjects attribute greater responsibility to another when a positive outcome of their interaction is expected but a negative outcome occurs.

OSA has been found to influence the attributions of both actors and observers in a situation. Arkin and Duval (1975) reported that in non-OSA situations the usual pattern for attribution is that actors attribute more causality to the situation than observers. However,the introduction of OSA prompts actors to attribute less causality to the situation than observers. Also, OSA actors attribute less causality to the situation than non-OSA actors, and OSA observers attribute more causality to the situation than non-OSA observers. Wegner and Finstuen (1977) have argued that an observer's attention toward another person may have counterparts to OSA and SSA. They found that when observers focus on an actor rather than actor's situation, the subjects tend to focus more on internal motivations than external stimuli for predicting another's attitude change in a forced compliance situation.

G. OSA and Deindividuation

While it is not the purpose of this paper to describe all of the various approaches to deindividuation, a number of theorists have noted similarities between an increase in deindividuation and a decrease in OSA. Diener (1977, p. 145) has noted that deindividuation is accompanied by internal changes such as "feeling indistinguishable from one's environment and reduced self-consciousness, self-evaluation and concern for negative consequences from others." He notes that such changes are often prompted from lessened OSA. Similarly, Dipboye (1977, p. 1059) writes that, "deindividuating inputs have been predicted to release restraints against many behaviors by lessening a person's self-focused attention and concern for how he or she appears to others."

Empirical research is somewhat supportive of the relationship between OSA and deindividualation. Ickes et al. (1977) found that subjects in the OSA state (particularly low self-monitors) made more individuated responses on a "Who Am I" questionnaire then low OSA subjects. In other words, OSA made them more aware of themselves as individuals resulting in more detailed self-descriptions. A number of studies have related OSA, and deindividuation to counternormative behavior. Diener and Wallbom (1976) reported that OSA subjects were less likely to engage in cheating than low OSA subjects. However, it should be noted that Vallacher and Solodky (1979) observed that OSA does not always inhibit cheating. OSA inhibited cheating on a task where success was attribued to luck but increased it when the task success was attributed to skill.

Beaman et al. (1979) found that OSA tends to reduce transgressions from a standard by children. This reduction was particularly pronounced for children whose identities had been recognized and were older. Children who were anonymous or younger, tended to transgress regardless of the presence or absence of OSA.

Johnson and Downing (1979) have offered a slightly different approach to OSA and deindividuation. They found that subjects who remained anonymous or deindividuated tended to engage in anti-social behavior only in the presence of cues indicating that anti-social behavior might be appropriate. Similarly, they also tended to engage in pro-social acts in the presence of other pro-social cues. These researchers suggest that deindividuation due to anonymity and possibly group involvement may reduce OSA and subsequently, increase the salience of cues in the environment for determining behavior. Heightened OSA and therefore, reduced deindividuation may increase the salience of internal cues for determining behavior. As such, deindividuation may not produce counter-normative behavior unless situational cues prompt it.

H. OSA and Behavior

While the previous research focused largely on the relationship between OSA and other cognitive processes (e.g., self-perception, self-affect, attitude change, causal attribution, and deindividuation), some research has focused on the relationship between heightened OSA and a variety of overt behaviors. One of the more controversial studies related OSA to cigarette-smoking. Liebling et al. (1974) found that subjects who believed that they smoked significantly more cigarettes than they should smoked slightly more cigarettes in the OSA state than when not in the OSA state. In addition, OSA subjects tended to engage in a number of smoking related behaviors (puffing, holding, and flicking) to a greater extent than low OSA subjects. Rather than reducing the discrepant behavior, the subjects tended to increase some related behavior contrary to versions 1 or 2 of the theory. In a subsequent debate Wicklund (1975a) suggested among other things that the design was flawed because the subjects were told that the experiment involved listening to music. As a result, the subjects were able to focus their attention toward the music and away from the discrepancy. Liebling et al. (1975) disagreed with Wicklund suggesting that sufficient cues were present to prompt the individual to focus on his/her cigarette smoking and in addition, if the person chose to be distracted from the discrepancy, other easier methods were available but not employed.

OSA has also been examined in relation to physical aggression. Carver (1974) reported that OSA subjects who were told that physical aggression was valued delivered significantly higher shocks to a confederate than low OSA subjects. Scheier et al. (1974) found that OSA induced by a mirror tended to reduce aggression by men toward women but OSA induced by an audience had no effect unless the audience frequently looked the man in the eye. Rule et al. (1975) found that OSA subjects aggressed against another more so when told of the positive value of aggression. This effect was much smaller when OSA was not induced. Rather than focusing on external standards of physical aggression, two studies have examined OSA and internal attitudes toward physical aggression. Carver (1975) found that OSA subjects who had punitive attitudes gave higher shocks than OSA subjects who did not have punitive attitudes. Subjects not in the OSA state did not differ in their shocks based upon punitive attitudes. Finally, Scheier (1976) reports that subjects who had been made angry by a confederate tended to administer shocks of greater intensity when in the OSA state than angry subjects who were not in the OSA state. Thus, OSA seems to increase the salience of standards toward aggression regardless of whether they stem from instructions from an experimenter or internal attitudes and emotions.

Just as OSA has been related to anti-social behavior such as cheating or aggression, it has also been studied in relation to helping behavior. Wegner and Schafer (1978) observed that subjects confronting a situation involving few potential helpers or many victims were more likely to experience OSA. Observers in a helping situation tended to focus more attention on the helper if there were many victims or few potential helpers. Consequently, an individual was more likely to help under those two conditions. Duval et al. (1979) combined an attribution explanation of OSA with helping. Subjects made objectively self-aware immediately before or after a presentation about a social problem tended to feel more personally responsible for the problem and were more likely to help resolve the problem than subjects made objectively self-aware 4 minutes before or after the presentation. When OSA is induced close to an appeal for help, the person will make more self-attributions about the cause and therefore, will increase assistance.

A number of studies have focused on the relationship of OSA to task performance. Initially, Wicklund and Duval (1972) argued that a person in the OSA state will tend to evaluate his performance against his ideal standard for performance and consequently, the individual will increase performance. Their research indicated that OSA subjects performed better than low OSA subjects. Liebling and Shaver (1973) replicated Wicklund and

Duval's findings but only in a task completed with little evaluation. However, in situations involving high evaluation, performance was worsened when experiencing OSA. Innes and Young (1975) observed task completion time under conditions of OSA and evaluation. Unlike Liebling and Shaver, they found that the combination of high evaluation and mirror presence tended to increase performance. In addition, the best performance was a subject who was alone with a mirror especially if evaluation is emphasized; the worst performance was a subject performing in front of a mirror with an audience observing.

Other researchers have examined the relationship between OSA, self-esteem and task performance. Shrauger (1972) reported that subjects low in specific self-esteem tended to perform better in a low OSA condition than in a high OSA condition. OSA had no impact on high specific self-esteem subjects. Brockner and Hulton (1978) observed that subjects high in chronic self-esteem performed better than subjects low in chronic self-esteem in the OSA condition. However, when instructed to concentrate on the task, low chronic self-esteem subjects outperformed high chronic self-esteem subjects. Brockner (1979b) extended this research by examining self-focusing or task focusing in the presence or absence of a mirror. Again, he found that low chronic self-esteem subjects performed better with task focusing instructions rather than self-focusing (OSA) stimuli. Low chronic self-esteem subjects manifested greater anxiety than high chronic self-esteem subjects in the OSA condition but not in the task focus condition. Brockner (1979a) pursued this research by adding previous success-failure. In the OSA state, high chronic self-esteem subjects performed as well regardless of previous success or failure; however, low self-esteem subjects performed significantly better in the success condition than in the failure condition. Interesting, low self-esteem subjects in the OSA/success condition performed as well as high self-esteem subjects in the OSA/success condition.

While not looking specifically at self-esteem, some researchers have looked at the relationship between confidence or expectation of success on task success. Carver and Blaney (1977) reported that confident subjects experiencing OSA by hearing what they believe to be their own accelerating hearbeat tended to approach a negative task more so than doubtful subjects in the same condition. When hearing a constant heartbeat, the groups did not differ in their approach. Interestingly, confident subjects reported thinking more about applying their behavior to the goal of the task when hearing an accelerating heartbeat than in hearing a constant heartbeat. Doubtful subjects reported paying less attention to their behavior and the goal when hearing the accelerating hearbeat compared with constant heartbeat. Carver et al. (1979) reported that OSA subjects with positive expectancies for the outcomes of a task tended to be more persistent in completeing the task than subjects not in the OSA state. In addition, OSA subjects with negative expectancies tended to withdraw from the task more frequently than subjects low in OSA.

I. OSA and Communication

Relatively little research has been reported relating OSA with communication. Duval and Wicklund (1972) do address some aspects of communication. They suggest that at different times during a communication sequence, the communicator may vary between OSA and SSA.

> It is consistent with our analysis that an individual who is actively involved in a monologue will be subjectively self-aware, and that when he pauses, or otherwise contemplates his remarks, objective self-awareness is likely to ensue. The implication is that people frequently will be objectively self-aware when preparing to send information, but subjectively self-aware when engaged in the communication process. There is a second implication. When exposing himself to information, the person who expects to convey that information to others should be more objectively self-aware than the person who simply expects to absorb the same information passively—the reason being that the communicator anticipates focused attention from his audience, and this anticipation will cause him to focus on the correctness and consistency of the material to be communicated (Duval and Wicklund, 1972, p. 172).

Consistent with their first implication, Wicklund et al. (reported in Wicklund, 1975b, p. 256) report that OSA subjects tended to have poorer recall of a memorized speech than non-OSA subjects. As one might expect, focus on self rather than task tended to reduce recall of material related to the task. Consistent with their second implication, Davis and Wicklund (1972) found that subjects made objectively self-aware by either expecting to deliver a message to an audience or having their behavior recorded tended to write more integrated speeches than subjects not made self-aware.

J. Diener and Srull:
Psychological and Social Perspective

Diener and Srull (1979) have suggested that a person experiencing OSA may also judge themselves from the perspective of others as well as internal standards. Indeed, they argue that an OSA person may be more likely to judge their behavior from a social than a personal perspective when both are varied. Consistent with their prediction, subjects in a task, rewarded themselves more when they surpassed their ideal but not the ideal of others in the non-OSA condition than in the OSA condition. In addition, subjects who surpassed the ideal of others but not their own rewarded themselves more in the OSA condition than in the non-OSA condition. Interestingly, OSA subjects felt that they had less choice in administering self-rewards than subjects in the non-OSA condition.

In essence, their approach argues that OSA may have a bigger impact by making subjects aware of themselves from the viewpoint of others rather than internal awareness. As we shall see later in this chapter, Diener and Srull may be arguing that there are two forms of self-awareness. One form of self-awareness may prompt an increase in personal standards whereas another prompts an increase in social standards.

K. Hull and Levy: The Organizational Functions of Self

Duval and Wicklund (1972) developed a model of self-awareness that Hull and Levy (1979) characterized as having four steps: (1) self-focused attention; (2) self-evaluation; (3) affective reaction; and (4) motivated discrepancy reduction. In contrast, Hull and Levy (1979, p. 757) describe self-awareness as the "encoding of information in terms of its relevance for the self and as such directly entails a greater responsivity to the self-relevant aspect of the environment." Information is self-relevant to the extent that it "specifies contingencies related to the individual's present activities or projects." Thus, if the situation prompts contingencies related to other's standards then the person should guide his/her behavior according to those standards. If the situation prompts contingencies related to similar processes in the past, then behavioral consistency should be observed. In addition, Hull and Levy argue that evaluative and affective information can be self-relevant prompting significant self-focus and response. However, they disagree with the assumption that self-awareness is naturally self-evaluative and affect-inducing.

They report two studies dealing with OSA, which support their position. In the first study, OSA females reported more negative self-descriptions when they knew that a female experimenter would see their responses and be able to identify the responses as theirs. In addition, OSA females reported more positive self-descriptions when they knew that a male would see their responses and could identify the responses as theirs. Interestingly, OSA did not affect the responses of females who felt that their responses could not be identified as theirs. OSA did not affect mood self-reports. Hull and Levy interpret this result as indicating that when subjects feel that their responses could not be traced back to themselves then sex of the experimenter was no longer self-relevant and the effects of OSA eliminated. In a second study, OSA subjects attributed more responsibility to self than non-OSA subjects, but again, the effect only occurred when subjects perceived that their responses would be observed by an experimenter and the responses would be traced back to them.

Thus, Hull and Levy (1979) suggest a more complex effect of self-awareness. Their approach requires not only an understanding of what prompts self-awareness but of the cues in the situation that might be interpreted as self-relevant and will affect behavior.

L. Carver: Cybernetic Model of Self-Attention Processes

Recently, Carver (1979) has proposed a model that focuses on self and environmental focus. Environmental focus is hypothesized to involve categorizing stimuli into a person's preexisting recognitory schemas. Self-attention often involves a similar situation in which a person examines him or herself according to a response schema.

While a number of similarities exist between OSA Theory and Carver's notions, some important differences are stressed by Carver. First, both version 1 and 2 of OSA put a great deal of stress on its aversive nature whereas Carver does not. Carver's position states that self-focused attention is only aversive when persons feel that they cannot reduce a negative discrepancy between ideal and real self. Second, OSA Theory posits a motivational drive state stemming from the realization of a within self discrepancy to alter behavior. Carver argues that his cybernetic model does not depend upon such a drive state but instead focuses on the realization that one is in a situation in which a salient standard exists. As a result of the recognition of a standard, a procedure similar to test-operate-test-exit occurs prompting the person to compare him or herself with the standard and under certain circumstances, attempt to reduce a discrepancy. Rather than positing an aversive drive state as a motivating factor, Carver simply focuses on realization as the stimulus. Finally, OSA Theory assumes that when persons encounter self-focus, their initial responses are to avoid the state due to the potential of recognizing within self discrepancies. Carver suggests that the initial responses of individuals are to compare their attitudes and behaviors with salient standards. Withdrawal is only posited to occur if the person develops a negative expectation of being able to reduce the discrepancy.

In summary, two versions of OSA Theory have been developed and extensive research conducted. In addition, three alternatives have been suggested to the theory.

IV. SELF-CONSCIOUSNESS

At the beginning of the previous section, we noted that Argyle (1969) has suggested that some situations prompt individuals to be more self-aware than usual. A variety of derivations of OSA Theory seem to validate Argyle's position. In addition to situational causes of self-attention, Argyle noted that some people are typically more self-aware or self-conscious than others. Again, a number of researchers have found that people do differ in their normal patterns of self-reflection. The next two sections focus on two individual difference measures of self-reflection: self-consciousness (SC), and self-monitoring (SM).

A. The Construct of Self-Consciousness

Fenigstein et al. (1975, p. 522) began with the assumption that people could be evaluated along a continuum ranging from persons who "constantly think about themselves, scrutinize their behavior, and mull over in their thoughts— to the point of obsessiveness," to persons "whose absence of self-consciousness is so complete that they have no understanding of either their own motives or of how they appear to others." Whereas, OSA can be described as a transient, situationally induced state, self-consciousness is a trait or chronic disposition toward self-reflection.

B. Self-Consciousness Research

In order to identify individuals of varying degrees of self-consciousness, Fenigstein et al. (1975) constructed and pretested a 23-item questionnaire. A factor analysis of the responses of college students found three factors of self-consciousness. Private SC reflected a tendency on the part of the individual to attend to one's internal thoughts and feelings. Public SC reflected an awareness of oneself as a social object. Social anxiety reflected a discomfort in the presence of others. The three subscales were somewhat intercorrelated with the no correlation larger than .26 ($p < .01$).

In order to futher refine the constructs, the subscales have been correlated with other personality inventories. Carver and Glass (1976) found that public and private SC were relatively uncorrelated with a variety of inventories including IQ, test anxiety, activity, and impulsivity. Public SC was significantly ($p < .05$) but modestly correlated with emotionality (.20) and sociability (.22). Social anxiety was negatively and significantly ($p < .05$) correlated with IQ (-.21), activity level (-.27), and sociability (-.46). Turner et al. (1978) observed that private SC was significantly ($p < .01$) correlated with thoughtfulness (.48), imagery (.30), emotionality (.21), and self-esteem (-.26). Public SC was significantly ($p < .01$) correlated with thoughtfulness (.22), femininity (.17), emotionality (.21), test anxiety (.20), masculinity (-.15), and self-esteem (-.26). Social anxiety was significantly ($p < .01$) correlated with femininity (.25), emotionality (.31), test anxiety (.23), social desirability (-.23), self-esteem (-.35), masculinity (-.39), and sociability (-.39). As one can see, even though the correlations are significant, their magnitudes are small. Turner (1978c) reports that subjects high in social anxiety had difficulty reporting the self-relevance of socially desirable and undesirable terms.

Private SC subjects only had difficulty reporting the self-relevance of socially undesirable terms and public SC was unrelated to response time. Hull and Levy (1979) found that subjects high in SC (all three scales combined) were better able to recall words they had analyzed previously than low SC subjects. This effects was particularly pronounced when they were asked to analyze the words for their self-relevance rather than length or meaning. In addition, Turner (1978b) reports that high private SC subjects used more descriptors to describe themselves than low privates. In other words, SC individuals seem to be sensitive to self-descriptors.

Some research has focused on the validity of self-reports of SC subjects. Turner and Peterson (1977) found that self-reports of anger and elation were more correlated with actual anger and elation for low public SC subjects than high publics. In addition, Turner (1978a) observed that high private subjects gave more accurate self-reports of dominance than low privates and low public SC subjects gave more accurate self-reports than high publics. Scheier et al. (1978a) reported that subjects high in private SC had higher correlations between self-report of aggressiveness and actual aggression than low privates.

Two studies have investigated the reactions of SC subjects to others. Scheier et al. (1978b) found that high private SC individuals provided more favorable evaluations of a handicapped person than low privates. In addition, high privates evaluated the handicapped person more favorably than a normal person with similar qualifications. Turner (1977) reports that people high in social anxiety were significantly more likely to engage in anticipated belief change than people low in social anxiety. They were more likely to agree with a persuader's announced position before hearing the arguments.

An interesting area of research has compared SC and OSA. While Wicklund (1975b) does not include SC as part of OSA, some similarities exist. Scheier and Carver (1977) found that high privates reported more favorable reactions to positive slides and more unfavorable reactions to negative slides than low privates. In addition, high privates put through a mood induction procedure reported feeling more depressed than low privates. In both experiments, high privates reacted in a similar manner to OSA subjects in similar experimental conditions. Fenigstein (1979) observed that high public SC women reacted more negatively to and were more likely to quit affiliating with a rejecting group than low publics. A similar reaction was observed, in a second experiment when OSA subjects were given negative feedback about self. Finally, Scheier et al. (1979) found high privates were less affected by expectations about the strength of taste of a substance than low privates and consequently gave more accurate assessments of the actual taste than low privates. A similar accuracy of self-report of reaction to slides was reported for OSA subjects.

Rather than looking for similarities between OSA and SC, others have examined their interaction. Buss and Scheier (1976) observed a complex and puzzling triple interaction between OSA, private SC, and outcome of a behavior on self-attribution. When made OSA, high privates made more self-attributions than low privates for negative outcomes than their non-OSA counterparts. However, non-OSA subjects who were high in SC made more self-attributions for positive outcomes than their OSA counterparts. Carver and Scheier (1978) report that a marginally significant interaction ($p < .08$) was found between OSA and private SC on self-focus sentence completions. The form of the interaction was such that low privates gave proportionately more self-focused completions in the presence of the mirror whereas high privates were unaffected by the mirror. Brockner (1979b) found that high SC (all three subscales combined) made more errors on a task than low SC subjects. This effect was pronounced when high SC subjects were placed in front of a mirror. Interestingly, high SC subjects improved their task performance when instructed to focus on the task while low SC subjects were unaffected. When examining the subscales, he reports that high social anxiety subjcts made more errors than low social anxiety subjects. This was particularly true when made OSA. Brockner (1979a) observed that while OSA, SC, and several others variables interacted, the important effect stemmed from the similar influence of OSA and SC when not occurring together. In the absence of OSA, high private SC subjects who were high in self-esteem performed equally well regardless of whether the receive positive or negative feedback; whereas, high private SC subjects who were low in self-esteem performed better when receiving positive feedback than low self-esteem subjects who received negative feedback. This pattern did not hold for low privates or subjects not in OSA.

Thus, the research on SC suggests that people differ in terms of their habitual self-reflection patterns. Individuals who are high in private SC typically experience similar patterns of self-reflection associated with OSA. In addition, subjects who are high in public SC or social anxiety exhibit greater sensitivity to interpersonal cues such as rejection from a peer group or disagreeing with a persuader.

V. SELF-MONITORING

The theory and research examined in this section is the outgrowth of Snyder's (1974) seminal work concerned with the role that self-monitoring processes play in social interaction situations. In this section we first consider the construct of self-monitoring itself and then review research which has examined the role that self-monitoring plays in interpersonal communication.

A. The Construct of Self-Monitoring

In his initial work, Snyder (1974, p. 528) characterized the high self-monitoring individual as follows:

> The self-monitoring individual is one who, out of a concern for social appropriateness, is particularly sensitive to the expression and self-presentation of others in social situations and uses these cues as guidelines for monitoring his own self-presentation.

In later work, Synder (1979, p. 89) described the prototypic low self-monitoring individual as one who,

> ...is not so vigilant to social information about situationally appropriate self-presentation. Neither does he or she have such well-developed repertoires of self-presentational skills. In comparison with their high self-monitoring counterparts, the self-presentation and expressive behavior of low self-monitoring individuals seem, in a functional sense, to be controlled from within by their affective states and attitudes (they express it as they feel it) rather than molded and tailored to fit the situation.

These characterizations of high and low self-monitoring individuals indicate that the self-presentation of the high self-monitor is likely to be contingent upon the situation and the persons in it, while the interpersonal behavior manifested by low self-monitors is likely to stem from internal dispositions like attitudes, values, and self-attributions. This difference in orientation between high and low self-monitors suggests that not only should the behavior of high self-monitors be more variable across different social situations, but that high self-monitors should be better able to achieve interaction goals by presenting themselves in ways that will make them more attractive to others. Since high self-monitors pay closer attention to relevant social cues and since high self-monitors are not locked into a self-presentation based upon relatively enduring internal dispositions, we would expect them to be more effective communicators than lows in terms of goal achievement across a wide variety of social interaction contexts. Lows might be effective in a limited number of contexts in which there is a match between situational demands and their internal dispositions; however, high self-monitors should be more effective in more different situations because of their greater flexibility in self-presentation.

There are some similarities between the self-monitoring construct and the construct of public self-consciousness discussed in the previous section.

Persons scoring high on both constructs are more sensitive to cues provided by others in social situations. However, in contrast to self-consciousness, self-monitoring emphasizes the degree of self-presentational *skill* possessed by the individual. It is one thing to be aware of situational demands, but quite another to be able to present one's self so that one meets the demands. The similarity between public self-consciousness and self-monitoring is evidenced by statistically significant but relatively low positive correlations between the two variables (Fenigstein, 1979; Scheier and Carver, 1977).

B. Self-Monitoring Research

Snyder (1974) found that his 25 item self-monitoring scale had acceptable levels of internal reliability and test-retest reliability. In addition, he reported a slight negative relationship ($r = -.18$) between the self-monitoring (SM) scale and social desirability. Nonsignificant relationships were found between SM and measures of achievement anxiety, machiavellianism, and inner-other directedness. He also reported the following differences between high and low SM persons:

1. Peers judged high SM persons to be better than low SM persons at learning what is appropriate in new social situations, to have better control of their emotional expressions, and to be persons who can use this control to create the impressions they wish.
2. Theatre actors scored higher in SM than did university students, while psychiatric patients scored lower than students.
3. Persons with high SM were better than those with low SM in expressing emotions intentionally in both verbal and nonverbal channels.
4. High SM persons were more likely than lows to seek relevant social comparison information about their peers when involved in a self-presentation task situation.

Although the above differences might suggest that high SM persons are more manipulative than lows, the lack of relationship between the SM scale and machiavellianism indicates that high SM persons do not have the kind of malevolent view of humanity which is part of the world view of the high machiavellian.

Subsequent research has provided general support for the characterizations of high and low SM persons discussed previously. For example, Snyder and Monson (1975) found that high SM individuals changed their levels of conformity in response to situational changes to a greater extent than did lows. Snyder and Swann (1976) reported that the degree of correlation between attitudes and behavior was significantly higher for low SM persons than for highs. When high and low SM persons were placed in a counterattitudinal advocacy situation under high choice conditions, low SM individuals displayed greater amounts of attitude change than highs. Finally, Rarick et al. (1976) found that high SM persons displayed more preferences for behavioral alternatives which conformed to situational demands than did their low SM counterparts. Taken together, these studies suggest that the behavior of low SM persons is directed by reference to internal dispositions; while the behavior of high SM individuals is more contingent upon situational cues. High SM persons appear to be able to say things they do not believe with little impact upon their private beliefs. By contrast, low SM individuals require some degree of consistency between their beliefs and behavior.

In his original studies, Snyder (1974) found that among persons who anticipated participating in a group discussion, who were given access to information about the population from which the group was drawn, high SM persons spent more time looking at the information than did lows. Berscheid et al. (1976) reported that when persons were given the opportunity to observe a videotape of a prospective date participating in a discussion group, high and low SM persons did not differ with respect to the amount of time they spent looking at the tape; however, post-viewing measures revealed that in contrast to their low SM counterparts, high SM persons: (1) recalled more details about their prospective dates, (2) made more confident trait ratings about their prospective dates, and (3) liked their anticipated dates more. Elliott (1979) found that high SM persons spent more money than lows in order to buy information about a person to whom they were asked to misrepresent their opinions on an issue. Geizer et al. (1977) assessed the ability of high and low SM persons to detect intentional deception using videotaped segments of the television show, "To Tell the Truth." High SM individuals were better able to identify the "real" individual. Jones and Baumeister (1976) concluded that high SM persons are more likely than lows to evaluate behavior in terms of its motivational context and that low SM individuals are relatively insensitive to shifts in context. Berger and Perkins (1979) performed two experiments in which persons made paired comparison judgments of the information value of slide pictures of a target person in a variety of situations. Subjects were asked to indicate which picture in each pair provided them with the most information about the target person. Multidimensional scaling analyses revealed that judges used two primary dimensions on which to base their judgments: (1) the degree of social involvement of the target person, and (2) the facial affect displayed by the target person. After making their judgments, subjects were asked to indicate the bases upon which they made their choices. In both experiments, significant positive correlations were found between the number of reasons given for choices and SM (.33 and .45).

Further analyses revealed that among low SM persons, there was a positive relationship between the degree to which the involvement dimension impinged on their judgments and the tendency to verbally mention the use of that dimension. This relationship was absent for highs. It appears that in the case of the involvement factor, high salience was a necessary condition for the verbalizations of the low SM subjects, while for the highs, high salience was not necessary for verbalization. These results suggest that high SM persons may have greater verbal access to some of the dimensions they use when making judgments of social stimuli.

The information processing studies reviewed above suggest that under certain conditions high SM individuals will seek more information when anticipating interaction with strangers. More importantly, however, are the findings which indicate that the highs remember more details about persons on whom their outcomes depend and may have easier verbal access to dimensions which underly their social judgments. It seems that high SM persons have more information available to them regarding those with whom they anticipate interaction. This skill combined with the ability to detect intentional deception no doubt gives the high SM individual a deeper understanding of others and the ability to achieve desired interaction goals.

Snyder (1974) reported that high SM persons are better able to express intentionally various emotional states through both verbal and nonverbal channels. Lippa (1976) had subjects play the roles of introverted and extraverted teachers. He found that the expressive behaviors of high SM subjects changed more when they shifted from one role to the other than did the expressive behaviors of lows. In addition, naive judges' ratings of the performances correlated most highly with the actual expressive behaviors for the highs. Thus, not only did the high SM subjects shift their expressive behaviors more when they moved from one role to the other, but audience members were better able to label accurately the behavior of the high SM subject-actors. These findings, when coupled with the information processing studies, indicate that high SM individuals are not only more perceptually "sensitive" to personal and situational cues, they are also better able to adjust their self-presentations to changes in these situational cues.

In the final study to be considered in this section, Ickes and Barnes (1977) covertly videotaped dyadic initial interactions between persons with either similar or dissimilar levels of self-monitoring. Their analyses revealed that high SM persons were more likely to initiate conversation. Dyads consisting of one high SM subject and one low SM subject displayed more breaks in the flow of their conversations than did dyads consisting of other combinations of SM levels. In addition, post-interaction ratings revealed that the high SM persons in the high–low SM dyads felt significantly more self-conscious than their low SM partners. These heightened feelings of self-consciousness may have been caused by the relatively high frequency of disruptions in the flows of their conversations.

C. Summary

The studies reviewed in this section clearly indicate that high SM individuals are able to control their expressive behaviors in ways which they desire, while their low SM counterparts are less adept in this respect. Moreover, high SM individuals are more perceptually sensitive to situational cues which aid in the development of a definition of the situation and they are apparently more sensitive to changes which act to define appropriate self-presentations in various situations. Because they tend not to be bound to act in accordance with internal beliefs, the behavior of high SM persons is more flexible across situations. These attributes and skills point to the general conclusion that high SM individuals are relatively adaptive interpersonal communicators.

VI.   IMPLICATIONS FOR COMMUNICATION THEORY, RESEARCH, AND PRACTICE

This final section traces some of the implications of the theory and research reviewed in this chapter for the development of communication theories and the conduct of communication inquiry and in addition, attempt to show how the theoretical and empirical issues raised in the chapter impact upon strategies for the improvement or optimization of communication in a variety of social settings. Obviously, these practical implications are more speculative in nature and research needs to be done to determine their applied utility.

A. Implications for the Development of Communication Theory

As has been noted, there are a number of communication oriented theories which carry with them the assumption that in social interaction situations persons interact with each other in states of high conscious awareness about what they are doing and saying. The research and theory reviewed in this chapter sheds considerable doubt on the viability of this assumption. One extreme extension of this position might be to assert that cognitive processes are not at all important in the study of interpersonal communication and that a behavioristic perspective should provide the base from which to launch communication inquiry. Under this extreme view, communication researchers would not attempt to employ cognitive mechanisms to explain communicative conduct. The notion of thinking would be foreign to such theories.

We do not advocate such an extreme response to the theory and research reviewed in this chapter. Rather, we feel that a more reasonable approach is to recognize that the amount of self-consciousness and conscious thought about communicative conduct varies considerably from interaction to interaction. Having recognized this fact, the next step is to determine what variables are responsible for these changes. Langer's work and the research on objective self-awareness both give us clues about the situational factors which might prompt conscious thought processes in social interaction situations. In addition, the research in the areas of self-consciousness and self-monitoring alert us to the fact that persons may be differentially self-conscious and thoughtful about their communicative conduct across a variety of interaction contexts. There may be additional variables such as cognitive complexity which are related to self-consciousness and self-presentation in face-to-face encounters.

Attention must also be directed to the communicative consequences of differential levels of thought and self-awareness in social situations. The scripts research and the objective self-awareness research both demonstrate the impact of thoughtfulness and self-awareness on information processing. Several of Langer's studies showed differential compliance as a function of mindlessness. However, more work needs to be done to specify the impacts that self-awareness and thoughtfulness have on *communicative conduct*. For example, Giles and Powesland (1975) differentiated between *overt* and *covert* accommodation of speech behaviors. They point out that during the course of an interaction, participants may *consciously alter* aspects of their speech to achieve some kind of effect, e.g., switch from one language code to another. By contrast to these conscious speech alterations, changes in such speech dimensions as speech rate, pauses, and accent might take place outside of the conscious awareness of both the source and the receiver. Whether the source consciously or unconsciously alters these dimensions may influence how these speech changes affect the receiver's perceptions of the source. For example, conscious alterations of speech behavior by the source may induce the receiver to attribute more responsibility to the source for any positive or negative interaction outcomes; since the source "knew" what he or she was doing.

Of course, the hypothesis advanced above assumes that conscious alterations of speech behavior can be discriminated from unconscious ones by auditors of communication. Such discriminations would seem to be possible since Lalljee and Cook (1973) found that in the context of an initial interaction situation, speech indicators of uncertainty in linguistic decision-making, e.g., filled pause rate and speech rate showed changes as the interaction progressed. Filled pauses decreased and speech rate increased;

indicating reductions in linguistic uncertainty. However, Lalljee and Cook did not determine whether auditors of the communication were able to discern these changes over time. If these speech changes are generally perceived by auditors, then it may be that "thoughtful speech" procedes in a somewhat discontinuous fashion, while "thoughtless speech," which might be scripted, creates the impression of smooth flowing fluency. Obviously, such differences might give rise to differential perceptions of source attributes, depending upon the particular communication context.

While the above hypotheses are of potential importance, there is an even greater need to develop a theory which systematically brings together the various research areas we have explored in this chapter and then specifies the relationships between these cognitive processes and communication variables. Above we have given some examples of how this might be done and some of the research reviewed earlier in this chapter dealt directly with communication related phenomena. However, general propositions linking cognitive phenomena to communication phenomena need to be developed. Until they are, research in this area will continue to consist of studies which test unrelated hypotheses.

B. Methodological Implications

Not only does self-awareness impact upon the kind of theories that we employ or develop but it also suggests new perspectives about the methodologies we use. Specifically, self-awareness has a direct influence upon self-report validity, demand characteristics, and measures of cognitive activity.

1. Self-Awareness and Self-Report Validity: Why Not Ask Them?

Harré and Secord (1973) have suggested that if we are to study human beings as human beings, we must accept their self-reports as basically authentic. Their suggestion seems to have been well-received by communication scholars. Many communication studies have relied upon self-reports of communication strategies (Miller et al., 1977), communication style (Norton and Pettegrew, 1979), communication apprehension (McCroskey, 1977), and self-disclosure (Wheeless and Grotz, 1976). While we are not advocating the wholesale abandonment of self-report measures, we are suggesting that their authenticity cannot always be assumed. While subjects often provide explanations and descriptions of their communication patterns, our analysis of self-awareness suggests that these responses may only reflect what subjects think they might have done or what seems appropriate for the situation.

However, our analysis does suggest certain procedures that a researcher might use to check the validity of self-reports when behavioral criteria cannot be used. First, research indicates that self-consciousness affects self-report validity (Scheier et al., 1978a; Turner, 1978a; and Turner and Peterson, 1977). If a sample contains a large number of high public SC subjects or low private SC subjects then the authenticity of self-reports might be questioned.

Second, researchers may find that they can use certain methods to increase self-report validity. Pryor et al. (1977) found that inducing OSA tended to increase self-report validity. Researchers may find that subjects will provide more valid self-reports when the conditions under which they provide such information prompts self-focus. In addition, Turner (1978a) and Turner and Peterson (1977) observed that self-report validity is enhanced by asking subjects to report their behavior in terms of what they are capable of doing rather than what they typically do. In other words, people may be more aware of their behavior in extreme situations than in typical ones.

Thus, we are arguing that researchers ought to be concerned with the authenticity of self-reports. Rather than asking "Why not ask them?" the more appropriate question may be "When do they know?"

2. Self-Awareness and Demand Characteristics: Is It Real?

The notion that researchers may create experimental situations that prompt atypical behavior from subjects is by no means new. A variety of scholars have noted the potential difficulties produced by experimental procedures (Orne and Gustafson, 1965; Rosenthal et al., 1966). The perspectives on self-awareness suggest new insights into this problem. Some individuals may be more affected by experimental procedures than others. Given the external orientations of public SC individuals, we may find that they are more likely to be aware of and responsive to perceived demands. Individuals high in social anxiety may be motivated to conform to perceived demands due to fear. Similarly, high SM subjects are sensitive to situational cues and to their self-presentations. Consequently, high SM subjects may be very reactive to experimental conditions and alter their responses to provide the best self-presentations possible.

However, it should be noted that the sensitivity of some subjects to demand characteristics may suggest a new area of theoretical development. Tedeschi et al. (1971) have argued that the tendency to respond to a situation based upon the impression one creates should be considered a valuable theory of human behavior in and of itself. High SM subjects may vary their response to experimental situations, just as they vary their response to any situation outside of the lab. Although not employing SC or SM, Bem and Funder (1978) found that perceptions by friends that a subject was a person who was helpful, cooperative and would strive to be a good subject in an experiment were a significant predictor of attitude change. SC and SM may provide a measure of this cooperativeness in experiments and real-life situations.

Finally, differences in self-awareness may decrease a subject's sensitivity to demand characteristics. Gibbons et al. (1979) and Scheier et al. (1979) found that OSA subjects were less influenced by expectations created by experimenters. Subjects engaged in self-focus may not be as susceptible to the demands of the experiment since their attention is focused inward.

3. Self-Awareness and Measures of Cognitive Activity: How Would I Know It If I Saw It?

Determining a person's cognitive activity level is crucial to assessing self-awareness. However, this process is inherently problematic. Asking subjects what they are thinking about should serve the function of increasing self-awareness whether or not it had previously existed. As a result, researchers have been forced to infer varying degrees of self-focus based upon a number of indirect indicators.

First, some researchers have relied upon methods that logically should prompt cognitive activity. OSA Theory assumes that procedures such as seeing one's reflection in a mirror or being videotaped should induce self-focus. But as Wicklund (1975b) has noted, a direct check on this effect may not be possible. He has suggested that using projective techniques such as use of first person pronouns or self-focused sentence completions may provide valuable indirect indicators of self-awareness.

Second, Langer and Newman (1979) assumed that subjects who could not recall parts of a communication were "mindless." However, this assumption may not always be valid. Some individuals may not retain information about a situation in a permanent memory. Consequently, a lack of recall may be a function of memory processes rather than a lack of cognition at the time.

Third, Langer et al. (1978) used compliance to typical or minor requests as indicators of "mindlessness." While it is possible that an individual may comply with such requests while "mindless" it is also possible that an individual may comply because of some perception of the situation. The person could recognize that the request is minor or is structured in a manner similar to typical requests and obey them. While perhaps not expending a great deal of cognitive energy toward an analysis of the request, they could still be thinking.

Fourth, Slovic and Lichtenstein (1973) have focused on discrepancies between objective indicators of thought processes and subjective reports of thought as indicators of self-awareness. Subjects who describe how they weighted certain traits in making a decision often provide self-reports that differ from the information about their decision-making process derived from a statistical analysis of their decision-making. The assumption of their approach is that the statistical models provide a more accurate reflection of their thought processes than their self-reports.

Finally, a new approach focuses on physiological measures of cognitive activity. Cacioppo and Petty (1979) recently reported that certain physiological processes occur concomitantly with thought. Subjects engaged in counterarguing tended to have increased oral muscle, cardiac, and respiratory activity. If it could be established that certain physiological processes are correlated with certain types of thought then their absence or presence may indicate the absence or presence of thought.

Obviously this problem is a complex one and this short discussion makes no pretense of resolving it. Each of the five measures have their strengths and weaknesses. We should seek to refine those that are most applicable to communication research.

C. Practical Implications

The theory and research reviewed in the present chapter has a number of implications for those interested in modifying communicative conduct. Highly repetitive communication routines take place in both organizational and family communication situations. Given the research reviewed, we would expect persons to become progressively less thoughtful about their own communicative conduct as well as the communicative conduct of others as these routines are repeatedly enacted. This lack of thoughtfulness should lead to increases in misunderstandings; which can be corrected only if persons are made aware of the patterns of communication in which they are engaged. It is also possible that persons may become so minimally attentive to the communication situation of which they are a part that they employ inappropriate scripts for that situation. Of course, these problems are exacerbated within the context of family communication situations because family members may have little energy left after a hard day at the office or school.

While the thrust of a number of interpersonal communication textbooks is toward increasing awareness of both self and others in interpersonal communication transactions, it might also be useful to teach persons to be appropriately mindless in certain kinds of situations. Some persons seem to have the difficulty of thinking too much about even the most routine communication transactions. As a result, they exhaust energy resources quickly and they are judged by others to be awkward. Since there are many everyday interaction situations which deserve only minimal attention, persons should be taught to deal with these situations in a relatively thoughtless fashion. The problem is to know exactly what classes of situations can be so treated and what classes of situations are deserving of greater attention.

Another problematic situation involves learning of dysfunctional scripts. Because of idiosyncracies in socialization, persons can acquire scripts for dealing with everyday situations which are perceived by others to be deviant. Persons who consistently respond to even the slightest frustration with intense anger have acquired such a script. The problem with such persons is not that they are "angry" individuals but that they have automated a sequence of actions for dealing with a particular configuration of situational conditions. The problem here is not necessarily to deal directly with the anger response, but to make the individual aware of the sequence of events which produces the response and how that sequence can lead to another set of responses. From all appearance, child abuse as well as spouse abuse appear to flow from a set of automated or scripted behavior sequences which may be acquired early in life.

Finally, it is interesting to consider the implications of objective self-awareness research for the teaching of communication skills like public speaking. Typically, in public speaking classes, persons are asked to give speeches on which they are graded before audiences. Anyone who has participated in such a class as a teacher or as a student knows of the stress manifested by most students in this situation. Obviously, the situation itself makes persons extremely self-aware; which may have the effect of actually lowering the self-esteem or self-confidence of some of those participating in the class. In other words, such classes may actually produce negative effects for students who are already highly self-aware in either the public or private sense discussed in Section IV. Although it is true that there is "no substitute for experience," it is also true that it may be easier or more pleasant to experience if one has a well developed script for the situation. Thus, it may be desirable to have persons practice developing public speaking skills in environments which do not promote excessive self-awareness so that they can deploy their attention to monitoring their performance rather than to monitor potential audience responses. Presentations to live audiences would occur only after a general public speaking script has been well learned and rehearsed.

In a recent article appearing in the *Chicago Tribune,* super model Cheryl Tiegs discussed the intense communication demands that are place upon well known, public figures. She stated,

> The other night, after appearing on the 'Merv Griffin Show,' I went home and fell asleep. I build up so much tension from having to think before I speak, trying to answer questions intelligently and clearly. A year ago, after appearing on 'The Tonight Show,' I pulled my car to the side of the road and took a nap— exhausted from the mental strain. (*Chicago Tribune,* 1 February 1980).

In view of the material discussed in this chapter, Ms. Tiegs might have a less strenuous time on interveiw programs if she were to develop a kind of talk show script which would allow her to deploy fewer resources for thinking about what she should say. Of course, it is also the case that some public figures might benefit from the closer monitoring of their verbal output; for example, the famous "Freedom in Eastern Europe" faux pas committed by Gerald Ford during the Ford-Carter debates. In short, overlearning may make it easier to carry out behavior sequences, but may also prove to be embarrassing because of inattention.

REFERENCES

Abelson, R. P. (1976). Script processing in attitude formation and decision making. *In* "Cognition and Social Behavior" (J. S. Carroll and J. W. Payne, Eds.), pp. 33–45. Lawrence Erlbaum Associates, Hillsdale, New Jersey.

Argyle, M. (1969). "Social Interaction." AVC, Chicago, Illinois.

Arkin, R. M., and Duval, S. (1975). Focus of attention and causal attributions of actors and observers. *Journal of Experimental Social Psychology, 11,* 427–438.

Arkin, R. M., Gabrenya, W. K., Jr., Appelman, A. S., and Cochran, S. T. (1979). Self-presentation, self-monitoring, and the self-serving bias in causal attribution. *Personality and Social Psychology Bulletin 5,* 73–76.

Beaman, A. L., Klentz, B., Diener, E., and Svanum, S. (1979). Self-awareness and transgression in children: Two field studies. *Journal of Personality and Social Psychology 37,* 1835–1846.

Bem, D. J., and Funder, D. C. (1978). Predicting more of the people more of the time: Assessing the personality of situations. *Psychological Review 85,* 485–501.

Berger, C. R., and Perkins, J. W. (1979). "Studies in Interpersonal Epistemology II: Self-Monitoring, Involvement, Facial Affect, Similarity and Observational Context Selection." (Paper presented at the annual convention of the Speech Communication Association, San Antonio, Texas.)

Berscheid, E., Graziano, W., Monson, T., and Dermer, M. (1976). Outcome dependency: Attention, attribution, and attraction. *Journal of Personality and Social Psychology 34,* 978–989.

Brockner, J. (1979a). The effects of self-esteem, success-failure, and self-consciousness on task performance. *Journal of Personality and Social Psychology 37,* 1732–1741.

Brockner, J. (1979b). Self-esteem, self-consciousness, and task performance: replications, extensions, and possible explanations. *Journal of Personality and Social Psychology 37,* 447–461.

Brockner, J., and Hulton, A. J. B. (1978). How to reverse the vicious cycle of low self-esteem: The importance of attentional focus. *Journal of Experimental Social Psychology 14,* 564–578.

Buss,. D. M., and Scheier, M. F. (1976). Self-consciousness, self-awareness and self-attribution. *Journal of Research in Personality 10,* 463–468.

Cacioppo, J. T., and Petty, R. E. (1979). Attitudes and cognitive response: An electrophysiological approach. *Journal of Personality and Social Psychology 37,* 2181–2199.

Carver, C. S. (1974). Facilitation of physical aggression through objective self-awareness. *Journal of Experimental Social Psychology 10,* 365–370.

Carver, C. S. (1975). Physical aggression as a function of objective self-awareness and attitudes toward punishment. *Journal of Experimental Social Psychology 11,* 510–519.

Carver, C. S. (1977). Self-awareness, perception of threat, and the expression of reactance through attitude change. *Journal of Personality 45,* 501–512.

Carver, C. S. (1979). A cybernetic model of self-attention processes. *Journal of Personality and Social Psychology 37,* 1251–1281.

Carver, C. S., and Blaney, P. M. (1977). Perceived arousal, focus of attention and avoidance behavior. *Journal of Abnormal Psychology 86,* 154–162.

Carver, C. S., and Glass, D. C. (1976). The self-consciousness scale: A discriminant validity study. *Journal of Personality Assessment 40,* 169–172.

Carver, C. S., and Scheier, M. F. (1978). Self-focusing effects of dispositional self-consciousness, mirror presence, and audience presence. *Journal of Personality and Social Psychology 36,* 324–332.

Carver, C. S., Blaney, P. H., and Scheier, M. F. (1979). Reassertion and giving up: The interactive role of self-directed attention and outcome expectancy. *Journal of Personality and Social Psychology 37,* 1859–1870.

Chiesi, H. L., Spilich, G. J., and Voss, J. F. (1979). Acquisition of domain-related information in relation to high and low domain knowledge. *Journal of Verbal Learning and Verbal Behavior 18,* 257–273.

Cooley, C. H. (1922). "Human Nature and the Social Order." Charles Scribner's Sons, New York.

Cushman, D. P., and Pearce, W. B. (1977). Generality and necessity in three types of theory about human communication, with special attention to rules theory. *Human Communication Research 3,* 344–353.

Davis, D., and Brock, T. C. (1975). Use of first person pronouns as a function of increased objective self-awareness and performance feedback. *Journal of Experimental Social Psychology 11,* 381–388.

Davis, D., and Wicklund, R. A. (1972). An objective self-awareness analysis of communication sets. *In* "A Theory of Objective Self-Awareness" (S. Duval and R. A. Wicklund, Eds.), pp. 180–184. Academic Press, New York.

Diener, E. (1977). Deindividuation: Causes and consequences. *Social Behavior and Personality 5,* 143–155.

Diener, E., and Srull, T. K. (1979). Self-awareness, psychological perspective, and self-reinforcement in relation to personal and social standards. *Journal of Personality and Social Psychology 37,* 413–423.

Diener, E., and Wallbom, M. (1976). Effects of self-awareness on antinormative behavior. *Journal of Research in Personality 10,*107–111.

Dipboye, R. L. (1977). Alternative approaches to deindividuation. *Psychological Bulletin, 84,* 1057–1075.

Duval, S. (1976). Conformity on a visual task as a function of personal novelty on attitudinal dimensions and being reminded of the object status of self. *Journal of Experimental Social Psychology 12,* 87–98.

Duval, S., and Hensley, V. (1976). Extensions of objective self-awareness theory: The focus of attention-causal attribution hypothesis. *In* "New Directions in Attribution Research" (J. H. Harvey, W. J. Ickes, and R. F. Kidd, Eds.), pp. 165–198. Lawrence Erlbaum, Hillsdale, New Jersey.

Duval, S., and Wicklund, R. A. (1972). "A Theory of Objective Self-Awareness." Academic Press, New York.

Duval, S., and Wicklund, R. A. (1973). Effects of objective self-awareness on attribution of causality. *Journal of Experimental Social Psychology 9,* 17–31.

Duval, S., Wicklund, R. A., and Fine, R. L. (1972). Avoidance of objective self-awareness under conditions of high and low intra-self discrepancy. *In* "A Theory of Objective Self-Awareness" (S. Duval and R. A. Wicklund, Eds.), pp. 16–21. Academic Press, New York.

Duval, S., Duval, V., and Neely, R. (1979). Self-focus, felt responsibility, and helping behavior. *Journal of Personality and Social Psychology 37,* 1769–1778.

Elliott, G. C. (1979). Some effects of deception and level of self-monitoring on planning and self-presentation. *Journal of Personality and Social Psychology 37*, 1282–1292.

Federoff, N. A., and Harvey, J. H. (1976). Focus of attention, self-esteem, and the attribution of causality. *Journal of Experimental Social Psychology 12*, 336–345.

Fenigstein, A. (1979). Self-consciousness, self-attention, and social interaction. *Journal of Personality and Social Psychology 37*, 75–86.

Fenigstein, A., and Carver, C. S. (1978). Self-focusing effects of heartbeat feedback. *Journal of Personality and Social Psychology 36*, 1241–1250.

Fenigstein, A., Scheier, M. F., and Buss, A. H. (1975). Public and private selfconsciousness: Assessment and theory. *Journal of Consulting and Clinical Psychology 43*, 522–527.

Froming, W. J. (1978). The relationship of moral judgment, self-awareness, and sex to compliance behavior. *Journal of Research in Personality 12*, 396–409.

Geizer, R. S., Rarick, D. L., and Soldow, G. F. (1977). Deception and judgment accuracy: A study in person perception. *Personality and Social Psychology Bulletin 3*, 446–449.

Geller, V., and Shaver, P. (1976). Cognitive consequences of self-awareness. *Journal of Experimental Social Psychology 12*, 99–108.

Giles, H., and Powesland, P. F. (1975). "Speech Style and Social Evaluation." Academic Press, New York.

Gibbons, F. X. (1978). Sexual standards and reactions to pornography: Enhancing behavioral consistency through self-focused attention. *Journal of Personality and Social Psychology 36*, 976–987.

Gibbons, F. X., and Wicklund, R. A. (1976). Selective exposure to self. *Journal of Research in Personality 10*, 98–106.

Gibbons, F. X., Carver, C. S., Scheier, M. F., and Hormuth, S. E. (1979). Self-focused attention and the placebo effect: Fooling some of the people some of the time. *Journal of Experimental Social Psychology 15*, 263–274.

Graesser, A. C., Gordon, S. E., and Sawyer, J. D. (1979). Recognition memory for typical and atypical actions in scripted activities: Tests of the script pointer + tag hypothesis. *Journal of Verbal Learning and Verbal Behavior 18*, 319–332.

Harré, R., and Secord, P. F. (1973). "The Explanation of Social Behavior." Littlefield, Adams & Co., Totowa, New Jersey.

Heider, F. (1958). "The Psychology of Interpersonal Relations." John Wiley and Sons, New York.

Hull, J. G., and Levy A. S. (1979). The organizational functions of self: An alternative to the Duval and Wicklund model of self-awareness. *Journal of Personality and Social Psychology 37*, 756–768.

Ickes, W., and Barnes, R. D. (1977). The role of sex and self-monitoring in unstructured dyadic interactions. *Journal of Personality and Social Psychology 35*, 315–330.

Ickes, W., Wicklund, R. A., and Ferris, C. B. (1973). Objective self-awareness and self-esteem. *Journal of Experimental Social Psychology 9*, 202–219.

Ickes, W., Layden, M. A., and Barnes, R. D. (1977). Objective self-awareness and individuation: An empirical link. *Journal of Personality 45*, 146–161.

Innes, J. M., and Young, R. F. (1975). The effect of presence of an audience, evaluation apprehension and objective self-awareness on learning. *Journal of Experimental Social Psychology 11*, 35–42.

Insko, C. A., Worchel, S., Songer, E., and Arnold, S. F. (1973). Effort, objective self-awareness, choice, and dissonance. *Journal of Personality and Social Psychology 28*, 262–269.

Johnson, R. D., and Downing, L. L. (1979). Deindividuation and valence of cues: Effects on prosocial and antisocial behavior. *Journal of Personality and Social Psychology 37*, 1532–1538.

Jones, E. E., and Baumeister, R. F. (1976). The self-monitor looks at the ingratiator. *Journal of Personality 44*, 654–674.

Jones, E. E., and Davis, K. E. (1965). From acts to dispositions: The attribution process in person perception. *Advances in Experimental Social Psychology 2,* 219–266.

Kelley, H. H. (1967). Attribution theory in social psychology. *In* "Nebraska Symposium on Motivation"(D. Levine, Ed.), pp. 192–238. University of Nebraska Press, Lincoln, Nebraska.

Kelley, H. H. (1972). Attribution in social interaction. *In* "Attribution Perceiving the Causes of Behavior"(E. E. Jones, D. E. Kanouse, H. H. Kelley, R. E. Nisbett, S. Valins, and B. Weiner, Eds.), pp. 1–26. General Learning Press, Morristown, New Jersey.

Kleinke, C. L. (1978). "Self-Perception: The Psychology of Personal Awareness." W. H. Freeman and Company, San Francisco, California.

Lalljee, M., and Cook, M. (1973). Uncertainty in first encounters. *Journal of Personality and Social Psychology 26,* 137–141.

Langer, E. J. (1978). Rethinking the role of thought in social interaction. *In* "New Directions in Attribution Research: Volume 2"(J. H. Harvey, W. Ickes, and R. F. Kidd, Eds.), pp. 35–58. Lawrence Erlbaum Associates, Hillsdale, New Jersey.

Langer, E. J., and Imber, L. G. (1979). When practice makes imperfect: Debilitating effects of overlearning. *Journal of Personality and Social Psychology 37,* 2014–2024.

Langer, E. J., and Newman, H. M. (1979). The role of mindlessness in a typical social psychological experiment. *Personality and Social Psychology Bulletin 5,* 295–298.

Langer, E., Blank, A., and Chanowitz, B. (1978). The mindlessness of ostensibly thoughtful action: The role of "placebic" information in interpersonal interaction. *Journal of Personality and Social Psychology 36,* 635–642.

Lefcourt, H. M., Hogg, E., and Sordoni, C. (1975). Locus of control, field dependence and the conditions arousing objective vs. subjective self-awareness. *Journal of Research in Personality 9,* 21–36.

Liebling, B. A., Seiler, M., and Shaver, P. (1974). Self-awareness and cigarette smoking behavior. *Journal of Experimental Social Psychology 10,* 325–332.

Liebling, B. A., Seiler, M., and Shaver, P. (1975). Unsolved problems for self-awareness theory: A reply to Wicklund. *Journal of Experimental Social Psychology 11,* 82–85.

Liebling, B. A., and Shaver, P. (1973). Evaluation, self-awareness, and task performance. *Journal of Experimental Social Psychology 9,* 297–306.

Lippa, R. (1976). Expressive control and the leakage of dispositional introversion-extraversion during role-played teaching. *Journal of Personality 44,* 541–559.

McArthur, L. Z., and Post, D. L. (1977). Figural emphasis and person perception. *Journal of Experimental Social Psychology, 13,* 520–535.

McCroskey, J. C. (1977). Oral communication apprehension. *Human Communication Research 4,* 78–96.

Mayer, S., Hensley, V., and Duval, S. (1975). "Causality and Commitment." (Unpublished manuscript, University of Southern California, Los Angeles, California.)

Mead, G. H. (1934). "Mind, Self, and Society." University of Chicago Press, Chicago, Illinois.

Miller, G. R., Boster, F., Roloff, M. E., and Seibold, D. R. (1977). Compliance-gaining message strategies: A typology and some findings concerning effects of situational differences. *Communication Monographs 44,* 37–54.

Minsky, M. (1975). A framework for representing knowledge. *In* "The Psychology of Computer Vision" (P. H. Winston, Ed.), pp. 211–277. McGraw Hill, New York.

Newtson, D. (1973). Attribution and the unit of perception of ongoing behavior. *Journal of Personality and Social Psychology 28,* 28–38.

Newtson, D. (1976). Foundations of attribution: The perception of ongoing behavior. *In* "New Directions in Attribution Research: Volume 1"(J. H. Harvey, W. J. Ickes, and R. F. Kidd, Eds.), pp. 223–247. Lawrence Erlbaum Associates, Hillsdale, New Jersey.

Nisbett, R. E., and Bellows, N. (1977). Verbal reports about causal influences on social judgments: Private access versus public theories. *Journal of Personality and Social Psychology 35,* 613–624.

Nisbett, R. E., and Wilson, T. D. (1977a). Telling more than we can know: Verbal reports on mental processes. *Psychological Review 84*, 231–259.

Nisbett, R. E., and Wilson, T. D. (1977b). The halo effect: Evidence for the unconscious alteration of judgments. *Journal of Personality and Social Psychology 35*, 250–256.

Norton, R. W., and Pettegrew, L. S. (1979). Attentiveness as a style of communication: A structural analysis. *Communication Monographs 46*, 13–26.

Orne, M. T., and Gustafson, L. A. (1965). Effects of perceived role and role success on the detection of deception. *Journal of Applied Psychology 49*, 412–417.

Paulus, P. B., Annis, A. B., and Risner, H. T. (1978). An analysis of mirror-induced objective self-awareness effects. *Bulletin of the Psychonomic Society 12*, 8–10.

Pearce, W. B. (1976). The coordinated management of meaning: A rules-based theory of interpersonal communication. *In* "Explorations in Interpersonal Communication" (G. R. Miller, Ed.) pp. 17–35. Sage Publications, Beverly Hills, California.

Pryor, J. B., and Kriss, M. (1977). The cognitive dynamics of salience in the attribution process. *Journal of Personality and Social Psychology 35*, 49–55.

Pryor, J. B., Gibbons, F. X., Wicklund, R. A., Fazio, R. H., and Hood, R. (1977). Self-focused attention and self-report validity. *Journal of Personality 45*, 513–527.

Rarick, D. L., Soldow, G. F., and Geizer, R. S. (1976). Self-monitoring as a mediator of conformity. *Central States Speech Journal 27*, 267–271.

Roloff, M. E. (1980). Self-awareness and the persuasion process: Do we really *know* what we're doing? *In* "Persuasion: New Directions in Theory and Research" (M. E. Roloff and G. R. Miller, Eds.), pp. 29–65. Sage Publications, Beverly Hills, California.

Rosenthal, R., Kohn, P., Greenfield, P. M., and Corota, N. (1966). Data desirability, experimenter expectancy and the results of psychological research. *Journal of Personality and Social Psychology 3*, 20–27.

Rule, B. G., Nesdale, A. G., and Dyck, R. (1975). Objective self-awareness and differing standards of aggression. *Representative Research in Social Pscyhology 6*, 82–88.

Rumelhart, D. E. (1976). Understanding and summarizing brief stories. *In* "Basic Processing in Reading: Perception and Comprehension" (D. La Berge and S. J. Samuels, Eds.), pp. 265–303. Lawrence Erlbaum Associates, Hillsdale, New Jersey.

Schank, R. C., and Abelson, R. P. (1977). "Scripts, Plans, Goals and Understanding." Lawrence Erlbaum Associates, Hillsdale, New Jersey.

Scheier, M. F. (1976). Self-awareness, self-consciousness, and angry aggression. *Journal of Personality 44*, 627–644.

Scheier, M. F. and Carver, C. S. (1977). Self-focused attention and the experience of emotion: Attraction, repulsion, elation, and depression. *Journal of Personality and Social Psychology 35*, 625–636.

Scheier, M. F., Buss, A. H., and Buss, D. M. (1978a) Self-consciousness, self-report of aggressiveness, and aggression. *Journal of Research in Personality 12*, 133–140.

Scheier, M. F., Fenigstein, A., and Buss, A. H. (1974). Self-awareness and physical aggression. *Journal of Experimental Social Psychology 10*, 264–273.

Scheier, M. F., Carver, C. S. Schultz, R., Glass, D. C., and Katz, I. (1978b). Sympathy, self-consciousness, and reactions to the stigmatized. *Journal of Applied Social Psychology 8*, 270–282

Scheier, M. F., Carver, C. S., and Gibbons, F. X. (1979). Self-directed attention, awareness of bodily states and suggestibility. *Journal of Personality and Social Psychology 37*, 1576–1588.

Schneider, W., and Shiffrin, R. M. (1977). Controlled and automatic human information processing: I. Detection, search, and attention. *Psychological Review 84*, 1–66.

Shrauger, J. S. (1972). Self-esteem and reactions to being observed by others. *Journal of Personality and Social Psychology 23*, 192–200.

Slovic, P., and Lichtenstein, S. (1973). Comparison of Bayesian and regression approaches to the study of information processing in judgment. *In* "Human Judgment and Social

Interaction" (L. Rappaport and D. Sommers, Eds.), pp. 16–108. Holt, Rinehart and Winston, New York.

Smith, E. R., and Miller, F. D. (1978). Limits on perception of cognitive processes: A reply to Nisbett and Wilson. *Psychological Review 85*, 355–362.

Smith, E. R., and Miller, F. D. (1979). Salience and the cognitive mediation of attribution. *Journal of Personality and Social Psychology 37*, 2240–2252.

Snyder, M. (1974). Self-monitoring of expressive behavior. *Journal of Personality and Social Psychology 30*, 526–537.

Snyder, M. (1979). Self-monitoring processes. *Advances in Experimental Social Psychology 12*, 85–128.

Snyder, M., and Monson, T. C. (1975). Persons, situations and the control of social behavior. *Journal of Personality and Social Psychology 32*, 637–644.

Snyder, M., and Swann, W. B. Jr. (1976). When actions reflect attitudes: The politics of impression management. *Journal of Personality and Social Psychology 34*, 1034–1042.

Spilich, G. J., Vesonder, G. T., Chiesi, H. L., and Voss, J. F. (1979). Text processing of domain-related information for individuals with high and low domain knowledge. *Journal of Verbal Learning and Verbal Behavior 18*, 275–290.

Steenbarger, B. N., and Aderman, D. (1979). Objective self-awareness as a nonaversive state: Effect of anticipating discrepancy reduction. *Journal of Personality 47*, 330–339.

Swart, C., Ickes, W., and Morgenthaler, E. S. (1978). The effect of objective self-awareness on compliance in a reactance situation. *Social Behavior and Personality 6*, 135–139.

Taylor, S. E., and Fiske, S. T. (1975). Point of view and perceptions of causality. *Journal of Personality and Social Psychology 32*, 439–445.

Taylor, S. E., and Fiske, S. T. (1978). Salience, attention, and attribution: Top of the head phenomena. *Advances in Experimental Social Psychology 11*, 249–288.

Taylor, S. E., Fiske, S. T., Close, M., Anderson, C., and Ruderman, A. (1977). "Solo status as a psychological variable: The power of being distinctive." (Unpublished manuscript, Harvard University.)

Tedeschi, J. T., Schlenker, B. R., and Bonoma, T. V. (1971). Cognitive dissonance: Private ratiocination or public spectacle. *American Psychologist 26*, 685–695.

Turk, J. L. (1974). Power as the achievement of ends: A problematic approach in family and small group research. *Family Process 13*, 39–52.

Turner, R. G. (1977). Self-consciousness and anticipatory belief change. *Personality and Social Psychology Bulletin 3*, 438–441.

Turner, R. G. (1978a). Consistency, self-consciousness, and the predictive validity of typical and maximal personality measures. *Journal of Research in Personality 12*, 117–132.

Turner, R. G. (1978b). Effects of differential request procedures and self-consciousness on trait attributions. *Journal of Research in Personality 12*, 431–438.

Turner, R. G. (1978c). Self-consciousness and speed of processing self-relevant information. *Personality and Social Psychology Bulletin 4*, 456–460.

Turner, R. G., and Peterson, M. (1977). Public and private self-consciousness and emotional expressivity. *Journal of Consulting and Clinical Psychology 45*, 490–491.

Turner, R. G., Scheier, M. F., Carver, C. S., and Ickes, W. (1978). Correlates of self-consciousness. *Journal of Personality Assessment 42*, 285–289.

Vallacher, R. R., and Solodky, M. (1979). Objective self-awareness, standards of evaluation, and moral behavior. *Journal of Experimental Social Psychology 15*, 254–262.

Wegner, D. M., and Finstuen, K. (1977). Observers' focus of attention in the simulation of self-perception. *Journal of Personality and Social Psychology 35*, 56–62.

Wegner, D. M., and Schaefer, D. (1978). The concentration of responsibility: An objective self-awareness analysis of group size effects in helping situations. *Journal of Personality and Social Psychology 36*, 147–155.

Wheeless, L. R., and Grotz, J. (1976). Conceptualizing and measuring self-disclosure. *Human Communication Research 2*, 338–346.

Wicklund, R. A. (1975a). Discrepancy reduction or attempted distraction? A reply to Liebling, Seiler, and Shaver. *Journal of Experimental Social Psychology 11*, 78–81.

Wicklund, R. A. (1975b). Objective self-awareness. *Advances in Experimental Social Psychology 8*, 233–277.

Wicklund, R. A., and Duval, S. (1971). Opinion change and performance facilitation as a result of objective self-awareness. *Journal of Experimental Social Psychology 7*, 319–342.

Wicklund, R. A., and Ickes, W. (1972). The effect of objective self-awareness on predecisional exposure to information. *Journal of Experimental Social Psychology 8*, 378–387.

Wilder, D. A. (1978). Effect of predictability on units of perception and attribution. *Personality and Social Psychology Bulletin 4*, 281–284.

Wilson, W. R. (1979). Feeling more than we can know: Exposure effects without learning. *Journal of Personality and Social Psychology 37*, 811–821.

2 Mind vs. Matter— Mass Utilization of Information Technology

John E. Bowes
School of Communications
University of Washington

I. INTRODUCTION

Considerable progress has been made over the past decade in the technologies of information science. In enthusiastic moments, our view of these developments warms to a future of multiservice systems and interactive information utilities offering quick answers to difficult questions. Technologically, this future is being realized as experiments in interactive media are being extended to homes in a half-dozen nations (*Intermedia,* 1979, p.3). Beyond the attraction of a profitable new industry is a substantial idealism by governments and social planners in the quality of life improvements such systems may bring:

- New technologies will extend information resources to the places they are needed, when they are needed, in a form that is tailored to the users' needs and skill levels. Compared to traditional media or libraries, the effort of searching and selecting out pertinent information in a form that can be used and understood will be greatly improved (Martin and Norman, 1970 p. 48).
- The level of information, hence life quality, will be enhanced throughout all sectors of society. Widely available, low cost information resources will bring a uniformity of access which significantly surpasses present technologies. There is in this at least the suggestion that especially the informationally and educationally disadvantaged will gain because of these innovations (Chen, 1977).

II. PRESENT REALITIES AND THE GAP

Realities, as presently understood, are less encouraging. Recent research on the effects of traditional media is beginning to show, for example, that higher levels of information input from such technologies may result in comparative deprivation. The rate of gain from technological improvements, while it may possibly help the disadvantaged, is occuring at a far greater pace for the educated (Donohue et al., 1975). This differentiation has and will continue to be traced to relative deprivation in power, both individually and collectively among the information poor (Katzman, 1974; Parker and Dunn, 1972). Others (Conrath and Thompson, 1973), have criticized the economic basis which often justify information technologies because of the social values they ignore. Concerns such is this provide a somber contretemps to enthusiasm over advances in information technologies.

This chapter examines research on social and behavioral questions in the mass use of these technologies. In doing so, the goal is to find common conceptual themes. Some simplifications are necessary, given the range of material it is possible to cover. Policy and regulatory questions, ethical problems, and the role of "new" media in relationship to old are vital concerns (see Parker, 1973). But the present focus is confined to "human factors" in the use of new technologies as predictors of mass use *potential*. This represents the ultimate constraint on what is possible.

Historically, several well-known trends have heightened expectation that new information technologies would provide better solutions to mass information needs:

- The development of high capacity, low-cost computing equipment to electronically manage the accelerating growth of information. Access, processor speed, cost, and size have improved exponentially over the past 25 years. Sophisticated information techniques are affordable by all but the smallest business or institution (Baer, 1978; Harkins, 1972).

- Convergence of function in information processing equipment. The once separate functions of (a) data base management, (b) mail, (c) word processing, and (d) data processing increasingly share the same system and are interdependent. For example, financial reports can be generated from an organization's transaction records in the data base, analyzed by acounting routines (data processing), be prepared and edited (word processing), and sent out (electronic mail). These developments are increasingly commonplace in the commercial and governmental sectors (Johansen, et al., 1979, p. 17ff).

- Improvements in switched networks. Intelligent communications networks which allow high speed data transmission at low cost make possible interconnection of data bases and other resources. Packet switching and satellite transmission have largely removed distance as a cost component. Local cable television systems provide wide-band interconnect potential capable of handling complex, high speed signals for household distribution (see Robinson, 1978; Sackman, 1971; Sackman and Citrenbaum, 1972).

- Experimentation with information utilities: Beginning with the development of Prestel (now Viewdata) in Britain, the concept of home terminal access to vast quantities of information as a profitable venture has attracted wide interest (Ford, 1980; Tyler, 1978). Experiments and trial systems are now being constructed in better than a half dozen Western nations and Japan (Edelstein et al., 1978; *Intermedia,* 1979, p. 3; Tomita, 1979). There is expectation among several of these governments that such systems will substantially improve the life quality of their citizens. Educators, news media, business data providers, pay-tv entertainment firms, post offices, public utilities all see such systems as important in the future evolution of their enterprises (Madnick, 1977).

- The increasing availability of basic social and economic data in machine readible form. Far before commercial potential was seen in the mass market for "information utilities," the advantage of machine-based record keeping, transmission, and compilation meant that much useful data was in a form that could be easily transmitted or reformatted for new clientele. Government agencies, financial and educational institutions, newspapers and wire services have been quick to use technology to manage information and its growth (Lave et al., 1978).
- The large amounts of data generated by complex organizations. This bulk combined with changing situations for its use have altered the pre1960s problem of mere information sufficiency, into one of managing potential overload. This situation presents growing problems in managing *selective* use of *appropriate* information (Bowes, 1975; Katz and Kahn, 1966, pp. 223–258). As manual search and selection methods have proven too slow to keep pace with mounting information, computer technology has taken up the slack. In doing so, however, the problem of overload becomes replaced by the problems of operating technologies (Morris, 1972).
- The advent of "personal" computers for the mass market. The gaining power, reliability, and low cost of microprocessors together with lower costs peripherals (terminals, memory, and communications) make personal computers practical. Consumer electronics firms such as Radio Shack, Texas Instruments, Mattell, RCA, and Zenith now sell computers and software through thousands of stores well within the price range of major household appliances (Caulkins, 1978).

Has the general public realized the needs these technologies were created to satisfy? It is difficult to track this with precision, as new technologies and the access afforded by lower costs enlarge the pool of potential users monthly. But speculation has rarely been in short supply.

III. FORECASTS

In the 1960s, a wave of optimism was built on the high potential seen for cable television as it moved from rural towns to major metropolitan markets. The home television was to become a medium for many services extending well beyond traditional programming fare. Combined with this movement were the quickening developments in high technologies spurred by aerospace advances. But disillusionment came in the mid 1970s as expectation and reality remained apart. Users of information technologies continued to be the well-educated and innovative, employing the capabilities of the technology for scientific or business use. Innovative cable television uses were to remain speculative, not operational, due to a host of regulatory, financial, and bureaucratic problems (Branscomb, 1975; Price, 1974).

The most recent surge of optimism began with the availability of microprocessors in 1975. As costs declined and capabilities increased, established consumer manufacturers began to develop simple-to-use (turn–key) computers for public consumption. The same innovations also permitted low cost, two-way data communications between households and central computers for a variety of services. By 1979 cable television services had been extended to 15 million subscribers, about a third of whom now take pay TV services. Only a handful of the 4,000 systems in place, however, currently provide the extensive services state-of-the-art technology permits (Schmidt, 1979).

The lesson in this recent history is caution in the quick acceptance of forecasts. Each recent wave of enthusiasm has been built largely on mass application of state-of-the-art *technology*, not the public's unmet needs or readyness to invest and train in the use of new media. Adoption of sophisticated in-home information technology is almost entirely experimental (as we will soon discuss) and has not met either marketplace or mass use tests.

IV.   RESEARCH TRADITIONS AND APPLICATIONS

New information technologies have short but active research traditions which can be classified according to application: (a) special services to the community, providing such capabilities as communication among the elderly (Moss, 1978), "audio books" for the blind (Steen, 1978) and workplace training for firefighters (Baldwin et al, 1978); (b) economic analysis, demonstrating information as a national economic force or the impact of new upon old information technologies (Machlup, 1962; Porat, 1977); (c) administrative studies, concerned with the role of information technologies in meeting national goals or the regulatory and policy problems they create (Bowes, 1979; Edelstein et al., 1978; Japan Computer Usage Development Institute, 1972; Takasaki, 1977); and (d) futurist's work concerned with making predictions of new technologies and their utilization based upon present trends (Harkins, 1972).

A comparatively slight fraction of this work builds a conceptual basis for understanding social and behavioral problems in mass use of information technologies. Applied engineering design research, marketing studies, and theoretical work in artifical intelligence vie side-by-side as relevant scholarship, but with little that is encompassing. Fortunately, there are several common themes, which, while not affording conceptual integration, do suggest some common purpose to the research and the seeds for organization:

A. Public Opinion Toward Information Technology

A major national survey of attitudes towards computer technology (American Federation of Information Processing Societies and *Time*, 1971) showed ambivalent, contradictory findings. Over half those interviewed believed they were becoming too dependent on computers and too dehumanized by them. Yet, three-quarters of the respondents felt information technologies improved their life. Not surprisingly, favorable respondents were higher income, better educated. For most respondents, direct experience with computers consisted of the more formidable aspects of billing, bank statements, credit cards, and mailing lists. Few had experienced computer assisted instruction or recognized assistance given them by computer retrieved employment information or poison control data. Less than half, for example, thought computer assisted instruction should be expanded. Fewer than 10 percent had any regular contact with computing equipment at all.

Beyond the few studies of this type, what remain are anecdotal accounts of horrors—real and imagined—suffered from computers to visionary speculation on their benefits. Questions of privacy, computer errors, depersonalization, and job obsolescence are commonplace themes which are often found together with highly speculative accounts of push button lives filled with automated convenience (Martin and Norman, 1970). This mix of unfamiliarity, awe and distrust suggests that information technologies like most innovations with little compatibility with existing public experience, will have difficulty in quickly finding widespread acceptance. By contrast, the well-educated and scientifically literate have repeatedly shown their ability to avoid superstitious or naive views of new technologies (Rogers, 1971).

B. Managing Information

The era of informational abundance has brought repeated fears of overload; that more available information will not yield greater benefit but will overwhelm and confuse instead. On one hand, this prospect has encouraged work in system design and programming techniques which allow one to easily segment and sort large data sets (see Shneiderman, 1979). On the other, it has prompted study into human cognition and decision-making mechanisms for handling information in problem-solving (Bruner, 1966; Hunt, 1973). The literature of either area is large indeed. The difficulty is the intersect of the two: little research beyond mere anecdote relates information system structure to how people use and process information.

Overload hypotheses are predicated on the notion that humans have a limited capacity to process and store information. And while there is a tradition of research to improve these capacities, individual differences cannot be erased or the individual's capacity indefinitely extended (Miller, 1956). As Katzman (1974) points out, individual differences would eventually disappear if "information rich" individuals achieved full use of new communication technology, allowing the "poor" to catch up. But this never happens as the capacity of even present information technologies is enormous, compared to the individual, and as new technologies create fresh gaps before the old ones close.

Much effort in human interface design is devoted to lessening the advantage to the skilled user by engineering information systems to be "approachable" by novices. Adjustments of both hardware and software are made to meet several goals (see Gaines and Facey, 1975; Holt and Stevenson, 1977; Kennedy, 1974; Shneiderman, 1979; Turoff et al., 1978):

- Familiarity: Can the technology be made to resemble a more traditional and familiar information source? Metaphore, for example, is frequently invoked to make word processing terminals appear to be mere typewriters, with illusory "carriages" and "typebars." Is there a "social quality" or conversationlike character to the machine's interaction?

- Decomposition into small steps: Can complexity be coped with by breaking down tasks into a hierarchy of small, easy-to-make decisions, which, hopefully, anyone can handle?

- Modality: Can several sensory channels be used—audio, graphics, and text, for example, to simultaneously reinforce the information presented?

- Feedback and error handling: Can the system be designed to be "forgiving?" Errors, when made, ideally prompt understandable instructions to fix matters. In practice, designers are forced by the complexity and machine overhead of error handling into restricting the amount of resources devoted to it.

- Closure and confirmation is a necessary part of computer interaction on a step-by-step basis. Incremental indications of proper operation of the system reinforce the user and his sense of control.

- Responsiveness: There is growing awareness that the time taken by an information system to respond or allow new input is quite important. Prompting by a system which is too fast may panic or press users into ill-considered decisions. Response which is late, particularly for simple demands, can frustrate in the same way sticking typewriter keys do.

- Constancy and expectation: Does a system behave in a consistent manner, regardless of its workload or other transient conditions of operation?

- Rate: Can the user speed or slow the rate of interaction with the system so the pace of each is synchronized?
- Position or stage: Can the user tell where he or she is in a complex series of processes? Are actions reversible by step or must the user start from the beginning again?
- Flexibility: The user should be able to accomplish what he or she wants without the need to compromise goals. Ideally, instructions for use should teach for understanding of system operations so they may be used as logical operators, not rote prescriptions.

The central theme of these points is control; that the user is running the system to his or her conditions; not the reverse. The obvious rub is that some points are contradictory. Constancy and familiarity can be upset by considerable flexibility, for example. Others are ideals which can only be attained to some degree, such as natural language response capability. Finally, cost and the machine overhead of improving human performance are restraints. In one sense, technology should provide a "natural" interface to accommodate mass users—so this is the hope. But the machine resources needed for this can otherwise provide greater amounts of information and alternatives at higher speed. In a sense there is competition between technological enhancements to serve the human interface and improvements in the basic function performed (e.g., retrieval of documents, or accounting). It is not unreasonable that basic functions are served first, in that there is little sense to a highly developed user interface which deteriorates the basic functions of the system.

While the capabilities noted above suggest the accommodation of individual differences, much of the advice given anticipates a restricted, homogenous population of students or programmers. What must be questioned is whether the conditions described above can be extended (or compromised well enough where conflicting) and applied to the degree necessary to create a comfortable setting for novices.

A contrasting, but considerably less well developed approach is to enhance the learning of the user to meet the demands of the technology. In this way, users are brought to a performance standard and the technology is partly relieved of human factors design needs. In short, designers of information technology can count on certain stereotypical behaviors of their users and design to them.

"Computer literacy" is achieving greater currency in higher education and to some extent at elementary and secondary levels as well (see Pohl, 1979; Seidel and Rubin, 1977). The idea is to train students to cope with information technologies in a manner analogous to present-day instruction in library usage.

Computer literacy has been attempted for many years in education as a by-product of computer assisted instruction where rudimentary knowledge of computer hardware was a prerequisite of instructional access. But this kind of application was not intended to teach use of the information system itself. Efforts to bring about widespread, facile use of information machinery are quite few, owing to the cost of providing access and the mastery required. Nearly universal computing access and high competence levels are present only on several college campuses (Gillespie, 1979). But as models for mass use, such instances are wanting. The mix of highly capable students, no cost access, required use of computing for course work and the supportive environment of the university for trying new technologies put considerable distance between these few examples and mass use.

C. Language

Creation of a "standard" literacy, keyed to a common language and set of operations, would likely be out of the question. Minsky (1977) points out that needed information handling capabilities are not the province of one programming language; rather, each possesses strengths different from others (as is true of natural languages). In an obvious way, programming languages may assist or interfere with certain logic processes or functions the user wishes to program. In a very subtle way, computer languages (as is true of natural language) condition one's thinking about problem solving. As Minsky comments (1977, p. 249), "a computer language, just like a natural language, can have a characteristic literature."

This forcing effect of language has been a matter of intensive concern for two decades. Traditional languages such as Fortran, Algol, and Basic, embody machine concepts of the 1950s: a concern with building data sets and step-by-step descriptions for manipulating them. The languages act in a sequential manner imposing a geometrically increasing complexity with only linear increases in function (Kay, 1977). Newer languages (Simula or Kay's Smalltalk, for example), have attempted to fulfill several previously unmet needs:

- Embodiment of concepts of ordering information which extend beyond the language's basic (or primitive) grammar. Thus LISP, for example, instructs in hierarchical data sets and lists as a product of its structure, allowing one to extend and elaborate these principles beyond an elementary set.
- Checking programming complexity by creating a parallel (not sequential) structure where several "activities" may be independently programmed without concern for mutual interference, yet may be joined with ease when desired. This capability makes it easier to represent simultaneous activities of a system (e.g., a landing spacecraft or children interacting).

- Providing a structure by which the user can build his or her own programming tools from a set of primitives. In a sense, in Kay's (1977) system, complex ideas could be given simple labels and manipulated as a block (see also Kay and Goldberg, 1977). Special graphics symbols could be created for screen display as a labelling shorthand (e.g., notes for music, simple ideograms). Beyond providing enough prepared tools so that the user need not start from scratch in designing an information system, the user otherwise takes on this responsibility.
- Allowing the viewpoint of the observer (the context) to be considered in controlling information machinery, the situational need of the individual can be addressed. Though "observer languages" (Kay, 1977, p. 242) are largely developmental, they allow classification of objects into families which are generalizations of their properties, e.g., "vehicles" can subsume the rather different elements: bicycles, wagons, and automobiles. The tag "vehicles" can be used to economically manipulate all elements belonging to that family. By allowing people to develop their own sets and relations, the effectiveness of the information system is optimized on an individual basis.

The common purpose of all these efforts is to allow individuals the tools to make information systems better conform to personal needs and styles—to make programming structures better parallel individual problem-solving structure.

The successes of these efforts are unassessed in a mass user setting. Kay's (1977) experiments with children perhaps come closest and claim considerable success from the facilitative, self-defining qualities of Smalltalk in giving children confidence and problem-solving abilities with computers.

D. Hardware Interface

Considerable energy has been devoted to terminals and related equipment to make them responsive in an industrial design sense to human factors. The motivation for this kind of improvement is among the strongest. The population using terminal equipment for air line reservations, telephone switching, accounting, point-of-sale transactions, and so on, vastly exceeds the group of machine-tolerant programmers and information search specialists. Great differences in educational level and machine tolerance must be accommodated. The inventive side of this effort is to break away from the keypunch or teletype-print mode that characterizes the traditional hardware interface (see Chapanis, et al. 1977):

- Natural speech: Low cost vocal interfaces for speech generation have become inexpensive and commonplace to the point where among the more innovative of this equipment is found in children's toys. The problems arise in speech *recognition* (Dixon, 1977). So far, only rather crude devices are available, with little ability to cope with the variety of accents, elocution problems, and room acoustics. Production equipment of this kind can recognize only a limited vocabulary of fixed commands uttered by trained workers, or are only able to recognize numbers voiced over telephones. Facile recognition of complex speech awaits advances in artificial intelligence research and linguistic analysis. Presently, such systems operate on a subset of natural language which is almost as much trouble as more machine adoptable Boolean languages (Price, 1974).

- Graphics and visual recognition: High resolution graphics terminals allow spatial manipulation of images, diagrams, and other pictorial information, opening a universe of options beyond text (Swallow, 1977). Color is used in complex systems diagrams to show subsystem distinctions, give visual indication of change (e.g., red for "warning") and so on. However, the input of images is considerably more difficult, either involving use of graphics capabilities in the terminal or by "reading" images from television and translating them (digitizing) to binary machine code. What is most difficult is creating low-cost machine intelligence that can recognize visual patterns. Even the comparatively simple and standard shapes of typefaces are recognizable only via expensive scanning devices. More complex images—recognition of handwriting, for example—requires considerable resources.

- Manual input: There have been numerous substitutions made for the modified typewriter/teletype keyboards of commonplace terminals. Some of these in response to the handicapped, but most are to better match hand–eye coordination or increase input speed. Graphic input is viewed as continuous data, not discreet characters or code. Lightpens used to "write" on terminal screens mimic pens. Multidirectional levers ("joysticks") allow users to move characters or objects about on screeens. A hand-held cup (or "mouse") resembling a toy car can be wheeled on a flat surface to synchronize the movement of objects on a screen with hand movements. In short, matching of the kinesics of body movement to manipulation of computer displays permits higher speed and greater accuracy.

- Tonal or musical synthesis at the most primitive level provides alarms and cues. At the most sophisticated level, such capabilities attain the status of musical instruments (e.g. synthesizers).

In short, there is a growing effort to increase level and variety of sensory output and to make it more "natural." It is on the "output" or machine-to-user link where the sophistication is greater. The problems of pattern recognition, decoding of natural speech and of matching input behavior to familiar physical acts are less developed, suggesting that users still have the upper hand in accommodating the equipment, rather than the reverse. Machines require of us fixed, formal behaviors in directing their operations. As a rule, few machines can even remotely cope with the variability of communication behavior common to human interaction.

E.   Industrial Evaluation of Efficiency and the Workplace

Much has been written on the structuring of information systems and the work environment. It remains the dominant milieu of complex information technologies. Concern starts with the criteria for assessing efficiency of information systems and extends to the attitudes and work patterns of the individuals who use them. Capable design, with costs in mind, constitute an optimal balancing of many of the factors previously discussed in this chapter. Regrettably, the criteria for evaluating quality of this balance can be rather narrow.

Most common measures trade on concepts of "precision" and "recall." Precision notes the proportion of materials yielded by the system to the user's demand which actually are judged relevant by the user. Recall is the obverse: how much information relevant to the users needs was left unfetched in the system? Tests of better systems (e.g., MEDLARS) show precision and recall both to be about 60 percent. Another study, completed by *Time* and IBM, pitted manual search against automated and gave automated retrieval a slight edge (Senko, 1969).

The efficiency of those who work with information technology is the other major focus. Variables such as the user's efficiency in terms of process (time to task completion, errors made, effort, or number of steps needed) or final product quality (organization, size, control structure, readability, and reliability) have been examined. Measures of this kind have been made largely upon professional programmers operating (experimentally) in different work environments (see Basili and Reiter, 1979; Weinberg, 1971). The influence of working alone or in groups or the level of discipline over workers are characteristics of these job environment variables which have long been fixtures of industrial research.

More recently, attitudinal, personality, and anxiety variables have been used especially to check the inhibiting effects of reluctance and anxiousness upon performance (Gannon, 1979; Walther and O'Neil, 1974). Fear of failure, the burden of detail in operating the equipment, fear of inadvertently erasing work, and time pressure contribute to anxiety and negativism. Software designers have responded in part by eliminating drastic error messages ("FATAL USER ERROR!") or those merely cryptic ("UNIDENTIFIED

UUO") by substituting more benign and useful expressions ("Job stopped, try again" or "Can't write on protected file"). Other needs, such as providing step-by-step feedback, seem essential to maintaining a psychological feeling of control and successful use. Faced with little feedback, novice users have been frequently observed "doing things the hard way" (Basili and Reiter, 1979), avoiding powerful, global instructions, just to proceed more slowly and incrementally with more feedback.

For the most part, these studies are limited to a specialist's environment—skilled librarians using complex data base management systems or programmers working in a university who are more concerned with rating a particular system than with systematically developing explanatory concepts.

Several more recent efforts (cf. Shneiderman, 1979) to check attitudinal measures and work conditions suggest a growing concern with the social psychology of information systems use and the development of organizing concepts to facilitate study. Assertiveness and external control (cf., Rotter, 1966) have been used to gauge self-confidence in adjustment to changes in complex information systems (Lee and Shneiderman, 1978). Basili and Reiter (1979) looked at the influence of "teamwork" and high discipline job environments on the work quality of programmers. But generalization from workplace studies to a leisure, domestic setting presents several distinct problems.

Most existing data bases or computer-based information systems serve expert clientele. Documents are categorized by established specialties in the field or have been coded by document authors according to a standard thesaurus adopted by professional groups. While such devices might work for organic chemists or aeronautical engineers, the variety and depth of information needs occuring among a mass public would quickly tax narrow schemes. Several useful efforts to adequately code citizen information needs have generally been elaborate in design and complex in development (Dervin, 1976). Few such schemes exist and the implementation of ones that do would present formidable complexity to most citizens attempting their use.

Second, systems are often machine adaptations of manual procedures in particular disciplines. The isomorphism between steps in human problem-solving and those exacted by retrieval systems is largely unknown and less easy to determine with the varied needs of a mass clientele. Theoretical understanding of why a procedure seems efficient is largely guessed at with very little controlled observation being done. With a public information utility, one cannot rely on professional training and common purpose to guarantee efficient use.

Third, there is a conflict between standardization of information systems which allow training to transfer easily across systems and having different features which permit a particular system to work best for certain problems and situations. However, as functions converge into the same system (for example, word processing and electronic mail) or are shared (networked) among systems, some standardization is at least forced by compatibility needs and technologies. Considerable attention is being given currently to the technical standards for videotext type information utilities to permit international sharing of information (see Ford, 1980). Doubtless, the technology will force common useage pattern where the standards are adopted. But it should be noted that the effort is based more on the economics of technologies than on understanding of how people best use such systems.

Finally, much of productive searching does not come about in a highly purposive and formal fashion. Studies of newspaper readership show considerable scanning of content for appropriate material (American Newspaper Publishers Association, 1973). Many readers do not have a definite search agenda in mind before reading. Library users have long been familiar with searching stack locations close to where catalog-directed searches led. It is a familiar occurance to leave libraries with many publications gained through browsing, not directed search. Computerized information utilities typically use branching search methods which require explicit knowledge of what you want before you search for it. By extensive cross referencing and by allowing users to define certain of their own search strategies, it may be possible to simulate a "browsing" atmosphere in a machine environment. The vast majority of existing systems either do not or are awkward at it (Tyler, 1978).

F. Cost/Benefit Analysis

It is somewhat ironic, given the extent of visionary speculation on in-home information utilities, the lack of sound forecasts showing the market potential and delivery costs to citizens. In an abstract economic sense, it is argued that world economies are becoming largely information based (see Porat, 1977), but present evidence for mass information utilities in this growth remains largely speculative. Caulkins (1978) cites a study by Vantage Research showing accelerating growth rates for personal computers of about 120 thousand units/year after 1981. Estimates for sales of British teletext receivers forecast 250 thousand units in place in that nation by 1980. The more complex Viewdata system installed by the British Post Office presently has 1500–2000 sets in place on a subsidized, experimental basis. A similarly designed U. S. commerical system, QUBE (Columbus, Ohio), is reputed to have about 20,000 terminal-equipped subscribers. Experimental systems in Japan (e.g., Tama CCIS, Hi-Ovis, and CAPTAINS) offer collectively more varied services (Facsimile transmission, emergency notification, personal message service) but are also of small scale and large subsidy (as of 9/79, see Edelstein et al., 1978; Glued to the Qube, 1978; Zite, 1979).

What complicates prediction is the strength of competing assumptions which underlie forecasts. Dordick (1980) characterizes three scenerios for the future of information networks, the prime technological underpinnings of information utilities:

- Technology Drive Future: This is a diversified, fragmented marketplace, served by special service networks providing services at a cost beyond the reach of average households.
- Market Drive Future: Transportation and labor costs will make the use of information networks financially attractive as functional substitutes. New services, such as remote sensing of fire, protection, merchandising, and expanded entertainment offerings will become an increasingly attractive market.
- Policy Driven Future: Information inequality will become a consumer issue as well as a locus of business potential. Public data networks in other nations will serve as an example for regulation to improve access, develop technological standards, and control rates.

Because it is difficult to identify the comparative weight of such forces, longterm forecasting remains quite speculative.

Even present economics are unclear. There is little doubt that existing information utilities are heavily subsidized owing to their low fees, low volume, experimental nature, and expensive gear. QUBE taxes its customers a monthly service charge of about $12 in addition to charges for requested services (ranging from college credit work to feature movies). These costs, in addition to terminal purchase or rental appear average for similar systems being created for mass use in other nations (Tyler, 1978). Receiver costs alone (the interactive equipment necessary to access information utilities) range in present costs from between $400 and $1500, depending on its features and whether it is integrated into other household telecommunications devices (e.g., part of the telephone or television set). Added to that, the heavy costs of head-end and networking hardware make for a considerable expense with few economies of scale. How soon and to what extent these provider expenses will be passed along to the user is difficult to say. When they are, the information poor, to the extent they are also financially poor, will be disadvantaged.

Finally, a major and persistent enticement is the potential for new services. Home protection, shopping by TV, videophone, educational services, data processing all have been targets of previous speculation (Excerpts from..., 1968; Lachenbruch, 1968). Their potential, even after passage of a decade or more, remains untested and largely unrealized; a complex matter of services offered, cost reductions owing to volume and technological advance, and mass acceptance. It remains open to question if the attraction for new information technologies rests with powerful interactive information utilities or, rather, with their ability to provide more and better traditional TV fare and other passive-use services (pay TV moves, satellite "super" station reception). As a passive system, it seems unlikely that the information poor would be improved by it at a faster rate than the rich, simply through providing more of the same media fare they presently consume.

V.   THE MASS INFORMATION ENVIRONMENT

Extrapolation of computer information systems which successfully service an elite of private and institutional users must be tested against the machine interaction capabilities and information needs of the public. What is clear from considerable research is that problems in handling and appreciating information, as problem solutions, increases with distance from this information able elite (Dervin, 1971, 1972; Katzman, 1975). These problems argue strongly against a technology-based "wealth" for the information poor:

- Information processing skills decrease. Reading ability, skill with and knowledge of communication strategems (framing questions, for example), declines. Physical sensory abilities, due to health problems may be less acute.
- Increasingly restricted communication networks. Individuals are more locked into immediate personal acquaintences and local sources for advice and information. There is less tolerance of the specialized roles found in agencies offering "expert" advice. The impersonality and technological demands of information utilities could prove as formidable.
  - Increasing problems with control. Purposive behavior in dealing with problems—informational or otherwise—rests in part on a self-assurance (cf. Rotter, 1966) that that what one does can affect future successes. Lacking this self-assurance negates motivation to resolve information needs by whatever means offered.
  - Not seeing problem solutions in information terms. Problems may prompt several responses, only one of which may be information seeking. Resources, emotional support, or diversion (escape) are other mechanisms for dealing with problems. Seeking information-based solutions is a reflex of the educated which is not universal.
  - Unselective, inattentive media use. There is little doubt of the entertainment and escapism offered by leisure time media use. But attentive, selective use for information helpful to daily living, such as that found from news and public affairs programming, is less apparent. Use of information utilities could be more for entertainment than for self-help and education in this light.

These characteristics often inhibit information gathering from traditional institutional sources: libraries, social agencies, and schools. What must be questioned is the advantage offered by information technologies that will somehow remove old inhibitions for the mass user. .

VI. RESEARCH DIRECTIONS

Finding these advantages involves testing some of those assumed by providers of the technologies. In doing so, developers of information systems should be prepared to depart from the traditions of industrial testing. People in these contexts *have to* use information systems for job specific tasks. Use is not the voluntary sort exercised in mass access information utilities. Programmers, who seem to be ready test populations for many studies, may give some indication of man–machine problems, but are not ultimate tests of public acceptance. Their familiarity and tolerance for machine interaction makes the problems they encounter of a different order than those of first-time users.

Commercial and governmental experiments with mass use also must be viewed with some qualification. Subsidized home terminal equipment tested on experimental user groups does not really present true marketplace conditions. And one must consider that many systems such as QUBE present largely passive entertainment services—films or television programs. Their capability is not fully used for information retrieval and other services which place the user in complex interaction with information utilities. Moreover interaction is typically constrained to a simplified "multiple choice" selection of machine-based alternatives. This does not allow a complex dialogue, but may instead represent a shrewd estimate by system designers of the public's limited ability to interact.

What dazzles the observer of many information utilities is the technology— the interactive ability and the vast array of potential services available. But ultimately, these services have costs and the novelty of high technology in the home wears off. If they are to be more than elaborate pay TV networks offering rerun films, several hard questions will have to be pressed:

- What are consumer information needs and how are they more effectively served—in the user's terms—by new technologies? Marketing study cannot rest on entertainment prospects but must deal with what help to daily living such systems provide better than existing media. Past efforts (Brooks and Eastman, 1974; Levine, 1973) to use technologies for urban service centers have had only limited success and were usually operated by librarians or other professionals. Discovering needs of heterogenous populations and making information attractive even in an electronic package probably will remain difficult to do.

- What kinds of information-gathering will take place in a leisure situation? What proportion of time will be given to specific question answering vs. a "browsing" of information available? The purposive view of information gathering held in scientific or industrial environments cannot be expected to carry over into the home. Variables appropriate to a leisure context need better specification.
- Can interactive protocols be developed with assist users in defining a problem in information terms? To use system "answers", users must have questions. If gaps are to be closed between information rich and poor, the capabilities of these systems must cause improvement among the poor at an appreciably greater rate that among the rich, There seems very little development of explanatory concepts as to how this might be done.
- What forms of presenting and controlling information work best? Most current advice has little theoretical basis which relates cognitive processing of information to the systems which make information available. What is evident from recent advances in programming languages is effort to make a better fit between how the individual observes and solves problems and computer language. But this work is typically among professionals in the workplace, not the public at home.
- What should public terminal equipment be like? Present systems for mass use (QUBE, Viewdata, etc.) provide calculatorlike keypads of from twelve to thirty keys. None of these really resemble full typewriterlike devices for extensive user input. Rather, they are designed for limited check-list response and menu selection of services. This may be a reasonable fit to public use, but will alternatives—both more simple and complex—be tried? Identification of "human factors" variables in information equipment design is well developed in professional and office environments, but appears far less so in a mass marketplace.
- What should efforts at building "computer literacy" be like? Should this be left to the accident of an information market place (e.g., self-instruction or assistance via manufacturers) or should standards and curricula be developed in the public sector? The complexity of existing self-instruction materials makes them primarily of use to those already skilled with information technologies.
- Attitudinal and personality characteristics, remain largely untested, but have explanatory potential for mass use of information technologies. The difficulty remains in too few studies done overall and too many of these being based solely on computer professionals, not novices. "Control" is a recurrent theme both as a personality dimension and in what well-designed systems attempt to provide in the handful of studies currently done. It and other personality characteristics warrant considerable attention.

It is unlikely that any of these questions will meet with quick solutions. Common needs of enhancing personal control in a machine environment, of providing a natural, multisensory interface between citizen and system draw upon a short and erratic history of research. "Solutions," if they become available, certainly will be matters (as some presently are) of intense debate.

But this erratic record has been characteristic of many new scholarly pursuits. What is especially distressing here is the comparative lack of research amid the abundance of speculation on the mass benefits of information technologies. Demonstration projects at the hands of governments and commercial interests have tended to focus on the technologies involved, immediate policy needs and financing considerations, or the marketing of entertainment services. They have not yet shown a rich marketplace for information products which have great importance to the lives of the mass consumer. Attempts to do so have been more concerned with the cost, amount, and flow of information than with its quality and effect on people.

In a very real way, people and their information milieu must become a center of attention away from the intense interests about *possibilities* offered by new technologies. Many innovations—video-cassettes, local cable programming, pay TV, instant polling—offer little change from the present; the user is still largely a passive consumer of media services. But the power of "new media" to resolve problems, to close gaps between information rich and poor, will not be realized until the mass consumer becomes an initiator of complex demands upon technology.

Economically, and in terms of access, purposive, interactive use of new information technologies seems at the threshold. Whether a mass clientele awaits these prospects in an open marketplace and will use them effectively to improve life quality remains an open question.

REFERENCES

American Federation of Information Processing Societies and *Time* (1971). "A National Survey of the Public's Attitudes Towards Computers." Time–Life, New York.

American Newspaper Publishers Association (1973). "News and Editorial Content Readership of the Daily Newspaper." American Newspaper Publishers Association, Washington, D.C.

Baer, W. S. (1978). Telecommunications and technology in the 1980s. *In* "Communication for Tomorrow" (G. O. Robinson, Ed.), pp. 61–123, Praeger, New York. [note extensive bibliography on new technologies in this chapter]

Baldwin, T., Greenberg, B., Block, M., Eulenberg, J., and Muth, T., (1978). "Michigan State University–Rockford Two-way Cable Project: System Design, Applications and Public Policy Issues, Volume 1, Summary." Final Report, NSF Grant APR 75-14286, Department of Telecommunications, Michigan State University, East Lansing, Michigan. (ED172744.)

Basili, V. R., and Reiter, R. W., Jr. (1979). An investigation of human factors in software development. *Computer 12* (No. 12), 21–38.

Bowes, J. (1975). Media technology: Detour or panacea for resolving urban information needs. *Journal of Broadcasting 20,* 333–343.

Bowes, J. (1980). "Japan's Approach to an Information Society: A Critical Perspective."(Paper presented to the International Communications Association, Acapulco, Mexico.)

Branscomb, L. M. (1979). Information: The ultimate frontier. *Science 203,* 143–147.

Brooks, R., and Eastman, D. J. (1974). "Project IRMA: Development and Demonstration of a Computer Assisted Citizen Information Resource System to Enable Urban Residents to Make Use of Available Public Services." Final Report, H.E.W. Project #2-02-05. (ED 104 447-104 448.)

Bruner, J. (1966). "Toward a Theory of Instruction." Harvard University Press, Cambridge, Massachusetts.

Caulkins, D. (1978). Personal computer networks. *In* "Proceedings of the Sixth Annual Telecommunications Policy Research Conference" (H. S. Dordick, Ed.), pp. 297–306. Lexington Books, Lexington, Massachusetts.

Chapanis, A., Parrish, R. N., Ochsman, R. B., and Weeks, G. D. (1977). Studies in interactive communication, II: The effects of four communication modes on the linguistic performance of teams during cooperative problem-solving. *Human Factors 19,* 101–126.

Chen, T. C. (1977). Computing power to the people: A conservative ten year projection. *In* "Computers and Communication: Implications for Education" R. J. Seidel and M. L. Rubin, Eds.), pp. 53–58. Academic Press, New York.

Conrath, D. W., and Thompson, G. B. (1973). Communications technology: A societal perspective. *Journal of Communications 23,* 47–63.

Dervin, B. (1971). "Communication Behaviors as Related to the Information Control Behaviors of Urban Low Income Adults." Unpublished Dissertation, Michigan State University.

Dervin, B. (1972). "The Communication Environment of the Urban Poor." Project CUP, Department of Communication, Michigan State University.

Dervin, B. (1976). The everyday information needs of the average citizen: A taxonomy for analysis. *In* "Information for the Community" (M. Kochen and J. C. Donohue, Eds.), pp. 19–38. American Library Association, Chicago, Illinois.

Dixon, N. R. (1977). Automatic recognition of continuous speech: Status and possibilities for an operational system. *In* "Computers and Communication: Implications for Education"(R. J. Seidel and M. L. Rubin, Eds.), pp. 327–338. Academic Press, New York.

Donohue, G. A., Tichenor, P. J., and Olien, C. N. (1975). Mass media and the knowledge gap: A hypothesis reconsidered. *Communication Research 2,* 3–23.

Dordick, H. S. (1980). Information inequality: An emerging policy issue for the United States. *In* "Pacific Telecommunications Conference Proceedings" (D. Wedemeyer, Ed.), pp. 2C-27—2C-32. Honolulu.

Edelstein, A. S., Bowes, J., and Harsel, S. (1978). "Information Societies: Comparing the Japanese and American Experiences."University of Washington Press, Seattle, Washington.

Excerpts from Part of Communications Report on the Future of TV. (1968). *New York Times* (Dec. 10), 41.

Ford, M. L. (1980). "Experiences in the provision of Prestel Services in the United Kingdom and Abroad." (Paper presented to the Pacific Telecommunications Conference, Honolulu, Hawaii.)

Gaines, B. R., and Facey, P. V. (1975). Some experience in interactive system development and application. *Proceedings of the IEEE 63,* 894–911.

Gannon, J. D. (1979). Human factors in software engineering. *Computer* 12, (No. 12), 6–7.

Gillespie, R. (1979). "Issues and Opportunities in Computing and Higher Education." Comments on HR4326 to the Subcommittee on Science, Research, and Technology, U.S. House of Representatives, January, 1980.

Glued to the Qube. (1978). *The Economist 268* (No. 7039), 62–63.

Harkins, A. W. (1972). "World Information Systems and Citizen Participation." Office for Applied Social Science and the Future, University of Minnesota, Minneapolis, Minnesota.

Holt, H. O., and Stevenson, F. L. (1977). Human performance considerations in complex systems. *Science 195,* 1205–1210.

Hunt, E. (1973). The memory we must have. *In* "Computer Models of Thought and Language" (R. Schank and K. Colby, Eds.), pp. 343–371. Freeman, San Francisco, California.

Intermedia. (1979). *7* (May) [Entire issue examines Viewdata and Teletext.]

Japan Computer Usage Development Institute (1972). "The Plan for an Information Society: A National Goal Toward Year 2000." Tokyo. (Reprinted in *Data Exchange,* July–Aug., 1973, 4–43.)

Johansen, R., Vallee, J., and Spangler, K. (1979). "Electronic Meetings: Technological Alternatives and Social Choices." Addison–Wesley, Reading, Massachusetts.

Katz, D., and Kahn, R. (1966). "The Social Psychology of Organizations." Wiley, New York.

Katzman, N. (1974). The impact of communication technology: Promise and prospects. *Journal of Communication 24,* (No. 4), 47–58.

Kay, A. C. (1977). Microelectronics and the personal computer. *Scientific American 237* (No. 3), 230–244.

Kay, A. C., and Goldberg, A. (1977). Personal dynamic media. *Computer 10* (No. 3), 31–41.

Kennedy, T. C. S. (1974). The design of interactive procedures for man-machine communication. *International Journal of Man-Machine Studies 6,* 309–339.

Lachenbruch, D. (1968). Looking ahead. *TV Guide,* (April 13) 8–10.

Lave, L. B., Leinhardt, S., and Raviv, A. (1978). The demand for automated bibliographic systems: A diffusion model. *In* "Proceedings of the Sixth Annual Telecommunications Policy Research Conference" (H. S. Dordick, Ed.), pp. 329–344. Lexington Books, Lexington, Massachusetts.

Lee, J. M., and Shneiderman, B. (1978). Personality and programming: Time sharing vs. batch processing. *Proceedings of the Association for Computing Machinery Annual Conference,* 561–569.

Levine, M. M. (1973). "Information Needs in Milwaukee: Agencies and Groups." Milwaukee Urban Observatory, Milwaukee, Wisconsin. (ED 089 769.)

Machlup, F. (1962). "The Production and Distribution of Knowledge in the United States." Princeton University Press, Princeton, New Jersey.

Madnick, S. E. (1977). Trends in computers and computing: The information utility. *Science* 195, 1191–1199.

Martin, J., and Norman, A. R. D. (1970). "The Computerized Society." Prentice Hall, Englewood Cliffs, New Jersey.

Miller, G. A. (1956). The magical number seven, plus or minus two. *Psychological Review 63,* 81–97.

Minksy, M. (1977). Applying artificial intelligence to education. *In* "Computers and Communication: Implications for Education" (R. J. Seidel and M. L. Rubin, Eds.), pp. 245–252. Academic Press, New York.

Morris, DuB. S., Jr. (1972). "Information Technology Initiatives for Today: Decisions that Cannot Wait." The Conference Board, New York.

Moss, M. L. (1978). "Two-way Cable Television: An Evaluative of Community Uses in Reading, Pennsylvania." Final Report to the National Science Foundation, Grant #APR 75–1411A02, New York University–Reading Consortium, New York. (ED 162 625.)

Parker, E. B. (1973). Implications of new information technology. *In* "Mass Communication Research: Major Issues and Future Directions" (W. P. Davisons and F. T. C. Yu, Eds.), pp. 171–183. Praeger, New York.

Parker, E. B., and Dunn, D. A. (1972). Information technology: Its social potential. *Science 176,* 1392–1399.

Pohl, I. (1979). "Universal Computing Literacy: A Key to USCC in the '80s." Unpublished Manuscript, Department of Information Sciences, University of California at Santa Cruz.

Porat, M. U. (1977). "The Information Economy, Volume 1: Definition and Measurement." U.S. Department of Commerce, Office of Telecommunications, Washington, D.C.

Price, M. K. (1974). The illusion of cable television. *Journal of Communication 24* (No. 3). 71–76.

Robinson, G. O. (1978). Communications for the future: An overview of the policy agenda. *In* "Communcations for Tomorrow" (G. O. Robinson, Ed.), pp. 467–500 Praeger, New York.

Rogers, E. M. (1971). "The Communication of Innovations." Free Press, New York.

Rotter, J. B. (1966). Generalized expectancies for internal versus external control of reinforcement. *Psychological Monographs, 80* (Whole No. 609).

Sackman, H. (1971). "Mass Information Utilities and Social Excellence." Auerbach, Princeton, New Jersey.

Sackman, H., and Citrenbaum, R. L. (1972). "On Line Planning: Towards Creative Problem Solving." Prentice–Hall, Englewood Cliffs, New Jersey.

Schmidt, R. (1979). Cable: USA tests new uses. *Intermedia 7* (No. 6), (Nov.) 24–26.

Seidel, R. J., and Rubin, M. L. (1977). "Computers and Communication: Implications for Education." Academic Press, New York.

Senko, M. E. (1969). Information storage and retrieval systems. *Advances in Information Systems* Science 2, 257.

Shneiderman, B. (1979). Human factors experiments in designing interactive systems. *Computer 12* (No. 12), 9–19.

Steen, P. J. (1978). Providing specialized services through alternate broadcast and nonbroadcast technologies. *In* "Proceedings of the Sixth Annual Telecommunications Policy Research Conference" (H. S. Dordick, Ed.), pp. 219–224. Lexington Books, Lexington, Massachusetts.

Swallow, R. J. (1977). CHARGE and its potential in CAI. *In* "Computers and Communication: Implications for Education" (R. J. Seidel and M. L. Rubin, Eds.), pp. 303–312. Academic Press, New York.

Takasaki, N. (1977). "Our Study of 'Quality of Life' and Contribution of Telecommunications." Research Institute of Telecommunications and Economics, Tokyo, Japan.

Tomita, T. (1979). The search for a personal information medium. *Intermedia 7* (No. 2), 36–38.

Turoff, M., Whitescarver, J. L., and Hiltz, S. R. (1978). The human-machine interface in a computerized conferencing environment. *Proceedings of the IEEE Conference on Interactive Systems, Man and Cybernetics,* 145–157.

Tyler, M. R. (1978). New media in the information economy: Prospects and problems for Viewdata and electronic publishing. *In* "Proceedings of the Sixth Annual Telecommunications Policy Research Conference" (H. S. Dordick, Ed.), pp. 265–286. Lexington Books, Lexington, Massachusetts.

Walther, G. A., and O'Neill, H. F., Jr. (1974). On-line computer interface: The effect of interface flexibility, terminal type, and experience on performance. *AFIPS Conference Proceedings 43,* 379–384.

Weinberg, G. M. (1971). "The Psychology of Computer Programming." Van Nostrand Reinhold, New York.

Zite, T. (1979). TV seers take QUBE route. *Washington Post* (Aug. 24).

3

Communication Gaps and Inequities: Moving Toward a Reconceptualization

Brenda Dervin
School of Communications
University of Washington

I. COMMUNICATION GAPS AND INEQUITIES

A. The Ideas

In the recent literature in the communication and information science fields, one increasingly sees references to a set of terms that differ in nuance but essentially refer to the same hypothesized phenomena. The terms— knowledge gap, information gap, information inequity, information poor, and, most recently, communication gap—all have been used by theorists who have observed that when it comes to information/communication availabilities in society, there are those who are rich and those who are poor. Further, these theorists hypothesize as more information/communication becomes available, the rich get richer and poor get poorer.

These central ideas have been the focus of the work of a growing number of writers (Branscomb, 1979; Childers and Post, 1975; Dervin, 1977b; Dervin and Greenberg, 1972; Donohue et al., 1975; Galloway, 1977; Genova and Greenberg, 1977; Parker, 1978; Rogers, 1976; Smith, 1975; Tichenor et al., 1970, 1973).

Some writers have focused primarily on the static portrait—the observation that there are those that are information poor. Perhaps the most comprehensive treatment came with Childers and Post's 1975 book, *The Information Poor in America*. But the idea has been the focus of many. In their work on the communication environments of the urban poor, for example, Dervin and Greenberg (1972, p. 221) referred to the "information void" within which they saw the urban poor as living. In the same line, Smith (1975, p. 17) expressed a concern for the "...uneven distribution of information and communication" and suggested that some groups in society...

> ...have little access to our primary resources. They have no control of information, communication, production, or anything.

Along with these observations came an increasing concern for rectifying the situation. An example is Branscomb's question in his 1979 *Science* article:

> Food and energy challenge us because they are in short supply...Information is quite different. It is in quantitative surplus...the yawning chasm is between what some people have learned, yet others have not put to use...since so many individuals are information poor, how do you use the surplus of information in society to overcome the scarcity of information available to individuals? (Branscomb, 1979, p. 143).

Other writers have been more concerned with the impact of the growth of information societies, the so-called communication revolution, on these inequities. They are the ones who hypothesized that the poor get poorer while the rich get richer, a process now referred to with the label "the knowledge gap hypothesis." The best known, and first fully formalized presentation of the hypothesis was presented by Tichenor et al. (1970, pp. 159–160):

> As the infusion of mass media information into a social system increases, segments of the population with higher socio-economic status tend to acquire this information at a faster rate than lower status segments, so that the gap in knowledge between these segments tends to increase rather than decrease.

While in early formulations the inequity idea focused primarily on information inequity or knowledge gaps, Rogers (1976, p. 233) expanded the focus to the " communication effects gap" suggesting that the idea

> Should deal with the *attitudinal and overt behavioral effects* of communication as well as just "knowledge"; thus, I propose calling it the "communication effects gap" hypothesis.

The purpose of this chapter is to review the formulation of the communication gap and inequities ideas—their origins, their logical foundations, and how recent theoretic trends in the communication and information science fields are not only changing the nature of the ideas but, in some cases, making them no longer useful or appropriate perspectives.

B. The Context Within Which the Ideas Were Conceived

In understanding the nature of the inequity ideas, it is important to note that they came to the fore at the very same time that social scientists were becoming increasingly desenchanted with the traditional assumptions that suggested that communication of information into society was a powerful force. These traditional assumptions are typified well by Donohue et al. (1975, p. 3):

> A traditional viewpoint is that resolution of social problems is related to inputs of information. If a system is sufficiently saturated with information, according to this view, a general understanding of the topic will develop within the system.

As Donohue et al. point out, these traditional assumptions rested on two premises. One is that information availability leads to understanding. The second is, in their words:

> ...that higher levels of information input lead to general equalization of knowledge throughout the system.

The inequity or gap ideas were, of course, striking at the heart of the second assumption. It was no longer assumed that the presence of information served as an equalizer. In the mass media context, Tichenor et al. (1970, p. 170) stated in support of their knowledge gap hypothesis:

> ...the mass media seem to have a function similar to that of other social institutions: that of reinforcing or increasing existing inequities.

Roling et al. (1976, p. 160) provided a similar statement in the more general context of development. Diffusion processes, they said, "are imperfect equalizers."

More general than the strike at the equality idea, however, was the challenge to the root premise behind the idea—that information availability leads to use. This challenge was coming from a host of specific studies showing, for example, that mere availability of, or even exposure to, information did not necessarily bring about awareness or information gain (Allen and Colfax, 1968; Greenberg, 1964; McLeod et al., 1969; Robinson, 1972; Spitzer and Denzin, 1965). This challenge was also based on a growing number of reviewers who concluded from their own assessments of the literature that the power of communication campaigns was vastly overrated. It was the time, for example, of Bauer's (1964) "obstinate audience" seemingly impervious to the most persistent efforts of communications; and, of Klapper's (1960) "limited effects" statement suggesting that communication campaigns have effects only under limited conditions, for some of the people, some of the time.

The context was one, then, of disenchantment with the results of research, not with the research itself. It was assumed that the results showing the "obstinate audience" with "limited effects" were useful and accurate pictures of audience behavior. It was a time for trying to isolate the conditions within which one could not find effects. It was a logical time for the introduction of gap or inequity ideas as one explanation of why only limited effects were available. It was not yet a time for challenging the very premises that lead to the research that concluded that only limited effects were possible.

C. The Traditional Logic Supporting the Ideas: Receiver Deficits

The literature which posits gaps and inequities as existing is generated, almost without exception, within the frame of an explicit or implicit use of a traditional model of communication—a source is seen as having a message which he/she wishes to send to a set of receivers. The research then attempts to see whether the receivers got the message—which receivers didn't, which did, and how well. This description is a fitting summary of communication research of the 1950s, 1960s, and most of the 1970s. It is still estimated, in fact, that it is still a fairly standard perspective although one that is receding as alternate perspectives emerge (Dervin, 1978).

Within the frame of this traditional perspective, two questions have been "answered" with such a massive amount of evidence that the power of the generalizations seem almost irrefutable. One question is whether gaps exist. The second is why they exist. When one looks at research generated within the conceptual frame posited above, the evidence is clearly in agreement. Gaps do exist, according to the evidence. They exist, the evidence goes on to suggest, because some people are less able and less willing to take in information than others. While there is evidence that contradicts these conclusions, almost without exception that evidence comes from research using a different model of communication. These alternate models and their supporting evidence will be reviewed in later sections of this chapter.

When researchers using the traditional perspective of communication have gone out to ask whether some members of the audience are not receiving the sources' messages and, thus, suffer inequities, they have done so primarily using a structural or sociological framework, or with what Galloway (1977, p. 381) calls a substratum approach:

> Substrata are sectors of a social system which function to mediate distribution of communication effects, resulting in what are termed differential effects between substrata.

An important part of this approach is the attempt to isolate identifiable subgroups of the audience who are receiving or not receiving messages. In the early stages of the work, the groups were identified primarily in terms of socioeconomic variables (race, income, education). In the later stages, they were identified more by what Galloway (1977, p. 383) called "information-contextual variables" such as media exposure, social participation, or contacts with experts. In actuality, the literature is such that the distinction between these two classes of differentiators has not been terribly important. What has emerged is an almost tautological portrait of connection between the socioeconomic and information-contextual variables. Certain groups of people are identified as information poor. They are also identified as being those with less education and income and less able and willing to intake information both because of lower ability as well as less opportunity to gain and use information.

In their comprehensive review, for example, Childers and Post (1975) said that the same groups of individuals who suffer from economic poverty also suffer from information poverty. They identified these groups in the United States as Mexican American, Puerto Ricans, other Spanish, American Indian, Eskimo, poor Black and White, Appalachians, poor farmers, migrant workers, aging adults, prisoners, and the blind and deaf (Childers and Post, 1975, pp. 78-79). The groups they identify are those groups in the U.S. who have less education and lower incomes.

The Childers and Post emphasis is not unique to them. When research is conducted using the traditional communication model, the results consistently show that those with less education and lower incomes are less likely to be information seekers, use expert information sources, be informed generally, have informed interpersonal contacts, expose themselves to high information content print media, be aware of information sources, have organizational ties, have information processing skills, have sufficient background information that would allow them to become aware of and understand informational messages, or trust establishment and organizational sources. This portrait emerges clearly from reviews (Childers and Post, 1975; Dervin, 1976b; Dervin and Greenberg, 1972; Ettema and Kline, 1977; Greenberg and Dervin, 1970) and from the intersection of many articles (Block, 1970; Caplovitz, 1963; Hiltz, 1971; Hsia, 1973; Hurwitz, 1975; Key, 1961; Levine and Preston, 1970; Mann, 1973; Mendelsohn, 1968; Parker and Paisley, 1966; Rieger and Anderson, 1968; Smith, 1975; Spitzer and Denzin, 1966; Tichenor et al., 1970; Udell, 1966; Voos, 1969; Wade and Schramm, 1969).

Making the situation worse, according to these studies, is the evidence that showed that as with the vicious cycle of economic poverty which seems difficult to escape, information poverty has the same traplike quality. Studies, again using the traditional communication model, suggested that an information alienation can become established such that once an individual has failed in finding appropriate information for a problem he begins to believe that relevant information can never exist for him. (Bowes, 1971; Rotter, 1966; Seeman, 1966).

Again, the frame of the traditional communication model, the findings above have been extended to a wide range of contexts. Rogers (1976, p. 234) gave essentially the same portrait of the findings from the diffusion of innovation research. Higher status individuals, he said, were less likely to be receptive to change messages, more likely to be nonhomophilous (different from) the sources of the messages, and less likely to have the tight, informed interpersonal networks that allow change messages to "trickle down."

Similar findings have emerged from the field of education where myriad studies, looking at contexts ranging all the way from learning from Sesame Street broadcasts (Bogatz and Ball, 1971) to school achievement and intelligence testing (Fells et al., 1951; Hess, 1970; Ireton et al., 1970; Quay, 1974; Willerman et al., 1970) to the development and use of language (Bernstein, 1961; Deutsch, 1965) have confirmed, using the perspective of the traditional communication model, the presence of socio-economic status related gaps.

In summary, then, what appears in the literature that has emerged from those using the traditional communication model, is a strongly supported view of a phenomenon which is talked of as being real. As findings in the social sciences go, this phenomena is one of the more supported ones. These studies say: yes, the gap is real; yes, it is caused by the fact that some groups within society are less able and less willing to take in information. In their recent review of the literature on cause of the knowledge gap, Ettema and Kline (1977, p. 82) termed this the "deficit" explanation of gaps.

D. The Appearance of Contradictions

When one looks at this set of findings, there are two interesting things about them. The first is the sheer extent of the support behind them. This support has come in terms of both quantity and time. As early as 1947, Hyman and Sheatsley were offering a similar set of conclusions to explain "why information campaigns fail?" The second interesting thing about the findings is that there began to emerge in the mid 1970s, with spurts of activity prior to that, increasing evidence suggesting that the communication gap hypothesis is more idea than reality.

These contradictions came first in the form of descriptive evidences from studies which started out to replicate gap findings and found either no gap, gap reversals, or narrowing gaps (e.g., Galloway, 1974, 1977; Shingi and Mody, 1976; Tichenor et al., 1973). A call was issued for isolating the conditions under which one could or could not expect to find gaps (Ettema and Kline, 1977; Tichenor et al., 1973).

With this call, the theoretic circle became complete. Recall, the gap idea was one that emerged when research conducted within the traditional communication model found it had to explain why communication was not as powerful as expected, why direct effects could not be found, why only limited and indirect effects from information campaigns could be found. The call, then, was to isolate the conditions under which information impact occurred or did not occur. The gap research emerged as one thrust in that effort to isolate conditions. One condition seemed to be the existence of subgroup deficits—some people, it was assumed, just were not able or willing to process all the information that the information society made available. Yet, now, a call was out to explain the conditions under which the condition operated.

The response to this call came in two forms. The first was a more traditional reaction, an attempt to hang on to the hypothesis and explain the contradictory evidence. This took the form of what has become termed the "ceiling effects" explanation. Ettema and Kline (1977) ably review studies relating to this explanation (Cooke et al, 1975; Donohue et al., 1975; Galloway, 1977; Katzman, 1974; Kline et al., 1974; Shingi and Mody, 1975;

Tichenor et al., 1973). Basically, the idea is that there are conditions under which some kind of ceiling prevents the informationally/communicatively rich from acquiring more, giving the poor a chance to catch up, or, in some cases, reverse the gap. In this line of reasoning, the "ceiling" is seen as taking on several forms. One is a kind of saturation whereby the rich have all they want of a particular message/innovation so the poor have time to catch up. This kind of ceiling was seen by Galloway (1977, p. 382) as the major reason why he found narrowing gaps resulting from message dissemination:

> The most important influence leading to narrowing gaps appears to have been the operation of ceiling effects.... Restricted room for better-off segments suggests that other segments were able to catch up to reduce the differentials.

The second form of the "ceiling" idea has been more interventionist. The idea here is to give the poor an advantage by encouraging their exposure and planning information campaigns with them in mind. It is this kind of ceiling which Shingi and Mody (1975, p. 189) referred to when they said:

> ... the communication effects gap is by no means inevitable. It can be avoided if appropriate communication strategies are pursued in development efforts.

While the ceiling idea has taken on other interpretations, the two reviewed above form the major ones. What is important about the ceiling idea, however, is that it was a response to the call for explaining why the hypothesized gaps were not always present and, in particular, a response that arose within the frame of the assumptions which generated the gap hypothesis to start with. In essence, the ceiling idea accepted the source-receiver model of communication and continued to try to identify those conditions under which one could assure that receivers received the source's message.

But there was a second set of responses to the call for understanding the conditions of message receipt and, in this case, the conditions for the existence or absence of gaps. These responses, while not always identified as such, were generated from different models of communication. Because they were generated from different models, they were not concerned about explaining whether the gaps really exist or not. Rather, they say, if you start with the kind of assumptions the researchers using the traditional model did, you are bound to find the brunt of your evidence supports the gap idea. What is common to all the literature in this second set is that the authors agree that the traditional gap research (what Ettema and Kline, 1977, called "classical") has been asking the wrong questions.

Because the responses in this second set are, in essence, challenging the very framework within which most communication research is conducted, and thus, are relatively new in focus, the literature reporting them is not as organized. Essentially, though, the responses appear to be of two different but complementary types which come up with different explanations of why gaps or inequities occur, explanations with their roots not in empirical evidence but, rather, in conceptual perspectives. The first challenge to the traditional "deficit" explanation of gaps is one that changes the point of focus from receivers to sources. Here, rather than the receivers lacking, it is the sources who are seen as lacking, particularly in their responsiveness to the needs of receivers. The second challenge is, in actuality, a more fundamental challenge, for when pushed to its extreme it suggests that any data available on the presence of inequities and gaps is nothing more than numeric myths created by the use of inappropriate assumptions about the nature of human information seeking and use. Each of these challenges will be reviewed in turn below.

II. THE FIRST CHALLENGE: SWITCHING THE EXPLANATION TO SOURCE DEFICITS

This first alternative way of approaching the gap phenomena originates primarily through the efforts of Latin American and other third-world communication researchers. The essence of this thrust is its call for turning attention from receivers to sources/systems. Ettema and Kline (1977, p. 184) summarize it as a turning

> ... away from characteristics of the individual and toward the social system in the study of the factors which originate and maintain SES-related differences.

The fact that this thrust is identified primarily with third-world researchers does not mean there is a complete absence of the focus in the literature authored by U.S. researchers. An example of the U.S. emphasis is a series of studies which have suggested that the system is at least in part to blame for the existence of gaps. These studies suggest, for example, that the information systems within which citizens attempt to inform themselves are disorganized, overly bureaucratic, frequently humiliating in treatment of clientele, often unresponsive to more difficult needs and uninformed about the life styles of their users (Dervin and Greenberg, 1972; Dervin et al., 1977; Furman et al., 1965; Greenberg and Dervin, 1970; Grunig, 1972; Kurtz, 1968; Levin and Taube, 1970; Levine et al., 1963; Mendelsohn, 1968; Pratt, 1969; Scott, 1967; Sjoberg et al., 1966). There has been a turning of attention to media structure as a possible explanation with a concern for the fact that the most-used U.S. medium (television) places far less emphasis on disseminating helpful information than does the least used medium (newspapers) (Dervin and Greenberg, 1972; Wade and Schramm, 1969). Katzman (1974) made the point explicitly when he said that gaps may exist because of unequal access to communication technologies. This, he suggested, would be a gap resulting not from receiver characteristics but channel characteristics.

Despite the presence of some U.S. authorized research focusing on source behavior as a possible explanation of communication gaps, the emphasis by third–world researchers is different both in magnitude and kind. For U.S. researchers, the focus is simply one more possible explanation in addition to explanations rooted in the focus on receivers. For the third–world researchers, in contrast, the focus is not simply central and pervasive but also the obvious consequence, in their eyes, of their concern for the development of their countries and for the fact that until very recently the only research perspectives available to them were those they learned during their U.S. training (Beltran, 1976; Díaz Bordenave, 1976; Röling et al., 1976). These perspectives, they challenge, do not meet the development needs of their countries. Rogers (1976, p. 217) summarized it when he said that the traditional (now called "classical") approach to development research started with the assumption

> ... that poverty was equivalent to underdevelopment. And the obvious way for less developed countries to develop was for them to become more like the developed countries.

One aspect of this acceptance was an acceptance, the researchers challenged, of a persuasion oriented focus on receivers and getting them to accept messages from sources. In Beltran's (1976, p. 108) view, the research tradition which guided the early years of development research placed

> ... a high emphasis on the receiver so that research could determine how the commercial or political persuasion was effectively exerted on him.

Díaz Bordenave (1976, p. 137) made the same observation when he suggested that up until recently in development research ...

> *Communication was seen still as the long arm of the government's planners, and its main function was supposed to be that of obtaining people's support for, and participation in, the execution of development plans.*

Essentially, then, these writers challenge that the communication context that guided development research until recently was the source-sending-messages-to-receivers model which has traditionally guided communication research in the U.S. generally. They see this research paradigm as being a product of the U.S. which is not useful in the third-world context because it has embedded within it some assumptions about the nature of social systems which, they feel, either do not apply in the third world or ought not to be applied. More generally, they see these same assumptions as having pervaded all the U.S.

generated social sciences. As Beltran (1976, p. 115) puts it, the U.S. has created

> ... sciences for *adjustment*—essentially addressed to studying conformity with the prevailing needs, aims, values, and norms of the established social order, so as to help its ruling system to attain "normalcy" and avoid "deviant" behaviors.

These writers see, then, the focus on the receiver that has been traditional in U.S. communications research generally and in the gap research in particular as being tied in with the emphasis in U.S. research on attaining source goals and trying to manipulate receivers to those ends. Further, the authors see that research emphasis as being a reflection of the society which has generated it. In the severest form of ciriticism, for example, Beltran (1966, p. 115) challenged that the research paradigm is product of

> ... a society where individuality was predominant over collectivism, competition was more determinant than cooperation, and economic efficiency and technological wisdom were more important than cultural growth, social justice, and spiritual enhancement.

From the point of their agreement that U.S. communications research has emphasized source goals in its focus on the source-sending-messages-to-receivers paradigm, these researchers then suggest that a central focus of taking this perspective is the blaming-the-victim syndrome which they see as pervading U.S. communications research. In essence, this idea suggests that what U.S. researchers do is go looking at receivers to see if they got the sources message. When groups of receivers have not, it has been assumed, these writers challenge, that the receivers are deviant. As Rogers (1976, pp. 217–218) terms it, what has been operating is a kind of "intellectual ethnocentrism" or a "contemporary intellectual extension of social Darwinian evolution." In fact, Rogers suggests that the very idea of "underdevelopment" when seen in the context of the U.S. research paradigm is also a blaming-the-victim idea. In this context, Rogers (1976, p. 218) notes, underdeveloped nations are seen as deviant but always with the "hoped-for potential of catching up."

This idea—that the receiver has been blamed for gaps—is one that has been mentioned by a number of writers, both non-U.S. and U.S. (Beltran, 1976; Dervin, 1977b; Diaz Bordenave, 1976; Elliott, 1974; Hsia, 1973; McAnany, 1978; Mann, 1973; Mathiason, 1969; Nordenstreng, 1977). Increasingly, the authors agree that a major consequence of the use of the idea has been the development of communication programs which have led to greater rather than less development equity in third world countries. This is not an unexpected result given the fact that evidence shows the same impact in the U.S. as a result of communication campaigns guided by the same research paradigm. As Röling et al. (1976) explained it, the development research drew conclusions that reinforced the focus on progressive farmers who were more ready to change, more like the change agents to start with. As a result, the research generated development programs in which:

> The current practice ... is to provide intensive assistance to a small number of innovative, wealthy, large, educated and information-seeking farmers, and to expect that the effect of such assistance will reach other farmers indirectly by autonomous diffusion processes (Röling et al., 1976, p. 159).

The result, Röling et al. charge, is that inequities emerge and increase. Beltran (1976, p. 111) made the point more strongly when he suggested that ...

> Communication ... often works against development ... in favor of the ruling minorities.

Based on this reasoning, these writers come to primarily two conclusions. One is that much more attention must be placed on changing the structural conditions which leads to the potential for or actuality of inequities in the first place. Again, Beltran (1976, p. 111) makes the summarizing point:

> Communication itself is so subdued to the influence of the prevailing organizational arrangements of society that it can hardly be expected to act independently as a main contributor to profound and widespread social transformation.

A consistent theme that runs through these writings, then, is the idea that sources and systems must be changed and that these changes in the social structure are fundamental prerequisites for attaining development or equity.

The second conclusion is a corollary. It is that the agencies and individuals who launch development programs and information campaigns must change their communication strategies. As Röling et al. (1976, p. 168) put it:

> ... it is not the characteristics of farmers as much as it is the characteristics and deployment of government development services which are the prime determinants of diffusion efforts.

In the process of calling for this change, these writers agree that what is needed is a changed conception of the role of communication in development away from source-oriented message transmission to self-development (Diaz-Bordenave, 1976; Havelock, et al., 1969; Röling et al., 1976; Rogers, 1976; Rogers and Adhikarya, 1979). This change is, perhaps, best summarized by Freire's (1970) call for a move away from the "transmission mentality." Diaz-Bordenave (1976) sees it as a need for a more liberating type of communication education based on dialogue. Havelock et al. (1969) suggest that what is needed is to start with the needs of users, the ways they diagnose their problems, and the changes they want to initiate. Röling et al. (1976, p. 165) call for obtaining "preventive feedforward" about the needs for innovations and the conditions of receivers. In particular, they suggest that sources should learn not only about the "average" receiver but about the range of characteristics across all receivers. As they put it in the development context:

> The profile of the intended utilizer should reflect not only the characteristics of the average farmer, but also those of the farmer with the smallest resource base (Röling et al., 1976, p. 165).

With this call, the literature of the first challenge turns full circle back to a focus on receivers. The difference, however, is that in the deficit explanation literature, the focus is on source goals and receivers are blamed when they fail to get the message. In the challenge, the writers suggest, the focus should be placed on receiver goals with sources blamed if they fail to communicate and respond.

It is at this point that this literature tradition, authored primarily by third-world researchers, collides with a far more fundamental communication issue than the question of who is to blame for gaps and inequities. Rather, the issue becomes how can one design communication programs so they can be receiver-initiated and deal with the uniquenesses of the full range of receivers. While the literature reviewed in this section makes a call for turning away from the source-sending-messages-to-receivers model to a model where receivers are the initiators, as a body of literature it has not generated a cohesive theoretic way of looking at receivers so as to avoid the very pitfalls of the model it abhors. Atwood agrees (1980, p. 2) when she suggests that the avant garde of Latin American communication research is as plagued by the very same conceptual weaknesses that have been troublesome in traditional communications research. As she puts it:

> The most serious flaws evident in Latin American communication research are related to conceptual weaknesses which transcend cultural barriers, and cannot be attributed solely to culturally-based viewpoints.

Atwood sees these flaws as rooted in how it is that the researcher looks at the communicating of both sources and receivers. It is telling that when one looks at the literature reviewed in this section, one sees much mention made of the need for alternative communication strategies in general terms but very little mention made of the "how" of that communicating. At the most, one sees case examples of one particular kind of receiver-initiated effort or another (Röling et al., 1976).

It is this focus on the development of a cohesive theoretic net for looking at receivers that forms the second challenge to traditional foci on communication gaps and inequities. This second challenge is represented by a large and growing body of literature that, like the literature of the first challenge, suggests that the traditional blame-the-receivers deficit explanation of gaps and inequities is conceptually wrong. This literature, too, calls for communication programs that are genuinely receiver-oriented.

What differs, however, is that the literature of the first challenge is, at root, less concerned with the nature of communicating and more concerned with the nature of power. It is in this context that the literature of the first challenge posits essentially a series of "mal-intent" charges suggesting that the sources-sending-messages-to-receivers paradigm was a product of a particular kind of society which then attempted to impose the paradigm on different kinds of society. The literature of the second challenge, in contrast, but not in contradiction, is concerned more fundamentally with the idea that no matter who is in power or what their goals, the nature of communicating is such that the problem of communicating will remain. At root, the second challenge is concerned not only with a changed conception of the role of communications, as the literature in the first challenge is, but more generally with a changed conception of the nature of man, his information seeking and use.

In a sense, the literature of the second challenge begins where the literature of the first challenge leaves off. It is ironic that, for the most part, the two literatures have existed independently of each other. It has been issues such as those raised by the literature of the first challenge that has generated much of the purpose and direction for the literature of the second challenge. And, it is the literature of the second challenge which will make the aims of the first challenge possible.

III. THE SECOND CHALLENGE: MOVING TOWARD COMMUNICATION FUNDAMENTALS

Any observer of the literature in the communications field with an interest in reading between the lines, and, particularly, between the lines of the voluminous quantitative results which still mark the field, can readily see that for the first time since the field became established in its own right, the literature of the field is beginning to be as typified by profound conceptual discussion as by the evidentiary results of observation. Further, at this juncture of time, the conceptual discussion is taking primarily the form of confrontation in efforts to tear the field away from what are seen as the unuseful paradigms of the past to the useful paradigms of the future.

These conceptual confrontations are themselves taking on numerous forms, sometimes implicit, sometimes explicit; sometimes embedded in a mire of seemingly irrelevant data, sometimes brought out for crystallized view. Further, the confrontations can be found taking place at different points of location within the field. It does not seem to matter if one focuses on traditional topical divisions (e.g., interpersonal communication, mass communication), geographical divisions (e.g., mid-west schools, eastern schools, western schools), or conceptual divisions (e.g., those focusing on process, rules, information). No matter where one looks in the literature the same evidence can be found of important conceptual discussion cast as confrontation.

In one sense, one can see much of the literature of the field of communication as being in the center of a conceptual cyclone. No matter where one looks into the center of the cyclone, one sees the literature increasingly focusing on fundamental issues dealing with the nature of communication. When looked at with this distance, it can be seen that the literature that has received the label as being focused on gaps and inequities is but one of a series of literatures that are being challenged in the communication field. Yet, it is appropriate to see the gaps and inequities literature as being more central in the conceptual confrontations that are occurring for the gap and inequity literature focuses, by definition, on evidence showing that some people, some times, under some conditions just don't get the source's messages. When one looks at the nature of the conceptual confrontations occurring in the field, one sees that they are also dealing with this same issue. The question has become, however, whether one should believe the evidence or see it as an artifact of a series of assumptions that have been made about the nature of communication.

The basic assumptions about the nature of communication are nested symbolically in the phrase "sources-sending-messages-to-receivers." The image the phrase conjures is very much one of sources-sending-messages as if messages can be tossed like bricks to receivers. This analogy is a brief description of a host of assumptions which are being torn down as the result of the conceptual confrontations now going on in the eye of the cyclone. While the literature focuses on these confrontations in a variety of forms, for purposes of this chapter it is useful to present them in two major categories. The first category deals with different perspectives on the nature of the message that the source is sending—whether it can be looked at as a "brick" or as something quite different. The second category deals with the nature of receivers and whether they can be looked at as catchers of messages or as something quite different. Each of these categories will be reviewed in turn.

A. Observer vs. User Constructions of Information

While the various gap or inequity statements differ in terms of whether they are focusing primarily on information/knowledge gaps or on a wider variety of assumed message effects (e.g., adoption, attitude change), they all assume implicity or explicitly that they are concerned with the impacts of messages or communications. And, without exception, they implicitly or explicitly concur on the widely accepted idea of traditional communications research that information exchange or transfer is at the center of the communicative act or "... the stuff of communication" as Schramm (1973) puts it.

In essence, then, the gap or inequity idea has been one that comes from an observer looking at the world to catch in his/her vision some hoped-for-impacts of message or information transfer, whether those hoped for impacts be greater knowledge gain, greater self-development, or greater adoption. The idea of looking for impacts requires that some standard be established. It requires that an observer be able to look across a large number of receivers and measure each of them against the standard. In the gap and inequity research, as in communication research generally, the standard has been implicitly assumed to be the message. The sources send the message. It is then seen, traditionally, as existing much as a brick exists. One then looks for impacts from the existence of the message.

This line of reasoning has embedded in it a host of assumptions. It assumes that messages cause impacts, that they exist independent of sources or receivers, that messages have lives of their own. More fundamentally, however, these assumptions are tied to a host of assumptions about the nature of information, the thing that is said to be the "stuff of communication." Actually, it is not so much the message that is seen as having a life of its own but the information it imparts. It is this conception of information that provides the standard against which observers can judge whether some people suffer from communication gaps.

It is also this conception of information that is at the root of most of the confrontations going on in the conceptual cyclone. So, while the cyclone manifests itself in the form of a variety of arguments pro and con, the arguments that focus on the nature of information are the most fundamental ones.

Dervin (1977a, p. 18) summarizes the traditional assumptions that have been made about information in her critique of how the communication and information science disciplines have used this concept:

> Information is essentially seen as a tool that is valuable and useful to people in their attempts to cope with their lives. Information is seen as something that reduces uncertainty. As the individual moves through... the time-space continuum that makes up life... it is assumed that information can both describe and predict that reality and thus allow the individual to move more effectively.

This suggests that traditionally, information has been seen as a valuable resource, something that describes reality, reduces the uncertainty about it, and allows people to cope more effectively. Like most underlying or fundamental assumptions, proof of their use abound but are found between the lines rather than stated explicitly.

These assumptions about information have behind them a set of even more fundamental assumptions. Dervin et al. (1980) summarize them as "the absolute information" or "objective information" assumptions. (See also Dervin 1976a, 1977a,b.) Essentially, these assumptions are the very assumptions that have been most often associated with logical positivism or positivisitic science. The idea here is that the world can be seen as discoverable, describable and predictable and the purpose of information is to so describe it and predict it. As Dervin (1976a, p. 327) says:

> If we assume that we are discovering reality, then the acquisition of more and more information about reality will make a better fit.

What is important about this complex of assumptions is that they all rest on one fundamental assumption—that information can exist independent of the observer. When brought out for stark examination like this, the fundamental assumption, of course, runs counter the basic relativity tenent in the communication field that:

> ...an accurate understanding of the human communication process must begin from the recognition that persons subjectively perceive their world—a principle now accepted as a truism in virtually every communication text (Stewart, 1978, p. 198).

Despite the presence of the truism, ideas about absolute information persist. As Dervin (1976a, p. 324) suggests, it is a symptom of a kind of "disciplinary schizophrenia" that has yielded a flood of confusing and contradictory results not only about gaps and inequities but about communicating in general:

> We are at the same time, and sometimes almost in the same breath, both communication relativists and communication determinists. On the one hand, our research data and our practitioner experiences say "relativism" loud and clear. Meanings are in people. Messages sent do not equal those received. The same person is different across time and space. On the other hand, we commit ourselves to research and action efforts which seek deterministic answers. We continue to look for normative, nonvarient rules.

Other examples of recognition of this confrontation exist in the literature. Clarke and Kline (1974, p. 228), for example, challenged that most communication research "adopts a strictly normative definition of 'knowing.'"

What appears to have happened in the **gap and equity** literature, in particular, and in communications research generally is that researchers unknowingly accepted absolute information assumptions and imposed them on their respondents. It has been suggested by several that the assumptions themselves were derived from positivistic science with its belief in a deterministic world that could eventually, given enough effort, be fully described. Increasingly, these same positivistic assumptions are seen as being the root source of limited progress not only in the communications field where the concept of information and how it is defined is so central but to all of the social sciences. What seems to be happening, then, is that fundamental changes are occurring not only in the way the conception of information is viewed but in the way social scientists look at man and his use of information. In reviewing psychological research, for example, Allport (1960, p. 65) warned that:

> The designs we have been using in our studies of motivation, of symbol and hence of the foundations of moral behavior are not...sufficiently iconic with our subject matter. Addiction to machines, rats or infants leads us to overplay those features of human behavior that are peripheral, signal-oriented or genetic. Correspondingly, it causes us to underplay those features that are central, future-oriented and symbolic.

Weimer (1978, p. 57), in reviewing the use of psychological models of man in communications research, made a related charge:

> A conceptually adequate approach can result only if the positivistic conception of science found in logical empiricism and related philosophies of science is recognized to be inadequate and abandoned, and if the behavioristic-information processing model of man is recognized to be inadequate and replaced by an adequate cognitive psychology.

Weimer concludes that the confrontation between positivistic views and those that are not is a major confrontation facing the communications field and social science generally and fears "polarizations." A merging can occur, he suggests, but the dominant models of "both methodology and man" must be abandoned to achieve it.

Brown (1979, p. 64) reviewing communication theory agrees with Weimer but sees little reason for optimism when he says:

> ...contemporary social science seems content in its search for absolutes and ultimates, confidently proclaiming itself in the forefront of scientific thought while at the same time standing mired in the metaphysics of a previous epoch.

The conflict that emerges in these comments is an interesting one. First, it suggests that the charges made by the literature reviewed in the first challenge may be too simplistic. It is one thing to suggest that too much attention is paid to source goals and too much blame placed on receivers. It is another to challenge the very meaning of the term "information" and to suggest that the term has been used deterministically rather than relativisitically. It is also a different kind of challenge to suggest that this deterministic treatment of the information concept has roots that extend beyond the confines of a given country's approach to the study of human behavior.

Interestingly, the challenge to social science takes its roots from science, what might be termed the relativistic sciences of the 20th century. It is from this science that the idea of information takes on a new form. All observation is inherently biased, we are told. No observation can be made as a statement of "absolute truth." Information is a construction, a product of observer and observation. Myriad authors have made the point:

> ...information is associated with the *relation* between message and receiver (Conant, 1979, p. 179).

> ...knowledge is always the knowledge of the observer and therefore inescapably rational in nature (Holzner, 1968, p. 28).

> Information is necessarily about fragments of the cosmos and of history....At any time a man has some collection of pieces of information fitted into various systems of thought or accepted stereotypes of experience. He cannot know, except in regard to the most immediate physical effects, whether his information is all that exists which bears on his choice of action (Shackle, 1974, p. 10).

> ...the objective world is, it does not happen. Only to the gaze of my conciousness, crawling upwards along the life line of my body, does a section of this world come to life as a fleeting image in space which continuously changes in time (Weyl, 1963, p. 216).

In general terms, then, what is happening in the literature is that conceptions of information are moving from observer constructions to user constructions. The essence of the reasoning is that any piece of information is merely the product of the observing of one or more humans that has been made public and shared (Wilson, 1977). The observations of one or more humans are always constrained. First there are the obvious constraints of human physiology; man's perceptual equipment is limited. But even beyond these constraints, there are others. There are the constraints of time; no person can observe from every point in time. There are the constraints of space; no person can observe from every possible vantage point. There are the constraints of change; observations of one moment do not fit the next.

It has been reasoning of this type that has propelled what is being called the "phenomenological" thrust in the communications field. In his review of some of the phenomenological literature, Stewart (1978, p. 198) summarizes the main conclusion drawn from the reasoning presented above:

...the accurate study of human phenomena, specifically the study of human communicating, not only may be subjective and experiential but *must* be.

There is a major implication of the reasoning that goes beyond Stewart's phrases "subjective" and "experiential." The implication is that human communicating—in terms of this chapter, the use of information—can not be seen merely as a passive process where the receiver catches messages thrown by sources. Rather, information use is inherently a creative process. Given the observational constraints of time, space, change, and physiological limitations, no amount of information provided by another can provide an individual with the instruction he/she needs to cope with even the limited reality of a personal existence. This is, in Gorney's terms (1972), a human imperative; in Bruner's terms (1964, 1973), the human necessity of "going beyond the information given;" in Carter's terms (1972, 1973, 1974a,b, 1975; Carter et al., 1973), the mandate of "gap bridging" or "construction" necessitated by the absence of "instruction;" in Dervin's terms (1979a,b), the mandate of "making sense when none is given;" in Shackle's terms (1974, p. 2), the need for origination rather than calculation.

Two quotes, one from Dervin (1976a) and one from Shackle (1974) catch the essence of these ideas:

> Humankind's information is some unknown combination of information about reality and information that is the creative product of people. Since both adaptation and creation are simultaneous and continuing human activities (in the collective sense), no amount of "objective" information can possibly describe reality. Indeed, humankind's creations of today make maladaptive the adaptive behavior of yesterday. Given a picture of the universe that allows for the possibility that "objective" information cannot completely describe reality, the avoiding of accidents ... is not a matter of simply getting more "objective" information. Rather, it is a matter as well of humans being able to create and operate with their own instruction and understanding (Dervin, 1976a, pp 325-326).

> ...the sequel of an action chosen by one man will be shaped by circumstance, and its circumstances will include the actions chosen now and actions to be chosen in time to come by other men. If, therefore, choice is effective, it is unpredictable and thus defeats, in some degree, the power of choice itself to secure exact ends." (Shackle, 1974, p. 2).

This idea—that human information processing is inherently creative—has one additional implication. This implication has to do with the issue of whether anything in a message can cause the behavior of a receiver and is best summarized by Stewart (1978, p. 199):

> This insight into the nature of the most fundamental human process, perceiving, can also be seen as the grounding for the rejection by many communication scholars of causal models of communications.

One sees in the literature, thus, a significant movement away from traditional causal assumptions about communication behaviors to assumptions that place the control of outcomes of communication situations in the hands of receivers. As Berlo (1977, p. 11) states it:

> We have begun to move away from the hypodermic metaphor of communication as something a source sticks in a receiver, and moved toward concentrating on relationships other than the relationship of causally dependent change.

Others have not been so optimistic but have made the same call (Atwood, 1980; Carter, 1974b; Grunig, 1975, 1978a,b; Grunig and Disbrow 1977). Others (Blumler, 1979; Katz et al., 1974; McQuail et al., 1972; Swanson, 1979) have not spoken to the causality issue directly but have spoken indirectly in their growing body of work in the "uses and gratifications" tradition. One of the major premises of the tradition is that the receiver takes "initiative in linking need gratification and media choice" (Katz et al., 1974, p. 21). This quote from McQuail et al. (1972, pp. 162–163) states the position:

> ... the relationship between content categories and audience needs is far less tidy and more complex than most commentators have appreciated. It is not just that most popular programmes are multidimensional in appeal. It is also the case that we have no single scale by which we can reliably attach a value to any given content category. Given the heterogeneity of materials transmitted over the broadcast media, not only is one man's meat another man's poison, but one man's source of escape from the real world is a point of anchorage for another man's place in it.

In summary, then, a core of arguments against traditional assumptions about the nature of information and information use are emerging from the literature. These arguments suggest that the very notion of communication-produced gaps and inequities rests on the assumptions that the informational content of messages exist independent of either sources or receivers and can have impacts on receivers independent of any intervention by receivers. The analogy of sources throwing bricks at receivers aptly summarizes the traditional assumptions. Information existing independent of sources and receivers is set up as a standard against which all receivers are measured. Those receivers who do not catch the message are then labelled as being in gap or inequity.

In the context of the arguments that are attempting to tear down traditional assumptions about the nature of information and its use, the idea of using a conception of "absolute information" as a standard for assessing the success or failure of messages is both a theoretically unsound idea as well as a self-defeating one. It is a theoretically unsound idea when juxtaposed with our understanding of the nature of human perception and its inherent constraints.

It is a self-defeating idea because it means that when assessed in absolute information terms most information campaigns will necessarily fail. And with such a standard, one will find the most failure when sources attempt to send messages to those people most different from them. Logically, any source's messages will be least useful informationally to members of the audience who observe the world from points in time-space most different from those with which the source observes the world.

It is possible to posit the use of "absolute information" assumptions as an alternative explanation of why gaps have been found. Unlike the deficit explanation discussed earlier, this explanation is more a product of conceptualization than evidence. This explanation suggests that the ideas of gaps and inequities are:

> ...not so much summary of human communication behavior as summary of things observed using these paradigms (Carter et al., 1973, p. 36).

More specifically, one can see that what has happened in the gaps and inequities literature as well as communication research generally is that researchers have accepted absolute information assumptions and imposed them on their respondents. Since absolute information is unobtainable, what has really occurred is that researchers have imposed their views of what is informing (and, thus, to them "information") on receivers and called it "the" information. Clarke and Kline (1974, pp. 228–229) make this observation:

> ...most research...adopts a strictly normative definition of "knowing." To be informed means to grasp the kind of facts about public events that usually interest educators. The identities of statesmen, date of events, and awarenesses of sanctioned viewpoints figure prominently...Most often these kinds of cognitions are measured concerning public events that are salient to researchers, who are educators themselves—whether or not the events are relevant to mass publics.

Dervin (1979c, p. 11) makes much the same point:

> One begins to understand that much of the social sciences is based on mythical data collected by asking people to care about and make sense of things that have nothing to do with their own lives as they see them.

When one looks at the literature dealing with human information use, its one most outstanding characteristic is how little it has told us about when, how, and why people use information. This observation has been made by many (Brittain, 1970; Carter et al., 1973; Dervin 1976a,b; Dervin et al., 1976; Donohew et al., 1978; Hollis and Hollis, 1969; Rees and Schultz, 1967; Warner et al., 1973; Zweizig and Dervin, 1977).

In fact, if one were to believe the literature, one would think that people used information hardly at all. Yet, the evidence runs counter to the nature of human existence. The evidence has been produced primarily in the context of absolute information assumptions. Several authors (Moore and Newell, 1974; Rees and Schultz, 1967) have challenged that the reason that so much literature has yielded so little worth is that the literature has been constrained by its acceptance of the research techniques valued in logical positivistic science. More specifically, the challenge has been made (Carter et al., 1973; Dervin, 1976a) that the literature has rarely focused on the constructing of information and, instead, has implicitly assumed, contrary to relativistic assumptions, a kind of isomorphic relationship between external reality and the ideas that people construct about it and then share as information. This assumption is a logical outcome of a belief in absolute information. Swanson (1979, p. 42) states this well:

> For only if we assume perception to be a passive process of registering unproblematic content are we relieved of the necessity of investigating meaning created in perception.

As the literature moves into the 1980s, research is beginning to emerge that looks at information as a user construct rather than an observer construct. Clarke and Kline (1974, p. 229) describe the transition away from normative or absolute information assumptions:

> One remedy is to inquire how people become informed about issues that are important to them. A corollary need is to measure "knowledges" about those issues that are of value to respondents, as well as the researcher. This calls for respondent-centered and open-ended measurement techniques.

In their study of what they called "information holding," Clarke and Kline tapped the thoughts respondents articulated about issues of interest to them. Dervin et al. (1980) took a similar approach when they defined information as the answers respondents created to their questions in situations they personally faced. Edelstein (1974) used the same approach when he had his respondents identify problems of personal interest and then articulate their thoughts on possible solutions and how the problem compared to other problems.

In each case, the researchers have defined "information" as a user construct or, in the terms of Hollis and Hollis (1969) as "personalized information." In each case, the researchers created a context within which respondents could report on how they informed themselves for their unique worlds.

As one looks at the assumptions about information that have guided social science, they seem like the top of an iceberg. Yet, more properly, they should be seen as the foundation of the iceberg. With each step that is taken in understanding the implications of having used absolute information assumptions additional implications emerge. An important set of implications focus on the ways in which information behaviors can be predicted.

Linking issues of how information behavior can be predicted back to a root in absolute information assumptions is not something generally done in the literature. Exceptions are found in the articles by Dervin (1976a, 1977a,b) and Dervin et al. (1980) who see the efforts at predicting information use as being a direct reflection of the nature of the assumptions being made about information. While no other authors were found who made the same explicit connection, numerous citations were found in which writers have been wrestling with the issue of how to best predict information behaviors.

The very fact that prediction of information use is necessary is, in itself, proof of the failure of the absolute information assumptions. The hypodermic model was a direct manifestation of these assumptions. It is assumed that the presence of information was both a sufficient and necessary condition of information use. When it was found that the hypodermic model only fit some of the people, some of the time, a variety of predictive structures were introduced to attempt to explain why this was so. Basically, these structures have traditionally assumed that when a person does not get a message, this person can be seen as prevented from getting the message by a series of barriers that stand between the person and the message. Since absolute information was assumed, the only possible explanation of why these barriers existed was that they were barriers the individual had attached in some way to his/her person. The barriers were all seen as standing between the individual and "the" information that existed in an orderly, well-described world, a world in which the use of absolute information was an assumed necessary and sufficient condition of existence.

In this description, then, the traditional use of "deficit" explanations for explaining why some people attend to media information while others do not can be seen as a result of a blame-the-victim syndrome, as charged by those writers reviewed in the literature of the first challenge, or as a result of a more fundamental error in thinking—assuming that information describes an orderly and constant world that is knowable in an absolute sense.

From Dervin's point of view (1976a, 1977a,b), there is a definite parallel between conceptions of information and attempts to predict impacts of communication. She sees the communication literature as having started with absolute information assumptions that do not require a concern for the conditions of information use. Rather, one can look at information as being able to drop into receivers like bricks into buckets.

The absolute information assumptions did not work, however, and evidence of their failure was all too apparent. As has been the pattern in the field, the attempts to explain the contradictions and contrary evidence then focused not on the assumptions behind the evidence but on trying to isolate that subset of receivers who were not behaving like buckets. Only when persistent efforts in the line failed has attention been placed on changing the underlying assumptions.

Not surprisingly, the change was one that moved from attempting to predict information use, first, as a straightforward, unchanging, mechanistic process to a process that is now beginning to be seen as occurring at specific points in time, space, and as changing over time and space.

In broad perspective, then, the moves in attempts to predict information use have paralleled the ways in which information has been defined. And, in particular, the move has been toward incorporating the very constraints and time, space, and change that were so crucial to the move from observer to user constructions of information. This movement in approaches to predicting information use will be reviewed below.

B. Observer vs. User Constructions of the Predictors of Information Use

In the 1960s, when it became clear that the hypodermic model of communication did not hold, the first response was, as suggested above, to assume that the model held for some people and not for others. This assumption opened the door to essentially two decades of attempts to predict information use, specifically, and communication behavior, generally, on the basis of individual traits. The traits ascribed to receivers were of two types: personality traits, with the reigning definition being that of Allport (1960) as relatively stable, highly consistent attributes of people that exert widely generalized causal effects on behavior; and, demographic traits, generally defined as accepted indicators of a person's so-called station in life (e.g., education, income, socio-economic status, age, race).

Commonly, the trait approach was based on the idea of cross-situational consistency. This meant that the traits were assumed to predict behavior regardless of time, space, or change. As Bem and Allen (1974, p. 506) stated, the assumption of cross-situational consistency is "virtually synonymous with the concept of personality."

Given the logic presented in the last section of this chapter that unravels the absolute information assumptions, it is not surprising that the trait approach has simply not worked. At this juncture in the literature, many writers are trying to come to grips with this failure. While the postures shown in the literature vis-a-vis the cross-situationality issue vary, there is clear and growing agreement that the idea of cross-situationality in its current form does not work. The challenge has come from many quarters (Bem, 1972; Cappella, 1977; Carter, 1974b; Clarke and Kline, 1974; Davis, 1977; Dervin, 1976a, 1977a,b; Dervin et al., 1976, 1980; Endler and Hunt, 1969; Grunig,

1973a,b; Grunig and Disbrow, 1977; Hewes and Haight, 1979; Miller, 1963; Mischel, 1968, 1973; Rotter et al., 1972). Typical statements include the following:

> ... empirical evidence obtained over a wide variety of constructs does not support this [cross-situational] assumption (Hewes and Haight, 1979, p. 262).
>
> ... behaviors appear to be "idiosyncratically organized in each individual." (Endler and Hunt 1969, p. 20)
>
> When it comes to dealing with individuals as individuals ... [trait] attributes are but labels imposed by the outside world. The attributes may or may not be relevant to the individual. Furthermore, whether they are relevant or not, attributes are not the reason an individual may intersect with [a message] ... at a given point in time (Dervin, 1977a, p. 27).
>
> Response patterns even in highly similar situations often fail to be strongly related. Individuals show far less cross-situational consistency in their behavior than has been assumed by trait–state theories. The more dissimilar the evoking situations, the less likely they are to produce similar or consistency responses from the same individual. Even seemingly trivial situational differences may reduce correlations to zero (Mischel, 1968, p. 177).

Endler and Hunt (1969, p. 20) state that behaviors appear to be "idiosyncratically organized in each individual."

The extent of the challenge is best shown by the statements made by Mischel (1968, 1969, 1971, 1973) that suggest that regardless of improvements in measuring instruments the amount of variability that personality variables can predict across situations is never likely to exceed 10 percent. Even without the limitation suggested by Mischel, there is growing agreement that a shift from cross-situational predictors to situationally-bound predictors should greatly improve the prediction situation. As Grunig and Disbrow (1977) suggest, a cross situation approach may work some of the time because individuals with common demographic characteristics and common personality traits often are found in similar situations. But, such traits are too far removed from the actual situations in which information use occurs. Dervin (1977a, p. 19) makes this point when she suggests that the irony of the use of cross-situational approaches as a means of trying to improve the prediction of individual behavior is that it is, in itself, a normative response "attempting to correct the damages" of a normative, absolute information approach. She continues:

> In the normative approach, the individual is treated as irrelevant to the situation. In the use of across time-space demographic predictions, the situation is treated as irrelevant to the individual.

It is clear in the literature that the move away from cross-situational approaches and toward situationally-bound approaches came first as post hoc explanations of why expected results did not occur and then as piecemeal, primarily atheoretic attempts, to obtain better predictability. Long before the concept of situationality was bantered about, researchers were introducing variables such as "level of importance" and "degree of interest" and "life situation context" into their predictive statements. And, consistently but still out of the collective research consciousness, these variables—bound to the perceptions of situations at given moments in time-space—proved to be powerful predictors. Study after study showed significant relationships between interest or relevance and information seeking and use (Adams et al., 1969; Atkin et al., 1973; Bishop, 1973; Clarke and Kline, 1974; Donohue et al., 1975; Fitzsimmons and Osburn, 1969; Genova and Greenberg, 1974; Hanneman and Greenberg, 1973; Johnson, 1973; Levy, 1969). Other studies have shown a strong relationship between the presence of receiver uses for information and actual information seeking and use (Dervin et al., 1976, 1980; Edelstein, 1974; Grunig 1975, 1978a,b; Grunig and Disbrow, 1977; Sears and Friedman, 1967). Other studies have focused specifically on the presence of interpersonal uses for potential information and have found relationships between the presence of such uses and information seeking and use (Chaffee, 1970, 1972; Chaffee and Atkin, 1971; Clarke, 1965; McLeod and Wackman, 1967; Milbrath, 1965).

This move toward situationally-bound approaches on the basis of post-hoc explaining and piecemeal predicting was characteristic of the communication field generally and characteristic specifically of the gaps and inequities research. The first sign of the move came with the introduction of a gaps and inequities explanation that was presented as an alternative to the "deficit explanation." This alternative—called the "difference" explanation—was presented by Ettema and Kline (1977, p. 187):

> The major thrust in the difference interpretation is...that persons from different social strata and/or cultures manifest their abilities in different circumstances and, further, that these circumstances are predictable and reasonable given the differences in status or culture.

In this statement, Ettema and Kline are explaining why gaps occur and, while still adhering to the cross situational use of social strata and culture, they show the first signs of using situational explanations.

The second sign of the move toward situationality came in the face of contradictory results that disproved the existence of gaps or even found gap reversals. As has been the pattern in communications research generally, attempts were made in the gaps and inequities research to isolate the conditions of these variations in the gap phenomenon. The studies of Donohue et al. (1975) and Tichenor et al. (1973) are best known for this attempt. They isolated a variety of conditions that related to reduced or dampened gap effects in communities. Prominent among these conditions were degree of community interest, presence in the community of social conflict, and degree of community homogeneity. Each of these conditions attempts to capture some of the uniquenesses of specific points in time and space and, in particular, the points in time and space when there would be reason to expect that media messages would have broad general interest and use in a community.

It was research such as this that led to what might be called a situational restatement of the gap hypothesis:

> As the infusion of mass media information into a social system increases, segments of the population motivated to acquire that information and/or for which that information is functional tend to acquire that information at a faster rate than those not motivated or for which it is not functional, so that the gap in knowledge between these segments tends to increase rather than decrease (Ettema and Kline 1977, p. 188).

In sum, then, both in communications research generally and gap research specifically, the first move toward situationality was primarily an inductive one. At some point a critical mass of evidence was reached and one began to see explicit statements calling for situational theory. Typical examples of the call are shown below in quotes by two psychologists, Mischel and Rotter, and one communications scholar, Cappella.

> Given the overall findings . . . on the complexity of the interactions between the individual and the situation, it seems reasonable . . . to look more specifically at what the person *constructs* in particular conditions, rather than trying to infer what broad traits he generally *has,* and to incorporate in descriptions of what he does the specific psychological conditions in which the behavior will and will not be expected to occur (Mischel, 1973, p. 265).

> It is the position of [our theory] . . . that most predicative instances require an adequate description of the situation before useful predictions can be made. To rely solely on internal determinants or states results in either highly general predictions or else inaccurate ones (Rotter et al., 1972, p. 4).

> Situational factors seem to act as catalysts or attenuators so that relationships hypothesized and validated in one context are modified or perhaps reversed in other contexts. . . . personality traits can no longer be expected to predict communication behaviors . . . unless situational factors are accounted for (Cappella, 1977, p. 44).

The nature of the calls obviously varied. For some (e.g., Cappella, 1977; Hewes and Haight, 1979). the introduction of situational approaches was part of an attempt to find ways in which to retain cross-situational ideas. In these cases, the idea of situationality is, in actuality, simply one more case of the cross-situational idea. It is assumed that somehow the observer can judge the nature of the situation and that these observer-ascribed situational attributes will be helpful in the predictive realm. In actuality, however, given the perceptual constraints within which all communicative activity occurs, observer constructed ideas of situationality can be no better than observer constructed ideas of demography or personality.

The stronger theoretic call for situationality is typified by the quote by Mischel (1973) with its emphasis on "...what the person constructs in particular conditions." Mischel makes his call for the field of psychology. Dervin et al. and Grunig have made the same call for the field of communication when they suggest that in the context of the situationality assumption:

> ...predicting and understanding how people use information and cope with events must be based on their perceptions of how they see the situations they are in (Dervin et al., 1980, p. 00).

> ...a person's perception of a situation is the best explanation of when and how he or she will communicate about that situation (Grunig, 1978a, p. 42).

Edelstein (1974, p. 242) reflects the same underlying assumption in his definition of the situational approach:

> What is significant about the approach is that it takes the point of view of the individual who is attempting to cope with problems he defines for himself. He deals with a problem as it affects him at a particular time. He is thus defining a situation in his own terms.

With this call for a situational approach came a series of explicit tests pitting a variety of situational measures against more traditional cross-situational demographic or personality measures. With few exceptions—these exceptions being explained by the fact that researchers mistakenly used observer assessments of situations—the situational predictors proved more powerful than cross-situational predictors (Chaffee and McLeod, 1973; Clarke and Kline, 1974; Dervin et al., 1976; Donohue et al., 1975; Genova and Greenberg, 1974; Grunig and Disbrow, 1977; Hewes and Haight, 1979; Stamm and Grunig, 1977; Tichenor et al., 1973). Typical results show, for example, that message discrimination (respondent recall of messages voluntarily exposed to) was a stronger predictor of information holding than education (Clarke and Kline, 1974); personal interest was a better predictor of knowledge than education (Genova and Greenberg, 1974); situational measures were more powerful predictors of information seeking than across time-space attitudinal measures (Stamm and Grunig, 1977). Relevant studies in this roster, of course, are the explicit tests of the impact of situational measures on gap effects (Donohue et al., 1975; Tichenor et al., 1973).

With these tests, the beginning of coherent ideas about situationality began to emerge. Yet, strangely, most of the emerging ideas still lacked a generalizable base. This was due, in part, to the fact that there seemed to be in some quarters a sense of disbelief about what was happening. An example can be found in this statement by Hewes and Haight (1979, p. 265):

> If we fail to circumvent the cross-situational problem, a major reassessment of communication research priorities and paradigms must be forthcoming.

What seemed more crucial to coherent development of a situational approach, however, was full recognition of the need for user-constructed perceptions of situations and, more fundamentally, full recognition of and allegiance to the ideas of user-constructed information. Because the root assumptions about information are so frequently implicit, confusions over these issues abound in the recent situational literature. Yet, like most confusions tied to implicit assumptions, there frequently isn't enough direct statement to ferret out the confusions.

It is clear in the literature, though, that while more and more researchers are accepting user-defined situational assumptions, they frequently attempt to do so while retaining observer-defined information assumptions. Interestingly, it is those studies that have moved fully out of old observer perspectives into user perspectives that have made the most progress in developing a coherent situational perspective.

The core issue in developing a coherent perspective is how to select the situational variables. Some writers have suggested that the task is impossible. Dervin et al. (1980, p. *00*) summarizes the dilemma:

> The enigma, of course, is that each situation is seen by each participant uniquely. The research problem becomes how to tap this uniqueness in a way that allows it to be dealt with and, yet, at the same time, does not revert back to nonsituational, absolutist assumptions. The task is one of tapping variable classes . . . in such a way that the resulting measures can be seen as existing in *all* situations while at the same time tapping the very elements of uniqueness in specific situations.

It is this juncture that a solid hold on user-defined information assumptions has proven helpful. It is the constraints of time, space, and change that mandate the requirement of user-defined information and, in turn, user-defined situationality. It is these very same constraints that provide the basis for developing a coherent approach to situationality. The theoretical work of Carter (1972, 1973, 1974a,b, 1975) and its applications suggests that what is common to all situations is that the individual can be seen as moving through time and space. In Carter's terms, the individual has a mandate—to construct sense of the world in order to move through it. Sense is not seen as being "out there" but rather as being something that the individual constructs. The individual operates on available sense—the ideas made in the process of experiencing life, being educated, listening to others—only as long as available sense works. Since life is inherently unmanageable, available sense frequently runs out and the individual must ask questions and seek answers in order to design the next movement.

This viewpoint provides a conceptual context within which to hypothesize when people will seek to inform themselves. It is the point of the need for gap-bridging, when old sense has run out. It is the point when, for some reason, movement straight ahead through time and space cannot continue unfettered.

A number of researchers have made profitable use of this theoretic base. This use has taken three forms. One is predicting the "when" of information seeking; the second is predicting the nature of the situations in which the seeking occurs; the third is predicting the "what" of information seeking.

In terms of predicting the "when" of information seeking, the "gap-bridging" perspective suggests, quite simply, that individuals will move to inform themselves at the point of need, when old sense has run out, when there is a missing piece in a picture of a situation (Dervin, 1976a, 1977a; Grunig, 1975). Using this line of thinking, a number of researchers have found visible evidence of active information seeking by audience members where other researchers found little or none. Chaffee and Choe (1978), for example, isolated political information use where others found little by isolating those points when citizens do their deciding; Stamm and Grunig (1977) did the same on environmental issues by isolating citizens in situations where they had gaps to bridge; Dervin et al. (1976) compared their respondent references to information as traditionally defined in absolute terms to their references to need for sense-making and found that while only 6 percent of their respondents indicated they needed some form of objective, absolute information while facing a recent everyday, troublesome situation, 42 percent of them reported reading something relevant to their situations, and 75 percent or more spend time thinking and talked to someone.

The second use of the moving through time-and-space perspective has been in isolating the kinds of situational measures appropriate to studies of information behaviors. Here, the "gap-bridging" idea suggests that these situations should be those when the mover sees movement as somehow deterred or fettered. Grunig (1975, 1978a,b) and Grunig and Disbrow (1977) have applied these ideas in the development of a situational typology which, in its simplest form, juxtaposes a respondent's perception of the existence of a problem with his perceptions of the existence of constraints limiting movement. Grunig predicts, and the evidence shows successfully, that, for example, those people who recognize problems and don't see themselves as constrained will be active information seekers for they are ready to move on a recognized problem. Dervin (1976a, 1977a) and Dervin et al. (1976, 1980) develop a related situational typology although their explicit predictions differ from Grunig's. In the Dervin typology, movement through time and space is looked at in terms of whether the respondent is stopped from moving because he/she sees more than one road ahead (decision situation), sees no road ahead (worry situation), sees the road blocked by something or someone (barrier situation), or sees self as being propelled along a road of someone or something else's choosing (problematic situation). This typology has also been highly successful in predicting information use.

The third use of the moving through time-and-space perspective in developing coherent situational theory has focused on the "what" of information seeking. The basic idea here is that since informing behaviors are rooted in situations, the focus of these behaviors should be predictable based on assessments of these situations. The research cited above by Dervin provides an example of this application. Dervin (1979b, p. 20) lists the kinds of questions people try to get answers to in situations as:

Where am I? Where am I going? How can I get there? Where have I come from? Am I alone? How can I control me?

She hypothesizes a direct connection between the kinds of situations people see themselves as being in and the kinds of questions they ask. Dervin et al. (1980) gave an explicit test to this hypothesis in their recent study of sense-making by patients and found clear and significant relationships between how a person described his/her situation and the questions asked. They found, for example, that patients who saw their health situations as "barriers" more frequently asked questions on why things were happening while, in contrast, patients who saw their health situations as decisions more frequently asked questions focusing on the how of getting to where they wanted to go.

The important thing about these theoretic developments is not so much their specific characteristics or their results, but the fact that for the first time hypotheses are emerging, predicting the conditions of information use rather than assuming it will be used and then trying to comprehend why it isn't. More important than this, however, is the fact that these hypotheses are highly generalizable because they speak, in the terms of Dervin et al. (1980) to the uniquenesses of situations that can be applied across situations; or, in Grunig's terms (1975) to conditions that apply across systems. In a sense, it can be said that these hypotheses speak to the imperatives of the human condition, generated as they are by an understanding of the constraints on human experience of time, space, and change.

IV. CONCLUSIONS

This chapter has attempted to track through time a number of related but relatively isolated themes in the communications and information science literature and set them in the context of the fundamental assumptions upon which they rest. It has been concerned with communication gaps in the most generalizable sense. First, the "gaps" seen by observers between potential message receivers and the hoped-for-impacts of those messages. Second, the "gaps" seen by receivers between the pictures they now have in their heads and the sense they require to design movements for their lives.

Both types of "gaps" are communication gaps. In the former, it is assumed that communication occurs when sources throw messages at receivers. In the latter, it is assumed that communication occurs when receivers reach out to use input useful in their lives. The contrast between the traditional perspective on "gaps" and the recent, phenomenological perspective, is not idiosyncratic to research focusing on gaps per se. The "gap" idea is a central idea in any concern for communicating. For this reason, a review of literature dealing with the idea is, in itself, a review of the trends of the literature in general.

In looking at the movement toward reconceptualization of the "gap" idea, this chapter has reviewed two significant challenges to traditional conceptualizations. The first of these—expounded primarily by third world researchers—sees communications research as having primarily blamed receivers for being in "gap"—for not becoming informed, innovating, developing as a result of exposure to messages. In this view, research has been blaming the victim rather than focusing on the nature of systems which create gap conditions and the nature of communication campaigns which reinforce the rich while letting the poor fall further into gap. This first challenge draws two conclusions. One is that communication itself is limited in its power to change structural inequities in systems, that this requires a specific focus on system changing. The second is that communication campaigns must become receiver-oriented.

It is at this point where the first challenge leaves off that the second challenge enters. This challenge sees communications research as having been led astray by inappropriate assumptions about the nature of information, the thing that it is assumed is transmitted by messages. In this view, communications research is seen as having dealt with mythical gaps—those seen when an observer measures a receiver against a standard not relevant to that receiver—while ignoring the kinds of gaps that are crucial in communication—gaps that individuals see in their pictures of the world and sometimes try to fill with input from messages.

While these moves toward reconceptualization often seem cast as if they represent marked polarizations between points of view, this appearance is, in itself, more myth than reality. The literature of the first challenge does deal more with power while the literature of the second challenge deals more with fundamental premises. Yet, both call for a move to a more receiver-oriented social science and both call for more receiver-oriented communication programs. And, both contribute to the move toward reconceptualization in different but not contradictory ways.

The literature of the first challenge can be called the pragmatic literature. It presents the problems that need addressing in the arena of their sternest test, the arena of third world development where there is little disagreement about the enormous gaps that need bridging, individually and collectively, economically and informationally.

The literature of the second challenge can be called the philosophic literature. It presents the reasoning that supports the philosophic leap that will be required if new power structures, no matter how responsive to citizens in intent, are not merely to supplant old ones, leaving the worlds of citizens as isolated from the mainstreams of power as ever.

REFERENCES

Adams, J. B., Mullen, J. J., and Wilson, H. M. (1969). Diffusion of a minor foreign affairs news event. *Journalism Quarterly 46*, 545–551.

Allen, I. L., and Colfax, J. D. (1968). The diffusion of news of LBJ's March 31 decision. *Journalism Quarterly 45*, 321–324.

Allport, G. W. (1960). "Personality and Social Encounter." Beacon Press, Boston.

Atkin, C. K., Bowen, L., Nayman, O., and Sheinkopf, K. (1973). Quantity vs. quality in televised political advertising: Patterns of reception and response in two gubernatorial campaigns. *Public Opinion Quarterly 37*, 209–224.

Atwood, R. (1980). "Communication Research in Latin America: Cultural and Conceptual Dilemmas." (Paper presented at the Annual Meeting of the International Communication Association, Acapulco, Mexico.)

Bauer, R. (1964). The obstinate audience. *American Psychologist 19*, 319–328.

Beltran, L. R. S. (1976). Alien premises, objects, and methods in Latin American communication research. *Communication Research 3*, 107–134.

Bem, D. (1972). Constructing cross-situational consistencies in behaviour. *Journal of Personality 40*, 17–26.

Bem, D., and Allen, A. (1974). On predicting some of the people some of the time: The search for cross-situational consistencies in behaviour. *Psychological Review 81*, 506–520.

Berlo, D. K. (1977). Communication as process: Review and commentary. In "Communication Yearbook I" (B. D. Ruben, Ed.), pp. 11–27. Transaction Books, New Brunswick, New Jersey.

Bernstein, B. (1961). Some sociological determinants of perception. *British Journal of Sociology 12*, 159–175.

Bishop, M. (1973). Media use and democratic political orientation in Lima, Peru. *Journalism Quarterly 50*, 60–67.

Block, C. E. (1970). Communicating with the urban poor: An exploratory inquiry. *Journalism Quarterly 47*, 3–11.

Blumler, J. G. (1979). The role of theory in uses and gratifications studies. *Communication Research 6*, 9–36.

Bogatz, G., and Ball, S. (1971). "The Second Year of Sesame Street: A Continuing Evaluation." Educational Testing Center, Princeton, New Jersey.

Bowes, J. (1971). "Information Control Behaviours and the Political Effectiveness of Low-Income Urban Adults." Unpublished dissertation, Michigan State University.

Branscomb, L. M. (1979). Information: The ultimate frontier. *Science 203*, 143–147.

Brittain, J. M. (1970). "Information and its Users: A Review with Special References to the Social Sciences." Bath University Press, Bath, England.

Brown, S. R. (1979). Perspective, transfiguration, and equivalence in communication theory: Review and commentary. *In* "Communication Yearbook 3" (D. Nimmo, Ed.), pp. 51–65. Transaction Books. New Brunswick, New Jersey.

Bruner, J. (1964). Going beyond the information given. *In* "Contemporary Approaches to Cognition" (Colorado Symposium), pp. 41–70. Harvard University Press, Cambridge, Massachusetts.

Bruner, J. (1973). "Beyond the Information Given." W. W. Norton, New York.

Cappella, J. N. (1977). Research methodology in communication: Review and Commentary. *In* "Communication Yearbook 1" (B. D. Ruben, Ed.), pp. 37–53. Transaction Books, New Brunswick, New Jersey.

Caplovitz, D. (1963). "The Poor Pay More." Free Press, New York.

Carter, R. F. (1972). "A Journalistic View of Communication." (Paper presented at the Annual Meeting of the Association for Education in Journalism, Carbondale, Illinois.)

Carter, R. F. (1973). "Communication as Behaviour." (Paper presented at the Annual Meeting of the Association for Education in Journalism, Fort Collins, Colorado.)

Carter, R. F. (1974a). "A Journalistic Cybernetic." (Paper presented at the Conference on Communication and Control in Social Processes, University of Pennsylvania, Philadelphia.)

Carter, R. F. (1974b). "Toward More Unity in Science." (Unpublished paper, School of Communications, University of Washington, Seattle, Washington.)

Carter, R. F. (1975). "Elementary Ideas of Systems Applied to Problem-Solving Strategies." (Paper presented at the Annual Meeting of the Far West Region of the Society for General Systems Research, San Jose, California.)

Carter, R. F., Ruggles, W. L., Jackson, K. M., and Heffner, M. B. (1973). Application of signaled stopping technique to communication research. *In* "New Models for Mass Communication Research" (P. Clarke, Ed.), pp. 5–44. Sage Publications, Beverly Hills, California.

Chaffee, S. H. (1970). "Parent–Child Similarities in Television Use." (Paper presented at the Annual Meeting of the Association for Education in Journalism, Washington, D.C.)

Chaffee, S. H. (1972). The interpersonal context of mass communication. *In* "Current Perspectives in Mass Communication Research" (F. G. Kline and P. J. Tichenor, Eds.), pp. 95–120. Sage Publications, Beverly Hills, California.

Chaffee, S. H., and Atkin, C. K. (1971). Parental influences on adolescent media use. *American Behaviorial Scientist 14*, 323–340.

Chafee, S. H., and Choe, S. (1978). "Time of Decision and Media Use During the Ford-Carter Campaign." (Paper presented at the Annual Meeting of the Association for Education in Journalism, Seattle, Washington.)

Chaffee, S. H., and McLeod, J. M. (1973). Individual versus social predictors of information seeking. *Journalism Quarterly 50*, 237–245.

Childers, T., and Post, J. (1975). "The Information Poor in America." Scarecrow Press, Metuchen, New Jersey.

Clarke, P. (1965). Parental socialization values and children's newspaper reading. *Journalism Quarterly 42*, 539–546.

Clarke, P., and Kline, F. G. (1974). Media effects reconsidered: Some new strategies for communication research. *Communication Research 1*, 224–239.

Cooke, T. D., Appleton, H., Conner, R. F., Shaffer, A., Tamkin, G., and Weber, S. J. (1975). "'Sesame Street' Revisited." Russell Sage Foundation, New York.

Conant, R. C. (1979). A vector theory of information. *In* "Communication Yearbook 3" (D. Nimmo, Ed.), pp. 177–194. Transaction Books, New Brunswick, New Jersey.

Davis, D. K. (1977). Assessing the role of mass communication in social processes. *Communication Research 4*, 23–34.

Dervin, B. (1976a). Strategies for dealing with human information needs: Information or communication? *Journal of Broadcasting 20*, 324–333.

Dervin, B. (1976b). The everyday information needs of the average citizen: A taxonomy for analysis. *In* "Information for the Community" (M. Kochen and J. C. Donohue, Eds.), pp. 19–38. American Library Association, Chicago, Illinois.

Dervin, B. (1977a). Useful theory for librarianship: Communication, not information, *Drexel Library Quarterly 13,* (No. 3), 16–32.

Dervin, B. (1977b). Communication with, not to, the urban poor. Eric Clearinghouse on Urban Education, Institute for Urban and Minority Education, Columbia University, New York. (ERIC/CUE Urban Diversity Series, No. 50).

Dervin, B. (1978). The human side of communication. *Theory and Methodology Division (Association for Education in Journalism) Newsletter,* November, 5–14.

Dervin, B. (1979a). "A Pre-requisite for Information Equity: Individual Sense-Making." (Paper presented at the Conference on Indicators of Equity in Information Dissemination Programs in Education, National Institute of Education, Washington, D.C.)

Dervin, B. (1979b). "Sense-Making as a Prerequisite for Information Equality" (Paper presented at the 7th Annual Telecommunication Policy Research Conference, Skytop, Pennsylvania.)

Dervin, B. (1979c). "Meeting Individual Information Needs in the Midst of the Information Explosion of the 1980s." (Paper presented at the Coliquium-Visiting Lecture Series, All University Gerontology Program, Syracuse University, Syracuse, New York.)

Dervin, B., and Greenberg, B. S. (1972). The communication environment of the urban poor. *In* "Current Perspectives in Mass Communication" (F. G. Kline and P. J. Tichenor, Eds.), pp. 195–234. Sage Publications, Beverly Hills, California.

Dervin, B., Zweizig, D., Banister, M., Gabriel, M., Hall, E., Kwan, C., with Bowes, J., and Stamm, K. (1976). "The Development of Strategies for Dealing with the Information Needs of Urban Residents: Phase I—Citizen Study." (Final report on Project No. L0035JA to Office of Libraries and Learning Resources, Office of Education, U.S. Department of Health, Education,and Welfare.) (ED 125 640.)

Dervin, B., Zweizig, D., Hall, E. P., Kwan, C., Lalley, K., with Banister, M., Gabriel, M., Gray, V. A., Schnelle, R., and Yung, J. (1977). "The Development of Strategies for Dealing with the Information Needs of Urban Residents: Phase II—Information Practitioner Study." (Final report on Project No. 475AH50014 to Office of Libraries and Learning Resources, Office of Education, U. S. Department of Health, Education, and Welfare.) (ED 136791.)

Dervin, B., Harlock, S., Atwood, R., and Garzona, C. (1980). The human side of information: An exploration in a health communication context. *In* "Communication Yearbook 4" (D. Nimmo, Ed.), in press. Transaction Books, New Brunswick, New Jersey.

Deutsch, M. (1965). The role of social class in language development and cognition. *American Journal of Orthopsychiatry 25,* 78–88.

Diaz-Bordenave, J. (1976). Communication of agricultural innovations in Latin America: The need for new models. *Communication Research 3,* 135–154.

Donohue, G. A., Tichenor, P. J., and Olien, C. N. (1975). Mass media and the knowledge gap: A hypothesis reconsidered. *Communication Research 2,* 3–23.

Donohew, L., Tipton, L., and Haney, R. (1978). Analysis of information-seeking strategies. *Journalism Quarterly 55,* 25–31.

Edelstein, A. S. (1974). "The Uses of Communication in Decision Making: A Comparative Study of Yugoslavia and the United States." Praeger, New York.

Elliott, P. (1974). Uses and gratifications research: A critique and a sociological alternative. *In* "The Uses of Mass Communications" (J. G. Blumler and E. Katz, Eds.), pp. 249–268. Sage Publications, Beverly Hills, California.

Endler, N. S., and Hunt, J. M. (1969). Generalizability of contributions from sources of variance in the S-R inventories of anxiousness. *Journal of Personality 37,* 1–24.

Ettema, J. S., and Kline, F. G. (1977). Deficits, differences, and ceilings: Contingent conditions for understanding the knowledge gap. *Communication Research 4,* 179–202.

Fells, N. W., Davis, A., Havighurst, R., Herrick, V., and Tyler, R. (1951). "Intelligence and Cultural Differences." University of Chicago Press, Chicago, Illinois.

Fitzsimmons, S., and Osburn, H. A. (1969). The impact of social issues and public affairs television documentaries. *Public Opinion Quarterly 32,* 379–397.

Freire, P. (1970). "Pedagogy of the Oppressed." Seabury Press, New York.

Furman, S. S., Sweat, L., and Crocetti, G. (1965). Social class factors in the flow of children to outpatient psychiatric clinics. *American Journal of Public Health 55* (No. 3), 12–18.

Galloway, J. J. (1974). "Subcultural rates of change and adoption and knowledge gaps in the diffusion of innovations." (Unpublished dissertation, Michigan State University.)

Galloway, J. J. (1977). The analysis and significance of communication effects gaps. *Communication Research 4,* 363–386.

Genova, B. K. L., and Greenberg, B. S. (1979). Interests in news and the knowledge gap. *Public Opinion Quarterly 43,* 79–91.

Gorney, R. (1972). "The Human Agenda." Simon and Schuster, New York.

Greenberg, B. S. (1964). Person-to-person communication in the diffusion of news events. *Journalism Quarterly 41,* 489–494.

Greenberg, B. S., and Dervin, B. (1970). "The Use of the Mass Media by the Urban Poor." Praeger, New York.

Grunig, J. E. (1972). Communication in community decisions on problems of the poor. *Journal of Communication 22,* 5–25.

Grunig, J. E. (1973a). Information Seeking in Organization Communication: A Case of Applied Theory. (Paper presented at the Annual Meeting of the International Communication Association, Montreal, Canada.)

Grunig, J. E. (1973b). New Directions for Research in Communications and International Development: From the Study of Individuals to the Study of Formal Organizations. (Paper presented at the Annual Meeting of the International Communication Association, Montreal, Canada.)

Grunig, J. E. (1975). A multisystems theory of organization communication. *Communication Research 2,* 99–136.

Grunig, J. E. (1978a). Accuracy of communication from an external public to employees in a formal organization. *Human Communication Research 5,* 40–53.

Grunig, J. E. (1978b). Defining publics in public relations: The case of a suburban hospital. *Journalism Quarterly 55,* 109–118.

Grunig, J. E., and Disbrow, J. (1977). Developing a probabilistic model for communications decision making. *Communication Research 4,* 145–168.

Hanneman, G. J., and Greenberg, B. S. (1973). Relevance and diffusion of news on major and minor events. *Journalism Quarterly 40,* 433–437.

Havelock, R. G., with Guskin, A., Frohman, M., Havelock, M., Hill, M., and Huber, J. (1969). "Planning for Innovation through Dissemination and Utilization of Knowledge." (Report from Center for Research on Utilization of Scientific Knowledge, University of Michigan, Ann Arbor.)

Hess, R. D. (1970). Social class and ethnic influences on socialization. *In* "Carmichael's Manual of Child Psychology" (P. H. Mussen, Ed.), Vol. II, pp. 457–558, John Wiley, New York.

Hewes, D., and Haight, L. (1979). The cross-situational consistency of measures of communicative behaviours. *Communication Research 6,* 243–270.

Hiltz, S. R. (1971). Black and white in the consumer financial system. *American Journal of Sociology 76,* 987–998.

Hollis, J. W., and Hollis, L. U. (1969). "Personalizing Information Processes." MacMillan, New York.

Holzner, B. (1968). "Reality Construction in Society." Schenkman Publishing Company, Cambridge, Massachusetts.

Hsia, H. J. (1973). "A Preliminary Report on Motivation and Communication Patterns of the Black, Chicano, White, and Affluent White in a Typical Southwest U. S. City." (Paper presented at the Annual Meeting of the Association for Education in Journalism, Fort Collins, Colorado.)

Hurwitz, N. H. (1975). Communication networks of the urban poor. *Equal Opportunity Review,* Eric Clearinghouse on Urban Education, Columbia University, New York. (ED 109292.)

Hyman, H., and Sheatsley, P. (1947). Some reasons why information campaigns fail. *Public Opinion Quarterly 11,* 412–423.

Ireton, H., Thriving, E., and Graven, H. (1970). Infant mental development and neurological status, family socioeconomic status and intelligence at age four. *Child Development 41,* 937–945.

Johnson, N. (1973). Television and politicization: A test of competing models. *Journalism Quarterly 50,* 447–455.

Katz, E., Blumler, J. G., and Gurevitch, M. (1974). Utilization of mass communication by the individual. *In* "The Uses of Mass Communications" (J. G. Blumler and E. Katz, Eds.), pp. 19–32. Sage Publications, Beverly Hills, California.

Katzman, N. (1974). The impact of communication technology: Promises and prospects. *Journal of Communication 24,* 47–58.

Key, V. (1961). "Public Opinion and American Democracy." Knopf, New York.

Klapper, J. T. (1960). "The Effects of Mass Communication." Free Press, Glencoe, Illinois.

Kline, F. G., Miller, P. V., and Morrison, A. J. (1974). Adolescents and family planning information: An exploration of audience needs and media effects. *In* "The Uses of Mass Communication" (J. G. Blumler and E. Katz, Eds.), pp. 113–136. Sage Publications, Beverly Hills, California.

Kurtz, N. R. (1968). Gatekeepers: Agents in acculturation. *Rural Sociology 33,* 63–70.

Levin, J., and Taube, G. (1970). Bureaucracy and the socially handicapped: A study of lower-class tenants in public housing. *Sociology and Social Research 54,* 209–219.

Levine, F. J., and Preston, E. (1970). Community resource orientation among low-income groups. *Wisconsin Law Review 80,* 80–113.

Levine, S. L., White, P. E., and Paul, B. D. (1963). Community interorganizational problems in providing medical care and social services. *American Journal of Publich Health 53,* 1184–1195.

Levy, S. (1969). How population subgroups differed in their knowledge of six assassinations. *Journalism Quarterly 46,* 685–698.

McAnany, E. G. (1978). The role of information in communication with the rural poor: Some reflections. *In* "Communication with the Rural Poor in the Third World: Does Information Make a Difference?" (E. G. McAnany, Ed.) (Report from Institute of Communication Research, Stanford University, California.)

McLeod, J. M., and Wackman, D. B. (1967). "Family Communication: An Updated Report." (Paper presented at the Annual Meeting of the Association for Education in Journalism, Boulder, Colorado.)

McLeod, J. M., Rush, R. R., and Friederich, K. H. (1969). The mass media and political information in Quito, Equador. *Public Opinion Quarterly 32,* 575–587.

McQuail, D., Blumler, J. G., and Brown, J. R. (1972). The television audience: A revised perspective. *In* "Sociology of Mass Communications (D. McQuail, Ed.), pp. 135–165. Penquin Books, Harmondsworth, England.

Mann, D. (1973). "Shared Control in Urban Neighborhood Schools." (Report from Teachers College, Columbia University.) (ED 083 355.)

Mathiason, J. R. (1970). "Communication Patterns and Powerlessness Among Urban Poor: Toward the Use of Mass Communications for Rapid Social Change." (Paper presented at the Annual Meeting of the Association for Education in Journalism, Washington, D.C.)

Mendelsohn, H. (1968). "Operation Gap–Stop: A Study of the Application of Communication Techniques in Reaching the Unreachable Poor." (Report from Communication Arts Center, University of Denver.)

Milbrath, L. W. (1965). "Political Participation: How and Why do People get Involved in Politics." Rand McNally, Chicago.

Miller, D. (1963). The study of social relationships: Situation, identity, and social interaction. *In* "Psychology: A Study of Science" (S. Koch, Ed.), pp. 639–737. McGraw Hill, New York.

Mischel, W. (1968). "Personality and Assessment." Wiley, New York.

Mischel, W. (1969). Continuity and change in personality. *American Psychologist 24,* 1012–1018.

Mischel, W. (1971). "Introduction to Personality." Holt, Rinehart, and Winston, New York.

Mischel, W. (1973). Toward a cognitive social learning reconceptualization of personality. *Psychological Review 80,* 252–283.

Moore, J., and Newell, A. (1974). How Merlin can understand. *In* "Knowledge and Cognition" (G. Lee, Ed.), L. Erlbaum, Potomac, Maryland.

Nordenstreng, K. (1977). European communications theory: Review and commentary. *In* "Communication Yearbook I" (B. D. Ruben, Ed.), pp. 73–78. Transaction Books, New Brunswick, New Jersey.

Parker, E. B. (1978). An information-based hypothesis. *Journal of Communication 28* (No. 1), 81–83.

Parker, E. B., and Paisley, W. J. (1966). "Patterns of Adult Information Seeking." (Report from Institute of Communications Research, Stanford University.)

Pratt, L. (1969). Level of sociological knowledge among health and sociology workers. *Journal of Health and Social Behavior 10,* 59–65.

Quay, L. D. (1974). Language, dialect, age, and intelligence-test performance in disadvantaged black children. *Child Development 45,* 463–468.

Rees, A. M., and Schultz, D. G. (1967). Psychology and information retrieval. *In* "Information Retrieval: A Critical View" (G. Schecter, Ed.), pp. 143–150. Thompson Press, Washington, D.C.

Rieger, J. H., and Anderson, R. C. (1968). Information sources and need hierarchies of an adult population in five Michigan counties. *Adult Education Journal 18,* 155–177.

Robinson, J. P. (1972). Toward defining the functions of television. *In* "Television and Social Behaviour" (E. Rubinstein, G. A. Comstock, and J. P. Murray, Eds.), Vol. 4, pp. 568–603. National Institute of Mental Health, Rockville, Maryland.

Rogers, E. M. (1976). Communication and development: The passing of the dominant paradigm. *Communications Research 3,* 213–240.

Rogers, E. M., and Adhikarya, R. (1979). Diffusion of innovations: An up-to-date review and commentary. *In* "Communication Yearbook 3" (D. Nimmo, ed.), pp. 67–82. Transaction Books, New Brunswick, New Jersey.

Röling, N. G., Ascroft, J., and Chege, F. W. (1976). The diffusion of innovations and the issue of equity in rural development. *Communication Research 3,* 155–170.

Rotter, J. B. (1966). Generalized expectancies for internal versus external control of reinforcement. *Psychological Monographs 80* (No. 1), Whole Number 609.

Rotter, J. B., Chance, J. E., and Phares, E. J. (1972). "Application of a Social Learning Theory to Personality." Holt, Rinehart, and Winston, New York.

Schramm, W. (1973). "Men, Media, and Messages." Harper and Row, New York.

Scott, R. A. (1967). The selection of clients by social welfare agencies: The case of the blind. *Social Problems 14,* 248–257.

Sears, D. O., and Freedman, J. (1967). Selective exposure to information: A critical review. *Public Opinion Quarterly 31,* 194–213.

Seeman, L. (1966). Alienation, membership, and political knowledge. *Public Opinion Quarterly 30,* 353–367.

Schackle, G. L. S. (1974). Decision: The human predicament. *Annals of the American Academy of Political and Social Science 412*, 1–10.

Shingi, P. M., and Mody, B. (1976). The communication effects gap: A field experience on television and agricultural ignorance in India. *Communication Research 3*, 171–190.

Sjoberg, G., Brymer, R. A., and Farris, B. (1966). Bureaucracy and the lower class. *Sociology and Social Research 50*, 325–336.

Smith, A. G. (1975). The primary resource. *Journal of Communications 25* (No. 2), 15–20.

Spitzer, S. P., and Denzin, N. K. (1965). Levels of knowledge in an emergent crisis. *Social Forces 44*, 234–237.

Stamm, K. R., and Grunig, J. E. (1977). Communication situations and cognitive strategies in resolving environmental issues. *Journalism Quarterly 54*, 713–720.

Stewart, J. (1978). Foundations of dialogic communication. *Quarterly Journal of Speech 64*, 183–201.

Swanson, D. L. (1979). Political communication research and the uses and gratifications model: A critique. *Communication Research 6*, 37–53.

Tichenor, P. J., Donohue, G. A., and Olien, C. N. (1970). Mass media flow and differential growth of knowledge. *Public Opinion Quarterly 34*, 159–170.

Tichenor, P. J., Rodenkirchen, J. M., Olien, C. N., and Donohue, G. A. (1973). Community issues, conflict, and public affairs knowledge. *In* "New Models for Mass Communication Research" (P. Clarke, Ed.), pp. 45–80. Sage Publications, Beverly Hills, California.

Udell, J. G. (1966). Prepurchase behaviour of buyers of small electrical appliances. *Journal of Marketing 30* (No. 4), pp. 50–52).

Voos, H. (1969). "Informations Needs in Urban Areas: A Summary of Research in Methodology." Rutgers University Press, New Brunswick, New Jersey.

Wade, S., and Schramm, W. (1969). The mass media as sources of public affairs, science, and health knowledge. *Public Opinion Quarterly 33*, 197–209.

Warner, E. S., Murray, A. D., and Palmour, V. E. (1973). "Information Needs of Urban Residents." (Final report on Contract No. OEC-0-71-455 to Division of Library Programs, Office of Education, U.S. Department of Health, Education, and Welfare.) (ED 088 464.)

Weimer, W. B. (1978). Communication, speech, and psychological models of man: Review and commentary. *In* "Communication Yearbook 2" (B. E. Ruben, Ed.), pp. 57–77. Transaction Books, New Brunswick, New Jersey.

Weyl, H. (1963). "Philosophy of Mathematics and Natural Science." Atheneum, New York.

Willerman, L., Broman, S. H., and Fiedler, M. (1970). Infant development, pre-school IQ, and social class." *Child Development 41*, 70–77.

Wilson, P. (1977). "Public Knowledge, Private Ignorance." Greenwood Press, Westport, Connecticut.

Zweizig, D., and Dervin, B. (1977). Public library use, users, and uses: Advances in knowledge of the characteristics and needs of the adult clientele of American public libraries. *Advances in Librarianship 7*, 231–255.

4

Information
and Work*

William Paisley
Institute for Communication Research
Stanford University

---

*Preparation of this chapter was supported in part by NSF grant no. IST-77-28242-A1.

I. INTRODUCTION

Their sin was not so much that they were ignorant (although they might have done more to acquaint themselves with the facts), but that they acted as if they *did* know, and by their laws imposed their ignorance upon the settlers (Boorstin, 1958, p. 81).`

A. Historical Context

At the dawn of history, humans were already acquiring and using information in their work. The earliest human activities revealed by drawings and other prehistoric artifacts required ability in "reading" natural signs and coordinating group effort. Unnumbered generations taught their offspring these communication skills before the first hieroglyphic texts and calendars supplemented oral instruction in what to do and when to do it. Examples of "primitive" language that still exist in parts of the world today indicate that early speech was rich in words and phrases for describing work.

New information requirements accompanied the rise of commerce five thousand years ago. Trading societies needed records of transactions, debts, contracts, ownership, etc. Cuneiform tablets unearthed in the ancient cities of Mesopotamia were largely business records, each bearing the details of a transaction and the seals of buyer and seller.

The Code of Hammurabi, preserved as 3,600 lines of cuneiform, regulated not only social conduct but also commerce. Of the roughly 280 sections of the Code, 40 dealt with trade and commerce, 16 with professional services, 38 with wages and rates of hire, etc.

Urban crafts were specialized even in the ancient world. The craft guilds that flowered in Medieval Europe had their roots in Greece and Rome. Craft information passed from masters to apprentices; the latter graduated to the status of journeymen and waited for the guild to confirm them as masters qualified to renew the cycle of instruction. Guilds were a primary channel of *vocational information* for more than two thousand years, but they could not adapt to the new divisions of labor that the Industrial Revolution created.

Commercial and *financial information* was also entrusted to guilds—in this case, the merchant guilds that evolved into trading monopolies like the Hanseatic League in the Baltic countries. The first public channel of commercial and financial information in Renaissance Europe were the *Fuggerzeitungen* (Fugger newsletters), which relayed information from a network of "correspondents" to business associates of the wealthy Fugger family. The newsletters represented the challenge of rising capitalism to the waning power of the leagues.

Well into the sixteenth century, *scientific information* (to be distinguished from the guarded *scientific knowledge* of investigators like Leonardo) had not progressed much beyond Aristotle and Pliny. Between 1543 and 1638, however, the published writings of Copernicus, Vesalius, Harvey, and Galileo created scientific revolutions in astronomy, anatomy, and physiology. By 1670 the *Philosophical Transactions of the Royal Society of London* were read by scientists throughout Europe.

The rise of technology after 1700 provides historical markers of the role of information in work. Newcomen's steam engine of 1718 was little improved until 1764, when James Watt applied principles of heat transfer that he had learned as an assistant in Joseph Black's chemical laboratory to the design of a separate condenser. The practical problem of increasing the efficiency of steam engines attracted scientific attention after 1800 and led directly to the formulation of the First and Second Laws of Thermodynamics by Carnot, Joule, Kelvin, and others.

When the technological problem was novel, as in the construction of the first successful canal in America, it was necessary to import information in the head of an engineer. Morison, in his history of American technology (1974, p. 22), describes the quandary of the builders of the Middlesex Canal, connecting the Charles and Merrimack rivers in Massachusetts, in 1793:

> They found they did not know how to excavate a ditch with expedition, that is, how to proceed through rock, how to dig earth in quantity and dispose of it in appropriate places. They found they did not know how to seal the ditch effectively so that water would not run out through the bottom and sides. . . . They found they did not know how to build retaining walls that would keep their form. They found they did not know how to design a canal lock and what to build it out of. . . . They found they could not design the machinery for the opening and closing of the valve gates for the locks. . . . They found, in sum, that they did not know anything about how to build a canal.

The builders called in the engineer William Weston, who had built canals and bridges in his native England. In the successful phase of canal building that followed, contemporary English practices merged with older wisdom, as in the mixing of a hydraulic cement that would retain its strength under water. Roman engineers had used hydraulic cement two thousand years earlier, but its ingredients and proportions were forgotten until the middle of the eighteenth century, when they were rediscovered in an account by Vetruvius.

Interspersed among spectacular feats of technology in the past two hundred years are many mistakes and even disasters that can be traced to a lack of information. Canals leaked, bridges collapsed, dams crumbled, locomotives exploded, ships sank. More insidiously, factories disabled workers and poisoned the countryside. As Morison (1974, p. 37) states mildly, "slippages and wastes in the system for distributing information produced damaging inefficiencies." However, information emerged after the fact if not before. Morison (1974, p. 67) describes the Erie Canal as "a six-year engineering school. For a generation after, many of the dams, bridges, and railroads built in this country were designed by graduates of this school."

At the beginning of the nineteenth century, the role of information in construction and industry was to correct the failures of intuitive practice. By the end of the nineteenth century, structures and machines had become too complicated to be created intuitively.

The first industrial laboratory charged with producing information to lead rather than follow technological innovation was probably the "steelworks analytical laboratory" attached to the Bessemer converter in Wyandotte, Michigan. Built in 1864, it did not last long; it was burned by steelworkers who feared the experiments it was conducting (Morison, 1974, p. 108).

Adapting models such as Edison's Menlo Park laboratory in the United States and Helmholtz's Reichsanstalt in Germany, a number of American companies established laboratories around 1900. The romance of these early laboratories, embodied in popular images of Steinmetz at General Electric and Tesla at Westinghouse, may obscure the shift in the role of information that they represented. *Learning by doing* was giving way to *learning by experimenting*. Henceforth experimental data would be incorporated in the design of technological innovations. All workers from the drafting department to the production line would need to know facts and figures that were not generated by their own work but came "from the lab." Interdepartmental flows of information became indispensable.

In the laboratory itself, problems became too complicated for individual researchers to solve. Interdisciplinary teams of researchers were recruited. The academic tradition of disciplinary exclusiveness could not be tolerated in the industrial laboratory. Managers needed to ensure communication within the laboratory as well as from the laboratory to the plant.

Industrial laboratories at the turn of the century were beginning to produce information on machines and processes. At the same time, in a more amazing departure from previous research, engineers began to produce information on *work* itself. Taylor's *Principles of Scientific Management* (1911) objectified work, showing that work could be analyzed as a process and the worker as a machine. Taylor conducted time-and-motion studies at the Bethlehem Steel Company from 1898 to 1902. At the end of this period, each worker in the operation that Taylor studied was performing, at increased wages, the work that four workers had done previously.

Industry secured the knowledge capital for a new century of technological expansion by borrowing heavily from academic science. A few decades later, when high-technology warfare brought science and industry into urgent collaboration, the debt was repaid. The industrial laboratory, with its timetables and teams of researchers, served as a model for academic fields undergoing the transition from "little science" to "big science" (Price, 1963).

Federal management of the wartime science-industry collaboration was entrusted to two academic scientists, Vannevar Bush and James Conant. In the postwar period they and fellow scientists labored to secure a new footing for science vis-a-vis industry and the government. Their accomplishment was a peacetime program of support for science from the new National Science Foundation. The peacetime program answered a question posed by Bush (1945, p. 101) in the last month of the war:

> This has not been a scientist's war; it has been a war in which all have had a part. The scientists, burying their old professional competition in the demand of a common cause, have shared greatly and learned much. It has been exhilarating to work in effective partnership. Now, for many, this appears to be approaching an end. What are the scientists to do next?

In 1941, on the eve of American involvememt in the war, federal expenditures for all research and development were only $370 million. By 1951 federal expenditures had reached $2 billion. By 1971 they were $15 billion, and by 1979 they exceeded $25 billion. Industry's support for research and development rose nearly as fast, from $510 million in 1941 to $11 billion in 1971 and $23 billion in 1979 (Machlup, 1962; National Science Foundation, 1978). The effects of these expenditures on the flow of information have been prodigious.

The concept *knowledge industry* was introduced by Machlup in 1962 to denote work performed in research and development laboratories, educational institutions, publishing houses, communication media, etc., all of which produce or distribute information in some form. The extent of American investment in information was further described by Drucker (1969, p. 321):

> The "knowledge industries," which produce and distribute ideas and information rather than goods and services, accounted in 1955 for one-quarter of the U.S. gross national product. This was already three times the proportion of the national product that the country had spent on the 'knowledge sector' in 1900.... In the late 1970's it will account for one-half of the total national product.

Porat (1976) updated Machlup's 1962 data, showing that more than half of national income and nearly half of the gross national product now originate in the "production, processing, and distribution of information goods and services" (Porat, 1976, p. 1). In much less than a century, *information work* has grown from a small set of specialized activities to a dominant economic factor in American society. A present-day disciple of Frederick Taylor cannot concentrate on anything as simple as the flow of materials on a production line. The much more complex flow of information now determines the productivity of industry and even the vigor of science.

B. Definitions

Information, work, and *information work* are distinct but related concepts. *Information* can be defined both structurally and functionally. Structurally, information denotes an encoding of symbols (e.g., letters, numbers, pictures) into a message of any mode, communicated through any channel. Functionally, information denotes any stimulus that alters cognitive structure in the receiver. The functional definition is more readily understood through its converse: something that the receiver already knows (i.e., a stimulus that does not alter cognitive structure) is not information.

Work is commonly defined as effort that is productive or instrumental. Work is usually but not always remunerated; much work is done for the benefit of others without payment except for reciprocated effort, gratitude, respect, etc. Some kinds of work can be distinguished from play only by determining if the activity is being done out of necessity or for payment rather than for pleasure (as Robert Frost wrote of woodchopping, "I had no right to play / With what was another man's work for gain)". The use of sophisticated machines is often self-reinforcing, with the result that work and play are intermingled in established jobs. For example, computer programmers can be seen working "playfully" with their machines.

Information work denotes effort involving the production, distribution, transformation, storage, retrieval, or use of information. Many jobs (e.g., researcher, writer, editor, teacher) are almost exclusively information work, and many other jobs (e.g., engineer, physician, attorney, manager) combine a large proportion of information work with other "hands-on" activity.

The increasing number of jobs that are wholly or largely information work is a fact of interest to economists and historians. Drucker (1969, pp. 321–322) contrasted the American workforce of the 1930s and 1960s:

> Thirty years ago, on the eve of World War II, semiskilled machine operators, the men on the assembly line, were the centre of the American workforce. Today the centre is the knowledge worker, the man or woman who applies to productive work ideas, concepts, and information rather than manual skill or brawn.

Of equal interest but less discussed is the growing importance of information in work that is otherwise product- or service-oriented. Electricians, machinists, mechanics, and other skilled workers now depend as much on their manuals as on their tools. The shop owner's mail and the executive's in-basket are heavy with newsletters, notices, policy directives, etc. Printed specifications and regulations—"specs" and "regs"—now govern work of many kinds.

Studies of workers in various jobs show that they spend at least half and in some cases more than two-thirds of their time dealing with information (Chapanis, 1971, p. 952). Such findings have two implications. First, distinctions are disappearing between information workers, service workers, production workers, etc. Second, we need a conceptual taxonomy of *information tasks* as they enter into work *of all kinds* rather than the unitary concept of *information work*.

C. Framework for Analysis

Information tasks are more generic than each type of work that includes them. They are common denominators in the work of scientists, professionals, managers, technicians, and even service workers and production workers. More effective arrangements for the performance of any information task can benefit workers in many fields.

Information tasks occur in *sequences,* and a sequence of tasks is generally named after the focal task that it contains. For example, *decision making* is an information task in itself, but it also names a sequence of tasks that includes searching for information, selecting and processing relevant information, comparing alternative decisions with respect to their probable outcomes, and making the decision. To name a sequence after its focal task is a convenient synecdoche, just as the phrase "driving home from the office" implies entering the car, starting the engine, parking, shutting off the engine, and exiting the car as well as the actual behavior of driving.

Sequences of information tasks are also qualified by *content* and *context.* For example, much of medical practice consists of decision-making sequences qualified by the content of patients' needs and by the context of individual or group practice in an area with ample or meager medical resources. "Diagnosis" and "treatment selection" are two forms of medical decision making. They differ from other forms of medical decision making (e.g., managing the medical practice as a business) insofar as their content and context differ. Medicine as information work consists of various decision-making sequences, together with learning sequences, instrumentation and data-gathering sequences, patient–feedback sequences, etc.

Sequences of information tasks are best understood in the framework of cognitive *plans*. Miller et al., (1960, p. 16) define a plan as *"any hierarchical process in the organism that can control the order in which a sequence of operations is to be performed ."* They further define a plan as the action consequence of an *image,* which they define as "all the accumulated, organized knowledge that the organism has about itself and its world" (Miller et al., 1960, p. 17).

Plans elicit what Miller et al. describe as *searching and solving* behavior. Searching and solving behavior yields information, which in turn changes images: *"The meaning of a message is the change which it produces in the image"* (Boulding, 1956, p. 7). Changed images lead to new plans. With new plans, the cycle of behavior begins again.

Miller et al. further state that planful behavior is often the execution of hierarchically related subplans, each of which yields information that changes images governing subsequent subplans. This is another way of saying that information directs behavior.

Thus, much can be learned about the role of information in work by investigating:

1. What sequence of information and noninformation tasks the work consists of;
2. How each information task is performed;
3. What the effects of information tasks are on the performance of noninformation tasks;
4. What the effects of information tasks are on the productivity of the work overall.

II. PROPERTIES OF INFORMATION AND ITS USE

A. Quantity

The fact that the "information explosion" is an over-used metaphor should not obscure its essential validity. The accumulation of new information in many fields continues at a rate that far exceeds the *input processing rate* of workers. Derek Price (1963, p. 7) estimates that printed information in a field like experimental psychology has doubled every ten years through most of this century. At that rate a modest literature of *5,000* documents at the beginning of the century has already grown beyond *500,000* and will pass *5,000,000* before the century's end.

Strategies for coping with information overload include specialization of work (narrowing of attention frame) and sampling rather than systematic review of available information (episodic attention). Among the consequences of these strategies are further isolation of fields that could be cross-productive and duplication of information missed by workers in their sampling of the information store.

The *information input dilemma* created by the accelerating rate of information production has been well stated by two pioneering information scientists:

...let us assume that one one-thousandth of all science and technology constitutes a field of specialization; and let us consider the plight of a scientist who reads 3,000 characters a minute, which is a rate more appropriate for novels than for journal articles. Suppose that he gathers together the literature of his field of specialization (10^{10} characters) and begins now to read it. He reads 13 hours a day, 365 days a year. At the end of 12 years, he sets down the last volume with a great sigh of relief—only to discover that in the interim another 10^{10} characters were published in his field. He is deterred from undertaking 12 more years of reading by the realization that not only the volume but the rate of publication has doubled (Licklider, 1966, p. 1044).

...let me make just one observation about the volume of literature in my own highly specialized subfield of psychology. A compulsive, well-versed engineering psychologist would have to read, I estimate, somewhere on the order of 30 to 40 articles, books, theses, and technical reports every day of the year merely to keep abreast of the current literature, much less catch up with things that have been published in the past (Chapanis, 1971, p. 953).

There is no single solution to information overload. Solutions ranging from the computerization of information (to facilitate precise retrieval) to the creation of human networks (to facilitate interpersonal sharing of information) have been proposed, tested, and implemented successfully. However, these "first generation" solutions become less efficient with further growth in computerized information banks and human networks. Weinberg (1967, pp. 3–6) characterized as a "second Malthusian dilemma" the roughly exponential—$(n)(n - 1)/2$—ratio of the number of two-person linkages to the number of persons in a network. As a network of 100 persons grows to 200, the number of linkages grows more than fourfold from 4,950 to 19,900. If the original 100 persons represent a field of specialization that doubles in size every 10 years, the first decade's growth from 4,950 to 19,900 linkages is followed by a second decade's growth from 19,900 to 79,800 linkages. Early in the fourth decade, when the network passes the 1,000–member mark, it has 499,500 linkages. A tenfold increase in the size of a human network results in an approximately hundredfold increase in the number of two-person linkages that the network must accommodate.

B. Quality

The *quality* of information is a composite attribute based on the information's *relevance, timeliness, comprehensiveness,* and *authoritativeness.* Quality does not reside in the information itself but rather in the judgment of users qualified by need. Information that is relevant, timely, comprehensive, and authoritative according to the need of one user may not be so according to the needs of other users.

Information quality should be distinguished from information *value,* to which it contributes. In addition to the four aspects of quality mentioned above, value is a function of *specifiability* (distinctness of representation), *locatability* (distinctness of physical location), *acquirability* (ease of acquisition, including cost), and *usability* (suitability of form and content for the intended use).

Common sense and empirical studies agree that the amount of high-quality information in a field does not increase linearly with the quantity of information. In one respect this is a fortunate fact for the worker, whose information overload would be that much worse if the exponentially larger information store contained a constant fraction of high-quality items. In another respect the declining fraction of high-quality items adds to the information-processing burden of the worker, who must somehow discover these items in the mass of unwanted information. Written critiques of information quality have indicative titles such as "Is the Literature Worth Retrieving?" (Goudsmit, 1966) and "Management Misinformation Systems" (Ackoff, 1967).

First-generation solutions to the problem of information *quantity* have tended to exacerbate the problem of information *quality.* The real cost-efficiency of computerized information lies not in "hands-off" processing but in "heads-off" processing. Computerized information banks grow by millions of items per year precisely because the items are casually refereed and are not returned to the authors for revision. Information has been extensively computerized for a quarter of a century, but the computer is not yet able to influence or even distinguish the quality of the information it processes.

C. Structure

McLuhan's famous but overstated dictum, "the medium is the message" (McLuhan, 1964, p. 23), applies to technical information as well as public information and entertainment. If, as Kenneth Boulding (1956, p. 7) asserted, *"The meaning of a message is the change which it produces in the image,"* then we can make McLuhan's dictum consistent with the findings of information studies by paraphrasing it: *the change that a message produces in the receiver's image of the world is affected by the medium of communication.*

Studies of scientific communication indicate that the same research results are communicated many times and in many ways during the later stages of a research project. These communications differ in *mode* and *channel,* two concepts that define the structure of oral vs. print vs. electronic, and formal vs. informal communication. Messages communicated via different combinations of mode and channel have different meanings for the receiver.

The *mode* of information is the physical state in which it is encoded. The first technical information in prehistory was encoded in the oral mode.

Thousands of years later technical information was encoded in handwritten mode. Printed, audiovisual, and electronic encodings have all been invented in the recent past, relative to this time span.

The *channel* of communication is the medium or other arrangement by which information is conveyed from sender to receiver. Information in the oral mode can be conveyed in a casual conversation, in a briefing or seminar presentation, in a formal speech, etc. Information in the printed mode can be conveyed in a letter, in a photocopied paper, in a journal article, in a book, etc.

Mode and channel, defining the structure of communication events related to work, can be recorded as data in analyzing the performance of information tasks. For example, in a study of engineers reported by Lindsey (1979), data were recorded on as many as six combinations of mode and channel that each engineer turned to *consecutively* in dealing with a problem that arose in his or her work. The mode-channel combinations that were coded for response are listed below because they illustrate the range of an engineer's potential information sources:

Colleague in work group
Colleague in company
Colleague outside company
Consultant
Info. specialist in company
Info. specialist outside company
Representative of a
   supplier
Handbook
Book of collected papers
Scientific/technical book
Textbook
Internal company report
Other company's
   internal report
Technical report—published

Monograph—published
Trade publication
Professional journal
Scholarly journal
Popular science/
   technology serial
Library in company
Library outside company
Professional meeting/
   conference
Continuing education
   course
On-line computer
   search
Current awareness service

The fact that not all of these 25 modes and channels are available to every worker leads us to the concept of the *information environment*. Individual initiative, professional "connectedness," and organizational policies with respect to information services create rich or poor information environments for workers. Profiles of information environments are useful data in accounting for the performance of information tasks.

Workers who are favored with rich information environments receive information via many modes and channels. Studies of the acquisition of scientific information (notably Menzel, 1959, 1966) have shown that workers in rich information environments are desultory information searchers. Knowing that the information they need will reach them "spontaneously" not once but many times, they exhibit what can be called information nonchalance.

Workers who are out of the information mainstream account for more than their share of subscriptions to information services, computerized searches, reprint requests, etc. Their efforts to overcome deficient information environments help to explain what would otherwise be a paradoxical distribution of services (one example: Stanford University, with a top-rated school of education, does not subscribe to the ERIC educational database, while nearby California State University campuses at Hayward and San Jose do).

D. Function

Information alters cognitive structure in the course of information task sequences that focus on *learning, decision making, problem solving, calculation,* and *verification.* These five concepts have overlapping definitions because they are, in effect, molecules that consist of the same atoms or *elementary information processes* (discussed below). It is useful to define them as follows:

1. Learning is the process of *expanding cognitive structure* by incorporating new first-order, second-order, or higher-order information. First-order information consists of facts about the world. Second-order information consists of relations established among first-order facts. Third-order information consists of relations established among second-order relations. Etc. The truth status of the facts or relations is either *probable* or *determined,* depending on the learner's need for inference or what Bruner et al. (1956, pp. 182–230) call "categorizing with probabilistic cues." A contrasting hierarchy of learning consists not of facts vs. relations but of concrete learning vs. abstract "learning to learn." Gregory Bateson (1972, p. 293) defines five *levels* of learning, beginning with:

   Zero learning is characterized by *specificity of response,* which—right or wrong—is not subject to correction. *Learning I* is *change in specificity of response* by correction of errors of choice within a fixed set of alternatives. *Learning II* is *change in the process of Learning I, e.g.,* a corrective change in the set of alternatives from which choice is made. That is, Learning I is the level of learning the facts and relations that make adaptive behavior possible. Learning II is the level of developing a style of learning.

2. Decision making is the process of *deducing a course of action* from the relative advantages and disadvantages of alternatives. More graphically, each alternative can be thought of as a bundle of attributes that are judged to be relevant to the advantages and disadvantages of the alternative. Each attribute is judged to have a particular weight in determining advantages and disadvantages. The "loading" of each alternative on each attribute can be expressed as a coefficient or figure of merit. In the case of a simple two-alternative decision, weights and figures of merit combine in the following diagram:

Criterial attributes	*Attribute weights*	*Figures of merit for alternatives X, Y*		*Weighted figures of merit*	
1	w1	X1	Y1	w1X1	w1Y1
2	w2	X2	Y2	w2X2	w2Y2
3 ———————→	w3 ———→	X3 ——→	Y3	w3X3	w3Y3
$\hat{k}$	w$\hat{k}$	X$\hat{k}$	Y$\hat{k}$	wk$\hat{X}$k	wk$\hat{Y}$k

Weighted advantages and disadvantages: w.X.   w.Y.

3. Problem solving is the process of *inducing a solution* by examining facts and relations that are judged to be relevant to the problem and finding in them a *solution path* (Newell and Simon, 1972, p. 76). The cognitive step that actually produces the solution is somewhat mysterious, despite decades of psychological research on problem solving. The Gestalt principle of *insight* (Kohler, 1947) is still invoked in explanations of problem solving, but insight will also be a mystery until it can be traced to the information events that are its necessary and sufficient conditions. Although in everyday language "problem" denotes any circumstance in need of remedy, it is important in information-task analysis to restrict the definition of problem to those circumstances that have complete or highly satisfactory solutions. Otherwise problem solving as the process of finding an incomplete or partially satisfactory solution is too similar to decision making as the process of selecting the best alternative.

4. Calculation is the process of *applying algorithms* to combine facts into derivative facts or relations. Arithmetical operations are familiar examples of calculation; rules of additon, multiplication, etc., can be applied to produce sums, products, etc., that are derivative facts. However, calculation is also the process by which we plan activities, schedule time, lay out a travel route, fix things, etc. Note that most "arithmetic problems" are not problems in the problem-solving sense discussed in #3 above. If we know which algorithm to apply and how to apply it, then the process is one of calculation.

5. Verification is the process of *testing the truth status* of a previously known fact or relation, a previously made decision, a previously solved problem, or a previously completed calculation. Different cognitive steps may be required in each case. For example, we can verify a fact by finding an independent and credible statement of it in an information source. We can verify a decision by collecting information on its outcomes. We can verify a solution by demonstrating that another person who is informed of it can also solve the problem. Depending on the nature of the algorithm, we can verify a calculation by replicating it either "forward" or "backward."

The "atoms" that underlie these "molecular" information tasks are sequences of *elementary information processes.* As described by Newell and Simon (1972, pp. 20–38 and 787–809), elementary information processes are the throughput of an adaptive *information processing system* (IPS) which can be a person or computer with the following characteristics:

1. At a minimum, an IPS consists of receptors that make it cognizant of its environment, a processor, a memory, and effectors by which it can operate on its environment.
2. The processor consists of elementary information processes, a short-term memory that serves the elementary information processes, and an interpreter that determines the sequence of elementary information processes to be executed according to information stored in short-term memory.
3. Elementary information processes consist of discrimination tests and comparisons, symbol creation, symbol structure writing, external reading and writing, symbol structure designation and storage. "The entire behavior of the IPS is compounded out of sequences of these elementary processes."
4. The IPS also has a long-term memory and generally has access to an external memory.
5. The IPS has a program that is goal-directed, "where a goal is a symbol structure with certain characteristics: (1) a goal carries a test to determine when some state of affairs has been attained ...; (2) a goal is capable of controlling behavior under appropriate conditions" (Newell and Simon, 1972, pp. 806–807).

A dynamic concept that complements the somewhat static IPS is the *TOTE* (test-operate-test-exit) *unit,* proposed by Miller et al. (1960, pp. 26–38). The TOTE unit is a recurring four-step cycle of information processing:

1. Given a plan with a goal state or success criterion embedded in the plan, a person tests the environment to determine his or her progress toward

the goal state. The person may test external conditions via sensory receptors as well as internal conditions via proprioceptors. The test outcome is simply one of congruity or incongruity with the goal state.

2. When the test reveals incongruity with the goal state, the person operates on the internal or external environment in a way that the plan indicates will result in progress toward the goal state. Such operation may take the form of cognition (e.g., thinking it over), perception (e.g., searching the environment for a more successful approach), motor behavior (e.g., manipulating objects), symbolic behavior (e.g., communicating with someone), or combinations of these.

3. Following the operation, the person again tests congruity with the goal state.

4. When the test finally reveals congruity, the person exits from the TOTE unit and continues on to the next step of the plan—that is, to a different TOTE unit and goal state.

A simple integration of the Newell–Simon IPS and the Miller et al. TOTE concepts appears in Figure 1. Newell and Simon (1972, p. 822) further state: "plans are structurally identical to programs. They are symbolic structures ... that are used to guide action in exploring the problem space."

The TOTE unit occupies a useful middle ground between fundamental perceptual/cognitive processes and plans for accomplishing information tasks. "Plans for searching and solving" (Miller et al., 1960, pp. 159–175) can be analyzed as hierarchies of information-processing subplans. Subplans can

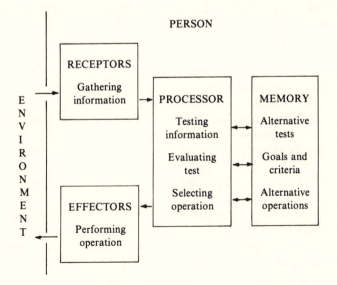

FIG. 1. Integration of the *IPS* and *TOTE* concepts.

be analyzed at several levels of hierarchical reduction. For example, the *information-input* subplan within a *decision-making* plan consists of steps by which information is sought, selected, and processed. One level down, the subplan for a single step such as *information selection* consists of TOTE units for testing incoming streams of information against a relevance criterion, sampling more deeply into the relevant streams, and selecting items for processing into memory. Another level down, the TOTE unit for testing information against a relevance criterion draws upon several perceptual/cognitive processes from the following list: *scanning, fixating, feature extracting, decoding, comparing, deciding, inducing, deducing, retrieving* (from memory), *selecting, transforming,* and *producing* (see Paisley and Butler, 1977, for an explication of these processes in relation to work).

What is important in the present discussion is a *principle of reduction:* information tasks can be analyzed in terms of the plans, subplans, TOTE units, and ultimately perceptual/cognitive processes that improved information systems should accommodate. The principle of reduction is illustrated in Figure 2.

E. Normative vs. Actual Information Use

A possible criticism of the Miller et al. (1960) *plan, subplan,* and *TOTE* concepts applied to information tasks is that workers do not seem to use information so purposefully. What about the unplanned events that bring information (e.g., corridor conversations at conventions)? What about the searches that are abruptly discontinued, to be resumed months later or not at all (e.g., see James Watson's account of interrupted and abandoned searches in *The Double Helix* [1968]? Do individuals engage in enough "planful" information use to justify the analysis framework described above?

This question is an information specialist's conundrum. Imagine that you have established an information system to serve researchers, engineers, supervisors, and other workers in an organization. Management holds you accountable to the simple test that workers' productivity will increase with their use of the system. However, the data show a slight but unmistakably negative correlation between productivity and system use. You dig deeper and uncover facts like the following:

1. The new system significantly augments the information resources of the organization, but...
2. Some workers were previously productive because they mastered the strategy of *reinvention*— that is, they learned now to decide, solve, calculate, and verify for themselves without much assistance from the literature or other workers.

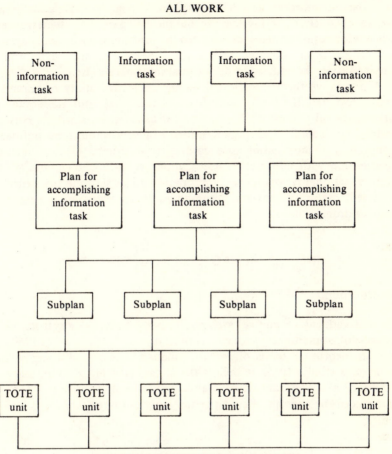

FIG. 2. Analytic reduction of information tasks.

3. Other productive workers cultivated *external information resources.*
   Some subscribed to journals, abstract services, newsletters, etc. Others
   were unusually active in professional and trade associations.
4. Still other productive workers cultivated *internal information
   resources*—"gatekeepers" in their own work teams and in other
   divisions of the organization.
5. Most productive workers were slow in supplementing these strategies
   with use of the new information system. At the same time, many of the
   less productive workers became regular users of the system.

In themselves, these facts do not explain the negative correlation between worker productivity and system use, but they are part of a pattern that recurs when information systems are installed in companies, government agencies, universities, associations, etc. In each case, a *normative* theory of information use is likely to be contradicted by actual information use.

A normative theory predicated on the subjective utility of uncertainty reduction usually treats individual differences and the social and organizational context of information use as *exogenous* factors. However, individual, social, and organizational factors should be defined as *endogenous* to information use according to two criteria: (1) their functional relationship with information use is apparent, once shown; and (2) they restore "rationality" to observed information use by showing how behavior is directed by individual searching-and-solving plans in a social and organizational context.

III. INDIVIDUAL FACTORS IN INFORMATION USE

A. Cognition

Three decades ago cognitive psychologists began to break away from "nickel-in-the-slot, stimulus-response conceptions of man" (Miller et al., 1960, p. 2) and to theorize in terms of *cognitive* maps (Tolman, 1948) and *personal constructs* (Kelly, 1955) as well as the *images* (Boulding, 1956) and *plans* (Miller et al., 1960) that we have already discussed. Tolman (1948, p. 193) introduced the concept of cognitive mapping in this statement:

> [The brain] is far more like a map control room than it is like an old-fashioned telephone exchange. The stimuli... are not connected by just simple one-to-one switches to the outgoing responses. Rather, the incoming impulses are...elaborated...into a tentative, cognitivelike map of the environment.

Kelly, (1955, pp. 8-12) viewed the cognitive map as a measurable "construction of the world" that differs among individuals:

> Man looks at his world through transparent patterns or templates which he creates and then attempts to fit over the realities of which the world is composed....Let us give the name constructs to these patterns that are tentatively tried on for size. They are ways of construing the world (Kelly, 1955, pp. 8-9).

Personal construct theory has stimulated research on individual *construction systems* and *cognitive complexity* (Adams–Webber, 1979; Bannister and Mair, 1968; Bieri, 1955; Scott, 1962). While people seem to share common dimensions for "constructing" experience, individuals place different emphases on these common dimensions and add unique dimensions according to the persons, places, events, and ideas in their lives. Differences in construction systems persist because of our reliance on past constructs to interpret the present and anticipate the future. Tennyson's *Ulysses* alludes to constructs in all three roles: "I am a part of all that I have met/Yet all experience is an arch wherethro'/Gleams that untravelled world...."

Differences in construction systems are already present among children in school. Cronbach and Snow (1977, p. 411) state that, "The learner brings abilities, information-processing habits or styles, and mental sets to the scene. These prove to be well or badly aligned with the task..." Information-processing habits or styles that cause students to choose different fields of work are then reinforced by training in the fields. For example, differences in verbal vs. numerical thinking that cause college students to choose linguistics vs. mathematics as their majors will be much smaller than differences found between midcareer linguists and mathematicians.

Roe (1952) studied differences in information-processing style among 61 biologists, experimental physicists, theoretical physicists, and social scientists. Roe explains that she did not intend to include information-processing style (her word is *imagery*) in her research on the development of scientists, but interviews made her realize that:

> ... their minds did not seem to be working the way mine does. They seemed to be able to call up in mind in detail the most intricate visual patterns and shapes, in two or three dimensions, so that they could compare mentally, say, the skull of one reptile (which is an amalgamation of a large number of bones, worse than a jigsaw puzzle) with that of another (Roe, 1952, pp. 141–142).

Roe's data on visual, auditory-verbal, kinaesthetic, and "imageless" thought are presented in Table 1. Roe (1952, p. 145) notes that biologists and experimental physicists particularly engage in visual thinking, while theoretical physicists are more likely to engage in verbal, symbolic, or imageless thinking. The kinaesthetic imagery that only social scientists reported is described as "feelings of muscular tension."

Closely related to differences in imagery across fields of science are differences in *paradigms* (Kuhn, 1962), which can be defined as structures of causal relationships that organize knowledge in a field. In fact, differences between the wave theory and particle theory of light in physics (for example) have as much to do with imagery as with the empirical phenomena. Like dominant images, dominant paradigms have the advantage of facilitating convergent thought in a field but also the disadvantage of impeding divergent thought.

According to Schroder, (1971, p. 242), the first problem in relating information processing to *individual differences* in cognition is "to discover

TABLE 1
Modes of Information-Processing Style Reported by Scientists

	Biologists	Experimental Physicists	Theoretical Physicists	Social Scientists
Visual				
Concrete, usually three-dimensional	11	7	3	3
Diagrams, geometrical figures, etc.	3	3	2	0
Symbols, visualized	3	3	2	0
Auditory-Verbal				
Formulae, etc., verbalized	0	1	3	1
Verbal imagery	6	0	4	11
Kinaesthetic	0	0	0	4
Imageless Thought	7	6	6	15

Source: Roe, (1952, p. 147)
Notes: Cell frequencies sum to more than the 61 scientists because of some multiple classification. In another table (p. 148), Roe reports unduplicated totals for visual and verbal imagery only:

	Visual	Verbal	Total
Biologists	10	4	14
Experimental Physicists	6	0	6
Theoretical Physicists	3	4	7
Social Scientists	2	11	13

the number and nature of dimensions along which a person scales a set of stimuli." Schroder elaborates:

> For example, in evaluating or making judgments about a set of people... person A might perceive information about intelligence and friendliness and person B about friendliness, wealth, helpfulness, and reliability.

Schroder proposes two measurements of individual difference: *differentiation* ("number of categories or kinds of information extracted from a given domain of stimuli") and *labeling* ("labels or names for the different ways we order stimuli").

Other cognitive variables may also explain individual differences in information processing. Witkin (1959) found differences between individuals on the variable of *field dependence,* which can be defined roughly as reliance on external cues for orientation to situations. Persons who are field-dependent seem to gather more and different kinds of information than persons who are field-independent, while the latter seem to have more analytic ability.

Pask and Scott (1972, p. 218) distinguish between *serialist* and *holist* information processing in this definition:

Serialists learn, remember and recapitulate a body of information in terms of stringlike cognitive structures where items are related by simple data-links: formally, by "low order relations." Since serialists habitually assimilate lengthy sequences of data, they are intolerant of irrelevant information... Holists, on the other hand, learn, remember and recapitulate as a whole: formally, in terms of "high order relations."

Characterization in terms of opposites such as "serialists" and "holists" is useful if somewhat misleading. In research on information seeking in gambling, players have been characterized as "pragmatists," those who collect only as much information as the payoff probabilities require, and "rationalists," those who collect enough information to understand the situation (Scodel et al., 1959).

A final example of a cognitive variable that affects information processing is that of *dogmatic* thinking. Rokeach (1960, p. 16) summarizes the findings of several studies in this characterization:

[Dogmatic persons] are more rigid in their problem-solving behavior, more concrete in their thinking, and more narrow in their grasp of a particular subject; they also have a greater tendency to premature closure in their perceptual processes and to distortions of memory, and a greater tendency to be intolerant of ambiguity.

With clear implications for information processing, Rokeach (1960, p. 286) states that the nondogmatic person exhibits "a willingness to relinquish old [belief] systems, a capacity to entertain and enjoy new systems and actively to synthesize new materials into an integrated whole."

Thus, returning to the questions raised in Section II.E, it may be difficult to grasp an individual's plan for information use unless we also know his or her *differentiation* and *labeling* of constructs, tendency toward *field dependence*, style of *serialist* or *holist* thinking, etc. Individuals who differ on these dimensions will probably differ in their conception of the task, in the number and heterogeneity of information sources they consult, in the length of time that decision alternatives are weighed, etc. If cognitive factors are not taken into account, differences in information use may seem random.

B. Personality and Motivation

The concepts of personality and motivation come together in *need theories* that define personality as a pattern of beliefs and behaviors produced by a different configuration of needs in each individual. The best-known *need theory of personality*, encompassing twenty needs ranging from sex and play to nurturance and understanding, was proposed by Murray (1938).

Murray's needs include several that affect information processing. For example, need for *achievement* affects perseverance in information use, and need for *understanding* takes an individual down avenues of inquiry that may unsettle his or her need for *infavoidance* (need to avoid failure) and need for *order*. Counteracting needs for *affiliation* and *autonomy* affect an individual's willingness to turn to other persons for information.

Needs proposed by Murray and other investigators can be categorized as follows:

1. Needs related to the self. Murray's needs for *order* and *understanding* fall in this category, as does, for example, the need to *reduce cognitive dissonance* (need to reconcile contradictory cognitions—Festinger, 1957).
2. Needs related to the task. *Conservation of effort, achievement,* and *avoidance of failure* are examples of task-related needs.
3. Needs related to people. In addition to Murray's *affiliation* need, these interpersonal needs are exemplified by the need for *coorientation* (Newcomb, 1953) and the need to *equalize power* in two-person interaction (Wheeler, 1964). Homans' (1961) *exchange theory,* discussed in Section IV.A, proposes a simple but powerful need for *distributive justice,* which is met when an individual's "outputs" from relationships with people equal his or her "inputs" to the relationships.

The role of motivation in the performance of information tasks was studied by Pelz and Andrews (1976). Their samples of scientists, engineers, and other information workers were measured on scales of involvement and satisfaction as well as needs for autonomy, professional status, organizational status, financial compensation, etc. The criterion variable of productivity was derived from supervisors' and coworkers' evaluations and from counts of papers, patents, and reports produced in a five-year period.

Self-reliance (oneself as a source of ideas) and a need for autonomy were strongly correlated with productivity in all groups. A "science orientation" or motivation to accomplish the task for its own sake was most prevalent among scientists in universities; this group was also highest in "professional orientation" (motive to advance professionally). In contrast, organizational and financial motives were strongest among engineers in industry. However, the professional, organizational, and financial motives were weaker correlates of productivity than were self-reliance and a need for autonomy.

Pelz and Andrews wondered whether the productive workers who emphasized self-reliance and a need for autonomy were "loners." A "loner" index, based on the general attitude of "I'd rather do it myself," was added as a control variable but did not correlate with productivity either positively or negatively. Pelz and Andrews (1976, p. 104) then concluded that self-reliance and a need for autonomy "does not mean isolation from people but an independence of *thought*—confidence in one's own judgment."

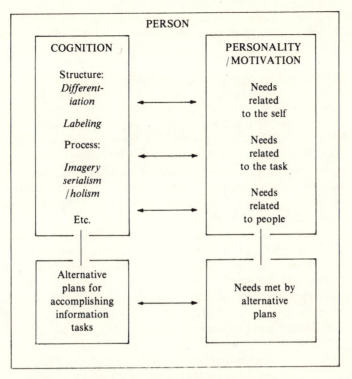

FIG. 3. Summary of individual factors affecting information use.

Cognition and personality/motivation can be discussed separately, but their effects on information processing are systemic, as Figure 3 suggests. One interrelationship among these factors is proposed by Bateson (1972, pp. 297–298) in his essay on the five levels of learning (see Section II.D):

> In describing individual human beings, both the scientist and the layman resort to adjectives descriptive of "character." It is said that Mr. Jones is dependent, hostile, fey, finicky, anxious, exhibitionistic... All [these adjectives] are descriptive of (possible) results of Learning II, and if we would define these words more carefully, our definition will consist in laying down the contingency pattern of that context of Learning I which would expectably bring about that Learning II which would make the adjective applicable.

IV. SOCIAL FACTORS IN INFORMATION USE

Older and newer views of the importance of social factors in the performance of information tasks are succinctly stated by Pelz and Andrews (1976) in their landmark study of "Productive Climates for Research and Development:"

One view of a laboratory is that it is a facility which provides services and equipment so that its scientists can conduct R&D activities. A somewhat different view is that it is a system of interacting scientists (and other components) in which the inhabitants stimulate each other to produce high-quality R&D (Pelz and Andrews, 1976, p. 35).

Co-workers in laboratories, offices, departments, etc., comprise the smallest social system that a worker participates in as a worker. For lack of a broader term, we will call this system the *work team.* Other social systems whose memberships overlap the work team are the *employing organization,* the *reference group,* and the *discipline* or *profession.* Cutting across these systems, which are homogeneous in their concern for task performance, are the heterogeneous systems of the *family,* the *religious group,* the *ethnic group,* the *community* the *nation,* etc.

The more strongly an individual identifies with each of these social systems, the more accountable he or she feels to the goals and norms of the system. Systems whose goals and norms may conflict, such as the employing organization and the profession, place the individual at the center of *cross pressures.* For example, information exchange between members of a professional group who work in different organizations is cross-pressured by the professional norm of disclosure and the organizational norm of secrecy.

Social systems have six primary functions with respect to work: they *mandate, justify, enable, guide, evaluate,* and *reward* work. Each social system is responsible for most of these functions, but each social system carries out the functions in its own way. For example, an organization enables work by providing space, equipment, and material; a work team enables work by providing know-how and direct assistance. An organization rewards work with pay and advancement; a work team rewards work with esteem and an exchange of services.

Information aspects of the functions of enabling, guiding, and evaluating work are noteworthy in four social systems: work teams, employing organizations, formal professional groups, and informal professional groups. Some studies of information flow within each of these systems is discussed below.

A. Work Teams

Studies of information flow in work teams date from 1953, making them the oldest literature on information and work apart from library circulation counts. Hertz and Rubenstein (1953) used questionnaires and diaries to study information flow within work teams in several R&D laboratories, finding that the amount of communication varied with function (e.g., higher among workers with administrative functions than among workers with design functions), with project duration (higher in long-term projects than in short-term projects), with team size (highest in medium-size teams, somewhat lower in large teams, much lower in small teams), etc. Diary entries indicated an average of two communication events per hour, but later studies based on participant observation suggest that the diarists forgot to record numerous communciation events. Two cycles of activity were noteworthy: communication was heaviest during the middle of the day and the middle of the week.

Ackoff and Halbert (1958) reported findings from approximately 25,000 participant–observations of the activities of about 1,500 chemists in 50 laboratories. Each observation was coded into one of the following categories: (1) scientific communication; (2) business communication; (3) thinking or planning alone; (4) set-up and maintenance of equipment; (5) use of equipment; (6) data treatment; (7) personal and social activities; (8) none of these; and (9) out of the laboratory.

Scientific communication was the most commonly observed activity. Chemists were engaged in scientific communication for an average of 33 percent of their time. The next most common activities were use of equipment (23 percent), business communication (10 percent), and personal/social activities (10 percent). No other activity was observed more than 6 percent of the time.

General discussion accounted for 31 percent of the chemists' total scientific communication, followed by giving/receiving instructions and advice (28 percent of scientific communication), working with unpublished materials (28 percent), and working with published materials (15 percent). Other chemists were involved in 64 percent of the chemist's scientific communication, followed in declining order by nonscientific company personnel (21 percent) and scientists other than chemists (8 percent).

Martin (1962) improved on the method of randomly timed participant observations by equipping scientists with pocket-sized "random alarm mechanisms" (RAMs) that alerted them to record their communication behavior several times a day. Since the RAM could be carried by a scientist anywhere, it provided for a more comprehensive sampling of communication behavior than a participant observer could record. Samples of about 300 chemists and 400 physicists collectively logged more than 33,000 self-observations over a two-week period. Unfortunately, only a subset of communication behavior was coded for analysis, making the study less interesting for its findings than for its methodology.

These monitoring studies produced excellent data on information flow in work settings, but they left a number of questions unanswered. For example, what are the *social dynamics* of communication behavior—that is, *who* exchanges information with *whom,* and what is the *quid pro quo* of the exchange? What *functions* does the information serve? What are the effects of information use on *productivity,* analyzed by the source and content of the information? In the past two decades, other studies have focused on the dynamics of exchange, on functions served, and on productivity effects.

Based on detailed interviews with about 75 biochemists, chemists, and zoologists, Menzel (1958) proposed a taxonomy of functions that scientific communication serves: (1) providing scientists with available answers to specific questions; (2) keeping scientists abreast of current developments in their chosen areas of attention; (3) enabling scientists to review recent years' work in an area; (4) giving testimony to the reliability of a source of information; (5) broadening a scientist's area of attention; (6) furnishing scientists with feedback in the form of responses to their own statements; and (7) helping scientists to orient their work within the totality of research endeavors.

Menzel's scientists proved to be proficient but unsystematic information users. Their case histories of information obtained (often without being sought) showed that they knew *whom* to talk with if not always *what* to talk about. In many cases, information was obtained on apparatus and procedures not covered in journal articles or books.

The "Menzel principle" that has guided much research on scientific communication for the past two decades is stated in a 1959 report:

> ... the news which comes to the attention of scientists is not restricted to the information obtained when they intentionally "gather information," as it is called. Fortunately so! For a good deal of the news which comes to their attention in unplanned and unexpected ways, during activities undertaken and on occasions sought out for quite different purposes, proves to be of considerable significance to them (Menzel, 1959, p. 202).

No deliberate study of scientific communication exemplifies the "Menzel principle" as well as Watson's *The Double Helix* (1968). This famous and much-debated memoir of the 1951–1953 period of research on DNA at the Cavendish Laboratory suggests that crucial information kept finding Watson rather than vice versa. Conversations among half a dozen people in London and Cambridge provided most of the pieces of the DNA puzzle, while a forgotten and unsought journal article and a few handbook references filled in the remaining pieces. A functional analysis would indicate that conversations provided alternative models for the DNA molecule, while the journal article and handbook references, together with fresh X-ray crystallographs, provided data for choosing among the alternative models. Each information source was essential, but scores of hours were spent in conversation for each hour spent in reading.

Crick, Watson's collaborator, asserts in a 1979 article that *The Double Helix* was ingenuous for literary effect. On the one hand, the truth of the matter seems to be that a number of fortunate information accidents occurred, including accidental juxtapositions of people. On the other hand, Watson and Crick were mentally prepared to seize upon leads that other researchers overlooked.

Pelz and Andrews (1976) gathered several kinds of data from more than 1,300 scientists and engineers in 11 industrial, government, and university laboratories. Some of this study's findings concerning the motivations of individual workers were discussed in Section III.B. Of particular interest here are the scientists' and engineers' average level of communication with their coworkers, the correlation of communication with productivity, and the effects of ancillary variables such as work–team composition, coordination, and age.

The criterion variable of productivity, described in Section III.B., was a composite measure of scientific performance, usefulness to the organization, and output of papers/patents. This is a robust measure of productivity that allowed a scientist or engineer to score well whether the work normally led to individual- or team-produced papers or products.

Respondents in the Pelz and Andrews study were asked to name their five most important colleagues (colleagues were defined as professionals with whom they worked in the laboratory). The question then followed: "As a general rule, how frequently do you communicate with [each of the named colleagues] on work-related matters?" Both engineers and scientists in development laboratories reported high levels of contact—several times a week or more. Scientists in research laboratories reported somewhat lower levels of contact—the median frequency was about weekly.

The correlation between frequency of contact and productivity was statistically significant for engineers and for scientists in both research and development laboratories, although for engineers the relationship peaked at semiweekly contact rather than daily contact. The productivity component of "overall usefulness" was most highly correlated with communication among engineers and scientists in development laboratories, whereas for scientists in research laboratories it was the "scientific contribution" component.

Two other measures of work–team communication in the Pelz and Andrews study focused on the number of coworkers frequently contacted (the previous question asked about the five most important coworkers only) and the actual number of contact hours. Productivity was highest when engineers and scientists in development laboratories had a large number of coworkers (15 to 20 or more). Scientists in research laboratories were most productive when they had from five to ten coworkers.

Irrespective of the number of coworkers, scientists were most productive when they spent from 6 to 10 hours a week communicating with each of their most important coworkers. Engineers were most productive when they spent from 8 to 15 hours a week communicating with each of their most important coworkers. These breakdowns help us to understand how scientists and engineers can spend from one-third (Ackoff and Halbert, 1958) to two-thirds (Chapanis, 1971) of their time in work-related communication.

Pelz and Andrews (1976) acknowledged the possibility that communication was an *effect* of productivity rather than its *cause*. That is, other workers may seek out the productive worker for advice. (This certainly happens to a considerable extent; it has been documented in many studies since Blau's *The Dynamics of Bureaucracy*, 1963.) Respondents in the Pelz and Andrews study were asked who typically initiated the contacts they reported. The correlation of communication with productivity was just as high among scientists and engineers who primarily initiated the contacts themselves as it was among scientists and engineers who were primarily contacted by others.

Several relationships between productivity and work–team composition, coordination, and age were also studied. The scientists' and engineers' similarity with their most important coworkers was measured on the dimensions of technical strategy, career orientation, style of approach to problems, and sources of motivation. In general, productivity was higher when the scientists and engineers were similar to coworkers with respect to motivation but dissimilar with respect to technical strategy, career orientation, and style of approach. Pelz and Andrews (1976, p. 141) view the technical dissimilarities as sources of productive "dither." ("Having colleagues who think differently from oneself may be one source of intellectual jostling needed for innovation.") On the other hand, similar motivations are viewed as "sources of emotional support" which, for the productive scientist or engineer, counterbalance the "anxieties that accompany creative thinking" (Pelz and Andrews, 1976, p. 147).

Tightness or looseness of work–team coordination was correlated with productivity, but the correlation was affected by an individual's need for autonomy. In the loosest situation, autonomous scientists and engineers began to be cut off from "outer stimulation...stimuli which might have enhanced their performance" (Pelz and Andrews, 1976, p. 237). In the tightest situations, autonomous individuals received ample stimulation but the rigidities of the situations interfered with their productivity. Pelz and Andrews (1976, p. 237) concluded that "only in the middle-range situations were two essential conditions present: (a) high autonomy was accompanied by a number of strong motivations and stimulations, and (b) the setting was flexible enough to allow these factors to improve performance."

The age of a work team was defined as the average number of years that its members had been working together. The productivity component of "scientific contribution" was highest in teams that had been working together two years or less. The productivity component of "overall usefulness" was highest in teams that had been working together from four to five years. Teams older than five years were lower on both measures.

Pelz and Andrews sought an explanation for the declining productivity of older work teams, and they found part of the explanation in communication data. The frequency of communication among coworkers in old teams (10 years or more) was nearly three times less than in young teams (3 years or less). Communication with the team leaders dropped even more, indicating a decline in the important factor of team coordination. Cohesiveness—the proportion of "significant colleagues" that a worker chooses from within the team—was highest in teams that had been working together from four to five years, while cohesiveness was even lower in old teams (ten years or more) than in teams that had just formed (one year or less).

The bright exceptions to the rule of declining productivity were a few older teams that "communicated often, and retained a zest for broad pioneering." They "continued to be competitive and a little secretive" (Pelz and Andrews, 1976, p. 259).

In summary, the Pelz and Andrews study is unparalleled in its analysis of the several ways in which work–team communication correlates with productivity. Although survey data cannot "prove" the hypothesized causal relationship between communication and productivity, Pelz and Andrews performed many control analyses to test alternative hypotheses. These control analyses reveal contingencies in which the correlation between communication and productivity is higher or lower, but they do not invalidate the basic hypothesis.

A second major study of communication in work teams was conducted by Allen (1977). This study differs from the Pelz and Andrews study in three interesting respects:

1. Cases were identified in which teams working in different organizations were attempting to solve the same engineering problem at the same time (as in parallel government contracts for design studies).
2. Instead of long-term individual productivity, the performance variable was the quality of the engineering solution produced by each team.
3. In addition to interviews and monitoring data obtained from work teams engaged in parallel projects, social networks were measured in several other laboratories and evaluations were conducted of experimental modifications of laboratories as communication environments.

The analysis of parallel projects involved 33 teams working on 17 engineering problems. (A typical problem called for the design of a large space-communciation antenna reflector.) Team members participated in three forms of data gathering: (1) a time allocation form, showing the amount of time spent in literature searching, consultation with persons inside and outside the organization, and analytic design; (2) a solution development record, showing the subjective probability of success that an individual assigned to each potential solution as the project progressed; and (3) interviews at the beginning and end of the project, providing data on background, information sources used, critical incidents affecting the choice of the final solution, etc.

The time allocation forms indicated that team members spent about 16 percent of their time in communication, 77 percent in analysis and experimentation, and 6 percent in other activities. Slightly less than half of the communication time was spent reading written materials. Unpublished reports and other informal written materials accounted for three-fourths of the reading time. Books, journals, and other formal written materials accounted for one-fourth. Textbooks and trade journals headed the list of formal literature read; professional engineering journals were in fourth place. Allen (1977, p. 73) comments:

> The publications of the professional engineering societies are little used by their intended audience . . . [because they] are utterly incomprehensible to the average engineer. . . . The articles . . . are written for a very limited audience, usually those few at the very forefront of a technology. Just as in science, the goal of the author is not to communicate to the outsider but to gain for himself the recognition of his peers.

The quality of each engineering solution was evaluated by physical test, by simulation, or by the judgment of government contract monitors. When solution quality was tabulated against information sources used, there was a slight negative correlation between solution quality and literature use—that is, more literature was used to generate the *lower*—rated solutions than the higher-rated solutions.

A major focus of the parallel-projects study was interpersonal information flow. Analysis of the source of 494 solution-facilitating ideas indicated that personal contact (other than federal contract monitors) accounted for more than 40 percent of the ideas. Personal contact with federal contract monitors accounted for another 25 to 30 percent of the ideas. In contrast, only 10 percent of the ideas were obtained from the literature.

Personal contact inside the organization, labeled "internal consulting" by Allen, was highest at the beginning of projects and at the two-thirds completion point, when decisions were being made concerning the final products of the project. Although teams with higher-rated and lower-rated solutions reported about the same amount of internal consulting at the beginning of projects, higher-rated teams reported more than twice as much internal consulting at the two-thirds completion point than did lower-rated teams.

Higher-rated teams communicated significantly more *within* themselves than did lower-rated teams (about 2.5 times as much communication). Even more striking is the finding that higher-rated teams communicated far more with *other* technical staff in the laboratory than did lower-rated teams (more than ten times as much communication).

It was also found that the technical staff contacted by higher-rated teams represented greater diversity in disciplines and functions than technical staff contacted by lower-rated teams. Higher-rated teams were involved in about 10 times more communication with other discipline/function groups in the laboratory. Allen (1977, p. 123) comments: "On complex projects, the inner team cannot sustain itself and work effectively without constantly importing new information from [other groups in the laboratory]."

Persons outside the organization were often contacted for information or, as in the case of equipment vendors, they contacted the work team on their own initiative. Both higher-rated and lower-rated teams obtained about the same proportion of their solution-facilitating ideas from equipment vendors, but the *lower*—rated teams made much greater use of the other outsiders. This finding corroborated the negative correlation between solution quality and use of outside consultants found by Allen (1964) in an earlier study of 22 proposal competitions for federal R&D contracts.

One of the most interesting aspects of Allen's research is the *network analysis* of communication within laboratories. Measures of "who talks with whom" produced graphic patterns of the connectedness of individuals in each laboratory. The most-connected individuals, labeled "communication stars" by Allen, were then compared with other laboratory members on measures of reading behavior and contact outside the laboratory.

Across several laboratories, the "communication stars" did not differ from other laboratory members in their reading of trade journals, but they read a significantly greater number of referred professional journals. The "stars" also made significantly greater use of persons outside the laboratory as information sources.

There was sufficient evidence in their communication behavior to rename the most-connected individuals "technological gatekeepers." They are critical links in a two-step or multistep flow of information into the laboratory from the professional literature and the outside world. Furthermore, by virtue of the greater number of journal articles they publish and the greater number of conference papers they present, they are also links from the laboratory *outward.*

Other measures indicate that technological gatekeepers are more likely than other laboratory members to hold the doctorate, to have longer tenure in the laboratory, and to be first-line supervisors (i.e., to direct the work of bench scientists or engineers). They are more likely to serve on outside committees formed by professional societies or government agencies. They also receive higher scores from their supervisors and peers on "contribution to knowledge."

It is clear why the technological gatekeepers are often contacted for information and advice by other laboratory members, but why, and how willingly, do they give their time to this gatekeeping function? In many of their characteristics of status and communication behavior, the technological gatekeepers resemble senior agents in a federal office studied by Blau and reported in *The Dynamics of Bureaucracy* (1963). *Exchange theory,* which derives from the work of Blau and that of Homans (1961), asserts that work-related information is a *good* that enters into interpersonal exchange with other goods and services. Sometimes the same good is offered in the exchange by both (or all) participants, as when coworkers communicate information of value to each other.

Often, however, the information is exchanged for other goods or services. In the federal office studied by Blau (1963), the junior or less competent agents could not offer information to the senior agents that equaled the value of the information they received. Nor were the senior agents "bargaining" for information in return; they were already well-informed. Instead, they were bargaining for esteem, status, or reciprocated services of other kinds.

When the exchanged goods or services are of approximately equal value, the participants in the exchange will perceive that *distributive justice* exists and the probability of further exchanges will increase. However, if the exchange is unbalanced, the probability of further exchanges will decrease.

The senior agents in Blau's study and the technological gatekeepers in Allen's study may also have derived what Homans calls *psychic profit* from the belief that they were "paying their dues" to the organization or profession by providing information to junior or less knowledgeable coworkers. It may be more accurate to say that they were paying back as senior professionals some of the information goods they received earlier in their careers. A study of univeristy scientists (Hagstrom, 1965) identified a number of service roles, involving communication with junior colleagues and students, that senior scientists play.

If technological gatekeepers did not exist in R&D laboratories, it would be necessary to invent them. They provide coworkers with information not only from the unread professional literature and from other organizations but also from other groups within the laboratory itself. Allen (1977, p. 155) found that technological gatekeepers form their own network: "The gatekeepers thereby maintained close communication among themselves, substantially increasing their effectiveness in coupling the organization to the outside world."

After conducting several studies on the effects of architecture on communication, Allen had an opportunity to measure communication in a three-division laboratory before and after the staff occupied a new building that was designed to facilitate communication among the three divisions. The "before" social networks clearly showed the effects of the 34, 85, and 104 meters separating the divisions. In particular, the third division, separated by 85 and 104 meters from the other two divisions, had only two ties to one of the divisions and none to the other.

In the new building, the mean intergroup distance was reduced by more than 70 percent. The formerly isolated division reported eight ties to one of the other divisions and seven to the other. Because of carefully planned traffic flow to and from the laboratory space, managers' offices, lunchroom, library, etc., communication within each division also improved markedly. However, there was an inadvertent reduction in communication between the laboratory divisions and other parts of the company (e.g., manufacturing, sales) that were left behind in the old building.

The convergent findings of the Pelz and Andrews (1976) and the Allen (1977) studies tell us, first, that productivity—at least in laboratory settings— is highly correlated with communication *within* the work team as well as *between* the work team and other groups in the organization and elsewhere. The findings also tell us that communication is affected by a number of factors such as the status and role of individuals, the size and composition of work teams, and even the physical layout of the workplace. Other studies that have investigated these factors less comprehensively report similar findings (see, for example, Berul et al., 1965; Report #11 in Garvey and Griffith, 1963–1969; Hagstrom, 1965; Herner, 1954; Lindsey, 1979; Lingwood, 1975; Rosenbloom and Wolek, 1967; Shilling et al., 1964; Whitley and Frost, 1973).

McClure (1978) reviewed the findings of research on technological gatekeepers in an article entitled "The Information Rich Employee and Information for Decision Making." Drawing upon 15 studies of gatekeepers, McClure summarized the personal characteristics that are ascribed to gatekeepers and the communication functions they perform. McClure notes that some "job types *demand* that an employee maintain contact with diverse and numerous types of information sources" (McClure, 1978, p. 388) and hypothesizes that many gatekeepers are organizational decision makers who extensively seek information not because of personal style (which is sometimes described as a *cosmopolitan* rather than *local* orientation) or because of the exchange "capital" that information represents but because of the information requirements of their jobs. In other words, the cosmopolitan orientation and the information-relaying activity of gatekeepers are corollaries rather than causes of their information richness. They are information rich simply because their jobs demand the information.

Network analyses identify another communication role which sometimes overlaps with the technological gatekeeper. This is the *liaison* between two work teams. Such a person has communication ties with members of both teams but does not belong to either. Informal communication between teams partly depends on liaisons; furthermore, liaisons account for many of the new ideas that reach a team. Research on the "strength of weak ties" (Granovetter, 1973) gives prominence to the liaison role.

B. Employing Organizations

We cannot readily separate the communication dynamics of work teams from those of employing organizations. In particular, an organization's *structure* and *policies* affect the development of its communication infrastructure, including the links connecting work teams with each other and with external information sources.

Any study of information and work in more than one organizational setting offers a potential comparison of the influence of organizational structure and policies on information flow and work performance. However, most studies in multiple settings confound organizational differences with task differences, since the personnel in the different organizations are performing different tasks, even within an equivalent category of work such as "engineering research." This was probably the case in one of the first good studies of information flow in organizational settings, which compared a university school of engineering and an applied physics laboratory (Herner, 1954). Engineers in the two settings differed markedly in their preferred sources of information; only two sources appeared on both composite lists of the five most preferred sources. To what extent these information-source preferences should be attributed to organizational differences rather than task differences could not be determined.

A later study of researchers in two settings, conducted by Garvey and Griffith (1965) as part of the American Psychological Association's Project on Scientific Information Exchange in Psychology, also showed the confounding effect of task differences on what appear to be organizational differences in information flow. Psychologists at a federal research laboratory differed from psychologists in a university department in many communication behaviors such as convention attendance and journal usage. However, they also differed in the substance and motivation of their work. For example, laboratory psychologists were more likely than academic psychologists to attribute their current research efforts to "continuation, replication, or extension of a past project" (77 percent versus 58 percent) while academic psychologists were more likely to attribute their current research efforts to a "particular need for... information in an area" (58 percent versus 37 percent). Garvey and Griffith (1965, p. 103) concluded from their analysis that: "Apparent in both settings was the fact that persons in the same general research area could have entirely diverse and divergent interests and that a researcher would communicate with [researchers in other settings] representing those interests as often, if not more often, than with [researchers in his or her own setting]."

Another study (Shilling et al., 1964) brought organizational effects into sharper focus. Questionnaires completed by 673 bioscientists working in 64 laboratories provided data on personal characteristics of the scientists, their communication behaviors, and organizational policies affecting information flow. Productivity, defined as number of papers presented and number of projects completed, was also determined for each scientist. Some findings relating information flow and productivity to organizational policies were:

1. Unrestricted long-distance telephoning correlated highly with success in obtaining information (or "information efficiency") but not with productivity.
2. Unrestricted travel correlated highly both with information efficiency and with productivity.
3. Availability of assistants was uncorrelated with information efficiency or productivity.
4. Information efficiency and productivity were positively correlated with diversity of research interests in each laboratory, defined as the number of scientists in the laboratory who claimed to be alone in their interests.
5. Productivity was negatively correlated with the use of outside consultants (see reference to Allen, 1964, in Section IV.A).

Reviews of research on organizational communication (Goldhaber et al., 1978; Porter and Roberts, 1976; Rogers and Agarwala-Rogers, 1976) show that weaknesses in this perspective are both methodological and substantive. Porter and Roberts list several methodological weaknesses in the pre-1976 research, including the prevalence of single-organization/single-method studies, the lack of integration between field studies and laboratory experiments, and the lack of longitudinal (time-lagged) measures and analyses. Substantively, the greatest weakness in most organizational communication studies is the lack of a measure of productivity or effectiveness. For example, one of the most ambitious organizational communication studies now underway is the International Communication Association's Communication Audit, which as of 1978 had gathered data from more than 8,000 employees in 17 organizations (Goldhaber et al., 1978). While the ICA Communication Audit seems to provide excellent data on information flow and on attitudes (e.g., job satisfaction), it does not indicate which individuals, teams, or organizations are more productive or effective than others.

C. Formal Professional Groups

Association and societies of scientists, technologists, adminstrators, practitioners, etc., are complex social systems that inform, motivate, and reward members while upholding standards of practice and protecting their

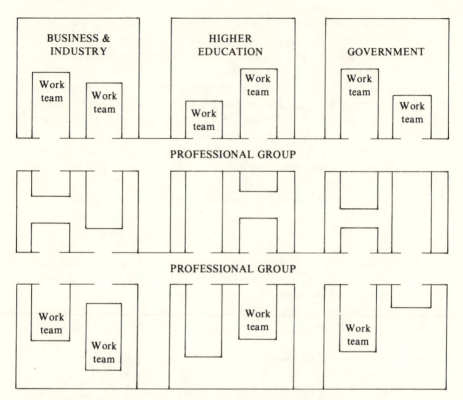

FIG. 4. Contrasting stratification of organizations and professional groups.

fields from external criticism. Professional groups have heterogeneous memberships drawn from business and industry, higher education, government, and private practice or consulting. Emphasizing disciplinary rather than organizational ties, professional groups draw "horizontally" stratified memberships from "vertically" stratified organizations (see Figure 4).

Not all information that flows horizontally (i.e., to members of a professional group) is sponsored by a professional association. However, in addition to the face-to-face contact that a professional association facilitates through its conferences, the association usually publishes a yearbook or annual review of its field, a set of journals, and a monograph series. In some fields, little information flows outside the professional association except for commercially published books. In other fields, the size and/or diversity of the membership motivates the commercial sector to publish journals and trade magazines as well as books. Two others contemporary developments that cause information to flow outside professional associations are government information systems and commercially sponsored symposia. In comparison with the thousands of communication events and products sponsored each year by professional associations, the federal information systems and the commercial symposia still play a minor role in the overall communication system of each discipline. (There are exceptions to this rule. For example, the federal ERIC system augments the publication programs of several education associations by cosponsoring reviews and by archiving conference papers. Also, in fast changing fields such as computer technology, commercial symposia travel the circuit of major cities to bring information that engineers and managers need to know immediately.)

What may have been the first study of disciplinary communication was conducted in the early 1950s (Michigan University. Survey Research Center, 1954). Approximately 5,400 physiologists completed a questionnaire that asked about a number of professional activities, including their use of information. The findings chiefly reveal the physiologists' dissatisfaction with publications (too many, too slow, too inaccessible), secondary services (inadequate indexes, abstracts, and reviews), and interpersonal communication (too little contact with colleagues).

The landmark study of disciplinary communication was begun in 1961 by the American Psychological Association. The APA's Project on Scientific Information Exchange in Psychology, which continued until the early 1970s, began with a series of descriptive reports on APA conventions, journals, annual reviews, books, and technical reports (Garvey and Griffith, 1963–1969). The project then initiated a series of innovations in the psychological communication system. Some innovations required only minor modifications in the system; an example is the practice of listing titles and authors of manuscripts accepted by journals with long publication lags. The project evaluated the effects of this innovation both on authors and on readers, who could now request a copy of the manuscript as much as a year prior to publication.

Some innovations required major modifications in the psychological communication system. The publication of brief papers in a *Proceedings* of the APA convention and the computerization of *Psychological Abstracts* are two examples. A careful evaluation of these innovations by the APA project staff confirmed the value of the *Proceedings* and *Abstracts* in terms of *primary* effects but also revealed a number of *secondary effects* of the innovations on other components of the psychological communication system.

Particularly noteworthy were the effects of the *Proceedings* publication on later submission to APA journals of articles based on convention presentations. The APA project undertook the *Proceedings* with two objectives: (1) to reduce the amount of lost information represented by convention presentations that were never published in journals; and (2) to reduce the manuscript backlog of APA journals by substituting the *Proceedings* as a refereed, archival publication in its own right. Lost information in convention presentations had been a topic of concern at the 1958 International Conference on Scientific Information (Liebesny, 1959), where it was estimated that about 48 percent of the presentations at conventions of the American Physical Society, the American Optical Society, and the Institute of Radio Engineers were left unpublished. The APA project staff found, prior to the *Proceedings* experiment, that more than 50 percent of APA convention presentations were left unpublished. A parallel concern for manuscript backlogs was based on th 18- to 24-month publication delay in some APA journals. If future manuscripts based on convention presentations could be diverted into a refereed, archival *Proceedings,* then the journals might be able to reduce their backlogs and even moderate their rejection rates (as high as 80 percent in some APA journals).

The *Proceedings* experiment accomplished both of its objectives—the formerly unpublished half of all APA convention presentations were made permanently available, and a considerable number of authors who would otherwise have added their manuscripts to the APA journal backlogs were satisfied with the publication of their brief papers in the *Proceedings.*

In a recent experiment, the American Chemical Society sought to reduce the average cost of the *Journal of the American Chemical Society* to chemists by publishing both an archival version with full-length articles and a summary version with two-page synopses of the articles. Assuming that the archival version would be purchased mainly by libraries and the summary version by individual chemists, the "dual journal concept" promised to lower the information costs of individual chemists while slightly increasing costs for libraries.

Specimen issues of the dual journals were published, distributed, and evaluated (Terrant and Garson, 1977). Overall, the authors, librarians, and readers who were questioned were about equal in their support or opposition to the dual journals. However, whereas reader groups such as research managers and graduate students were more often strongly in favor than strongly opposed, an increasing ratio of opposition was found among college faculty members (2:1 more strongly opposed than strongly in favor), American Chemical Society editors (2.4:1 strongly opposed, librarians (2.7:1), reviewers (3.3:1), and "prolific authors" (16:1). On the average, "outsiders" favored the innovation and "insiders" opposed it.

The role of a professional association in facilitating information exchange among members often conflicts with its role in certifying the work of the profession. Rapid publication (e.g., preprint distribution) schemes are generally favored by the "rank and file" but opposed by an association's editors and officers. The former value timeliness and are willing to screen out the occasional unreliable information that rapid publication schemes pass through. The latter are less concerned about timeliness and more concerned about the integrity of the association's information system. For the past decade a line of resistance has been drawn between refereed brief papers (e.g., in "letters" journals) and unrefereed preprints or other manuscripts.

In fast-moving fields, demands upon associations to sponsor rapid publication schemes lead to extended and often acrimonious debate. A landmark case involved the exchange of preprints in high-energy physics, which was strongly supported by a well-known physicist and strongly opposed by the editor of the *Physical Review* (Moravcsik and Pasternack, 1966). In order to avoid sponsoring unrefereed information exchanges, associations have introduced early announcement services of various kinds, such as the American Psychological Association's prepublication announcement of titles accepted, with names and addresses of authors.

Professional associations must also try to solve problems that arise later in the communication process: How can the separate social systems and information systems of scientists, technologists, and practitioners be interconnected in their fields? How can new facts, concepts, and procedures be digested from the research literature? Herring (1973) argued the case for critical reviews by plotting the normal curves of "range of awareness" versus "range of relevant information" surrounding the specialty of a typical scientist, technologist, or practitioner in the 1930s and at the present time. Whereas (normatively speaking) the range of awareness extended about as far as the range of relevant information in the 1930s, at the present time a large proportion of the range of relevant information lies beyond a person's range of awareness. The purpose of published reviews, conference pressessions, and similar arrangements is to extend the range of awareness by identifying the best or most useful information that would otherwise escape notice.

The larger the representation of practitioners among members of an association, the greater its investment in reviews and continuing-education activities is likely to be. For example, the American Educational Research Association, which has a large proportion of school administrators and faculty in its membership, publishes both the quarterly *Review of Educational Research* and the annual *Review of Research in Education* and also conducts presessions and postsessions at its annual meeting (nine such events at its 1980 meeting).

D. Informal Professional Groups

As fields and professional associations grow, they are victims of the "second Malthusian dilemma" described by Weinberg (1967, see Section II.A). For example, the number of psychologists affiliated with the American Psychological Association in 1978 was 46,891. APA memberships in individual states (California, 5,804; New York, 6,667) exceeded the size of the entire association before World War II.

Just as work teams are the social units in organizations that directly facilitate work, there are informal groups or "invisible colleges" of professionals in each discipline that directly facilitate communication. Although the term "invisible college" dates from the 17th century rivalry between scientists in Oxford, Cambridge, and London, the rise of invisible colleges in the 20th century was traced by Price (1963, p. 62–91) in this analysis:

1. All available yardsticks show that science reached its present size through a cycle of doublings that still continue. For example, the literature of many fields of science doubles every ten years; the number of "important discoveries" in science doubles every 20 years or so (actual doubling periods vary by field).

2. In a normally productive field, a scientist may be able to monitor the output of a few hundred colleagues. Because of limitations inherent in scientists themselves (e.g., reading speed), this number remains relatively constant although the fields with which they identify double in size three or more times during their careers. "When in the course of natural growth [a field] begins sensibly to exceed the few hundred members postulated, each man will find himself unable to monitor the field properly" (Price, 1963, pp. 72–73).

3. "[A] noteworthy phenomenon of human engineering is that new groups of scientists emerge, groups composed of our maximal 100 colleagues. In the beginning, when no more than this number existed in a country, they could compose themselves as the Royal Society or the American Philosophical Society. At a later stage, they could split into specialist societies of this size. Now, even the smallest branches of subject matter tend to exceed such membership, and the major groups contain tens or hundreds of thousands. In a group of such size . . . there are likely to be a few groups of magnitude 100, each containing a set of interacting leaders. We see now such groups emerging, somewhat bashfully, as separate entitles" (Price, 1963, p. 83).

4. " . . . these groups devise mechanisms for day-to-day communication. There is an elaborate apparatus for sending out not merely reprints of publications but preprints and prepreprints . . . . For each group there exists a sort of commuting circuit of institutions, research centers, and summer schools giving them an opportunity to meet piecemeal . . . " (Price, 1963, pp. 84–85).

The term "invisible college" connotes scientific or academic work, but similar informal groups are found in all professions and technical specialties. The sparse geographic distribution of scientists in most fields of research causes scientific invisible colleges to be national or international in membership. In contrast, informal groups of engineers, physicians, teachers, etc., tend to be local.

Referring to Figure 4, we may say that invisible college and other informal groups are "horizontal" extensions of work teams, just as organizations are "vertical" extensions of the work teams. When work is performed outside an organization, as in the case of solo medical practice, informal groups are among the most important information sources.

Because informal groups extend, with few eligibility rules, across organizational and disciplinary boundaries, they are largely defined by communication behavior itself. That is, they *exist* because they *communicate*. Measures of communication define the groups and also indicate the extent of their activity in facilitating work.

The technique of sociometry has been adopted and broadened in research on informal groups. Networks of links based on collaboration, friendship, advice, or discussion have been analyzed, producing patterns of cliques with more central and less central members, liaison persons spanning cliques, etc. In some studies, surrogates of social contact such as journal citations provide data for network analysis.

Two early studies of informal groups using sociometric techniques focused on school administrators and physicians. Carlson (1965) analyzed the rate of adoption of "new math" in an Eastern county as a function of the cliques revealed in a sociogram of friendship choices among the county's school superintendents. The great majority of superintendents adopting "new math" in the first three years belonged to a central clique or were connected to that clique by friendship choices. A majority of superintendents who adopted "new math" after the third year did not have a friendship connection to the central clique.

Coleman et al. (1966) studied the diffusion of a new antibiotic drug among physicians in four small Midwestern cities. Each physician's first prescription of the drug was verified in pharmacy records. They asked:

> Where does the crux of the [adoption decision] lie—between people or within people? ... The alternative explanations have very different policy implications. [One] focuses attention upon the links *between* doctors as the crucial elements in the adoption of new drugs. [The other] focuses on something *within* each doctor's individual make-up, behavior, or experience (Coleman et al., 1966, pp. 92–93).

It was found that individual characteristics had much less effect on the timing of the physicians' adoption decision than their affiliation with other physicians in friendship, discussion, and advice networks. When pairs of choosing-chosen physicians were analyzed together, their adoption dates coincided closely during the early months of the new drug's availability. In more abstract terms, physicians' involvement in informal groups was strongly related to one aspect of their work, the adoption of a new practice.

Several studies have charted the size and composition of invisible colleges within research fields. Mullins (1968) began a "snowball sample" by obtaining sociometric data from 50 university biologists. After two further waves of data gathered from scientists named by the initial sample and from scientists they in turn named, Mullins found that the sociogram spread across 64 disciplines ranging from the social sciences to the physical sciences. In other words, later respondents did not "close" the sociogram by naming the scientists who had named them. However, some interconnected groups did appear against a background of one-way linkages extending from discipline to discipline.

Other sociometric studies (e.g., Crawford, 1970; Gaston, 1969; Griffith and Miller, 1970; Lingwood, 1968) led to a definitive book on invisible colleges by Diana Crane (1972). Crane used data from the fields of mathematics and sociology to test the relationship between sociometric connectedness and productivity. "High producers" were much more likely than "moderate producers" to be the chosen rather than the choosers. They were also much more likely (88 percent versus 9 percent) to be credited with influence in the selection of a research topic by other researchers. Of the combined "high producers" from both fields, 93 percent received 11 or more direct choices. Of the combined "moderate producers" from both fields, only three percent received 11 or more direct choices.

Studies of invisible colleges continue, often with larger samples and better analysis techniques than were found in the early studies. For example, Judith Blau (1974) used choice data from almost a thousand theoretical high-energy physicists to analyze factors that choosing and chosen scientists have in common. She found that, "while the prestige ladder of academic departments and other institutional and personal characteristics affect [choice] across specialties, shared interest in a highly specialized field overrides these considerations and brings together individuals who in other respects are quite different" (Blau, 1974, p. 401). That is, similar personal characteristics were associated with dissimilar research interests and vice versa.

V.   CONVERGING ISSUES

A. The Evolution of Work

In nature, all animals work, although some have easier jobs than others. What sets humans apart from other animals is not our need to work versus their prerogative to play but rather *our* prerogative to transform work as we wish, even into play. Animal behavior is largely encoded in "nonerasable memory" (the genes) and remains constant over a thousand generations of a species. Human behavior is largely encoded in "erasable memory" (the brain) and changes when new instructions replace the old.

Furthermore, traditional and modern human societies change at different rates. In traditional society, a lack of alternative behavior models combines with tradition-conserving norms to retard change. In modern society, many alternative behavior models vie for attention and norms promote change; each generation chooses its own "lifestyle."

Work is increasingly amorphous. When sophisticated machines are involved, the outcomes of work are no longer related functionally to the human operations that achieve them. The blacksmith's hammer, the shoemaker's awl, the machinist's lathe, and even the physician's stethoscope are now an operator's console. Yet the versatility of these extensions of the worker's muscles and senses demands a clearer understanding than before of the *algorithmic* nature of work. That is, whereas a blacksmith can pause after each hammer blow to *intuit* the angle and force of the next blow, a computer-controlled metal press can only follow instructions; the computer must *calculate* the angle and force of the stamping.

Intuitive judgment yields to calculation not only in craftwork but also in the professions. A surgeon can still rely on fingers and eyes to repair an organ, but a radiotherapist cannot guess at the amount of radiation a tumor should receive. Many of the most powerful engines of technology work too quickly, precisely, or invisibly for humans to guide them at the time the work is being done. Calculations must be completed and instructions specified beforehand.

B. Sanctions for Remediable Ignorance

In the past, workers needed little information that was not produced on the job by the work itself. They now need increasing amounts of "off the job" or external information that reaches them through print, electronic, and interpersonal channels. Dependence on external information is unsettling to workers both because they are experiencing information overload and because they believe that others (i.e., the producers of the information) are interfering with their way of doing work.

Workers who want to avoid the effort of processing external information can play "overload" against "interference" and vice versa:

> I know there's information out there that might be useful in my work, but it's the old needle-in-a-haystack problem.

> Researchers [or government agencies, or industry standards committees, etc.] have no business telling me how to do my work, so I ignore that kind of information whenever possible.

It was noted some time ago that there are few "sanctions for remediable ignorance" to inhibit researchers from duplicating or overlooking existing knowledge (Paisley, 1968, p. 20). Beliefs that the literature is unsearchable, that experts are unlocatable, etc., also justify inferior practice in the professions and "seat of the pants" decision making in business and government.

In many cases these beliefs have outlived the actual problem. Publicly searchable information systems now combine document files, data files, and "people files." Answers *are* at hand. Coworkers and supervisors can know that a worker's error or omission was not justified, that the needed information was locatable.

C. Modes of Cognition

It can be misleading to contrast "seat of the pants" intuition with external information which, by virtue of the contrast, is assumed to be empirical and rigorous. The actual content of external information ranges from hearsay to reliable knowledge. The shift from internal to external information is not an end in itself but rather a corollary of the shift from intuitive to analytical modes of cognition.

Hammond (1978, pp. 15–18) defined a six-step scale of cognitive modes found in decision making:

1. Strong analytical experimentation "refers to the form of inquiry typified by the traditional laboratory experiment carried out by physical scientists."
2. Moderately strong analytical experimentation "refers to the experiments that are carried out by biologists, psychologists [etc.]. Because this random-assignment experimental-control-group method is based on the logic of statistical inference, it involves elements of judgment...a less powerful mode of inquiry..."
3. Weak analytical experimentation "refers to the quasi-experiments and surveys carried out by social scientists and others when strict random assignment [and other controls] are not feasible."
4. Strong quasi-rational judgment, which involves the "disentanglement of causal relations by (passive) cognition instead of (active) experimentation, is subject to a variety of psychological factors, such as memory loss, information overload [etc.]. Mode 4 refers to the cognitive activity of persons aided in three ways [statistical analysis, computer simulation, decision algorithms]."
5. Moderately strong quasi-rational judgment "refers to the cognitive activity of persons who base their decisions on a known, delimited set of data, but who must act on those data largely in a passive and intuitive fashion; physicians...provide an example."

6. Weak quasi-rational judgment "represents the kind of judgment most of us engage in most of the time. It involves an uncertain data base, no manipulation of variables, no statistical controls, and inconsistent logical rules never made explicit.... Mode 6 is not only the weakest means for solving problems; it is the most dangerous one."

Hammond (1978, p. 27) concludes this discussion by stating that "Modes of inquiry weaker that Mode 3 must be prohibited by someone, somehow," but asserts that "there is no imaginable institution that can drive Modes 5 and 6 out of use." Institutions may be ineffective against quasi-rational judgment, but information itself defies Gresham's Law: other things being equal, the empirical construction of events prevails over the intuitive. (However, intuition often prevails over empiricism in public decision processes for the same reason that a Colt six was the high card in Western poker games.)

D. Information Equity

The concept of an "information poor" has appeared in the literature of information science in the past dozen years. Both nations (Price, 1967) and individuals (Childers and Post, 1975) may be information-poor. An equity issue arises in the relationship of information to power:

> In the "knowledge society" of contemporary America, resources and power accrue to those who have information. It is no less true that information accrues to those who have resources and power.... We may be optimistic about the long-term effects of community information networks, cable television information services, home computers, etc., but thus far the introduction of new communication technology has widened rather than narrowed the gap between the information "haves" and "have nots" (Paisley et al., 1979, p. 1).

Unlike economic or political equity, "information equity" can be achieved without the conflicts of redistribution. Information is not a fixed-sum commodity; no one is required to give up information so that the information poor can have more. In fact, much information is a by-product of work activities that would continue whether or not the information was produced. Such information has no accountable production cost; it incurs costs only for "packaging and handling."

It is true that communication technologies of the post-war era have not narrowed the gap between the information rich and the information poor. However, it is also true that post-war communication technologies—notably broadcast television, cable television, video recording, and communication satellites—have taken over little of the information burden from print media. Most information that flows outside of interpersonal channels is still printed on paper as it has been for the past 500 years. Only as we turn the corner into the 1980s does it appear that new communication technologies are becoming widely available *information* technologies.

Since much work-related information is almost free except for "packaging and handling" costs, it makes a difference how much each page of paper or microform, each byte of computer memory, each minute of connect time, etc., costs. In general, the costs of mechanical processing are rising while the costs of electronic processing are falling. At the end of the 1970s the relative costs of the two technologies began to diverge dramatically.

Although electronic information is cheap, access to it has been limited by the high cost of terminals and datalines. Microcomputers, television-based videotext systems and videodiscs promise to lower the access costs of electronic information far below the access costs of the same information in paper or even microform copy. For example, the videodisc now in production can store the contents of about 200 average books. The holdings of a foremost scientific or professional library can be duplicated on a small set of videodiscs and distributed cheaply throughout the world.

Social, economic, and political equity are disputed in proportion to the scarcity of the resources that are to be shared. If a previously rare and costly resource becomes abundant and cheap, it is then shared freely by groups that previously contested each other's claim to it.

Abundant and cheap information does not bring about information equity by itself. On the worker's side, there are information skills to be learned. Young workers will enter the workforce with training in the use of electronic technology; they will use information "tools" proficiently. Some older workers will not adapt readily to electronic technology or to the new role of information in work. However, within one generation of workers or less, the information equity issue as we know it may be forgotten.

E. From Description to System Design

A description of the role of information in work is not an end in itself but a prelude to system design. Case studies, interviews, questionnaires, journal citation counts, sociometric analyses, and other sources of data show us that quality, timeliness, cost, and other attributes of information used on the job are correlated with productivity. Generally speaking, *individual* messages (items of information), modes, and channels are neither necessary nor sufficient causes of productivity. There are dramatic stories about the single fact that averted a disaster or led to a scientific breakthrough, but workers (i.e., all of us) know how to get on with their work whether or not they can locate the single fact. Instead, *aggregates* of messages, modes, and channels, comprising a *system* of thousands of information transactions per worker per year, have measureable effects on productivity.

In order to think about improving the system of information transactions related to work, it helps to develop a framework for specifying *who* is processing *what kinds* of information for *what purposes.* One such framework, consisting of three *process dimensions* and three *analysis dimensions,* is sketched below:

1. People involved, the "stakeholders." Information systems exist to serve groups of workers. Work can be classified as *information-dependent, information-sensitive, information-related,* or *information-independent.* Information-dependent workers include not only scientists, technologists, and practitioners in the professions but also decision makers, consultants, brokers, etc., in many fields. Information-sensitive workers include managers, craft workers, etc., whose work must adhere to specifications and regulations. Information-related workers are those who create and process information but may not use the substance of the information in their own work; editors, word-processing staffs, and computer programmers are examples. Information-independent workers are the vanishing breed who can do their day's work without knowing or caring what is happening in the research laboratory, in Washington, or on Wall Street. Information-independent workers do not need to be counted as stakeholders in this framework.

2. Information functions. Information serves workers by keeping them abreast of developments in their fields; instructing them about new procedures, policies, specifications, regulations, etc.; helping them to solve problems or make decisions; etc. Information can be defined functionally as *current-awareness information, policy information, procedure information, problem-solving information, decision-making information, information for finding further information,* etc.

3. Information modes and channels. One list of information modes and channels appears in Section II.C. More simply, the modes and channels of much work-related information can be enumerated as *oral exchange, correspondence, articles in technical journals, articles in trade magazines, books, bulletins, computer records, personal files, etc.*

4. Objectives of system functioning. This first analysis dimension is concerned with the weight that should be given to various aspects of system functioning, such as *efficiency* ("streamlined" approach), *economy* (least cost, may not equate with efficiency), *convenience* (least effort, "human-factored"), *compatibility* (minimum disruption of related systems), *equity* (equal or fair provision for everyone), *adaptability* (able to change to meet future requirements), *accountability* (system performance monitorable by stakeholders), etc.

5. Perspectives or frames of reference. This analysis dimension is concerned with how the information system will affect or interact with other systems in which work takes place, including the *perceptual/cognitive, affective* (involving feelings), *social, organizational, technological, economic,* and *legal/political* systems.
6. System design phases. We may be trying to improve the performance of an existing system or introducing an entire new system. Attention focuses successively on the phases of *assessment* of task requirements, needs and values of participants, etc.; *design; implementation; evaluation;* and *modification,* which cycles back in the short term to evaluation and in the long term to assessment.

These process dimensions and analysis dimensions are juxtaposed in Figure 5.

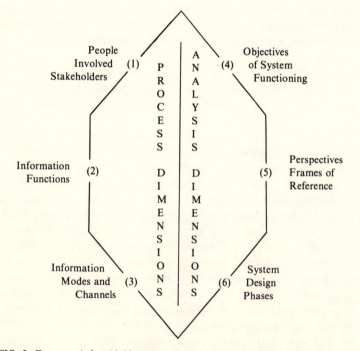

FIG. 5. Framework for thinking about information transactions related to work.

F. Lessons from *Memex*

Memex, a desk-sized electronic and micrographic device envisioned by Vannevar Bush in 1945, has challenged information system designers for more than three decades. Bush (1945) prophesied that *memex* would display an entire library of information at the user's command and process the user's own written work into instantly accessible personal files. Several features of *memex,* including extensive interlinked memories for documents and user-generated work, have been implemented on digital computers.

Exciting as the protean concept of *memex* is, we can recognize its limitations: support of exploration and learning but not of analysis and decision making; lack of networking or communication capability; lack of transformative power over the data in its memory. A 1980 *memex* would support work by integrating the features of at least six kinds of information systems which, unfortunately, do not interconnect at the present time: (1) *information storage and retrieval systems,* (2) *numerical analysis systems,* (3) *teleconference systems,* (4) *instruction systems,* (5) *decision support systems,* and (6) *editorial support systems.*

The very labels by which we are forced to identify these systems indicate the limited range of work functions that they support. A 1980 *memex* assembled from the best features of these systems would seem "sheer miracle to the multitude," as Yeats said, and yet *follow* rather than *lead* the evolution of work.

Taylor's method (1911, see Section I.A) of studying each movement in the work process in order to fit the machine to the process was based on the assumption that the work process was the most immutable of the three elements involved in the adaptation: the work process, the worker, and the machine. However, sophisticated machines change work so fundamentally that it would be better to base adaptations only partly on existing work processes. The other part of the adaptation should be based on what the machine will cause the work to become.

Arguably, the *memex* that was never built has provided more insight into the relationship of information to work than many information machines of the past three decades that had their brief use and have now been superseded. The concept of *memex* is as amorphous as the concept of work itself. In 1945 it was daring to propose that the difficult tasks of scholarship and other information-dependent work could be supported by *memex.* In 1980, when it is finally possible to build *memex,* we understand that an equally significant role for information technology is to foster tasks which, because of the extraordinary amount of information manipulation that they require, have not even been included in taxonomies of tasks to be adapted or augmented.

If we say that improved information systems will allow us to do our present work more efficiently, then *that* work becomes a part of our vision of the future. If we say that improved information systems will allow us to do work that isn't feasible or doesn't occur to us to do now, then we are envisioning an Information Revolution that truly parallels the Industrial Revolution.

REFERENCES

Ackoff, R. (1967) Management misinformation systems. *Management Science 14*, B147–B156.

Ackoff, R., and Halbert, M. H. (1958). "An Operations Research Study of the Scientific Activity of Chemists." Case Institute of Technology, Cleveland, Ohio.

Adams-Webber, J. R. (1979). "Personal Construct Theory: Concepts and Applications." John Wiley and Sons, New York.

Allen, T. J. (1964). "The Utilization of Information Sources during R&D Proposal Preparation." Massachusetts Institute of Technology, Cambridge, Massachusetts.

Allen, T. J. (1977). "Managing the Flow of Technology." MIT Press, Cambridge, Massachusetts.

Bannister, D., and Mair, J. M. M. (1968). "The Evaluation of Personal Constructs." Academic Press, London.

Bateson, G. (1972). "Steps to an Ecology of Mind." Ballantine Books, New York.

Berul, L. H., Elling, M., Karson, A., Shafritz, A. B., and Sieber, H. (1965) "DOD User Needs Study." Auerbach Corporation, Philadelphia, Pennsylvania.

Bieri, J. (1955). Cognitive complexity–simplicity and predictive behavior. *Journal of Abnormal and Social Psychology 51*, 263–268.

Blau, J. R. (1974). Patterns of communication among theoretical high-energy physicists. *Sociometry 37*, 391–406.

Blau, P. M. (1963). "The Dynamics of Bureaucracy." University of Chicago Press, Chicago, Illinois.

Boorstin, D. (1958). "The Americans: The Colonial Experience." Alfred A. Knopf, New York.

Boulding, K. E. (1956). "The Image: Knowledge in Life and Society." University of Michigan Press, Ann Arbor, Michigan.

Bruner, J. S., Goodnow, J. J., and Austin, G. A. (1956). "A Study of Thinking." John Wiley and Sons, New York.

Bush, V. (1945). As we may think. *Atlantic Monthly 176* (July), 101–108.

Carlson, R. O. (1965). "Adoption of Educational Innovations." Center for the Advanced Study of Educational Administration, University of Oregon, Eugene, Oregon.

Chapanis, A. (1971). Prelude to 2001: Explorations in human communication. *American Psychologist 26*, 949–961.

Childers, T., and Post, J. (1975). "The Information Poor in America." Scarecrow Press, Metuchen, New Jersey.

Coleman, J. S., Katz, E., and Menzel, H. (1966). "Medical Innovation: A Diffusion Study." Bobbs-Merrill, Indianapolis, Indiana.

Crane, D. (1972). "Invisible Colleges: Diffusion of Knowledge in Scientific Communities." University of Chicago Press, Chicago, Illinois.

Crawford, S. (1970). "Informal Communication among Scientists in Sleep and Dream Research." Unpublished dissertation, University of Chicago.

Crick, F. J. (1979). How to live with a golden helix. *The Sciences 19* (No. 7), 6–9.

Cronbach, L. J., and Snow, R. W. (1977). "Aptitudes and Instructional Methods." Irvington Publishers, New York.

Drucker, P. F. (1969). "The Age of Discontinuity: Guidelines to Our Changing Society." Pan Books, London.

Festinger, L. (1957). "A Theory of Cognitive Dissonance." Stanford University Press, Palo Alto, California.

Garvey, W. D. (1979). "Communication: The Essence of Science." Pergamon Press, New York.

Garvey, W. D., and Griffith, B. C. (1963–1969). "Reports of the American Psychological Association's Project on Scientific Information Exchange in Psychology." American Psychological Association, Washington, D.C.

Gaston, J. (1969). "Big Science in Britain: A Sociological Study of the High-Energy Physics Community." Unpublished dissertation, Yale University.

Goldhaber, G. M., Yates, M. P., Porter, D. T., and Lesniak, R. (1978). Organizational communication: 1978. *Human Communication Research 5*, 76–96.

Goudsmit, S. A. (1966). Is the literature worth retrieving? *Physics Today 19* (No. 9), 52–56.

Granovetter, M. S. (1973). The strength of weak ties. *American Journal of Sociology 78*, 1360–1380.

Griffith, B., and Miller, A. J. (1970). Networks of informal communication among scientifically productive scientists. *In* "Communication among Scientists and Engineers" (C. Nelson and D. Pollack, Eds.), pp. 125–140. D.C. Heath Company, Lexington, Massachusetts.

Hagstrom, W. O. (1965). "The Scientific Community." Basic Books, New York.

Hammond, K. R. (1978). Toward increasing competence of thought in public policy formation. *In* "Judgment and Decision in Public Policy Formation" (K. R. Hammond, Ed.), pp. 11–32. American Association for the Advancement of Science, Washington, D.C. (AAAS Selected Symposia Series.)

Herner, S. (1954). Information-gathering habits of workers in pure and applied science. *Industrial and Engineering Chemistry 46*, 228–236.

Herring, C. (1973). Dissemination and the use of information in physics. *In* "Physics in Perspective, Volume II, Part B: The Interfaces," pp. 1265–1452. National Academy of Sciences, Washington, D.C.

Hertz, D. B., and Rubenstein, A. H. (1953). "Team Research." Department of Industrial Engineering, Columbia University, New York.

Homans, G. C. (1961). "Social Behavior: Its Elementary Forms." Harcourt, Brace, and World, New York.

Kelly, G. A. (1955). "The Psychology of Personal Constructs, Vol.I. A Theory of Personality." Norton, New York.

Kohler, W. (1947). "Gestalt Psychology." Liveright Publishing Corporation, New York.

Kuhn, T. S. (1962). "The Structure of Scientific Revolutions." University of Chicago Press, Chicago, Illinois.

Licklider, J. C. R. (1966). A crux in scientific and technical communciations. *American Psychologist 21*, 1044–1051.

Liebesny, F. (1959). Lost information: Unpublished conference papers. *In* "Proceedings of the International Conference on Scientific Information," pp. 475–480. National Academy of Sciences-National Research Council, Washington, D.C.

Lindsey, G. (1979). "An Analytic Model for Assessing the Information Orientation and Behavior of Scientists and Engineers." Unpublished dissertation, Stanford University.

Lingwood, D. A. (1968). "Interpersonal Communication, Scientific Productivity, and Invisible Colleges: Studies of Two Behavioral Science Research Areas." Unpublished dissertation, Stanford University.

Lingwood, D. A. (1975). A study of research utilization in the U.S. Forest Service. *In* "Technology Transfer in Research and Development" (J. A. Jolly and J. W. Creighton, Eds.), pp. 37–48. Naval Post-graduate School, Monterey, California.

Machlup, F. (1962). "The Production and Distribution of Knowledge in the United States." Princeton University Press, Princeton, New Jersey.

McClure, C. R. (1978). The information rich employee and information for decision making: Review and comments. *Information Processing and Management 14,* 381–394.

McLuhan, M. (1964). "Understanding Media: The Extensions of Man." McGraw–Hill, New York.

Martin, M. W. (1962). The use of random alarm devices in studying scientists' reading behavior. *IRE Transactions on Engineering Management EM-9,* 66–71.

Menzel, H. (1958). "The Flow of Information among Scientists: Problems, Opportunities, and Research Questions." Bureau of Applied Social Research, Columbia University, New York.

Menzel, H. (1959). Planned and unplanned scientific communication. *In* "Proceedings of the International Conference on Scientific Information," pp. 199–243. National Academy of Sciences-National Research Council, Washington, D. C.

Menzel, H. (1966). Scientific communication: Five themes from social science research. *American Psychologist 21,* 999–1004.

Michigan, University. Survey Research Center (1954). "The Attitudes and Activities of Physiologists." Survey Research Center, Ann Arbor, Michigan.

Miller, G. A., Galanter, E., and Pribram, K. (1960). "Plans and the Structure of Behavior." Henry Holt, New York.

Moravcsik, M. J., and Pasternack, S. (1966). A debate on the preprint exchange. *Physics Today 19* (No. 6), 60–73.

Morison, E. (1974). From Know-How to Nowhere: The Development of American Technology. Basic Books, New York.

Mullins, N. C. (1968). The distribution of social and cultural properties in informal communication networks among biological scientists. *American Sociological Review 33,* 786–797.

Murray, H. A. (1938). "Explorations in Personality." Oxford Press, New York.

National Science Foundation (1978). "National Patterns of R&D Resources." Government Printing Office, Washington, D.C.

Newcomb, T. M. (1953). An approach to the study of communicative acts. *Psychological Review 60,* 393–404.

Newell, A., and Simon, H. A. (1972). "Human Problem Solving." Prentice-Hall, Englewood Cliffs, New Jersey.

Paisley, W. (1968). Information needs and uses. *Annual Review of Information Science and Technology, 3,* 1–30.

Paisley, W., and Butler, M. (1977). "Computer Assistance in Information Work." Applied Communication Research, Palo Alto, California.

Paisley, W., Butler, M., and Cirksena, K. (1979). "Conceptualization of Information Equity Issues in Education." (Paper presented at the Conference on Information Equity in Education, National Institute of Education, Washington, D.C.)

Pask, G., and Scott, B. C. E. (1972). Learning strategies and individual competence. *International Journal of Man–Machine Studies 4,* 217–253.

Pelz, D. C., and Andrews, F. M. (1976). "Scientists in Organizations: Productive Climates for Research and Development." Revised ed. Institute for Social Research, University of Michigan, Ann Arbor, Michigan.

Porat, M. U. (1976). "The Information Economy." Unpublished dissertation, Stanford University.

Porter, L. W., and Roberts, K. H. (1976). Communication in organizations. *In* "Handbook of Industrial and Organizational Psychology" (M. D. Dunnette, Ed.), pp. 1553–1589. Rand McNally, Chicago, Illinois.

Price, D. DeS. (1963). "Little Science, Big Science." Columbia University Press, New York.

Price, D. DeS. (1967). Nations can publish or perish. *International Science and Technology 70,* 84–90.

Roe, A. (1952). "The Making of a Scientist." Dodd, Mead and Company, New York.

Rogers, E. M., and Agarwala–Rogers, R. (1976). "Communication in Organizations." The Free Press, New York.

Rokeach, M. (1960). "The Open and Closed Mind." Basic Books, New York.

Rosenbloom, R. S., and Wolek, F. W. (1967). "Technology, Information, and Organization: Information Transfer in Industrial R&D." Graduate School of Business Administration, Harvard University, Cambridge, Massachusetts.

Schroder, H. M. (1971). Conceptual complexity and personality organization. In "Personality Theory and Information Processing" (H. M. Schroder and P. Suedfeld, Eds.), pp. 240–273. Ronald Press Company, New York.

Scodel, A., Ratoosh, P., and Minas, J. S. (1959). Some personality correlates of decision making under conditions of risk. Behavioral Science 4, 19–27.

Scott, W. A. (1962). Cognitive complexity and cognitive flexibility. Sociometry 25, 405–414.

Shilling, C. W., Bernard, J., and Tyson, J. W. (1964). "Informal Communication among Bioscientists." Biological Sciences Communication Project, George Washington University, Washington, D. C.

Taylor, F. (1911). "Scientific Management." Harper and Row, New York.

Terrant, S. W., and Garson, L. W. (1977). "Evaluation of a Dual Journal Concept." American Chemical Society, Washington, D. C.

Tolman, E. (1948). Cognitive maps in rats and men. Psychological Review 55, 189–208.

Watson, J. D. (1968). "The Double Helix." Atheneum Publishers, New York.

Weinberg, A. (1967). "Reflections on Big Science." MIT Press, Cambridge, Massachusetts.

Wheeler, L. S. (1964). Information seeking as a power strategy. Journal of Social Psychology 62, 125–130.

Whitley, R., and Frost, P. (1973). Task type and information transfer in a government research laboratory. Human Relations 25, 537–550.

Witkin, H. (1959). The perception of the upright. Scientific American 200 (No. 2), 50–70.

5 Communication of Scientific Information to Nonscientists

James E. Grunig
College of Journalism
University of Maryland

I. PROBLEMS AND THEORY IN
SCIENCE COMMUNICATION

Philosophers of science have gradually given up the idea that the purpose of science is to develop theories that articulate, or explain, regularities inherent in nature. Even though most social and behavioral scientists continue to cling to this positivistic view of science, most contemporary philosophers of science now reject it as an inadequate view of science (Suppe, 1977). Science, in the view of contemporary philosophers of science, is a problem-solving enterprise (Laudan, 1977).

A scientist as a problem-solver does not arbitrarily choose some aspect of nature to study. Neither does he hit upon a theory in a burst of inspiration and then spend years attempting to falsify the theory. All scientific theories are false, at least in part, because they are always incomplete and idealized. The test of a theory, therefore, is not whether it is true. Rather, the test of a theory is whether it can solve the problems important to a domain of scientific research. Scientists begin with vague, general ideas that offer promise in solving important problems in a domain and then gradually test, refine, and restructure those ideas to increase both the accuracy and the problem-solving ability of the theory.

In basic fields of science, such as astronomy or physics, scientists often view problems as important simply because the problems puzzle a large number of scientists—such as the problem of explaining a black hole. But scientific problems do not always arise within science itself, even in the basic, physical sciences. Often, scientists turn their attention to problems that society in general deems to be important. Both kinds of problems are equally valid concerns for scientific research, however. In the new philosophical view of science, the distinction between basic and applied research disappears. All scientists solve problems, and the source of those problems makes little difference in the way a scientist should behave.

Applied research, however, often leads to less scientific progress than basic research because the applied scientist less often develops deep, powerful theories which solve more and more problems. One of the most frequent criticisms of the social and behavioral sciences is that they fail to develop deep, powerful theories (see, for example, Lakatos, 1970, pp. 175–176; Popper, 1970, p. 58; Shapere, 1977, p. 521; Toulmin, 1972, p. 380). Social scientists probably fail to develop deep, powerful theories because society asks them to address more problems and more diversified problems than it asks physical scientists to address. In addition, the subject matter of social science—human beings—can control its own behavior, whereas the subject matter of the physical sciences cannot (Machlup, 1978). Because human beings can control their own behavior, the problems addressed by social scientists change more frequently than those addressed by physical scientists.

The communication sciences probably confront even more diverse and changing problems than the other social sciences. Like other social scientists, communication scientists address problems important to society. They also serve a number of communication professions, each of which has problems it wants solved. Many of these problems are quite narrowly defined, however. They trouble one profession but not another, or they trouble only a small part of one profession. The result is a great deal of atheoretical communication research or research that leads to narrow and shallow theories. That, unfortunately, has been the case with research on the communication of scientific information to nonscientists.

Scientists and scientific organizations have asked communication researchers to tell them how to gain more public understanding of science so that the public will accept science and be willing to pay tax dollars to support it. Professional science writers in the media or working in a public relations position in a scientific organization have asked how they can write about science to gain better understanding of science among their readers. They have also asked who their audiences are so that they can target their messages to those audiences. Publishers of science magazines, books, and reports also have asked who makes up the audience for their publications. Communication researchers have addressed these questions and produced a great deal of research. But seldom have the results of that research been linked together by a deep theory with the power to provide an integrated picture of communication between scientists and nonscientists and with the power to indicate how to facilitate that process.

This paper, therefore, has two purposes. The first is to review the research literature on science communication in an attempt to learn what is known and not known about problems of communicating scientific information to nonscientists. The second is to use a theory of communication behavior to explain these research results and to solve the problems which the research has addressed. Because this theory has also been used to solve communication problems other than those of science communication, the paper will also end with an evalaution of that theory and of its promise for communication science in general.

A. A Science Communication Domain

The first step in developing a deep theory to explain as many problems of science communication as possible is to find a conceptual mechanism to bring diverse areas of research together. Shapere's (1977) concept of a scientific domain provides such a mechanism.

According to Shapere, a domain consists of a number of "items" that scientists attempt to explain. The items in a domain do not consist only of empirical observations, however. They also include the theories that have been used to explain different empirical observations. To call a collection of theories and observations a domain, there must be reason to suspect a deeper unity among the facts, theories, and observations that make up the domain. Shapere points out that scientists working in a domain typically try to solve three types of problems: (1) domain problems—to clarify the domain, (2) theoretical problems—to find a theory to explain the observations and theories in the domain, and (3) theoretical inadequacies—to improve an unfinished theory.

Although one might conclude that the field of science communication constitutes a domain, it is probably safer to say that there are many domains in the field. Few, if any, communication scientists have even begun to address the domain problem of developing a single science communication domain. That is, few have thought beyond the narrow communication problems they have attempted to solve. Solving this domain problem is a necessary first step in developing a deep theory of science communication. We must know the items in the domain, that is, before we can develop a deep theory to explain them.

A similar situation confronted the field of persuasive communication research in the 1940s and 1950s when there was a great deal of research on the effects of communication, but little research designed to construct an integrated theory. Some theorists began their search for deeper, more general theories by constructing the communication models that we still use to describe communication—the source → medium → receiver → effects models. Originally those models were nothing more than attempts to categorize the results of communication research—to solve the domain problems of persuasive communication.

Although science communication researchers today can draw from many more communication theories than could communication researchers in the 1940s, few have made consistent use of the same theories and few have done cumulative studies on science communication problems. A useful way to make some sense out of the research on science communication, therefore, seems to be to construct a model of what goes on in science communication in order to classify the problems that need attention and to look for similarities in the research that can lead to a deep theory.

Figure 1 contains a model of a single domain of science communication that includes most of the subdomains that now populate the field. At present, each of the elements of the model has been characterized by a different research tradition. The model in Figure 1 looks like a source-message-receiver model, but actually it is quite different. The arrows in the model are all two-sided and there is nothing to indicate that information flows only in one direction. Rather, Figure 1 depicts the different behaviors and interactions that take place between scientists and audiences of scientific information. The model shows that scientists seldom communicate directly to audiences.

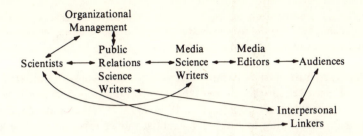

FIG. 1. A model of science communication behaviors and interactions.

Instead, they communicate through public relations and media science writers, media editors, and interpersonal linkers such as change agents, extension workers, salesmen, or community leaders. In addition, the model shows that the interaction between public relations science writers and scientists takes place within the context of organizational management.

The model in Figure 1 also helps to identify the problems that science communication researchers have attempted to solve. These problems fall into two general categories: (1) the individual behaviors of each of the actors in the model—scientists, science writers, management, editors, linkers, and audiences; and (2) the interactions between these actors, such as the relationship between scientists and science writers or between science writers, editors, and audiences.

Figure 1 helps, therefore, to identify the kinds of research results that should be in a science communication domain. We need to examine one more concept from the philosophy of science, however, in order to understand the nature of theories that should also be included in the domain and of the deep theory that will be proposed to explain the items in the domain.

B. Variables and Systems in Theory Building

In describing his concept of a domain, Shapere (1977, p. 521) also distinguished between "primitive" and "developed" science. In primitive science, "obvious sensory similarities or general presuppositions usually determine whether certain items of experience will be considered as forming a body or domain, this is less and less true as science progresses." In primitive science, scientists work directly with phenomena and with empirical generalizations; they have no deeper explanations of the domain. In advanced science this changes:

As part of the growing sophistication of science, such associations of items are subjected to criticism, and often are revised on the basis of considerations that are far from obvious and naive. Differences which seemed to distinguish items from one another are concluded to be superficial; similarities which were previously unrecognized or, if recognized, considered superficial, become fundamental....The items themselves often, in the process, come to be redescribed, often, for scientific purposes...

What a scientist must do to move from the "obvious sensory similarities" of primitive science to the deeper theories of developed science can be understood in terms of Suppe's (1972, 1973, 1974, 1977) semantic conception of theories. According to Suppe, a scientist moves through three levels of abstraction in developing a theory. These three levels include a *phenomenal system,* an abstracted or idealized *physical system,* and a *theory.* Phenomenal systems consist of "particulars"—real world objects—that scientists in a given domain want to explain. As a human being, however, a scientist cannot conceptualize a phenomenal system in its full complexity. Instead, the scientist constructs an abstract replica of the phenomenal system that Suppe calls a physical system.

A physical system consists of a limited number of defining parameters or variables that the scentist assumes exert the only influences on the phenomenal system. Other parameters may in fact exert influence on the behavior of the phenomenal system, but the scientist simplifies things by assuming they have no influence. Theories, then, do not explain the behavior of the phenomenal system; they explain the behavior of the abstracted physical system. Suppe defines a behavior as a change in state of the system.

A scientist can describe states of the physical system with elementary theoretical propositions that Suppe (1974, p. 50) calls the *language of physical description.* But, he adds, this language is too "impoverished linguistically" to describe changes in state over time. Changes in state—behaviors—require a *theory formulation language,* "a more comprehensive language, with augmented logic, which is able to express the laws of the theory, deduce various predictions, etc. from these laws...."

A primitive science, as described by Shapere (1977), thus can be characterized as a science that has not progressed from the language of physical description to the theory formulation language. That, indeed, seems to be the case with research on science communication. We have many descriptive studies of the parameters of the physical system, but few theories to explain changes in state of those parameters.

Moving from the language of physical description to a theory formulation language is not easy, however. Rapoport (1959, p. 351), for example, argued that the task is much easier in the physical sciences than in the social sciences, because parameters in the physical sciences are more evident and intuitive. He explained:

Nevertheless, the social scientist does try to select the fundamental entities of his field of interest. This process of selection, however, is so laborious and involved that it often constitutes the bulk of the social scientist's effort, so he hardly ever gets around to stating "postulates." He must first relate his terms to referents. These referents cannot be simply exhibited; they must themselves be abstracted from a rich variety of events, generalizations, and relations. By the time a number of these referents have been so abstracted and christened, one already has a bulky "system" before the work of seeking out "laws" has ever begun. Such "system," particularly in sociology, is sometimes taken to be "theories."

It is to this task, then, that we now turn. We will use the model of the science communication process in Figure 1 to identity the problems that have concerned researchers in various science communication subdomains. Then we will examine the literature to identify parameters and the language of physical description that has been used to date in the field. Then we will use a theory of communication behavior to integrate these domains into a single domain and to develop a theory formulation language to explain the domain.

II. STUDIES OF INDIVIDUAL BEHAVIORS

A useful way to begin an analysis of the studies of individual science communication behaviors is to classify them as descriptive (positive studies) or prescriptive (normative studies). This distinction is somewhat artificial, as a good positive study usually leads to prescriptive advice. Yet, researchers clearly have had different intentions when they have conducted these two kinds of studies. Positive researchers have attempted to explain why existing behaviors have occurred—such as why audiences use science information— while others have attempted to explain how to improve a behavior—such as how to write a science story better. Most studies of audiences, editors, linkers, scientists, and management have been descriptive, whereas most studies of science writers have been prescriptive.

Because the largest number of individual behavioral studies have been of audiences and science writers, we begin with those two elements of the model.

A. Science Audience Studies

Audience studies far outnumber studies on any other aspect of science communication. This should not seem strange, for in an applied, professional field such as communication the problems that researchers address often are those felt to be important by professionals or by agencies willing to put up money for research. In science communication, the media, professional science writers, and scientific organizations have wanted to know if there is an audience for science information, what that audience is like, what attitudes toward science its members have, how positive attitudes toward science can be created, or how new technology can be diffused to potential users.

1. General Audience Studies

One of the first and most extensive audience studies was a survey of 1,919 American adults commissioned by the National Association of Science Writers (NASW) and conducted by the University of Michigan Survey Research Center (Krieghbaum, 1967, pp. 146–148; Michigan, University Institute of Social Research, 1958; Swinehart and McLeod, 1960). Schramm and Wade (1967), Tichenor (1965), and Patterson et al. (1969) conducted similar studies.

These audience studies generally have shown that survey respondents will claim they like science news and would read more if it were available. For example, the Michigan study showed that 76 percent of the sample respondents could recall a specific science news story they had read in the media. Survey respondents also indicated they would be willing to cut down on crime and sports news to read more science news. Yet these same studies showed science audiences to be specialized. Members of science audiences tend to be more educated, to have higher incomes, and to be consistent users of the media—particularly the print media—for all types of news. In addition, members of the science audience have had some exposure to science courses, although that audience does not usually consist of people with advanced scientific training. Rather, science audiences consist of people with high school science courses and a curiosity or hobbyist interest in science. Similar results in studies done by the Mass Communication Research Center at the University of Wisconsin in the late 1950s and early 1960s led the then director of the center, Percy Tannenbaum, to tell a 1964 meeting of the National Association of Science Writers (quoted in Krieghbaum, 1967, p. 182; see also Tannenbaum, 1963) that science writers write for audiences that seldom if ever read science news if they write for broad general audiences:

> My suggestion, then, is that we recognize that only a part of the public is interested enough in science to want to select and attend to science information, and that we direct our attention to that select audience, rather than the vast audience of uninterested people.

Krieghbaum (1967, p. 183) went on, however, to cite a rebuttal from Martin Mann, then president of the NASW, who argued that the problem with Tannenbaum's approach is that science "'readers' and 'nonreaders' won't stand still" and each group "fluctuates rapidly, wildly, and erratically" with "the story, the time, politics, weather..." Mann can be interpreted as calling for a situational theory of science audience behavior. That is, the audience is not fixed for all types of science stories. Rather, stories about different science issues—situations—bring forth different types of audiences. It is such a situational theory that will be used in this paper to integrate the subdomains of science communication.

2. Consummatory vs. Instrumental Communication.

Before turning to the situational theory, it is necessary to understand the difference between consummatory use of science news (for pleasure or curiosity) and instrumental use (for solving a problem or dealing with a practical situation) (see Grunig, 1979a). Jack Reniree, a science writer at the National Science Foundation, has said that people read science news for one of two reasons: because of curiosity or because the news affects them in some way. Science communication research bears him out. The Michigan survey, for example, found that men more often read about science and that women read about medicine. Krieghbaum (1967, p. 149) interpreted that finding as follows:

> Both men and women were chiefly attracted to science/medical news because they want to keep up with things that were going on. However, slightly more men found science and medicine "interesting" and slightly more women found such information "helpful to me in everyday life." Thus, the males tended to stress intellectual curiosity while women favored the utility of learning about science and medicine.

In a recent study (Grunig, 1979a), I attempted to explain audience news preferences by correlating these preferences with the way in which people spend their time during the day. Only for nonworking women reading "women's" news could I find any evidence that newsreading was functional to everyday life. Preference for what were essentially home economics articles correlated with such time uses as child care, doing the laundry, or cleaning the house. For other types of articles, including science, readership could be explained better by the amount of free time available than by correlation with specific uses of time that seemed related to news articles.

Similar evidence that use of science new is consummatory rather than functional can be found in Tichenor's (1965) dissertation study. He found knowledge of science to be higher among readers whose interest in science was based on curiosity rather than on practical, utilitarian value. Similarly, an extensive review of the literature on environmental communication (Grunig, 1977a) and two studies of environmental communication (Grunig, forthcoming) provided a great deal of evidence that most people do not actively seek out environmental information. They take in—passively process—information in the media about environmental problems because the media have put it on the public agenda. (See Shaw and McCombs, 1977, for an introduction to the agenda setting idea.) But the average member of the public seldom makes much use of environmental information unless he or she is an active environmentalist or unless it relates directly to his or her own life (such as information on the energy crisis). That conclusion was also supported by Robinson (1963) who found that readers of science news do not internalize that information rapidly or extensively in spite of all the attention which the media pay to science.

One study (Shaw and Van Nevel, 1967) suggested that medical specialists first learn of research news in the mass media and then seek more information from specialized sources. But the weight of the evidence is that people do not read science news *in the mass media* for its utilitarian value. Rather they read it because it is there and it arouses their curiosity. We may ask, however, whether people read science news in other media, especially in specialized magazines or other specialized publications for functional purposes. Evidence that people do use specialized media functionally can be found in my time budget study (Grunig, 1979a),which found magazine readership to be correlated with specific uses of time.

Murphy's (1960) review of readership research conducted by *Wallace's Farmer* strongly suggested that content was more important than stylistic characteristics of writing, use of color, readability level, etc. in explaining readership of agricultural articles. In Iowa, for example, beef articles always have higher readership scores than poultry articles, because more farmers raise beef and the information about beef has more functional value for them. Brown's (1970) study of the effectiveness of pictorial symbols in communicating with illiterate Chilean peasants showed relevance of content to be the most important reason why peasants used agricultural bulletins. Even illiteracy did not stop communication if the bulletin appeared relevant. Most peasants could find a literate neighbor or child to read the bulletin to them if the information was something they needed.

The most reasonable answer to the question of whether people read science for curiosity (consummatory) or functional reasons is a synthesis of the two positions. At times persons may read science information simply because it interests them, at other times, they may read it because they can use it. But why a person reads a particular article depends upon whether the situation described in an article involves him or her. Few people read an article on black holes or the behavior of polar bears because it relates to their life situation. But they do read about crabgrass for functional reasons if their lawn is infested with the weed. Thus people read different articles for different reasons. The research evidence strongly suggests, however, that people read about science in mass media more often for curiosity and in specialized media for utilitarian purposes.

3. Knowledge Gap Research

The use of science information for instrumental vs consummatory purposes also helps to explain what Tichenor et al. (1976) have called the knowledge gap or what Rogers (1976) has called the communication effects gap. Simply stated, the knowledge gap hypothesis is that people who already know the most about a subject will gain the most from an information campaign or from media coverage of that subject. The "information poor" will learn something but not as much as will the "information rich," thus widening the knowledge gap. Donohue et al. (1973) also suggested that the apparent selectivity by the information rich leads to social control because only those who are already knowledgeable about science seek science information.

Later the same research team discovered, however, that the knowledge gap in a local community existed only on scientific issues from outside the community. When an issue directly affected the community, nearly everyone was well informed about it (Donohue et al., 1975). These results suggest that when most people in an audience use science information for functional purposes a knowledge gap does not result. A knowledge gap develops when only a few people find the information functionally relevant, or when only those who are more educated find the information has curiosity value.

These results show that there is no single audience and no single reason why audiences use scientific information on a particular topic. Changing the topic may change the audiences and their reasons for using the information. What is needed, then, is an explanatory theory that explains why these patterns emerge.

4. The Situational Theory

The two theories that have dominated research on the effects of science communication—attitude theory and diffusion theory—do not explain this picture of the audience well, if at all. The domain of diffusion research (e.g., Rogers and Shoemaker, 1971) boasts over 1,500 studies of how people hear about and adopt new ideas and practices. The end result of all this research adds little to the descriptive studies discussed above. These studies show that some people (the innovators and early adopters) hear about new technology before others and that people first hear about new ideas from the mass media. At later stages of the adoption process people seek information from interpersonal sources before adopting the new idea. One can deduce from this research that early adopters use information provided by agencies promoting new ideas and practices for functional purposes and that later adopters either do not hear about the information until nearly everyone is using it or that they use it for consummatory purposes. But why? Diffusion research really does not say, as it offers little deep explanatory theory.

The most important shortcoming of diffusion research, however, is its presupposition that communication is something that a person or agency does to get other people to do what he or she wants them to do. Agricultural colleges want farmers to adopt hybrid seed corn. Drug companies want doctors to use their products. Educational researchers want teachers to use new techniques they have developed. Diffusion researchers find out who followed the advice of these agencies. Diffusion studies describe information flow to audiences. They do not *explain* the communication behavior of audiences.

Attitude research has the same problem (for a review, see Oskamp, 1977). It is designed for agencies with a fixed model of how others should behave and who look at communication as a "quick fix" for eliciting that behavior. Attitude theory has a simple appeal to the quick fixers. According to the theory, communications change attitudes which in turn program people's behavior. Thus, a researcher with a surefire method for changing attitudes would seem to have a solution for many of the behavior problems scientific agencies face—people not using their new ideas, not buying their products, not accepting nuclear power, opposing taxes for science, etc. I call the attitude model the domino model of communication. If we can just communicate with people, according to the model, the communication domino will topple the attitude domino and that will topple the behavior domino. Research suggests that attitude theory has little explanatory power. It does show that people who communicate about an issue are more likely to have *an* attitude on that issue and are more likely to do *something* (behave) about that issue (Grunig and Stamm, 1979). But one message seldom leads to one attitude and one behavior. The dominos do not always fall in the same direction. People have free will. They control their communication, their attitudes, and their behavior. We cannot control all three with a quick communication fix.

I have worked for over 10 years on a theory which I believe overcomes the faulty presuppositions of diffusion and attitude theory and which explains the communication behavior of science audiences. The theory assumes that people *can* control their own behavior and that in many situations they communicate in an effort to improve that control—that is, they communicate for functional reasons. In other situations, communication is the behavior they control. That is, people may simply communicate because they enjoy the communication—they communicate for consummatory purposes. The theory is a situational theory because it assumes that people communicate about specific situations or issues. It assumes that attitudes, personality traits, and similar cross-situational concepts do not explain the reasons why people communicate. Attitudes and personality traits do not program people to communicate. People communicate when a situation arouses their interest or when they must deal with a problem in the situation. The theory states that how a person perceives a situation affects *whether* he or she communicates about a situation and *how* he or she communicates. Thus, the theory seems to explain well when audiences will communicate about science topics and whether that communication will be instrumental or consummatory. The theory explains communication behavior. It does not explain attitude change or adoption.

Three variables of the theory explain *when* a person communicates. These are called problem recognition, constraint recognition, and presence of a referent criterion. *Problem recognition* represents the extent to which persons recognize that something is missing or indeterminant in a situation so that they stop to think about the situation. The concept essentially derives from John Dewey's (1938) idea that people do not think or inquire (communicate) about a situation unless it is problematic to them. Thus problem recognition increases the probability that a person will communicate about a situation and have a need for information about that situation. In actual studies, problem recognition has been measured by presenting survey respondents with a list of eight to twenty situations related to an organization or problem and asking them if they often, sometimes, rarely, or never stop to think about each situation.

Constraint recognition represents the extent to which persons perceive constraints in a situation that limit their freedom to construct their own behavior. If persons realize that their freedom to do something about a situation is limited, then information which helps them to plan and make decisions about what to do in that situation has little value. Constraint recognition has been measured by asking subjects, for each of the same eight to twenty situations, whether anything they might do, personally, would make a great, some, little, or no difference in the way the situations are handled.

A *referent criterion* is an "attitude" which a person can use to decide what to do about a situation. It is a different kind of attitude, however, from that described by social psychological theories of attitude. In contrast to attitude theory, which assumes that attitudes control the behavior of people in different situations, the referent criterion is assumed to be a guide or rule learned in previous situations that the person uses with discretion in a new situation. In a new situation the person may apply the referent criterion as an initial guide for resolving the situation. If the old criterion seems to work the person will use it. If it does not seem to work he or she develops a new solution—a new criterion—to guide his or her behavior in the new situation. The referent criterion influences a person's communication behavior because it subsumes what he or she has learned in previous, related situations and thus reduces a need for new information to deal with a new situation. Presence of a referent criterion has been measured by asking whether each respondent had a very clear, somewhat clear, hazy, or no idea of what to do about each situation.

The fourth variable in the theory, *level of involvement,* also explains *when* a person will communicate but, more importantly, it explains *how* he or she will communicate. Level of involvement is defined as the extent to which a person perceives a connection with the situation. It is measured by asking if the respondent sees a strong, moderate, weak, or no connection with the situation. The stronger the connection with a situation, the more probable it is that the person will communicate about it.

Level of involvement also predicts whether a person's communication behavior will be active or passive. I define passive communication behavior as *information processing* and active communication behavior as *information seeking*. A person purposively seeks information that has functional utility in deciding what to do in a situation. Thus, information seeking occurs when the perceived level of involvement is high. In contrast, a person does not look for and generally does not need information that he or she processes. It is used for consummatory reasons. A person may take it in, however, as a means of passing time—such as watching TV or reading a magazine while waiting for an appointment—or for enjoyment—such as reading a novel or human interest story, watching some TV programs, or even reading science magazines.

The distinction between information seeking and processing is important in choosing a medium and communication strategy. If a public seeks information, specialized media such as booklets, magazines, seminars, or interpersonal contacts are most effective. When a person processes information, the most effective media are mass or generalized media which people use when they have available time. Style and creativity are important in facilitating information processing, because a message must get a person's attention and keep his or her interest if he or she is to process the information. Style and creativity are not as important for information seeking because the person then makes an effort to obtain and understand the message.

This theory seems to explain the communication behavior of audiences for science information. Level of involvement, in particular, seems to explain when people use science information for instrumental rather than consummatory purposes. A person who perceives a high level of involvement in a situation seeks science information for instrumental use. If crabgrass, for example, invades a lawn, the person will search for information on how to control it. But few people perceive an involvement with such scientific problems as black holes, whale populations, or animal genetics. If they have time available, people will process such low-involvement information when it comes to them randomly without any effort on their part, but they will internalize little of that information unless they are curious about the scientific problem—that is, recognize it as a problem. Those with high problem recognition, research shows, will seek out information related to the scientific problem and will remember the information they process. The theory also provides an explanation for the knowledge gap because research shows that people who recognize abstract science problems usually are more educated and have taken coursework related to science. They, in turn, are usually the information rich.

5. Applications of the Theory

The four independent variables of this theory have been developed, not only as basic theoretical concepts that explain communication behavior, but also as key indicators that a professional communicator should measure and use when preparing science information for different audiences. The theory has already been used for several science audience studies. In those studies we have generally measured each concept for eight to sixteen different situations. For example, in a study of environmental communication (Grunig forthcoming) we applied the model to eight environmental issues: air pollution, the energy shortage, flood control projects, extinction of whales, strip mining, pesticides, fertilizer run-off, and nuclear power plants. We then used a series of multivariate techniques (factor analysis, canonical correlation, and discriminant analysis) to locate specific combinations of perceived situations that define different publics. For example, the environmental study showed that extinction of whales, air pollution, and the energy crisis each brought about separate publics, whereas the other five situations brought about the same publics.

We have used the combination of the four variables for each public to develop probabilities that different kinds of publics will seek or process information (Grunig and Disbrow, 1977). These probabilities indicate the likelihood of successful communication—either seeking or processing of information—with each public as well as the topics most likely to bring about an audience large enough to make communication worth the professional communicator's effort. Most recently, I have developed the theory into a mathematical model which shows interactions between variables. That model indicates when it might be possible to use communication to intervene in communication behavior—that is, to use information processing that occurs randomly to increase problem recognition and level of involvement to in turn increase the probability that a person will seek or process information (Grunig 1979b). The results show that a professional communicator does not always have to be content with an existing audience and that under certain limited circumstances the audience may be enlarged through communication.

Of the most interest here, however, are the results of studies based on this theory which involve science communication. I first began to develop the theory after examining the role of information in economic decision making (Grunig, 1966). It's first application, however, was in two studies of communication programs aimed at large landowners (Grunig, 1969) and peasants (Grunig, 1971) in an underdevleoped country (Colombia). I developed the theory as an alternative to the then conventional wisdom that communication could bring about economic development by diffusing modern technology and by inculcating modern attitudes among traditional peoples (e.g., Rogers, 1969). The two studies in Colombia showed, in contrast, that constraints as defined in the theory are so strong in an underdeveloped country that few peasants had the latitude in their behavior to make use of technical information or to adopt innovations. Large landowners, in contrast, were faring quite well economically using traditional agricultural practices and, as a result, they recognized no problems in their situations. Thus, I concluded that unless economic development changed the situations to which technical information related, development communication programs would have little effect. In contrast to the then common attitudinal theory that communication brings development, my situational theory showed that development creates a need for communication.

Research on environmental publics using this theory (Grunig, forthcoming) showed that most people think about environmental problems but feel constrained from doing anything about the problems. In addition, all but active environmentalist publics perceive a low level of involvement with environmental issues. Only when an environmental issue directly involves most people does the nonactivist public actively seek information about the issue. The variables of the theory thus explain why most people have only a superficial knowledge of environmental issues but still know the issues are important to society. They process the information prominent in the media but, because of a low level of involvement, do not seek it out or think much about it.

In these environmental studies, Stamm and I (Grunig and Stamm, 1979; Stamm and Grunig, 1977) also developed a situational concept of attitude based on the assumption that people develop and change attitudes to fit situations. People control their attitudes, that is, the attitudes do not control them. Using this concept of attitude, we found that members of the public tended to use a pro-environmentalist attitude—to believe that the waste or deterioration of scarce resources should be simply stopped (what we called a "reversal of trends" position)—until their perceived level of involvement in the situation increased, as it did with the energy issue. (See Levy and Kilburn, 1979 for further evidence of the high involvement of people with the energy shortage.) On the involving issues people combined a "reversal of trends" attitude with a "functional substitutes" attitude which favors the use of an equivalent resource when a scarce resource is depleted. In our terminology, people "hedged" seemingly incompatible attitudes when the situation was one in which no single solution—"attitude"—seemed to resolve the situation.

A recent study compared university journalism and business students to determine whether the two groups fall into different kinds of publics for corporate economic education programs (Grunig, 1979c). Rightly or wrongly, corporations believe that the media are biased toward business and that the way to resolve the problem is to topple the dominos by "educating" journalism students and thus changing their attitudes and behaviors when they become working journalists. We thought this presupposition could best be tested by comparing journalism students with business students. We did find a difference in the two groups, but the difference was not attitudinal. Using our situational definition of attitude, we found that students in both groups were both pro- and anti-business, depending upon the issue. If anything, the business students were more anti-business on more issues than the journalism students.

The level of involvement and problem recognition variables showed, however, that journalism students would seek information only about business issues which directly affect the public, such as pollution and product price and quality. The results showed that business students, on the other hand, would be more likely to both seek and process information on business issues that are not likely to involve the public, such as government regulation, taxation, or size of corporate profits. The study suggests, therefore, that business-media conflict is not so much a difference in attitude as a difference in views of which issues should be reported. The media want to report the consequences of business actions on the public whereas business executives want the media to cover their pet issues even though the public is not interested.

Jenkins (1976) also used the theory in a study of the use of science news in the mass media by university students. His results were much like those found in other science audience studies, and they fit the theory in the way hypothesized here. The active information seeking students—with more problem recognition, etc.—were nonscience students with some science background. The science students did not seek science information from the mass media, presumably because they get it from more specialized sources such as journals or their major courses.

Jenkins' results link directly to the results of three studies of how scientists use the information provided to them by internal publications of the organizations for which they work (Grunig, 1977b; Pelham, 1977; Schneider, 1978). These three studies, as well as a study by Dunwoody and Scott (1979), showed that scientists have a high level of involvement only in science topics within their own narrow specialization. On other science topics scientists are as much laymen as are nonscientists. Scientists would seek information related to their own research from technical publications and seminars. But they spend little time with internal media that report other research done by the organization. We have found that scientists will process information about the work of other scientists only if it is easily available and they have time available. Thus, ease of access, timing, and brevity are especially important in preparing publications, newspapers, exhibits, etc. which are designed to facilitate communication among scientists doing different kinds of research within the same organization.

B. Science Writer Studies

Next in frequency to audience studies are studies of the behavior of science writers. Most of these studies make no distinction between media and public relations science writers, so they will not be separated here. These science writer studies can be placed into three smaller categories: studies of how to translate scientific language into lay language, studies of factors associated with the accuracy of science communication, and studies of story selection by science writers.

1. Translation of Scientific Language

These studies are normative studies. That is, they do not explain how science writers translate scientific language. Rather they test out ideas that have been proposed for translating science. For many years the dominant type of research on science writing involved measurement of readability scores with instruments such as the Flesch readability formula. Essentially the assumption behind these studies was that higher readability would make science more understandable (e.g., Funkhouser, 1967). Funkhouser (1969) found, for example, that articles on science in media intended for lay audiences had lower readability scores (were more readable) than articles in media intended for technical audiences. Murphy's (1960) *Wallaces Farmer* studies showed stories with lower readability scores had higher readership scores, although the differences were not great. Fewster (1966) hypothesized that people read books written by food faddists more often than books by recognized nutrition authorities because they were more readable. Her study showed no difference, however, in Flesch scores, sentence length, or number of verbs. Generally, then, the literature does not provide a great deal of support for the idea that shorter sentences and simpler words (the components of most readability scales) provide an easy solution to the problem of how to explain science to the layman.

Several studies were done at the University of Wisconsin (Powers, 1966) on the comprehensibility of graphs that parallel the readability studies. These researchers found that tables and graphs improve comprehension of science topics over text alone. They also found that graphs simplified in several ways also improved comprehension over graphs that were more difficult to read. In a similar "simplification" study, Witt (1976) found that an experimental group of students that read an article on pollution with quantitative statements were less likely to think the problem discussed could be solved than a control group that read a less quantified version of the same story. A number of studies (Felstehausen, 1965; Flippen, 1969; Kearl and Powers, 1961; Sorenson, 1957) measured audience undestanding of technical terms used in communicating scientific topics. Generally, the studies showed that frequent readers of articles related to the technical topic studied understood the terms better. The researchers also generally recommended that writers use scientific terms which their research showed audience members most often understood if they wanted to increase audience understanding of the topic.

Other studies have tested the effect of traditional writing advice generally given in journalism and English courses. For example, I found (Grunig, 1965) the percentage of active voice verbs to be very highly correlated with readability scores. Maurer (1963), however, found that use of active verbs does not have a significantly greater effect upon retention of information than use of passive voice verbs. Parker (1962) found that the widely used expository writing devices of a topic sentence and beginning and closing summaries improved scores on a recall test.

Although results are mixed, the research on writing techniques and on simplification of writing generally supports the advice traditionally given by writing teachers. Research also shows that both lay audiences *and scientists*— in contrast to what is generally believed—prefer simplified writing to complex and difficult writing (Funkhouser and Maccoby 1970, 1971b; Wales and Ashman, 1978). Nevertheless, the research evidence cannot support the conclusion that simplified and well organized writing will insure understanding of science information. There is more to the communication of an idea that stringing words together. Ideas are more than words (see e.g., Paivio, 1971), and the purpose of communication is to reconstruct one person's idea in another person's mind. When we communicate an idea we break it down piece by piece and explain it in words. But just as it is easier to take an automobile engine apart than it is to put it back together, so simplified words and style do not insure that the reader will be able to use the words to put the idea being communicated back together.

Science writing teachers and textbooks frequently claim that the rhetorical devices of analogies, examples, and parables help readers reconstruct a scientist's idea in their minds because these devices make it possible to relate an unfamiliar idea to a familiar idea. Several researchers, therefore, have studied the effects of these devices. In one study, Funkhouser and Maccoby (1970, 1971b) found that examples resulted in more "information gain" than did analogies, although analogies resulted in slightly more liking of the stories, attitude changes, and information seeking. In a later study, Funkhouser and Maccoby (1971a, 1973, 1974) found that analogies resulted in more information gain for less advanced students than did examples, but they could find no difference for advanced students. McCrosky and Combs (1969) also found that a message containing analogies resulted in more attitude change than did a no-analogy message.

These studies of rhetorical devices used such dependent variables as recall, information gain, or attitude change. Thus, the results indicate more whether words are remembered than whether ideas have been reconstructed. The studies, that is, measured recall rather than understanding.

In three studies of rhetorical devices (Grunig, 1974), I used Richard Carter's signaled stopping technique (Carter et al., 1973) to try to get at understanding. With the signaled stopping technique, experimental subjects read different versions of articles on economics, placed a slash mark at the points in the article where they felt like stopping, and indicated their reason for stopping—to agree, disagree, ask a question, to think about implications, to think because of confusion, or other reasons. I then reasoned that thinking about implications would be a logical antecedent to understanding and used the number of stops for that reason as my dependent variable. The more times someone stops to think about implications of what he is reading, I reasoned, the more likely he or she would be able to reconstruct the idea being communicated. I also asked the subjects, in a direct question, how well they thought they understood the articles they read. Initial results of these studies showed very little difference between stories containing analogies, examples, and parables and an article containing none of these devices.

As the research progressed, however, I began to control for level of problem recognition and constraint recognition, two of the variables from my theory. Then, significant results began to emerge. Subjects who had high problem recognition and low constraint recognition, who the theory predicted should seek and process information, stopped to think about implications more and reported a higher level of undertanding than subjects the theory predicted should be less likely to seek or process information, regardless of what kind of writing device was used. For the actively communicating subjects, however, analogies and parables stimulated thinking and understanding. Examples, however, stimulated less thinking than did writing using none of these devices.

Bartholomew (1973) replicated this study using analogies only. He had a group of journalism students and a group of physics students read articles on physics taken from Isaac Asimov's *Understanding Physics*. He found that analogies caused physics students to stop to think and to report more understanding, but the same was not true for the journalism students. He traced the cause to lack of communication by journalism students which he attributed to constraint recognition—fear of mathematics.

The results of these studies indicate that the style of a science story is less important than whether the content is relevant to the perceived situation of the reader. Thus the studies indicate that science writers should be most concerned with story selection if they hope to achieve understanding of science. But the findings also show the difficulty of communicating with people who do not perceive a problem to which the scientific topic relates or who cannot apply the information because of constraints in their situation. The students in these studies did not stop to think about the information even when an attempt was made to make the information more understandable and when the experimental condition forced them to read it.

In discussing the development of my theory, I pointed out that I had fit a mathematical model (a set of simultaneous equations) to data from environmental and economic studies to determine interactions between varaibles. The results of this effort (Grunig, 1979b) showed that random information processing could increase problem recognition which could in turn stimulate more information processing and seeking. But the regression coefficients showed these connections to be weak, a finding which explains the Grunig (1974) and Bartholomew (1973) results. At this point in our research we really do not know what communication techniques, if any, are most likely to get the interest of people who are randomly processing information. We know that analogies and parables help people who are actively communicating about science to understand it better. Yet we do not really have an adequate theoretical explanation of why.

I believe the problem of helping both interested and disinterested audience understand that science deserves a great deal more research attention. To find the answers, I believe we should look more into theories of cognitive psychology (for an overview, see Horton and Turnage, 1976). I also believe we can find some answers in the philosophy of language. Communication researchers, however, have paid little attention to these two bodies of theory.

2. Accuracy of Science Writing

The typical accuracy study is an after-the-fact check of how well a science writer has done his or her job. In the simplest study, the scientist whose ideas are discussed in an article reads the story and indicates on a check list of possible errors any errors found in the story. In the more sophisticated studies, these errors are crosstabulated with one or more writing or reporting practices—such as whether the writer showed the scientist the story before publication—to determine if that practice significantly affected accuracy.

Accuracy researchers have addressed the problem of whether science articles are less accurate than general news articles. Tankard and Ryan (1974), for example, found 6.2 errors per science story, compared to .77 to 1.17 errors which four other researchers had found in general news articles. Only 8.8 percent of the science stories were error-free, compared with forty to fifty-nine percent of the general news stories. Tankard and Ryan, however, used a check list with forty-two possible errors, as compared to about 14 in the general news studies. To see if the number of categories in the list made a difference in accuracy, Pulford (1976) replicated the Tankard and Ryan study using a list of eleven possible errors. This time the results showed 2.16 errors per story and 29.4 percent error-free stories. Pulford's results still showed science stories to be less accurate than general stories, but the difference was not great, especially considering the greater difficulty of science news.

Although this type of accuracy result is interesting to the science writer, it tells little about how to improve writing or reporting methods. Knowledge of the most common errors, however, can be useful. Both Tankard and Ryan and Pulford found errors of omission to be most common errors—omission of relevent information on results, methods, inferences, and qualifications. Generally, Tankard and Ryan and Pulford found each of these errors in about a third of the stories. Misleading headlines also represented frequent errors.

Broberg (1973) found essentially the same results using a different methodology. She classified the changes scientists at the National Institutes of Health made in press releases submitted to them for review. About half of the changes were additions made by the scientists—where deletions, corrections, word changes, and revisions were the other categories of changes. She also found that scientists made significantly more additions for inaccurate writers (those with more total changes) than for accurate writers. Her results thus suggest that the best science writers explain and interpret more, which is also indicated by the fact that in every case where extensions and applications of research were deleted the releases were written by accurate writers.

Although the Tankard and Ryan (1974), Pulford (1976), and Broberg (1973) results could indicate that scientists want the mass media to cover their results in the same detail as a technical journal, a better interpretation is that science writers err the most when they do not fully understand a story. It is possible to write a science story in good journalistic form, but still write it inaccurately. Results of these three studies support that observation. Broberg had conceptualized the changes made by scientists in science stories as a way of measuring Carter's signaled stops. She reasoned that scientists would make changes in articles when something stopped them in the story. Thus Broberg's results can be connected to Heffner's (1973) studies of stopping and accuracy by student news reporters. Heffner found that the more often writers stopped to question information they had received from a news source the less frequently readers stopped while reading the news story. Likewise, news sources stopped more often as they read less accurate stories, thus confirming Broberg's measure of accuracy.

We can infer that the best science writers are those who actively seek information while writing a story. They do not routinely write a story whether they understand it or not. They stop to think and to seek further information when there are gaps in the story. In other words, they look for and recognize problems (lack of unity) in their understanding of the story they are writing. But just as the journalism students in Bartholomew's (1973) study did not stop to think about what they were reading because of constraints (lack of background in mathematics), so Broberg's (1973) study suggests that inaccurate science writers may also fail to stop, think, and communicate while writing because of constraints resulting from inadequate science preparation. Broberg found that the accurate writers had experience or training in both journalism and science; the innaccurate writers were trained in only one area.

A study by Tichenor et al. (1970a) provides further support for the idea that frequent stopping and active communication by science writers increases communication accuracy. They found that organizational policies of both the organization that employs the scientists and the organization that employs the science writer improve communication accuracy. For example, they found that the more people involved in preparing a story, the more accurate the result. In their study, accuracy was measured by asking members of lay audiences to explain what a science article had said. Scientists discussed in the articles then indicated whether these statements were accurate or not. They found that writers who had written stories above average in accuracy had gotten information from press releases or journal articles rather than from public hearings, the story had been assigned by an editor, and the writer had checked back with the scientist during or after writing a story. In other words, the more people who read the story, and presumably stopped and corrected poor or unclear writing, the more accurate the final story.

Stories were also more accurate when the organization employing the scientist had a policy stressing the importance of communication with the public. Stories were most accurate when the scientist perceived a rigid policy for reporting research to the public and the scientist had some administrative or teaching duties. Tichenor et al. (1970a, p. 683) thus concluded that "factors that point to more specific, purposive, control of public communication in the science organization contribute to the production of more accurately understood messages when these scientists come into contact with media professionals."

The Tichenor et al. (1970a) study thus suggests that scientists will communicate more accurately if public relations science writers assist them in communicating. Dunwoody and Scott (1979), however, found that scientists who had worked through a public relations "mediator" did not evaluate science coverage more highly than scientists who had not worked through a mediator. Bassett et al. (1968) reached the same conclusion. General perceptions of media coverage measured by these latter researchers and accuracy of a specific message (measured by Tichenor et al., 1970a) are quite different dependent variables, however. These three studies taken together, therefore, probably show that public relations assistance does not change scientists' attitudes toward the media, even though public relations assistance can improve their communication.

The studies of accuracy bring us back to the basic theories developed thus far. The more active the communication, the more accurate that communication is. Although researchers have studied extensively the kinds of audiences that communicate actively, they had only begun to study why scientific organizations develop a policy for active communication, and why science writers behave as they do.

3. Science Writer Behavior

In contrast to studies of language and accuracy, which generally have had a normative purpose, studies of news selection patterns and other behaviors of science writers generally have had a positive or descriptive intent. Few such studies have been done, however. Whereas many funding agencies have been interested in quick–fix solutions to audience problems, few have had as much interest in the behavior of science communicators.

There has been a long tradition of "gatekeeper" research in mass communication—many studies of the reasons why journalists make the decisions they do. With increasing frequency these studies have shown that the decisions of journalists reflect organizational and societal controls and that they are not autonomous individual decisions (Tichenor et al., 1972). Donohue et al. (1973) applied this same perspective to science writers and concluded that science news will be controlled by the science system as "a function of the degree to which media channel members identify with the science system" (p. 655). If the science writer sees his role as accurately transmitting and interpreting science to the public, that is, he will be under the control of the science system. Thus, Donohue et al. (1973) conceded that their own study of accuracy showed how a science system can best assure "knowledge of" what it wants the public to hear when "knowledge about" the functioning of the science system and its impact upon society is what the public needs. They then argued that science coverage has begun to change from a "fairly descriptive, one-project-at-a time" coverage to more "critical, conflict-laden coverage of science" which resulted from the "growing relevance of scientific problems to the political system" (Donohue et al., 1973, p. 657).

Cole (1975) tested this hypothesis in a study which compared conflict vs. nonconflict coverage of science in four metropolitan newpapers in 1951, 1961, and 1971. As expected, the coverage of controversial topics increased over that period. Cole also found what was apparently a science writer tie to the science system. Science writers were less likely to cover controversial science stories than were reporters who seldom covered science or, especially, than were reporters who were part-time science writers. He speculated that this difference might have resulted from an institutional constraint of newspapers, which assign "hard" science news stories to science writers and controversial and political science stories to reporters who do not cover science on a regular basis.

In a similar study, Tichenor et al. (1976) asked residents of two Minnesota communities the extent to which they believed sicentific information should be widely disseminated in the community. In essence, the researchers want to know whether residents wanted "knowledge about" science. One of the two communities was more pluralistic than the other, the other more homogeneous. They found that residents of the more pluralistic community more often said they favored wide distribution of scientific information. Thus we can conclude that because residents in a pluralistic community experience more conflict they are more likely to recognize problems that do not involve them but do involve other community residents or groups. As a result, they are more likely to recognize the utility of different kinds of scientific information both to themselves and others in their community with different interests. Presumably, pluralistic communities would also have a demand for science writing that is not controlled by the science system.

In a study that traced science writer behavior to media influence rather than to science system influence, Dunwoody (1979) examined the behavior of science writers covering the annual convention of the American Association for the Advancement of Science. She found that the constraints of the newgathering organization itself also constrained science writers to what is essentially "knowledge-of" rather than "knowledge-about" science. Deadline pressure and competition with other media forced science writers to use press releases and news conferences set up by the AAAS, rather than original interviews and symposia, and to rely on a single news sources rather than multiple sources. Dunwoody (1979, p,. 18–19). explained:

> Respondents in this study viewed competition not as a journalist-vs-journalist battle but rather as a newspaper-vs-newspaper situation. Rather than pitting themselves against colleagues, they perceived competition as something their *editors* felt, as an organizational constraint that must be satisfied. Competition meant that their editors were gauging the quality of their work not on the basis of reporter originality but on the basis of what the competing newspaper or wire service was reporting... Science writers could minimize complaints from their city rooms, then, not by scooping each other on stories (which in fact would have increased complaints) *but* by *duplicating* each other. And press conferences provided the best place to accomplish this.

Being a member of the "inner club" of science writers and the expertise gained by interaction with these other science writers did not help science writers unless the constraints of deadlines and competition loosened. Under the same constraints inner club members generally selected the same stories as the reporters who were not part of the club. When constraints loosened, Dunwoody added, science writer interactions did improve the accuracy and quality of the stories reported.

In summary, the studies of science writer behavior suggest that both public relations and media science writers have a responsibility to report both "knowledge of" and "knowledge about" science. Constraints of the science system and the media, however, limit the ability of science writers to report "knowledge about" science. Scientific organizations with a stated and formal policy of communicating to the public effectively communicate "knowledge of" science. But the public relations science writer must be able to perceive the problems of science from the standpoint of the public as well as that of the science system if that organization is to exercise its social responsibility to the public. The research also suggests that as society becomes more pluralistic, publics will recognize more problems and increasingly seek out such "knowledge about" science.

Media science writers also are more successful in providing "knowledge of" science then in providing "knowledge about" science because of the constraints of the news gathering organization and their own identification with the science system. The studies cited here suggest that media science writers must do more than process the information which scientific agencies choose to disseminate. They must perceive the problems of society, stop to think about them, and seek out scientific information relevant to an increasingly pluralistic society.

We have now covered the two major areas of research in science communication, science audiences and science communicators. We can now look at the other elements of Figure 1, most of which have received less attention.

C. Editor Studies

Research on editor behavior in dealing with science articles have not been extensive, although editors have often been accused of being the weak link between scientists and the public. Editors supposedly doom many science stories to the overset, write the misleading headlines which scientists complain about, and fail to see the news value in science stories. Their lack of interest would also explain why newspapers devote less than 5 percent of their space to science (Nunn, 1979).

The research does, in fact, show that editors recognize different problems than scientists and science writers and apply different referent criteria, as I have defined these two terms (Johnson, 1963; Missouri University, 1973; Patterson et al., 1969; Tannenbaum, 1963). Scientists see science stories from the standpoint of scientific interests, while editors see them from what they perceive as the public interest, a conclusion which is supported by my study of journalism and business students and their interest in economic problems (Grunig 1979c). Science writers see science more like scientists than do the editors. These studies also show that scientists pay more attention to what is said, whereas editors pay attention to how it is said.

Although editors evaluate science stories from the perspective of what they think is the public interest, they are not very adept at predicting what will interest the public. Studies of editors show that the scientist, science writer, and public have similar views about science, but that the editor is out of tune with the others (Patterson, et al., 1969; Tannenbaum, 1963;). We can infer that the misperception of editors leads to media science content that is not of interest to the public. Research on editors thus suggests that editors may be the source of many of the inaccuracies which accuracy researchers have found to be common in science stories such as omissions and misleading headlines. Using the situational theory, we can hypothesize that the editor's unique science communication behavior results because he does not share the referent criteria of the science system. Editors could be the one actor in the communication link from scientist to public—or public to scientist—who forces science writers to provide "knowledge about" science to the public and to ask scientists socially relevant questions. Too often, however, editors do not understand the public's interest in science. Their gatekeeping decisions are based more on competition, deadlines, and writing style. To understand why, we need more studies of the science communication behavior of editors similar to those of the science communication behavior of audiences

It seems logical that editors process but do not seek science information and that they do not process science news enough to internalize it and understand it. Editors also seem to perceive political problems more often than scientific problems, unless the scientific problems have political implications. Editors also do not appear to believe the public is interested in science. We need research, however, to substantiate these conclusions. We also need research to place editors into different categories of communication behavior. Some, no doubt, communicate differently about science. Research into the comparative backgrounds of the different editors would help us to deal with the editor problem.

D. Scientist Studies

Scientists communicate with each other as well as with the lay public, and there have been studies of both types of scientist communication behavior. Studies of scientists communicating with other scientists (Crane, 1972; Garvey and Griffith, 1967; Garvey et al., 1970a, b; Nelson and Pollock, 1970) show that scientists communicate within specialized communities or "invisible colleges," although Garvey et al. (1970a) found that social scientists communicate more randomly than physical scientists. In addition to this literature from the sociology of science, there is also a great deal of literature in the philosophy of science which discusses the difficulty scientists from diffrent research traditions have in communicating with each other (e.g., Bohm, 1977; Kuhn, 1970; Popper, 1970). The theory that could be developed from the philosophy of science could, I believe, be quite similar to that used to explain the communication of science to laymen.

Most of this literature can be explained with the situational theory of communication behavior. Scientists are most likely to communicate with other scientists who are *involved* in research from the same scientific domains and who recognize similar *scientific* problems within those domains. Also, scientists communicate best with scientists who have the same theories (referent criteria) and who are constrained by the same research techniques. This is an area of research that should be pursued further to test these hypotheses. It is an area of research that would be useful to science writers who need to know how to identify scientific communities, compare and contrast different schools of thought, and locate sources of scientific information.

Of more relevance to the model in Figure 1, however, is the communication of scientists with the public. Krieghbaum (1967, pp. 160–177) has described some of the *constraints* which discourage scientists communicating with the public, such as the priority of journal publication, peer pressure against popularizing, and the necessity of peer review. Goodell (1977, pp. 19–38) studied seven "visible scientists" who actively communicate with the public on controversial issues. Her results also fit into the situational explanation of why a person actively communicates—in this case by explaining why people actively *give* information. Goodell's results suggest that a scientist must first free himself of the constraint of peer pressure by establishing himself as a credible researcher before he can be involved in public issues. (Boltanski and Maldidier (1970) reached the same conclusion from a study of French scientists.)

Goodell's research then suggests that actively communicating scientists recognize broad public problems (what she calls "hot topics") related to their area of expertise, and perceive a high level of involvement in the consequences of these problems on the public. Finally, she found that these scientists are articulate—able to communicate science in the language of the layman. One could interpret the inability to communicate as a constraint facing the average scientist and conclude that the visible scientists are more likely to communicate because they are free of that constraint. In addition, Goodell's research indicates that visible scientists are controversial and have a colorful image. Thus, they are likely to get the attention of people randomly processing information from the media—editors and casual readers of science in the media.

The assumption behind Goodell's research is that visible scientists are different from the average scientist. The average scientist, according to much of the literature on science communication, avoids contact with the media because of the constraints identified by Krieghbaum and others. A recent study by Dunwoody and Scott (1979) showed, however, that 75 percent of a sample of Ohio State and Ohio University scientists said they welcome contact with the mass media.

In a study of biological scientists in the Washington, D.C. area, Van Duzee (1977) likewise found that 90 percent of her sample said they would be willing to help a science writer get information, even though forty-three percent had never been interviewed by a science writer.

Why do scientists want to communicate with the public? It could be that they recognize a lack of public support as a problem related to financial support for their research. It could also be that the organizations they work for have a policy calling for communication with the public, which would be in line with the Tichenor et al. (1970a) findings discussed above. We can only speculate, however, until we have further research to apply such theoretical explanations to these observations.

The scientists in the Dunwoody and Scott (1979) study also said they preferred making contact with magazine journalists rather than newspaper journalists. This difference seems to reflect a preference for coverage by the instrumental media rather than the consummatory media. Consummatory coverage of science appears to be the source of the complaints of scientists about sensationalism and humorous treatment of science in the media. Van Duzee (1977) also found that scientists could distinguish between the news value and the scientific value of research—thus failing to confirm another accepted generalization about scientists. The stories the scientists in Van Duzee's study said had the greatest news value, however, generally were stories with the greatest consummatory value. This study, therefore, suggests that scientists think the media have an interest only in consummatory use of science news and not in science of functional use.

Research on the communication behavior of scientists, in conclusion, has often sought confirmation of common beliefs that science writers have about scientists. Many of those beliefs have not been confirmed. What we need are more attempts to develop theoretical explanations of why scientists communicate as they do.

E. Linker Studies

The concept of individuals who link together specialized groups has been most thoroughly researched in studies on communication within organizations (e.g., Farace et al., 1977, pp. 177–203). Linkers—"liaisons" and "bridges"—in an organization have been found to have diverse interests and group memberships and to serve as mediating communicators between specialized groups.

We do not do too much damage to the organizational concept of a linker if we apply it to individuals who serve a bridging function between scientists and publics. Examples of such linkers are agricultural extension agents, salesmen for technical products or medical supplies, community leaders, or specialized teachers such as physical education or health teachers. The relevant research question about linkers is "how do they communicate?"

Early diffusion research (Wilkening, 1956) showed that farmers most often communicate with agricultural extension agents and salesmen at the stage of decision making when they are trying to put a change into effect. Media, on the other hand, make farmers aware of possible changes, and other farmers help farmers decide whether to adopt a change. It is reasonable to conclude from diffusion research that members of the public are the active communicators, not the linkers.

I have theorized that people communicate most effectively with one another when their perceived situations are similar—when they recognize similar problems, face similar constraints, perceive involvement in similar situations, and have similar referent criteria. This hypohesis would explain research by Jain (1970) which showed that extension specialists whom their peers rated as most effective were those who engaged in *diverse* communication behaviors rather than in large *amounts* of communication behavior. The effective linkers, it would appear, perceived diverse situations in a way that stimulates communication, even if their communication behavior is only information processing. Then when farmers or other members of the public with more specialized interests come to the linkers for information, the linkers will be able to provide relevant information to diverse client groups. Research related to the "opinion leaders" by Atkin (1972) also supports this conclusion. Because of their role as an information source in a social system, opinion leaders recognize many different problems which in turn stimulate them to seek out information relevant to these problems. Opinion leaders recognize diverse problems because the social system expects them to.

Our normal conception of a linker, change agent, or opinion leader, however, is of an active disseminator of information, not as an active seeker of information and a passive disseminator of information. Miller (1978) wanted to know whether local physical education administrators act as active disseminators of information about physical education to members of the public. He hypothesized that physical educators who actively disseminate information would perceive communicating with the public, communicating with the media, and communicating with lawmakers as important problems which involve them and which they can do something about (they are unconstrained). These are situational perceptions the situational theory says should stimulate active communication. Miller found two types of physical education administrators who did perceive communication with the public as an important and involving problem. One type was in a large school system, with a public relations department to which the administrators delegated the responsibility of communicating with the public. The other type of physical educators with an interest in public communication were in smaller organizations. They did communicate with the public themselves.

Research on linkers thus suggests that if we want linkers to be good sources of information sought by others they should be able to perceive the problems and the constraints of the people they serve, variables that motivate linkers to seek out relevant information (see Grunig, 1978). If we want them to be active disseminators of information to the public we should define their role in the organization as that of a communicator so that they perceive communication with the public as a problem and feel involved with that communication process. We should also eliminate their perceived constraints to communication by teaching them how to communicate.

F. Management Studies

Public relations science writers work within a context structured by the management of the organization that employs them. We have already seen in the Tichenor et al. (1970a) study of communication accuracy that a management policy in favor of "purposive control of public communication in the scientific organization" results in more accurate communication from scientists to the public. An important research question then is why some organizations have such a policy and others do not.

I addressed this question in a study of 216 organizations employing public relations specialists in the Baltimore–Washington area (Grunig 1976a). Most of these 216 organizations were not scientific organizations, however. In that study, I reasoned that organizations would communicate through their public relations departments for the same reasons that individuals communicate. In particular, I hypothesized that organizations that continually recognize problems and that are not constrained by their technology or environment (which are dynamic rather than static) would have public relations departments whose function was both to give information to and seek information from the public. I called these organizations problem solving organizations. In contrast, organizations that did not recognize problems (new opportunities) and that were constrained by their technology and environment would use public relations practitioners to defend their fixed behavior, i.e., as propagandistic "flacks." I called these latter organizations fatalistic organizations.

The literature on the sociology of organizations (e.g., Hage and Aiken, 1970) indicated that problem-solving organizations would be relatively unstructured, with decentralized decision making, fewer formalized rules and job descriptions, and less stratification in rank and prestige among employees. Problem-solving organizations should also have been complex organizations with many professional employees. And, they should have been found in a complex, changing environment. Fatalistic organizations would be more structured—with centralized decision making, more formal rules, more distinguishable differences (stratification) between employees, fewer professional employees, and a static, unchanging environment.

In general, my results supported these hypotheses. I found that the role of public relations people in fatalistic organizations was to defend the organization if criticized, but not to actively provide information to publics. Public relations people in the problem-solving organizations did actively disseminate information to the public, but few actively sought out information from the public. Only in young and small problem solving organizations did the public relations people seek information from the public. In larger problem-solving organizations, management had defined the role of public relations in job descriptions as strictly the disseminiation of information—thus depriving the organization of an important public relations role. This was especially true in governmental organizations that hire a large proportion of the public relations science writers.

Miller (1978) applied the same organizational variables in his study of the public communication behavior of physical education administrators. He found two kinds of organizational structures: a large, decentralized school system and a small, more centralized school system. Because school systems are complex organizations with a large proportion of professional employees, however, both of these types of school systems were relatively unstructured. In the large school system the physical education administrator delegated public communication to the public relations department. These administrators, however, believed the goal of public relations to be one-way communication to the public. The administrators who communicated with the public themselves were found more often in small school systems. They, too, defined their public relations goal as one-way communication. As in my study of 216 organizations, Miller's study showed that even when organizational structure is favorable toward two-way public relations the organization often practices one-way communication only, primarily because administrative policy and perceptions limit it to that.

Hill (1979) most recently applied this research framework to a study of information personnel, scientists, and directors of forty-nine agricultural experiment stations in the United States. Hill's study showed that few experiment stations carry on full two-way public communication because of a combination of public relations personnel who are untrained to carry on the full public relations function and organizational structures that discourage such full communication.

Hill found four types of experiment station information people. One type was in an unstructured organization in which the public relations person could conduct two-way public relations. But, probably because of a strictly journalistic background, this person believed that information dissemination was the only important public relations function—press releases, press conferences, tours and events, etc. A second type of professional communicator also thought information seeking was an important part of his or her role—that he or she should do research on the information needs of the public—but was found in a structured organization that discouraged two-way communication. The third type of communicator was found in the structured organization, where the role was strictly to write press releases and prepare publications—at the beck and call of the administrators. A fourth type also did little more than write press releases and prepare publications, although in an open organization where more could be done.

It seems, therefore, that information personnel in agricultural research organizations do little more than disseminate information—provide "knowledge of" science—even when they are in open organizations where they could do research about audience information needs necessary to provide "knowledge about" science. Those who did see their role as two-way were, unfortunately, constrained by the organization from doing so. What is the solution to this dilemma? Public relations science writers should have training in modern-day public relations as well as in science writing. In addition, administrators of scientific organizations need a better understanding of the value of public communication to their organizations because the policies they set make a great deal of difference in how effectively scientific organizations communicate "of" science and, especially, "about" science to the public.

III. STUDIES OF INTERACTIONAL BEHAVIORS

Communication between scientists and members of the public must flow through several gates, as depicted in Figure 1. How useful that scientific information is to the public and how accurately it is communicated depends to a great extent on how well the actors in the chain understand each other and communicate with each other.

Thus far this paper has attempted to explain the communication behavior of each actor in this chain. The studies we will now examine have attempted to determine how well these individual communication behaviors mesh. Do the actors communicate with each other? Do the actors communicate effectively with each other?

Most of the research on interactions between the actors has been based upon, or can be interpreted in terms of, McLeod and Chaffee's (1973) coorientation model. Cooientation simply means that two actors simultaneously orient to and communicate about the same problem, topic, or situation. The McLeod and Chaffee (1973) model as revised and reconstructed in Figure 2 assumes that each actor has an idea (cognition) about the situation and a positive or negative evaluation of that idea (an "attitude"). Each actor also has a perception of the other person's idea and

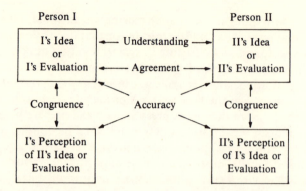

FIG. 2. A reconstruction of the McLeod-Chaffee coorientation model.

evaluation of that idea. The variables in the model can then be interpreted as effects of communication. Congruence is the extent to which each person thinks the other person's idea or evaluation is similar to his or her own. Accuracy is the extent to which one person's perception of the other person's idea or evaluation approximates the other person's actual idea or evaluation. Understanding represents the extent to which the two ideas are the same. Agreement represents the extent to which the evaluations are the same.

Several studies of science communication have measured levels of congruence, accuracy, understanding, or agreement between the actors in Figure 1, such as the accuracy with which science writers can predict the interest of audiences in different science topics or the understanding and agreement between scientists and science writers on the news value of scientific topics. Many of these studies have been designed to test out common assumptions of working professionals.

Most of these interactional studies have not provided a theoretical explanation for the presence or absence of one or more of the coorientational variables. For example, they have not explained why scientists and science writers do and do not understand each other. One possible theoretical explanation can be constructed from Rogers and Shoemaker's (1971) concepts of homophily (similarity) and heterophily (dissimilarity). Rogers and Shoemaker maintain that two people who are more alike in attitudes, values, or demographic characteristics will communicate more effectively. To me, however, Rogers and Shoemakers's concepts are too broad to provide meaningful explanations. In what ways should people be similar? What similarities are most likely to lead to effective communication?

Thayer (1968) theorized that two people will communicate more often and more effectively when *symbiosis* is possible—when both gain something from the exchange. I have added to that concept by arguing that people will be most likely to communicate and to communicate effectively when they have symbiotic *problems* and *constraints* (Grunig, 1976b). Under those conditions, a person can seek or give information that will help the other to solve important problems and to operate within constraints. Involvement in the same situations would stimulate communication, but it is not a necessary condition for communication. As long as two people are involved in symbiotic situations, communication can occur. Having similar referent criteria may make communication easier, but it is not a necessary condition for coorientation. Obviously, a person who does not recognize any science problems (as do editors) or who face constraints (such as fear of mathematics) will not communicate often with those who recognize science problems and who are not similarly constrained.

With this theoretical explanation in mind, we can now turn to specific interactional studies of science communication.

A. Interactions with Audiences

Several studies have measured the perceptions that several actors in the science communication chain have of audiences. The first of these, Tannenbaum (1963), was done before McLeod and Chaffee (1973) introduced their coorientation model, although it can easily be interpreted in terms of that model. Tannenbaum described one study that attempted to explain mass media coverage of mental health. A questionnaire which measured the knowledge of and attitudes toward mental health of psychiatrists and members of the public showed a great deal of understanding and agreement between members of these two groups. A content analysis of television and magazine coverage of mental health issues, however, showed a preoccupation with what Tannenbaum described as the "bizarre" aspects of mental health, a conception of mental health which neither the experts nor the public held. Interviews with key media personnel showed that they wrote about mental health in this way because they thought the bizarre slant would be similar to the attitudes and knowledge of the public. Journalists, in other words, sensationalized science because they thought, inaccurately, that that was what the audience wanted.

Tannenbaum also described another study which compared the semantic compatibility of scientists, science writers, editors, and science readers. He found all the groups to be compatible, except the editors. The editors generally preferred "exciting" science news, the others did not. This study thus would explain why the editors are the weak link in the science communication chain. They are not involved in science or do not recognize science problems. Thus they process consummatory science news which gets their attention while the others seek utilitarian science news or, at least, do not have to have their science news sensationalized before they will process it.

Lassahn (1967) did a similar study of actors in the agricultural science communication system. She compared the ability of university extension specialists, information service editors, county extension directors, and county newspaper editors to predict how farmers would rate science news items that might appear in the newspaper. The county newspaper editors and the information service editors were best at predicting farmer preferences, thus showing their value as mediators in the science communication chain. These two mediator groups would be more likely to have symbiotic relationships with both farmers and scientists than the farmers and scientists would have with one another. That is, the professional communicators can recognize the problems and constraints of both scientists and farmers.

Knodell (1976) conducted a coorientational study of food writers in a public relations agency, newspaper food editors, and food readers. Part of that study determined the ability of the public relations writers to predict the information preference of food readers. Q factor analysis revealed two kinds of food readers, which she called the "nutritionists" and the "chefs." Five of the nine public relations writers studied successfully predicted the nutritionist readers and three predicted the chef readers. None predicted both types, however, showing essentially that writers do not always know their readers, presumably because the food problems recognized by the writers are not the same problems recognized by all members of the audience.

B. Public Relations-Media Interactions

In the same study, Knodell (1976) asked food editors in newspapers to rate the news value of the food stories that had been rated by audiences and then asked the nine public relations food writers to predict the preferences of the newspaper food editors. Q factor analysis revealed three types of newspaper food editors: "traditionalists, transitionalists," and the "new guard." Traditionalists were interested only in recipes and menus. Transitionalists were interested in nutrition, canning, and economic items. The new guard, found in big city newspapers, were interested in nutrition, economy items, food laws and consumer education, wine, food additives, etc. The public relations writers predicted the traditional and transitional type, and their own story preferences were similar to those of the transitional type. They did not predict the new guard type. This study also can be interpreted as showing that science writers must determine what problems editors and audiences will recognize if they are to successfully meet the information needs of these clientele groups.

C. Scientist-Science Writer Interactions

Van Duzee (1977) used the coorientational model to test the common belief that there is misunderstanding and disagreement between scientists and science writers about media coverage of science. She asked a sample of biologists and a sample of science writer to rate the news and scientific value of articles on biological science.

Q factor analysis yielded two types of science writers and three types of scientists. Van Duzee also asked the scientists and science writers to predict how the other groups would rate the same articles and developed Q typologies from those predictions. Correlations of the self and predicted types revealed high levels of accuracy, congruence, and agreement among all of the science writer and scientist types. Her questionnaire did not ask, however, whether stories *should* have news value. Scientists could have believed that stories which have news value by journalistic standards should not have news value by their standards.

Ryan (1979) did a similar coorientational study based on a national sample of 122 science writers and 110 scientists whose research had been reported in ten daily newspapers. He asked these respondents to indicate their extent of agreement or disagreement with thirty-eight statements about the nature of science news coverage, science reporting practices, and science writers. As in the other studies discussed here, agreement was high. For thirty-two of the thirty-eight items, scientists and science writers were either on the same side of the agree/disagree scale or the differences were not significantly different. Congruence, however, was lower. Both scientists and science writers perceived a greater difference than actually existed.

The areas of disagreement, however, revealed an apparent desire of scientists to restrict science coverage to "knowledge of" science. Science writers strongly disagreed and scientists strongly agreed that scientists should read articles before publication, that headlines should be written by reporters, that the science writer should rely completely on the scientist to point out what is important in his or her research, that scientists should release results to the press only after scholarly publication, that a science writer should not interpret a scientist's research, and that science writers sensationalize news. In addition, both groups accurately perceived this disagreement.

Both Ryan's and Van Duzee's results suggest that science writers identify with the science system but not as completely as other research suggests. But Ryan's study does suggest that scientists believe science writers should identify with the science system. Ideally, science writers should straddle the fence between the problems of the public and the science system and Ryan's results suggest that they do. Nevertheless, the desire of scientists to restrict the reporters' coverage "about" science indicates that pressure from scientists may be one reason why science writers often come to identify with the science system.

D. Public Relations-Scientist-Management Interactions

Hill (1979) asked a sample of agricultural experiment station science writers, scientists, and directors to rate the importance of several activities and goals for the station's communication program. The results picture directors as isolated from both scientists and communications personnel in their understanding of the role of public communication in an organization.

Hill also used Q factor analysis to develop types of scientists, communication specialists, and directors as well as types based on the predictions of each group. Each communication specialist type had a high agreement score with at least one scientist type, although each also had one high disagreement score with another scientist type. The same pattern of agreement was found between communications personnel and director types. Agreement was also mixed between scientists and directors, although those two groups were generally more in agreement than the communication personnel and the scientists and directors.

Although the agreement scores showed relative agreement throughout the system, the congruency and accuracy scores showed that both scientists and communications personnel perceived incongruency with the directors and that neither could accurately predict how the directors would rate the importance of these public relations activities. On the other hand, congruency and accuracy between communications personnel and scientists was reasonably high. Directors of experiment stations, in other words, do not seem to have articulated a communication policy that is understood by scientists and science writers in the organization, although their perception of what that policy should be is reasonably close to that of the other groups. That policy was not generally one of two-way public communication, however. These results corroborate the studies cited above on management behaviors. Too often managers of scientific organizations do not understand public relations; therefore, they make it difficult for the professional communicators in that organization to effectively communicate with the public.

E. Scientist-Linker-Audience Interactions

Studies of coorientation between scientists and the public cited above confirmed the ability of science writers to perform a mediating function. Similar studies have been done on the mediating ability of interpersonal linkers. Groot (1970) found that extension workers in the Philippines fell between farmers and scientists in agreement, congruence, and accuracy—thus confirming that they do indeed serve as effective intermediaries.

Bowes and Stamm (1975), however, found that local community leaders were ineffective mediators between the public and agencies promoting resource development in North Dakota. Agency personnel could predict public cognitions of the development projects better than the community leaders—indicating that community leaders are not a good source of information about public opinion.

These two studies provide no indication of why some linkers are effective and others are not. We can only hypothesize that linkers serve as effective mediators only when they are able to recognize the problems, constraints, and involvements of both scientists and the public and are able to find a symbiotic relationship in those two sets of perceived situations. Presumably, training in how to accurately perceive the situations of their clients is the secret to successful linkage.

F. Public Relations-Audience Interaction

A common practice in public relations is to tell the public only good things about an organization and to be quiet about the bad things. Few public relations practitioners openly lie about environmental damage caused by their organization, for example, but many withhold negative information and overpromote the positive aspects of new projects or facilities.

In a study of an Army Corps of Engineers project in North Dakota, Stamm and Bowes (1972), found that people in a sample public who perceived advantages of the project also perceived that the Corps would perceive those advantages. The same was not true, however, for people who perceived disadvantages of the project. They generally could not say whether the Corps also perceived the disadvantages. One-way public relations, in short, left the public with the impression that the organization is too naive to perceive the negative consequences of its own policies. One-way public relations, as practiced by many scientific agencies, can be dysfunctional to the interests of those agencies.

IV.   SOME CONCLUSIONS

In this paper, I have presented a model of the science communication process and have fit the results of science communication research into that model. For each of the communication behaviors and effects of communication behaviors in the model I have used a situational theory to explain individual behaviors and the effects of communication interaction. The result, I believe, is a coherent picture of how the science communication process works.

This literature review shows that we do know a great deal about science communication. Many of the theoretical explanations presented, however, are speculative and have not been substantiated by research. Science progresses when researchers take what is originally a vague, general idea (a theory), test that idea, and then reconstruct the theory to improve the originally vague idea (Suppe 1977). I believe I have presented some reasonable theoretical ideas in this paper. What we still need to know, however, is whether these ideas can be improved further. In addition, there are some specific areas of the science communication chain where the most research is needed.

A. Recommendations for Research

1. I believe I have developed a useful way of conceptualizing and analyzing science publics and their information needs. There are may scientific problems, however, for which we have not yet developed typologies of publics and their information needs. We have not, for example, developed a typology of publics for energy issues, which should be a top priority because of the severity of the energy problem. We need to know what kinds of publics develop on issues such as nuclear power, solar energy, synthetic fuels, conservation of gasoline, etc. We also need studies of the communication behaviors of governmental officials who make decisions on scientific matters. We have little idea of what their information needs are.

2. We are far short of having an adequate explanation of how to communicate and gain understanding of unfamiliar, scientific ideas. The situational theory can identify the obstacles: we know that it is almost impossible for people who randomly process information to gain an understanding of a difficult idea. We know that simplification alone does not solve the problem. We know that traditional writing techniques generally work, but not why they work. I believe it is time to delve into cognitive psychology and the philosophy of language in the search for a solution to this problem. Those bodies of knowledge should extend the power of the situational theory from solving the problem of who communicates to the problem of how to communicate effectively.

3. I have presented some hypothetical explanations of the gatekeeping communication behavior of public relations people, science reporters, and editors. But communication researchers have paid far less attention to the behavior of professional communicators than to the behavior of audiences. I believe we need to further analyze the behavior of the communicators, using the same techniques and theory used to analyze the behavior of audiences. This would further develop the deep theory used here to integrate the science communication subdomains.

4. We have a few studies of the communication behavior of scientists. But we need more. The sociology and philosophy of science offers some rich resources for understanding the communication of scientists with one another. We should make use of it in designing future research. In addition, I think we should test out the theoretical explanations I have provided for the communication of scientists with the public. Existing descriptive studies seem to support the theory; we need to test the theory more, however.

5. Research has shown that administrators plan a key role in successful public communication by scientific agencies. We need more normative

research, however, on ways to provide administrators with a better understanding of public relations. Some questions this research might address include: Can properly trained public relations people communicate the role of public relations to their administrators so that administrators recognize and become involved with the problem of public communication? Or, will it be necessary to train administrators in formal public relations courses?

6. The coorientational studies have provided useful tests of many of the common assumptions of science communication, and the research has proven many of them to be wrong. I have suggested a theoretical explanation for the communication effects isolated by these coorientational analyses. Again, however, that explanation needs to be tested.

7. Research has made it clear that science writers often, but not always, identify more with the science system than with the public. Editors identify with the public but do not recognize the true information needs of the public. We need more research, therefore, on how professional communicators can become true mediators, able to interact with both scientists and the public. Again, I have provided some theoretical explanations that need to be researched further.

B. Do We Have a Deep Theory?

This paper has, I believe, successfully pulled together several disparate areas of science communication research into a single domain. Domains, it will be recalled, consist of both observations and theories. And, it will also be recalled, social science research seldom progresses beyond the identification of the parameters of the "physical system" to deep theories and laws that explain the behaviors of the physical system.

The domain of science communication does contain more observations and variables than it does theoretical statements. Most of the studies discussed in this paper did not go beyond the "language of physical description." But there are several theories in the domain: diffusion theory, attitude theory, system control theory, organizational structure theory, community structure theory, the concepts of homophily and heterophily, language and readability concepts, the concept of symbiosis, coorientation concepts, and, of course, the situational theory.

The question of whether the situational theory is a deep theory can be answered only by asking: (1) whether the theory can solve most of the problems in the science communication domain, (2) whether it can integrate the other theories in the domain, and (3) whether it can solve the anomalies the other theories cannot solve. We can take these questions one at a time.

The problems of the domain consist almost entirely of explaining when and how different actors in science communication communicate individually and in interaction with the other actors. These actors include audiences, science writers, editors, scientists, linkers, and management. Although research evidence was not always available to confirm the situational theory's explanation of those communication behaviors, the theory's explanation of the behaviors does seem logical. Suppe (1976) has claimed that historical evidence about science indicates that the best theories have always been "underdetermined by data." That is, the suggestive power of the theory usually goes well beyond the observations that scientists have had time to collect. Thus, I would conclude that the theory is indeed a deep one for this domain.

The major problem of the domain that the theory cannot solve is how to write, or otherwise communicate, to gain maximum understanding of difficult scientific concepts. The situational theory can explain when understanding will not be possible, namely when a symbiotic coorientational situation does not exist. Symbiotic problems and constraints, in other words, are a necessary but not a sufficient condition for understanding. The theory does not, however, explain how actors with symbiotic situations can best structure their messages to understand each other. For that problem a language-oriented theory must be added to the domain.

The second evaluative question asked whether the theory can also explain what the other theories in the domain explain—whether it can integrate the theories. The theory cannot explain effective language, as already stated, but it does not seem capable of integrating coorientation theory, attitude and decision theory, as well as those parts of system control theory, organizational theory, community theory, and theories of audience behavior that relate to communication. The situational theory also goes beyond these theories to make it clear the conditions under which these theories apply and do not apply.

That conclusion leads to the final question: can the situational theory explain the anomalies of the other theories, a question that Laudan (1977, p. 66) argues is the most important test of a new theory. The most important anomalies in the science communication domain are those left by attitude and diffusion theories. By assuming that people are in control of their attitudes and behavior, the situational theory explains why communication, knowledge, attitudes, and behavior are not linked deterministically, as assumed by attitude theory. The situational theory shows when and how people will communicate, when they will have different kinds of knowledge, when they will have *an* attitude, and when they will do *something* (behave).

The theory resovles the attitude anomaly by showing that one communicator's message does not lead, deterministically, to one kind of knowledge, one attitude, and one behavior—the toppling domino effect. In the case of diffusion theory, the situational theory goes well beyond the mere description of diffusion theory to explain why people seek or become exposed to new ideas and practices, something diffusion theory cannot do. The greatest anomaly of coorientation theory has always been its inability to explain the conditions under which coorientation takes place and which lead to effective communication. The concepts of homophily and heterophily cannot solve that anomaly because they are too general. The situational theory's connection of symbiotic problems and constraints with the extent and success of communication, on the other hand, seems to solve the anomaly.

Although this paper suggests that the situational theory still needs more testing and confirmation, this brief analysis does suggest that the theory has the potential to be a deep theory., It works well in the science communication domain. It also seems to work well in the domains of the agenda setting effect of media, media uses and gratifications, organizational communication, communication in communities, and the knowledge gap (see Grunig, 1975, 1979b). These domains, however, are beyond the scope of this paper.

REFERENCES

Atkin, C. K. (1972). Anticipated communication and mass media information seeking. *Public Opinion Quarterly 35,* 188–199.

Bartholomew, C. M. (1973). "Cognitive Effects from Using Analogies to Communicate Physics to Audiences in Different Decision Situations." Master's thesis, University of Maryland.

Bassett, G., Davison, W. P., and Hopson, A. L. (1968). "Social Scientists, University News Bureaus, and the Public." (Paper prepared for the Russell Sage Foundation, New York. Cited in Dunwoody and Scott 1979.)

Bohm, D. (1977). Science as perception–communication. *In* "The Structure of Scientific Theories," 2nd ed. (F. Suppe, Ed.), pp. 374–391. University of Illinois Press, Urbana, Illinois.

Boltanski, L., and Maldidier, P. (1970). Carriere scientifique, moral scientifique et vulgarisation. *Social Science Information 9,* 99–118. (Cited in Dunwoody and Scott, 1979.)

Bowes, J. E., and Stamm, K. R. (1975). Evaluating communication with public agencies. *Public Relations Review 1* (Summer), 23–37.

Broberg, K. (1973). Scientist's stopping behavior as indicator of writer's skill. *Journalism Quarterly 50,* 763–767.

Brown, M. R. (1970). Communication and agricultural development: A field experiment. *Journalism Quarterly 47,* 725–734.

Carter, R. F., Ruggles, W. L., Jackson, K. M., and Heffner, M. B. (1973). Application of signaled stopping technique to communication research. *In* "New Models for Communication Research" (P. Clarke, Ed.), pp. 15–44. Sage Publications, Beverly Hills, California.

Cole, B. J. (1975). Trends in science and conflict coverage in four metropolitan newspapers. *Journalism Quarterly 52,* 465–471.

Crane, D. (1972). "Invisible Colleges: Diffusion of Knowledge in Scientific Communities," University of Chicago Press, Chicago, Illinois.

Dewey, J. (1938). "Logic: The Theory of Inquiry." Holt, Rinehart and Winston, New York.

Donohue, G. A., Tichenor, P. J., and Olien, C. (1973). Mass media functions, knowledge, and social control. *Journalism Quarterly 50,* 652–659.

Donohue, G. A., Tichenor, P. J., and Olien, C. (1975). Mass media and the knowledge gap: A hypothesis reconsidered. *Communication Research 2,* 3–25.

Dunwoody, S. (1979). "The News-Gathering Behaviors of Specialty Reporters: A Comparison of Two Levels of Analysis in Mass Media Decision-Making." (Paper presented to the Association for Education in Journalism, Houston, Texas.)

Dunwoody, S., and Scott, B. T. (1979). "Scientists and the Press: Are They Really Strangers?" (Paper presented to the Association for Education in Journalism, Houston, Texas.)

Farace, R. V., Monge, P. R., and Russell, H. M. (1977). "Communicating and Organizing." Addison-Wesley, Reading, Massachusetts.

Felstehausen, H. (1965). "Economic Knowledge and Comprehension in a Netherlands Farming Community." Afdelingen Voor Sociale Wetenschappen Aan De Landoouwhogeschool. (Bulletin 26.)

Fewster, W. J. (1966). "Readability and Style Variables in Nutrition Books Written for the Public by Food Faddists and Recognized Nutrition Authorities." Master's Thesis, University of Wisconsin.

Flippen, C. C. (1969). "Verbs of the Stock Market: A Study in Connotative Meanings." Unpublished dissertation, University of North Carolina.

Funkhouser, G. R. (1967). "Readability in Science Writing." (Paper presented to the Association for Education in Journalism, Boulder, Colorado.)

Funkhouser, G. R. (1969). Levels of science writing in public information sources. *Journalism Quarterly 46*, 721–726.

Funkhouser, G. R., and Maccoby, N. (1970). "Communicating Science to Nonscientists: Phase I." Institute for Communication Research, Stanford University, Stanford, California.

Funkhouser, G. R., and Maccoby, N. (1971a). "Communicating Science Information to a Lay Audience: Phase II." Institute for Communication Research, Stanford University, Stanford, California.

Funkhouser, G. R., and Maccoby, N. (1971b). Communicating specialized science information to a lay audience." *Journal of Communication 21*, 58–71.

Funkhouser, G. R., and Maccoby, N., (1973). Tailoring science writing to the general public. *Journalism Quarterly 50*, 220–226.

Funkhouser, G. R., and Maccoby, N. (1974). An experimental study on communicating specialized science information to a lay audience. *Communication Research 1*, 110–128.

Garvey, W. D., and Griffith, B. C. (1967). Scientific communication as a social system. *Science 157*, 1011–1016.

Garvey, W. D., Lin, N., and Nelson, C. E. (1970). Communication in the physical and social sciences. *Science 170*, 1166–1173.

Garvey, W. D., Lin, N., Nelson, C. E., and Tomita, K. (1970b). "The Role of the National Meeting in Scientific and Technical Communication." Johns Hopkins University Center for Research in Scientific Communication, Baltimore, Maryland.

Goodell, R. (1977). "The Visible Scientists." Little, Brown, Boston, Massachusetts.

Groot, H. C. (1970). "Coorientation in Agricultural Development: The Interrelationship Between Farmers, Change Agents and Scientists." (Paper presented to the Association for Education in Journalism, Washington, D.C.)

Grunig, J. E. (1965). "A Test of the Relationship Between the Use of Passive Voice Verbs and Flesch Readability Scores." (Unpublished seminar paper, University of Wisconsin, Madison, Wisconsin.)

Grunig, J. E. (1966). "The Role of Information in Economic Decision Making." Association for Education in Journalism, Austin Texas. (Journalism Monographs No. 3.)

Grunig, J. E. (1969). Information and decision making in economic development. *Journalism Quarterly 46*, 565–575.

Grunig, J. E. (1971). Communication and the economic decisionmaking processes of Colombian peasants. *Economic Development and Cultural Change 19*, 580–597.

Grunig, J. E. (1974). Three stopping experiments on the communication of science. *Journalism Quarterly 51*, 387–399.

Grunig, J. E. (1975). A multisystems theory of organizational communication. *Communication Research 2*, 99–136.

Grunig, J. E. (1976a). "Organizations and Public Relations: Testing a Communication Theory." Association for Education in Journalism, Lexington, Kentucky, (Journalism Monographs No. 46.)

Grunig, J. E. (1976b). Communication behaviors occurring in decision and nondecision situations. *Journalism Quarterly 53*, 252–263.

Grunig, J. E. (1977a). Review of research on environmental public relations. *Public Relations Review 3* (Fall), 36–58.

Grunig, J. E. (1977b). Evaluating employee communication in a research operation. *Public Relations Review 3*, (Winter), 61–82.

Grunig, J. E. (1978). A general systems theory of communications, poverty, and underdevelopment. *In* "International and Intercultural Communication" (Fred Casmir, Ed.), pp. 72–194. University Press of America, Washington, D.C.

Grunig, J. E. (1979a). Time budgets, level of involvement, and use of the mass media. *Journalism Quarterly 56*, 248–261.

Grunig, J. E. (1979b). "A Simultaneous Equation Model for Intervention in Communication Behavior." (Paper presented to the Association for Education in Journalism, Houston, Texas.)

Grunig, J. E. (1979c). "An Assessment of Economic Education Programs for Journalism Students." (Paper presented to the Association for Education in Journalism, Houston, Texas.)

Grunig, J. E. (forthcoming). "Communication Behaviors and Attitudes of Environmental Publics: Two Studies." *Journalism Monographs.*

Grunig, J. E., and Disbrow, J. B. (1977). Developing a probabilistic model for communications decision making. *Communication Research 4*, 145–168.

Grunig, J. E. and Stamm, K. R. (1979). Cognitive strategies and the resolution of environmental issues: A second study. *Journalism Quarterly 56*, 715–726.

Hage, J., and Aiken, M. (1970). "Social Change in Complex Organizations." Random House, New York.

Heffner, M. B. (1973). "Communicatory Accuracy: Four Experiments." Association for Education in Journalism, Lexington, Kentucky. (Journalism Monographs No. 30.)

Hill, D. G. (1979). "A Coorientational Study of Communication Behavior Within Agricultural Experiment Stations." Master's thesis, University of Maryland.

Horton, D. L., and Turnage, T. W. (1976). "Human Learning." Prentice-Hall, Englewood Cliffs, New Jersey.

Jain, N. C. (1970). "Patterns and Effectiveness of Professionals Performing Linking Roles in Research Dissemination. Unpublished dissertation, Michigan State University.

Jenkins, L. (1976). "Uses of Science Information in the Mass Media by University Students." (Unpublished seminar paper, University of Maryland, College Park, Maryland.)

Johnson, K. G. (1963). Dimensions of judgment of science news stories. *Journalism Quarterly 40*, 315–322.

Kearl, B., and Powers, R. D. (1961). Estimating understanding of scientific terms. *Journalism Quarterly 38*, 221–223.

Knodell, J. E. (1976). "A Coorientational Study of Food Public Relations Practitioners, Editors, and Readers." Master's thesis, University of Maryland. (Also published as Matching perceptions of food editors, writers and readers. *Public Relations Review 2* (Fall), 37–56, 1976).

Krieghbaum, H. (1967). "Science and the Mass Media." New York University Press, New York.

Kuhn, T. S. (1970). "The Structure of Scientific Revolutions," 2nd ed. University of Chicago Press, Chicago, Illinois.

Lakatos, I. (1970). Falsification and the methodology of scientific research programs. *In* "Criticism and the Growth of Knowledge" (I. Lakatos and A. Musgrave, Eds.), pp. 91–196. Cambridge University Press, Cambridge, England.

Lassahn, P. H. (1967). Comparison of judgments about agricultural science news. *Journalism Quarterly 44,* 702–707.

Laudan, L. (1977). "Progress and Its Problems." University of California Press, Berkeley, California.

Levy, M. R., and Kilburn, H. Jr. (1979). "A Multidimensional Message Strategy for Energy Conservation." Center for Governmental Research and Services, State University of New York at Albany, Albany New York.

McCrosky, J. C., and Combs, W. H. (1969). The effects of the use of analogy on attitude change and source credibility. *Journal of Communication 19,* 333–339.

Machlup, F. (1978). "Methodology of Economics and Other Social Sciences." Academic Press, New York.

McLeod, J. M., and Chaffee, S. H. (1973). Interpersonal approaches to communication research. *American Behavioral Scientist 16,* 469–500.

Maurer, L. L. (1963). "The Effects of Verb Voice on Connotative Meaning and Retention of Material Presented in Four Newspaper Articles." Master's thesis, University of Wisconsin.

Michigan, University. Institute for Social Research. (1958). "Public Impact of Science in the Mass Media." University of Michigan, Ann Arbor, Michigan.

Miller, F. (1978). "A Nationwide Study Explaining the Public Relations Behavior of Public School Physical Education Administrators." Unpublished dissertation, University of Maryland.

Missouri, University. "Science Symposium Series for Editors—Report 1973." School of Journalism-National Science Foundation Project GM-34938, Columbia, Missouri.

Murphy, D. (1960). "What Farmers Read and Like." Iowa State University Press, Ames, Iowa.

Nelson, C. E., and Pollock, D. K. (1970). "Communication Among Scientists and Engineers." Health Lexington Books, Lexington, Massachusetts.

Nunn, C. Z. (1970). Readership and coverage of science and technology in newspapers. *Journalism Quarterly 52,* 465–471.

Oskamp, S. (1977). "Attitudes and Opinions." Prentice–Hall, Englewood Cliffs, New Jersey.

Paivio, A. (1971). "Imagery and Verbal Processes." Holt, Rinehart and Winston, New York.

Parker, J. P. (1962). Some organizational variables and their effect upon comprehension. *Journal of Communication 12,* 27–32.

Patterson, J., Booth, L., and Smith, R. (1969). Who reads about science? *Journalism Quarterly 46,* 599–602.

Pelham, K. L. (1977). Internal communication at the Naval Surface Weapons Center: An Analysis Using Grunig's Multisystems Theory. Master's thesis, University of Maryland.

Popper, K. R. (1970). Normal science and its dangers. *In* "Criticism and the Growth of Knowledge" (I. Lakatos and A. Musgrave, Eds.), pp. 51–58. Cambridge University Press, Cambridge, England.

Powers, R. D. (1966). Communicating with graphs. *Journal of Cooperative Extension 4,* 35–43.

Pulford, D. L. (1976). Follow-up of study of science news accuracy. *Journalism Quarterly 53,* 119–121.

Rapoport, A. (1959). Uses and limitations of mathematical models in social science. *In* "Symposium on Sociological Theory" L. Gross, Ed., pp. 348–372. Harper & Row, New York.

Robinson, E. J. (1963). Analyzing the impact of science reporting. *Journalism Quarterly 40,* 306–314.

Rogers, E. M. (1969). "Modernization Among Peasants: The Impact of Communication." Holt, Rinehart, and Winston, New York.

Rogers, E. M. (1976). Communication and development: The passing of the dominant paradigm. *Communication Research 23*, 213–240.

Rogers, E. M., and Shoemaker, F. F. (1971). "Communication of Innovations: A Cross-Cultural Approach." Free Press, New York.

Ryan, M. (1979). Attitudes of scientists and journalists toward media coverage of science news. *Journalism Quarterly 56*, 18–26, 53.

Schneider, L. (1978). "Employee Communication in a University-Based Research and Development Center: An Analysis Using Grunig's Theory." Master's thesis, University of Maryland.

Schramm, W., and Wade, S. (1967). "Knowledge and the Public Mind." Stanford University Press, Stanford, California.

Shapere, D. (1977). Scientific theories and their domains. *In* "The Structure of Scientific Theories," 2nd ed. (F. Suppe, Ed.), pp. 518–565. University of Illinois Press, Urbana, Illinois.

Shaw, D. L. and McCombs, M. E. (1977). "The Emergence of American Political Issues: The Agenda Setting Function of the Press." West Publishing, St. Paul, Minnesota.

Shaw, D. L. and Van Nevel, P. (1967). The informative value of medical science news. *Journalism Quarterly 44*, 548.

Sorenson, D. (1957). "Factors Influencing Knowledge of Technical Soils Concepts by Wisconsin Farmers." Department of Agricultural Journalism, University of Wisconsin, Madison, Wisconsin. (Bulletin 27.)

Stamm, K. R., and Bowes, J. E. (1972). Environmental attitudes and reaction. *Journal of Environmental Education 3* (Spring) 56–60.

Stamm, K. R., and Grunig, J. E. (1977). Communication situations and the resolution of environmental issues. *Journalism Quarterly 54*, 713–720.

Suppe, F. (1972). What's wrong with the received view on the structure of scientific theories? *Philosophy of Science 39*, 1–19.

Suppe, F. (1973). Theories, their formulations, and the operational imperative. *Synthese 25*, 129–164.

Suppe, F. (1974). Theories and phenomena. *In* "'Developments in the Methodology of Social Science" (W. Leinfellner and E. Kohler, Eds.), pp. 45–91. Reidel, Dordrecht, Holland.

Suppe, F. (1976). "Beyond Skinner and Kuhn." (Paper presented to the Committee on History and Philosophy of Science Colloquim, University of Maryland, College Park, Maryland.)

Suppe, F. (1977). "The Structure of Scientific Theories," 2nd ed. University of Illinois Press, Urbana, Illinois.

Swinehart, J. W., and McLeod, J. M. (1960). News about science channels, audiences, and effects. *Public Opinion Quarterly 24*, 583–589.

Tankard, J. W., and Ryan, M. (1960). News source perceptions of accuracy of science coverage. *Journalism Quarterly 51*, 219–225, 334.

Tannenbaum, P. (1963). Communication of science information. *Science 140*, 579–583.

Thayer, L. (1968). "Communication and Communication Systems." Richard D. Irwin, Homewood, Illinois.

Tichenor, P. J. (1965). "Communication and Knowledge of Science in the Adult Population in the U.S." Unpublished dissertation, Stanford University.

Tichenor, P. J., Olien, C. N., Harrison, A., and Donohue, G. A. (1970a). Mass Communications systems and communication accuracy in science news reporting. *Journalism Quarterly 47*, 673–683.

Tichenor, P. J., Donohue, G. A., and Olien, C. N. (1970b). Mass media flow and differential growth in knowledge. *Public Opinion Quarterly 34*, 159–170.

Tichenor, P. J., Olien, C. N., and Donohue, G. A. (1972). Gatekeeping: Mass media systems and information control. *In* "Current Perspectives in Mass Communication Research" (F. G. Kline and P. J. Tichenor, Eds.), pp. 45–79. Sage Publications, Beverly Hills, California.

Tichenor, P. J., Olien, C. N., and Donohue, G. A. (1976). Community control and the care of scientific information. *Communication Research 2*, 403–423.

Toulmin, S. (1972). "Human Understanding" Vol. 1. Princeton University Press, Princeton, New Jersey.

Van Duzee, D. (1977). "A Coorientational Study of Scientists and Science Writers." Master's thesis, University of Maryland.

Wales, L. J., and Ashman, M. G. (1978). What is preferred technical writing style today? *ACE Quarterly 61* (October–November), 13–22.

Wilkening, E. (1956). Roles of communicating agents in technological change in agriculture. *Social Forces 34*, 361–367.

Witt, W. (1976). Effects of quantification in science writing. *Journal of Communication 26* (No. 1). 67–80.

6 Computer Conferencing

Ronald E. Rice
Institute for Communication Research
Stanford University

I. INTRODUCTION: TERMS AND CAPABILITIES

A. Electronic Mail and Computer Conferencing

Before discussing various computer conferencing (c.c.) systems and related research, some clarification of terms will be helpful. Miller (1978) suggests that electronic mail and computer conferencing are a heterogeneous "third force" beginning to take its place alongside established data processing and newer word processing technologies. Even now, however, such distinctions are rapidly blurring as these technologies converge or are integrated in organizational or networked contexts. For the moment, we can agree with Price (1975) in stating that the third force (and particularly c.c.) is distinguished by using the computer for establishing controllable links between and among individuals and groups and *not* for the transfer or processing of data.

The distinctions *within* the force of electronic messaging and c.c. are important, however. This is primarily because c.c. has such considerable potential applicability and new characteristics that it should not be constrained by users' or regulators' preconceptions derived from simpler messaging media (such as letters or telephones) which may well describe electronic messaging usage (Turoff and Hiltz, 1977a).

Both media involve some terminal device (currently, a hard-copy print terminal or a cathode-ray video terminal); some communication link (direct cables, acoustic coupler and telephone lines, microwave, satellite, etc.); and a/several computer(s) (a local computer providing within-system links, or a local "node" computer interconnected via networks with other "nodes" and one or more "host" computers which provide the switching, software, and storage). Major network service providers are ADP, ARPANET, Control Data, General Electric, Telenet, and Tymnet. The "computer" in computer-based conferencing provides fundamentally new (as well as more elaborate, controlled, or efficient) capabilities to communicators, using switching and routing of the communications, storing, processing, retrieving, and monitoring.

Electronic/computer mail/messaging allows one user to transmit a message, in the form of a discrete file containing (usually) text, to another user, who does not have to be simultaneously operating a terminal, or to a number of other users on a particular "distribution list," perhaps according to preestablished distribution times. It is thus quite similar to sending a letter. Indeed, early systems were referred to as "electronic mailboxes." When a user activates the proper account via the terminal, the messaging program will inform the user of any mail in the "in basket" and then will print out, usually sequentially, the messages when instructed to do so. As Miller (1978) emphasizes, there is usually very little processing or preorganizing of the messages by the program. Topic- or task-related organization is usually performed by the users.

Computer conferencing, both because of its historical roots (see below) and its explicit capabilities, has been quite different from electronic messaging. (1) Technically, c.c. involves *shared* files; an entry is not a separate file transmitted to another user, but an addition to a multiaccessible data base. (Some users may not be *allowed* to access some parts of the file, however.) Thus the emphasis is upon the sharing, and not on the transmission, of communications. (2) This file and its contents can then be processed in various ways by the conferencing software according to the tasks and rules of the relevant conference. Hiltz and Turoff (1978a) particularly point out the use of the computer to structure and facilitate communication. (3) As one of several *teleconferencing* media (see Short et al., 1976), c.c. emphasizes communications between and among specified groups separated by time and space, (4) engaged in collective dialogues, perhaps with a given agenda.

B. Capabilities of Computer Conferencing Systems

Carter (1980), Hiltz and Turoff (1978a), and Miller (1978) provide the sources for describing the capabilities of a general c.c. system. In addition to shared files, computer processing, telecommunications and facilitation of group communications, c.c. systems usually offer the following.

(1) Public and private entries. A user may transmit an entry to one, several or all of a group's members via a "private" entry, which is identifiable as such and which nonaddressed members cannot read. Or, a user may transmit an entry to the whole group or a subset which is holding a (electronic) conference, and which may access such "public" entries.

(2) Labelling of user. Particularly for Delphi or sensitive decision analysis (see below), the ability to use anonymous or pen name identifications is important. Or, one's own name may be attached to an entry.

(3) Individual and group control. An individual may retrieve or delete one's own entries. A group or conference may continually retrieve, but usually not delete or alter public entries. A conference or group leader usually has that ability.

(4) Word-processing and searching. The c.c. system may allow text (not just "messages") to be edited, formatted, recopied, associated, retrieved by various indices (date, author, content, etc.), and printed. This usually implies the existence of private and public workspaces where text may be individually or jointly produced and processed. Other users may also be searched for, by their related identifying information.

(5) Synchronous and asynchronous modes. Sending and receiving entries in "real time"—synchronous interaction—allows users to emulate a live

conference or meeting. Some system conferences will require all members to be on-line simultaneously, and the commands will automatically deliver entries to others, delayed only by computer, networking, and text sequencing activities. In some systems, a special command will allow one to transmit a synchronous entry to another on-line user. Usually, however, entries are asynchronous, where receipt and response are delayed until the other user enters the system, is informed which entries are yet unread, reads them, and chooses to respond. This mode is somewhat similar to typical electronic messaging.

Other capabilities may include graphics, interfacing with computer programs and other systems, adaptable levels of command complexity, scheduling of users' accessibility, automated evaluation from system and conference traffic, etc. Additional capabilities of specific systems are noted in Section III.

C. Costs

Because of the rapidly changing technologies, designs, applications, and usage scales associated with c.c., providing costs would be an exercise in being specific to a future audience based upon generalizations from already past experience. The main points to note are that most traditional means of mediated communication are becoming more expensive (because they use materials such as paper, and energy such as labor); c.c. is becoming less expensive (because it involves increasingly efficient communications technologies and electronic signals); and c.c. can provide some old and some new communications more efficiently and powerfully. Therefore, cost-justifications will increasingly favor the use of computer-mediated communications. (These are not the only relevant evaluations, however; see Section IV.) Summaries and descriptions of costs are provided by Hiltz & Turoff (1978a), Infomedia (1979), and Panko (1978).

System and/or software may be bought or leased, or access to a commercial system may be gained through computer networks with a combination service, connect and usage charge. C.c. systems may reside in and be accessed through large time-shared computers, but even the EIES conferencing system (see below) requires only two minicomputers (one for backup and research) and a dual disk system, for a total less than $200,000.00 (Turoff and Hiltz, 1977b). Leased satellite links and rooftop antennae will avoid the high costs of telephone links.

II. HISTORY

It has been suggested that the first computer conferencing system was contemplated during the Berlin crisis when the State Department attempted (unsuccessfully) to join its teletypes on a central line. Indeed, by 1965, over 57 organizations had private, computer-based writing systems involving Telex and TWX (Panko, 1977). However, two major sources for c.c. are familiar to the literature.

The first motivating source was the development of Delphi analysis, used for forecasting and assessing information, usually by a panel of experts, in iterative rounds. Delphi analysis attempts to structure group communication so the process is effective in allowing a whole group to deal with a complex problem, particularly when accurate information is unavailable or costly, or when information is heavily subjective. Techniques involved include feedback, assessment of group views, opportunities to revise views, some anonymity, and controlled asychronous entries. Linstone and Turoff (1975) provide the definitive text on Delphi analysis.

Delphi was a spinoff of defense research in the early fifties, in the sixties was used to assess the long-range trends of science and technology, and then seeped into aerospace corporations and academic institutions. The wedding of computer-mediated communications with Delphi analysis was a marriage made at least in the highlands of Greece, as communications can easily be structured and sequenced, individuals do not need to travel to several conferences or wait for mail, and group results may be compiled and presented. Scientists including Paul Baran Norman Dalkey and Olaf Helmer at Rand Corporation and the Advanced Research Project Agency (ARPA) were involved early in systems which supported structured group interaction for futures research (Informed (a) 1979).

The second major motivating source was the needs of the Office of Emergency Preparedness (OEP) and the Defense community for communications during crises (Price, 1975; Turoff, 1972; Turoff and Hiltz, 1977a, b). Researchers including Richard Wilcox, Robert Kupperman, Tom Balden and Wallace Sinaiko were involved in early systems for crisis management. Turoff (in Hiltz and Turoff, 1978a) describes his rather underground and politic-laden development of OEP's EMISARI (Emergency Management Information System and Reference Index) and its precursors (DELPHI conference PARTYLINE and discussion). The crises involving the need for rapid assessment of the steel industry in 1970 and the need for regional monitoring of the 1971 wage-price freeze led the way in establishing such a system. Now known as RIMS (Resource Interruption Monitoring Systems), EMISARI included Delphi-like communications in a complex system providing particular tasks (such as report-generation, data collection, scheduling status transitory conferences, numerical estimation, and graphic presentation) matched to definite responsibilities located at known nodes.

The rise of computer networking (Hiltz and Turoff, 1978a), packet switching as a transmission strategy (Roberts, 1978) and inexpensive computer components met these historical needs to motivate the proliferation of computer-mediated communications systems. By 1979, there were over seventeen major computer-mediated teleconferencing systems in use, up from seven in 1975. Price et al. (1980) claim the number of computer-based electronic mail or teleconferencing services has risen to fifty. The Yankee Group estimates that by 1983, over two-thirds of the Fortune 500 corporations will have implemented electronic messaging systems. Dunn (1978), in discussing obstacles to market growth (user learning costs, regulatory policies, and network structures) is less optimistic—or more realistic.

III. SYSTEMS AND APPLICATIONS

An article in EMMS (An electronic mail and messenger system primer, 1978) provides a good technical introduction to electronic messaging and conferencing systems, while Hiltz and Turoff (1978a), Lipinski and Miller (1974), and Lipinski et al. (1979) describe the appropriate file structures and algorithmic strategies. The Hiltz and Turoff book is the major text on all aspects of computer conferencing. See Carlisle (1975), Hough (1976), Johansen et al. (1977), Price (1975), and especially Leduc et al. (1979) for system descriptions and bibliographies.

This section will mention a number of current and developing systems and then will describe in greater detail three major systems. Applications of these systems will be noted where appropriate. Some major commercial computer mail systems are:

— Telenet: TELEMAIL
— Bolt, Beranek and Newman (Cambridge, MA): HERMES
— Hewlett–Packard (Palo Alto, CA): HP-2026 and COMSYS
— Scientific Time Sharing Corporation (Washington, DC): MAILBOX
— Tymshare, Inc. (Cupertino, CA): ON TYME
— Computer Corporation of America (Cambridge, MA): COMET
— CITIBANK (NY): Integrated Electronic Office
— Cook Industries: Cook Administrative Message System

Some computer conferencing systems not described below are:

— University of Illinois: DISCUSS (part of PLATO)
— University of Michigan: CONFER (see Carter, 1974)
— National Technical Information Service (Washington, D.C.): DEP Conferencing System
— National Physical Laboratory (United Kingdom): CONFER (part of scrapbook)

— Northwestern University: ORACLE (conferencing as a component of education, combined with information files, computing and CAI) (see Schuyler and Johansen, 1972)
— Memo from Turner System and MINT, derived from DELPHI conference; later, General Conference System, LTD. (Canada) (see Hough, 1976)
  (in Canada) (see Irving, 1978)
— BELL'S TOPES (includes graphics) (see Pford et al., 1978)
— Bell Northern Research (in Canada): CMI, derived from DELPHI conference

As noted above, more integrated systems are devleoping along the lines of "automated offices" (see Keen and Morton, 1979; Uhlig et al., 1979). New York's CITIBANK has been experimenting with two such systems since 1976 (White, 1977), and a variety of other large corporations are beginning to develop and market massive systems. These include the U.S. Postal Service, Western Union, the Satellite Business System consortium, XEROX, AT&T's Advanced Communication Service, and Bell Northern Research's Integrated Electronic Office. Three systems with particular emphasis on conferencing will now be described in more detail.

A. Forum-Planet-Hub-Notepad

PLANET was developed at the Institute for the Future (IFF) (founded by several early DELPHI inventors) out of various versions of FORUM, which had been available on the ARPANET since 1973 (Amara and Vallee, 1974; Lipinski and Miller, 1974.) Also used on Tymshare and Telenet networks, these are relatively simple conferencing and messaging systems designed for groups of small to moderate size, and used extensively for evaluations of and experiments with conferencing. FORUM offers discussion or question and answer activities. In discussion activities, public, private, and anonymous entries are possible. The second activity allows answers in the form of numbers, probabilities, and essays, and can summarize and process numeric input for statistical tables. Several "help" or user information capabilities are provided, including a "skill rating" routine to require shorter system commands as the user becomes more familiar with FORUM.

PLANET is being used at the IFF for continued experiments and evaluations, and in various versions is offered by the first commercial computer conferencing company, Infomedia (1977). After typing the commands on a terminal to enter PLANET, the user types in a name and password. Some preliminary information is followed by a list of activities (or conferences) in which the user is participating, and who the other participants are. Then entries, activity summaries, etc. may be received and sent. If requested, PLANET collects and processes a group's responses to a question, and allows the user to review some or all of those responses (by date, last N entries, etc.) and their statistics, note the status of participants, or shift to another activity.

One particularly powerful PLANET facility is the MONITOR, a set of routines which collects and analyses user communication traffic and system data to provide a variety of insights into the use and evolution of a particular conference. These analyses may be used to help better structure the group's activities, identify users having difficulties, make cost-effectiveness choices, judge training effectiveness, etc. Some results of these analyses appear in Section IV.

The IFF has recently developed and begun testing a sophisticated system involving PLANET as one tool in issue formulation, problem identification, and quantitative modelling by research communities (Lipinski et al., 1979): HUB. Four modules are connected under the HUB program, which acts as an interface and switcher between the modules. PLANET is one module. Program Workspaces are entered to run modelling programs, from which results and program transcripts can be entered into PLANET via HUB. Shared Visual Workspaces allow the development and sharing of flowcharts and graphical output to conceptualize a problem. Finally, Documentation Workspaces allow documentation and reports to be developed and shared. The use of HUB by several modelling groups is currently being evaluated at the IFF.

Infomedia's NOTEPAD is somewhat similar to HUB, except that it is designed for larger organizations and does not require the user to pass through a central switcher to access another module. NOTEPAD provides specialized support to sets of working groups.

B. NLS-Augment

The OnLine System (NLS) was conceived and developed by Douglas Englebart at Stanford Research Institute (SRI) in the mid-1960s as a comprehensive knowledge augmentation workshop (see Bair 1973, 1974, 1980; Englebart et al., 1976; Uhlig et al., 1979). The intention of NLS development was to provide an extension of intellect by means of computer-based tools; later, group and organizational capabilities were added. As such, it includes messaging and conferencing capabilities but also many others. Messages can be stored, indexed, cross-referenced, and cataloged. Multiple authors may create journals and reports (including photo-composition), with internal cross-references automatically updated. Text structures are hierarchically and laterally indexed and may be retreived and associated in a variety of ways. Management information, personal notation and reminders, computer processing, custom-built subsystems, and organizational scheduling are also provided via one high-level grammar. Some innovative aspects developed and planned include a hand-held cursor control (called a "mouse") which activates execute, delete, and point commands; a one-hand binary key set which allows keying of alphanumerics on a video terminal; handwriting and voice input; and integrated text and image filing. NLS is implemented and supported in over 20 companies and government agencies, and will be marketed by Tymshare as its AUGMENT service.

C. EIES

The Electronic Information Exchange System (EIES), developed by Murray Turoff at the New Jersey Institute for Technology, is a comprehensive, continually evolving electronic world (see Hiltz and Turoff, 1978a). A wide variety of experiments and evaluations involving EIES has been supported by NSF in an attempt to understand the uses, impacts, and required designs of c.c. "EIES to date has logged almost 60,000 hours of use with about 700 users. This includes the writing of over 100,000 messages, 40,000 conference comments, and 15,000 notepad pages. In terms of items delivered this is about 200,000 messages, 400,000 conference comments and 20,000 notebook pages" (Hiltz and Turoff, 1980, p. 5). The philosophical motivation behind the development of EIES is that communication systems should be continually redesigned to reflect users' experiences, suggestions, and evolving behavior.

The EIES user network consists of ten or more formal groups (each with up to 50 members), "guest" users invited to participate in some of the numerous public or private conferences, user consultants who provide and revise system facilities and on-line explanations, special task-specific research groups, shifting sets of controlled experiments or demonstrations, newsletters, and more.

Some of the EIES features, in addition to the facilities basic to most c.c. systems already described, include: (1) the EIES menu, a hierarchical summary of the facilities or system actions available at each command step. Table I, a sample EIES session, shows some of the choices revealed by the first-level menu. An experienced user may string the choice numbers together, or use a preestablished system command instead of travelling through the menu. (2) A membership directory, which includes user-entered descriptions, addresses, and group memberships. (3) A sophisticated microprocessor which can be activated as a group member to provide analyses and graphics, interact with other computers, or mediate with other conferencing systems. (4) Self-defined sequences of operations in the form of a single command. (5) Special programs for specific group purposes, such as voting on terms to be used in negotiations, or providing on-line questionnaires and automated data-gathering and analysis, and various games. (6) Structured communication interfaces (such as the LEGITECH network of inquiries and responses about licensing, hazardous waste, etc.; users receive all current and future responses to selected inquiry topics). (7) Applications of EIES with

TABLE I
Sample *EIES* Session*

RONALD E RICE (RICE, 352) ON AT 2/8/80 5:00 PM EST ON LINE 11
LAST ACTIVE: 1/31/80 5:51 PM
EIES NEWS HEADLINE 2/3/80 6:45 PM
New era of cc opens with digitalized communication on ham radio! Also new feature: "observer" status in conferences and notebooks. Name a new public conference and win free hour of connect time. +WEEKLY for details in CHIMO.
LIST THOSE NOW ON-LINE(Y/N)?n
WAITING:
3 CONFIRMATIONS
3 PRIVATE MESSAGES
1 GROUP MESSAGE
ACCEPT ABOVE COMMUNICATIONS (Y/N/#)?y
M 4227 GEORGE CARTER (GEORGE, 402) 2/5/80 10:46 PM L:9
Ron, We are now neighbors. New address is in ++5,1,402. My...
DO YOU WISH TO:

GET ITEMS	(1)
DISPLAY ITEMS	(2)
SEARCH/FIND	(3)
SEND/COMPOSE/SUBMIT	(4)
EDIT/DELETE	(5)
ORGANIZE ITEMS	(6)
VOTE/FORM	(7)
SET/OPTIONS	(8)

MESSAGE CHOICE?+4
ENTERING SCRATCHPAD:
1? Alvin...a little late ressonding to your symposia notice,
2?/ress/resp/
1: Alvin...a little late responding to your symposia notice,...
TO (#'s/NAMES)? 386
    ALVIN WOLFE (WOLFE, 386)
ASSOCIATED MESSAGE (#)?1520
KEYS (/WORD/PHRASE/)?Symposia
OKAY TO SEND (Y/N/-)?y
...
INITIAL CHOICE?+gc 35
GROUP CONFERENCE: GENERAL CONFERENCE GROUP 35
THERE ARE NOW 1 MEMBERS ACTIVE.
272 ITEMS CC 272 WRITTEN ON 1/28/80 5:11 PM
NO ITEMS WAITING.
INITIAL CHOICE?++5,1,402
NAME: GEORGE CARTER
NICKNAME: GEORGE
TELEPHONE: [number]
LAST ACTIVE: 2/8/80 1:29 AM
ADDRESS: [address listed, and George's self-description printed]
...
MESSAGE CHOICE?+get N1000P282L22T

TABLE I
Sample *EIES* Session

EIES FACT SHEET #9
RESEARCH ON TECHNOLOGY FOR THE HANDICAPPED
EIES offers unique opportunities in the research and development of devices for physically
disabled people. [...] A multidisciplinary group involved in the research and development of
devices for the disabled has been using EIES since 1977 to explore....

....
INITIAL CHOICE?+WEEKLY
[... reading the weekly CHIMO (EIES newsletter) ...]

....
INITIAL CHOICE?--
TIME USED: 0:27
TOTAL USED: 39:50
RONALD E RICE (RICE, 352) OFF AT 2/8/80 5:27 PM EST

---

*This sample session illustrates only some very simple uses, and some EIES responses,
commands, etc. have been edited for clarity.

custom-designed structures as an office and management augmentation
system. (8) Programming languages allowing custom EIES structures (which
could, for example, emulate PLANET), and, in the future, BASIC for
computer processing.

Applications of EIES are already numerous and the possibilities are vast
(see Hiltz and Turoff, 1978a). Some of these include: controlled laboratory
experiments (Hiltz, 1978a); increased communication and productivity in
invisible colleges (Freeman and Freeman, 1979); joint discussion for
publishing articles (Computers and super-literates, 1980); international
communication (Turoff and Hiltz, 1978); structured group negotiation,
decision-making and simulation (Turoff and Hiltz, 1977a); communication
and information-retrieval services for the handicapped; and interactive
education and planning.

IV.   EMPIRICAL RESEARCH ON
COMPUTER CONFERENCING

This section will consider several areas of research on the use and effects of
c.c. (satisfaction, frequency and pattern style, etc.) comparisons with
alternative media (capacity, effects on group processes, appropriate uses) and
substitutability (for other media and experiences). The quite extensive and
growing research on computer-mediated conferencing indicates the potential
significance and fertile analytical environment of this new medium. The single
most comprehensive and influential review of research about the effects of
noncomputer-based teleconferencing media is by Short et al. (1976). Only

research relevant to conferencing mediated by the computer will be considered here. The two most accessible primary works in this area: Hiltz and Turoff (1978a) wrote the first major text on all aspects of computer conferencing, whle Johansen (1977) has provided the best organized and succinct review of teleconferencing meda comparisons to date. Other, less accessible, but useful overviews are Carlisle (1975) and Day (1975). The early major set of studies by the Institute for Defense Analysis (Bailey et al., 1963) remains useful for suggested variables and results from the use of computer conferencing in simulated crisis. For research designs in conferencing research, see Johansen et al. (1975, 1977).

A. Usage: Acceptance

Not all "users" actually use a computer-based conferencing system much! Difficult access to a terminal, unreliable telephone lines, or other professional activities with higher priority can be very significant reasons for limited use (Hiltz, 1978c; Johansen et al., 1977). Poor system reliability may lead to perceptions of decreased reliability of other tools used within a conference, increased status of technically expert members, and decreased emphasis on problem-solving (Lipinski et al., 1979). Also, perceptions of slow, unresponsive systems are manifested in more tangible ways; maintenance on terminals used to access such systems can be 50% higher than average (Bair, 1979b). A common objection, the necessity of typing skills, does not seem to be a major factor (Chapanis, 1975; Johansen et al., 1977; Miller, 1980), at least after the beginning period. Apparently most of the user's time is spent in nontyping activities or combines slow typing with mental composition. Neither the cost of use nor typing difficulties seem to be very important factors in acceptance—other than access, the social and work relationships and contextual factors such as conflict resolution and authority in an organizational usage setting are the major factors (Shulman and Steinman, 1978).

B. Usage: Patterns

There seems to be stages in acquiring c.c. facility:

1) culture shock, learning the commands, loss of interpersonal cues, new social dynamics
2) ability to use basic commands
3) push toward sociability, introduction of new cues and group norms, learning
4) serious use, perhaps dependence/addiction (Hiltz, 1978c,d; Hiltz and Turoff, 1978a, b; Turoff, 1978).

At early levels of usage, the textual styles of the first users within a conference appear to be imitated by following users, even if the later users belong to other conferences (Miller, 1980). In the beginning, entries are generally longer (Johansen et al., 1977) and in the form of private messages. At the second learning level a preference for group conferencing develops; at very high usage levels users tend to return to messaging and to begin to use private workspaces (Hiltz and Turoff, 1980; Turoff, 1978). Irving (1978) reported initial rises to high activity followed by a decrease and then levelling off to the end of a 9-month pilot use. Experienced users evaluate asynchronous conferencing more favorably than do new users. And, communication links among users tend to become more dense with use (Hiltz and Turoff, 1978b). In general, with increased hours of usage, items per session increase (from four to six), session length increases (from 15 to 40 minutes), the items sent/received ratio decreases (from ten to four), the number of conference comments rises then falls (Hiltz and Turoff, 1980), and the number of words per session may increase (Infomedia, 1979).

These usage patterns are based largely on pilot or subsidized applications; commercial uses can have planned, and rather different, patterns (see Carter, 1980; Infomedia, 1979). In the organizational contexts, private messaging seems to stabilize around 30 to 50 percent, and sessions are shorter (around 6 to 8 minutes with message length around 60 characters. It may be that the different systems used in these varying contexts perform similar *functions* but require different user *processes*. When synchronous use increases, so does the use of private messaging in organizational contexts (Miller, 1980). Synchronous use may lead to greater information overload, funnelling through one participant, more structured roles, yet better integrated information.

Although there is a high correlation between the number of private and group messages one sends (Johansen et al., 1978), these modes appear to be distinct, being preferrred differentially as users gain experience. Average group or public messages are 150 percent longer, and have four times the received/sent ratio, than private messages. Even several conference types have distinct received/sent ratios (Hiltz and Turoff, 1978b; Johansen et al., 1978). In general, these types include:

1) notepad (small group with no agenda)
2) seminar (a moderate-sized group with a strict agenda and a strong leader)
3) assembly (some real-time interaction within and among a series of seminars)
4) encounter (synchronous interaction of small group with time and crisis pressure)
5) questionnaire (for polling opinions, etc.)

The content threads of conversation or conferencing increase in a c.c. environment (Hiltz and Turoff, 1978b); and more threads are generated by messages directed to individuals (as opposed to undirected comments). Directed messages seem to receive slightly more responses. The number of entries per user is lowest, in general, for middle-sized groups (Johansen et al., 1977).

Not surprisingly, but importantly, users' attitudes to such systems change with use: satisfaction increases, sense of tediousness decreases, and impersonality of work environment decreases with increasing usage (Conrath and Bair, 1974; Hiltz, 1978d; Irving, 1978; Johansen et al., 1978.) It may be that new users view computer-mediated conferences as simple substitutes for familiar messaging media (such as a letter or a meeting), but develop an understanding that c.c. has its own advantages, uses, and constraints (Hiltz, 1979). With increased usage, perceived usefulness of features that facilitate long-term group communication, active control, tailoring of the system, and composition also increases (Hiltz and Turoff, 1980). A review of organizational use of teleconferencing arrives at a similar conclusion—once a work unit has established its coordination pattern, it first carries similar patterns over to a newly-implemented system (Shulman and Steinman, 1978) rather than seeks new applications.

In addition, users seem to need a "real" task to motivate use and favorable perception. Perhaps related to the professional priorities mentioned earlier (and the approach which professionals and researchers have toward tools of their trade), this importance of a cohesive group task explains usage amount far more than do costs, system characteristics, typing speed, or prior computer experience (Hiltz, 1979).

An important policy implication of this section is that a computer-based message/conferencing system should allow (and be allowed, by regulatory policy, to provide) different modes of communication precisely because the above modes receive demonstrably different emphasis by users. Implementors should also allow longitudinal development of system design because user behavior evolves and simple message systems become insufficient for regular, experienced users (Hiltz and Turoff, 1980). Regular applications should see c.c. as a different, but complementary, medium.

C. Comparisons: Capacity and Participation

As far as potential capacity is concerned, mathematical formulations show that c.c. word exchange can be about twice the level of face-to-face interaction (for about twelve people) (Hiltz and Turoff, 1977b). Because of the multiplicative effect of using a messaging system with a number of users, the number of characters passing through a user's account may be several times greater than possible through continuous typing to separate individuals (Irving, 1978; Vallee, 1976). Yet in problem-solving experiments, typing requires (or allows) fewer words (or less messages/time) than does face-to-face (Chapanis, 1975; Hiltz and Turoff, 1978a; Johansen et al., 1977), although the systems used by Chapanis and Johansen et al. were very restricted and would produce conservative figures.

Computer conferencing reduces the inequality of participation usually present in other forms of group interaction (Hiltz, 1978b; Hiltz and Turoff, 1978a, b; Johansen, 1977). Synchronous messaging reduces the inequality even more than does asynchronous mode (Miller, 1980). Participation inequality may be a natural characteristic of group discussion, and is clearly related to the stable personality trait of latency (and even more to duration) of verbal response (Koomen and Sagel, 1977). Thus more reserved group members may finally gain access to discussions and decision-making, while any one individual may have a harder time gaining the group's attention. In fact, the emergence of group leaders is different, and simply less likely, in teleconferencing (Williams, 1978). This has implications for decision-oriented applications of teleconferencing, as inequality of participation may be functional for such tasks, which require coordination and direction of comment flow by a leader. If, as Schwartz (1978) suggests, "*social organization is itself a network of interlocking queues.... a way of organizing obligations*" where "strategically placed delays are the preconditions of organizational efficiency," the resultant dequeuing by amorphous participation using immediate input with asynchronous response has major implications for social order. Inevitably, some tasks will fail, and in other instances new forms of gatekeeping will arise. Consensus may be harder to reach as the group gropes for organization (see below). An important issue is that shared or increased information is not the same as increased understanding of that information; indeed, understanding may even be masked by torrents of input (Lipinski et al., 1979).

D. Comparisons: Written Text

The form of c.c. communication is (presently) written text, whether by CRT or printer. The retrievability, associability, and indexibility of this text in a c.c. environment has major implications for decision- and judgement-oriented groups. Kaplan and Miller (1977) showed that "*in cases where all group members are exposed to the same information, differential memory* [and perceptions] *may be a mechanism for producing variety in the information shared during group discussion, and thus for affecting discussion-induced judgment shifts.*" In particular, more, and a different variety of, facts are recalled from one's most recent information sessions. With training, group members could retrieve and utilize past discussions and information to minimize such biases. Thus, some research comparing written communications, teletype, etc. provides a precedent for more specific c.c. studies.

Counter to most people's expectations, written media (as well as audio forms) can introduce more attitude change than face-to-face (or videotape) (Johansen, 1977), perhaps by masking cueing behavior and allowing unobtrusive shifts in opinion. Written material such as by teletype can be more effective for the communication of factual information than face-to-face, perhaps because of its preciseness and the greater comprehension gained from rereading text without pressure to overcome response latency. On the other hand, simulations involving the Prisoner's Dilemma show that the likelihood of a cooperative, as opposed to competitive, solution increases as the medium is altered from written through the more nonverbal media to face-to-face (Short, et al., 1976).

Most people in organizations tend to prefer face-to-face interactions to interactions over telephone or written channels (Conrath, 1973), yet Dewhirst (1971) suggested that perceived information-sharing norms were intervening factors. Perceptions of fellow-workers as sharers of information associated highly with preferences for the face-to-face channel (and the opposite relation for written). Perhaps to make up for missing interpersonal interaction, those who preferred written channels inside the organization tended to prefer face-to-face channels outside. International contexts for teleconferencing lead to a market preference for hardcopy—because text is much easier to translate than is voice (An electronic mail and message system primer, 1978)!

E. Comparisons: Direct Communication, and Decision Tasks

Many opponents of computer-mediated communication emphasize its loss of nonverbal communication and social presence. Certainly the channels wich c.c. does not provide typically allow cues for sequencing interaction rules, nonverbal feelings, intentions, physical relationships, etc. Immediate feedback is usually missing, and public or rhetorical questions often go unanswered. However, synchronous cnferencing does allow immediate response, and personal cues often appear in new forms, whle direct questions are almost always answered—even when addressed to strangers (Johansen, 1977). The absence of visual and nonverbal cues may be an advantage to some users—those with visual or speech handicaps, those usually intimidated by turn-taking conventions or rapid cross-fire. However, there are cases where the loss of such cues, mixed with rapid responses in synchronous mode, led to iteratively escalated misunderstanding (Uhlig, 1977). For those who object to delayed response, there are others who appreciate the break from eye contact so they can compose a thoughtful response (Hiltz and Turoff, 1978a). The face-to-face channel, when compared to c.c. (Johansen, 1977), does allow or provide

1) increased bandwidth and information types
2) more variance in message length
3) more questions
4) interruptions
5) ability to digress and lose thread
6) quicker adjustment to changes in interaction

A considerable amount of research has considered group decision processes in c.c. Using small groups given simple or complex group decision tasks, researchers have attempted to compare the effects of different communication media (usually face-to-face and c.c). In general, c.c. groups take longer to reach agreement (Hiltz, 1978a, b; Johansen, 1977), perhaps because more time is spent in noncommunicative acts, fewer items are exchanged, group problems are injected into the task, or a leader is less likely to emerge as quickly, if at all. There may be less consensus in c.c. groups for complex problems, or human-relations-oriented problems (Hiltz, 1979). For reasons of group coordination, mentioned earlier, it seems that unstructured problems require a strong leader, which c.c. suppresses somewhat. Interestingly, females change their opinions more easily in face-to-face contexts than do males, although there is no difference in c.c. groups.

Proponents of Delphi analysis claim it can improve results by structuring communication patterns dynamically and iteratively to exploit differential levels of expertise, although some evaluations are not excessively convincing (Brockhoff, 1975). The application of HUB (Lipinski et al., 1979) to the problem of quantitative modelling showed users' preference for asynchronous comments and the free formation of subgroups whose activities would still be accessible by others: capabilities possible most easily with c.c.

The comprehensive review and analysis by Short et al. (1976), although not involving c.c., provides good evidence that the level of "social presence"—how "real" the other person seems—a particular medium allows, interacts with the mix of interpersonal and task content a communication event requires. As the authors (Short et al., 1976, pp. 109, 156) write, the outcome of meetings, such as "the likelihood of reaching agreement, the balance of success, the nature of the settlement reached, the evaluation of the other side and the individual opinions after the discussion..." can be "significantly affected by the medium of communications used.... Some tasks are more sensitive than others: in particular those meetings involving conflict between the participants (e.g., attitude change or negotiation) or involving the function of impressions of strangers or slight acquaintances..." or in coalition formation. This latter may occur via the process of interpersonal "liking", as liking (and overt disliking) may decrease in media which transmit fewer nonverbal cues. For example, one simulation (Vallee, 1976) revealed significantly more within-group interaction for the winning, than the losing, coalition; in another example, people at the same teleconferencing nodes supported each other in a persuasion and decision task more than they supported individuals at other nodes (Short et al., 1976).

F. Comparisons: Generalizations and Appropriate Applications

Using a typology of group activities developed by Short et al. (1976), several researchers have arrived at very similar conclusions about the appropriate (or at least (modifying "uses"; qualifying "appropriate) positively evaluated) uses for c.c. In general, c.c. is at least as good as, and sometimes better than, face-to-face (in some experiments, video) for the following tasks:

1) exchanging (especially technical) information (especially for short bursts)
2) asking questions
3) exchanging opinions or orders
4) staying in touch
5) generating ideas
   (Hiltz, 1978c, 1979; Hiltz and Turoff, 1978a; Infomedia, 1979; Johansen et al., 1978; Short et al., 1976; Williams, 1978)

There are interactions which do not demand high interpersonal involvement and may be typified as cooperative in nature. C.c. is not nearly as satisfactory as face-to-face or video for

1) bargaining
2) resolving disagreements
3) getting to know someone
4) tasks requiring constant focussed discussion

However, for very embarrassing or conflictful interactions, c.c may be the medium of choice precisely because it minimizes the interpersonal dimension. The earlier point about changing attitudes with increasing use holds here as well: new users generally rate face-to-face higher on all group processes or tasks, while experienced users develop the ability to discriminate the appropriate uses listed above. Also intriguing is that users feel more confident in their perceptions gained from face-to-face meetings than by nonverbally poorer media, but they are in fact no more accurate (and sometimes less so) when using face-to-face (Short et al., 1976). Thus c.c. may be less favorably evaluated than face-to-face, and may create less favorable perceptions of others, even though it allows equally (or more) accurate transmission of behaviors and information.

G. Transferability, Substitutability and New Uses

Can an electronic system substitute for a centrally-located institution or laboratory? A promising set of results (reviewed in Hiltz and Turoff, 1978a), based on energy researchers' use of conventional and c.c. interaction in alternating periods, involved more flexible working hours, greater colleague contact, more efficient use of other media, and more precise text in the computer conferencing environment. The comprehensive EIES project included participant surveys which also indicated that respondents felt that c.c. increased their quality of work, variety of ideas, and contact with others' work (Hiltz, 1979). Researchers dispersed in "invisible colleges" tend to evaluate their use of c.c. positively, as contact with distant and extra-disciplinary members increases (Freeman, 1979; Freeman and Freeman, 1979; Johansen et al., 1977, 1978). However, some structural changes in communication patterns may be dysfunctional or divisive. The Freeman studies of their EIES group used network analysis (Rice and Richards, 1980) to show that communication links increased, c.c. had more effect than several face-to-face meetings, and for some people c.c. was substitutable for the kinds of experience upon which close friendships develop. However, inequalities in strengths of "friends" and "close friends" increased (perhaps a sign of intimate stratification) and interdisciplinary collaboration tended to force members of each discipline into defined stances, away from other disciplines.

There are a few studies which consider the effect of the introduction of a c.c. system on other media or communication activities in an organization. Johansen et al. (1978) report slight decreases in mail usage and work-related reading, but no decrease in telephone usage (although Conrath (1978) found a very small reduction). SRI's use of NLS, not explicitly a conferencing system, did result in increases in total communication and reductions of face-to-face and telephone, but not written, communication (Conrath and Bair, 1974). This type of change is also reported by Edwards (1978), Leduc (1979), McNurlin (1978), and Stanford University (1980). Williams (1978) suggests that teleconferencing might provide a reasonable substitute for 50 percent of current face-to-face meetings. Short et al. (1976) see a majority of meetings theoretically allocatable to a variety teleconferencing media, but the percentage is reduced by the favorable evaluation people have of face-to-face and video and the poor cost-effectiveness of video systems. Much lower figures are suggested by other researchers (in Williams, 1978; and see Edelstein et al., 1978). For example, analysing communication flow characteristics, Dormois et al. (1978) conclude that only 7 percent of meetings and 14 percent of telephone uses could be transferred to teleconferencing. This study involved 2000 respondents and 33,000 interorganizational communications in 60 organizations, generalizable to France! The exhaustiveness and sophistication of this study lend considerable credibility to the authors' conclusions. Factors involved in such substitutability in group contexts include the nature of the group task, the need for a leader, the sense of group task and cohesion, the importance of getting to know the other members, and, to a lesser extent, cost.

The impacts of word-processing systems, computerized conferencing, and "automated offices", from this communication perspective, are evaluated quite favorably in a series of papers (Bair 1973, 1979 a, b; Carlisle, 1970; Conrath and Bair, 1974; Uhlig, 1977). Their basic premise is that the potential economic and worklife benefits of "automated offices" are greatest for professional and managerial tasks, of which 75 percent involve communication (mostly oral and in meetings, however). For the most recent and comprehensive review since Mintzberg (1973) and Stewart (1967, 1976) of how managers allocate their time, media use and tasks, see Carter (1980). In the study of an Air Force secton's use of SRI's NLS, for example, the greatest organizational changes occurred in the users' communication patterns—increased connectivity, effectiveness, and productivity. At SRI itself, subjective analysis of 4 years' usage of NLS concluded that individual effectiveness, team consensus, intraorganizational collaboration, and overall communication increased, and time savings amounted to nearly two hours a day for a typical professional (in a very supportive environment for information augmentation).

Other general findings are a preference for using NLS for upward-flowing message (bridging authority links) and increased breadth of contact. A subtle but potentially consequential finding was that interruptions from outside the terminal were resisted, but not from within the terminal (as, immediate messages from other terminal users). Bell Canada's use of NLS resulted in better projected-oriented communication, and greater external links but little improvement in problem-solving. Other Bell results reported by Leduc (1979) are very similar to those of SRI's. Price (1975) refers to a study which explained that a computer messaging system dramatically altered the structure of a widely-dispersed information-intensive consulting and computer company. The very strong democratizing and flexible communication system allowed/required a shift from a hierarchical organization to one consisting mostly of constantly changing sets of teams.

The kinds of payoffs these authors foresee include: fewer kinds and number of transformations between media required, less nonproductive "shadow functions" such as redialing busy telephone lines, automation of manual processes (although the job enrichment of creative text-editing is offset by a factor of three to four increase in number of text revisions!), improved scheduling, and increased control (of information neeeded, span, etc.) Some of these studies claim that "no negative consequences of computer-mediated communication that would be cause for limiting usage have been uncovered.... no evidence to support fears of increased depersonalized communication, alienation, or loss of privacy..." (Bair, 1979b) and therefore their favorable cost-benefit analyses are sufficient justification for full implementation. Perhaps their respondents were too close to the change, or the environments were atypically supportive, but such statements are too all-encompassing for this author's taste.

Some new uses develop as well (Conrath, 1978), and these may be additional justifications for transferring some tasks (Short et al., 1976, Chapter 10). For example, over 50 percent of messages by the members of the U.S.-Canada Satellite project using the PLANET conferencing system occurred during times when telephone usage would have been impractical due to costs or scheduling (Infomedia, 1979). These new uses create new communication behaviors and habits. When one can work at home by computer-mediated communication media, what will become of the traditionally clear-cut distinction (in most occupations) between work-hours and leisure-hours (Johansen et al., 1978)? The very nature of information work, less dependent on material transformations and physical access to resources, makes such occupations quite amenable to flexible scheduling. Some preliminary experiences show that the transition between these activities can be very difficult and frustrating to family members and neigbors (American Association for the Advancement of Science, 1980).

V. CONCLUSION

This chapter has provided a basic introduction to computer conferencing, described several major systems, and summarized the empirical research on its usage and impacts. What are some of the future directions of this medium? Miller (1980) and others suggest that the next breakthrough is a collision, convergence, or wedding (perhaps shotgun) of technologies and approaches for data processing, telecommunications, human communication, and information retrieval. The variety of human communication functions (of which c.c. can only provided some) will be facilitated and integrated in such an approach. The developing "office of the future" is a large step toward this end. In Sweden, the telecommunications ministry is already experimenting with comprehensive interconnection of teletypes, telephone exchanges, computers, etc.

The 1980s have been predicted as the "interactive" decade. In communication systems, the goal will be to develop interactive systems for humans who may have no knowledge of computers, systems which can flexibly delegate various tasks to humans or machines according to the user's experience and skills. Thus the second breakthrough will be to design systems that bend with people. To promote this breakthrough, much emphasis needs to be placed on research into the behavioral factors of computer-based communications, to understand how users evolve with and react to particular systems. In addition, work needs to be directed toward supporting access to and knowledge of these new communications media, in order to enable people's attitudes toward computer-based communications to evolve in positive directions.

As we have seen, the research so far points to a very complicated mix of factors in some cases, and quite clear-cut responses in others. C.c. is a unique, but complementary, communication medium which has useful and positive attributes for appropriate tasks; in other uses it may be detrimental. For some of the appropriate tasks, c.c. may substitute for other media or even provide new applications. As Short et al. (1976) suggest in their chapter on "The Decision to Telecommunicate" the goal is a proper "communications diet" which mixes media usage for given organizational, task, and individual contexts. Carter's analyses (1980) and the EIES evaluations (Hiltz and Turoff, 1978a) are some of the very few cases where research results are used explicitly to guide computer-mediated technology design.

The issues surrounding this new medium are numerous and complex (see Bezilla, 1978; Hiltz and Turoff, 1978a) and policy decisions should be informed so that some potentially beneficial developments are not prevented. The equity of access—both input and output—to these information resources by all social segments is also a critical factor. Will computer-based conferencing replace physically-centered organizations and face-to-face meetings? Will they unilaterally reshape social and work communication behavior? How will the ability to discuss several topics simultaneously, to use delayed electronic messages to defuse negative reactions, or to process greater amounts of interaction (of a very particular sort) affect social communication rules? What will the effect on spelling standards by frequent informal messaging be? There are many questions yet to be answered, and many of them are important.

ACKNOWLEDGMENTS

I would like to acknowledge the helpful comments by Dr. William Richards, Jr., and the assistance in obtaining documents provided by Dr. Roxanne Hiltz, Dr. Murray Turoff and Dr. Sara Spang.

REFERENCES

American Association for the Advancement of Science. (1980). Computers and Telecommunications: Impacts on Society. (American Association for the Advancement of Science, Session on Computers, S. Roxanne Hiltz, Moderator, San Francisco.)

Amara, R., and Vallee, J. (1974). FORUM: A computer-based system to support interaction among people. *In* "Proceedings of the International Federation of Information Processing Congress," pp. 1052–1056.

Bailey, G. C., Nordlie, P. G., and Sistrunk, F. (1966). "Teleconferencing: Literature Review, Field Studies and Working Papers." Institute for Defense Analysis, Washington, D.C. (Research Paper P-113). (NTIS: AD 480 695.)

Bair, J. H. (1973). Experiences with an augmented human intellect system: Computer-mediated communication. *Proceedings of the SID 41* (No. 2), 42–51.

Bair, J. H. (1974). "Evaluation and Analysis of an Augmented Knowledge Workshop." (NTIS AD 778-835/9.)

Bair, J. H. (1979a). "A Communication Perspective for Identifying Office Automation Payoffs." (Paper presented at New York University Symposium on Automated Office Systems.)

Bair, J. H. (1979b). Communication in the office of the future: Where the real payoff may be. *Business Communications Review 9* (No. 1), 1–11.

Bair, J. H. (1980). Design problems and guidelines for human-computer communications in office automation systems. *In* "EURO IFIP 79: European Conference on Applied Information Technology" (P.A. Samet, Ed). North Holland Publishing, Amsterdam.

Bezilla, R. (1978). "A Discussion of Selected Aspects of Privacy, Confidentiality and Anonymity in Computerized Conferencing." New Jersey Institute of Technology Computerized Conferencing and Communications Center, Newark, New Jersey. (Report 11.)

Brockhoff, K. (1975). The performance of forecasting groups in computer dialogue and face-to-face discussion. *In* "The Delphi Method: Techniques and Applications" (H. A. Linstone and M. Turoff, Eds.), pp. 291–322. Addison-Wesley, Reading, Massachusetts.

Carlisle, J. H. (1975). "A Selected Bibliography in Computer-Based Teleconferencing." University of Southern California Information Sciences Institute, Marina Del Rey, California.

Carlisle, J. H. (1979). "How Can Office Automation Improved Administrative Productivity and Managerial Effectiveness?" Office of the Future Inc., Guttenberg, New Jersey.

Carter, G. (1974). "CONFER—A Preliminary Design Concept." University of Illinois, Department of Electrical Engineering, Urbana, Illinois.

Carter, G. (1980). "The Implications of Empirical, Managerial-Attention Data for Computer-Mediated Communication Systems." Chapter Two of the untitled dissertation, Carnegie-Mellon University, Department of Engineering and Public Policy.

Chapanis, A. (1975). Interactive human communication. *Scientific American 232* (No. 3), 36–42.

Computers and super-literates (1980). OMNI Magazine (forthcoming).

Conrath, D. W. (1973). Communications environment and its relationship to organizational structure. *Management Science 20,* 586–603.

Conrath, D. W. (1978). Organizational communication behavior: Description and prediction. *In* "Evaluating New Telecommunications Services" (M. C. J. Elton, W. A. Lucas, and D. W. Conrath, Eds.), pp. 422–425. Plenum, New York.

Conrath, D. W., and Bair, J. H. (1974). "The Computer as an Interpersonal Communication Device: A Study of Augmentation Technology and Its Apparent Impact on Organizational Communication." Stanford Research Institute, Menlo Park, California.

Day, L. H. (1975). "Computer Conferencing: An Overview." (Paper presented at Airlie House 1975 Conference on Telecommunications Policy, Washington, DC.)

Dewhirst, H. D. (1971). Influence of perceived information-sharing norms on communication channel utilization. *Academy of Management Journal 14,* 305–315.

Dormois, M., Fioux, F., and Gensollen, M. (1978). Evaluation of the potential market for various future communication modes via an analysis of communication flow characteristics.

In "Evaluating New Telecommunications Services" (M. C. J. Elton, W. A. Lucas, and D. W. Conrath, Eds.), pp. 367–384. Plenum, New York.

Dunn, D. (1978). Limitations on the growth of computer-communications services. *Telecommunications Policy 2,* 106–116.

Edelstein, A. S., Bowes, J., and Harsel, S., Eds. (1978). "Information Societies: Comparing the Japanese and American Experiences." University of Washington International Communication Center, Seattle, Washington.

Edwards, G. C. (1978). Organizational impacts of office automation. *Telecommunications Policy 2,* 128–136.

An Electronic mail and message system primer (1978). *EMMS (Electronic Mail and Message System Newsletter) 2* (No. 7), 1–12.

Englebart, D. C., Watson, R. W., and Norton, J. C. (1976). The augmented knowledge workshop. *In* "Computer Networking" (R. P. BLank and J. Prothro, Eds.), pp. 228–240. IEEE Press, New York.

Freeman, L. (1979). "Q-Analysis and the Structure of Friendship Networks." Unpublished paper, School of Social Science, University of California, Irvine.

Freeman, S., and Freeman, L. (1979). "The Networkers Network: A Study of the Impact of a New Communications Medium on Sociometric Structure." (Paper presented to Seminar on Communication Network Analysis, East-West Center, Honolulu.)

Hiltz, S. R. (1978a). Controlled experiments with computerized conferencing. *Bulletin of the American Society for Information Science 4* (No. 5), 11–12.

Hiltz, S. R. (1978b). The computer conference. *Journal of Communication 28* (No. 3), 157–163.

Hiltz, S. R. (1978c). The human element in computerized systems. *Computer Networks 2,* 421–428.

Hiltz, S. R. (1978c). "The Operational Trials of the EIES: An Overview of the Nature, Purpose and Initial Findings." New Jersey Institute for Information Technology Computerized Conferencing and Communications Center, Newark, New Jersey.

Hiltz, S. R. (1978d). The human element in computerized systems. *Computer Networks 2,* 421–428.

Hiltz, S. R., and Turoff, M. (1978a). "The Network Nation." Addison–Wesley, Reading, Massachusetts.

Hiltz, S. R., and Turoff, M. (1978b). "Electronic Networks: The Social Dynamics of a New Communications Medium." (Paper presented to American Sociology Association Seminar on Social Networks, San Francisco.)

Hiltz, S. R., and Turoff, M. (1980). "The Evolution of User Behavior in Computerized Communication Systems." (Paper presented to International Communication Association, Acapulco, Mexico.)

Hough, R. W. (1976). "Teleconference Systems: A State of the Art Review." Stanford Research Institute, Menlo Park, California.

Infomedia. (1977). "Planet System User's Guide." Palo Alto, California, Infomedia Corporation, Inc. (Manual.)

Infomedia. (1979). "An Introduction to Infomedia." Infomedia Corporation, Palo Alto, California.

Irving, R. H. (1978). Computer assisted communication in a directorate of the Canadian Federal government: A pilot study. *In* "Evaluating New Telecommunications Services" (M. C. J. Elton, W. A. Lucas, and D. W. Conrath, Eds.), pp. 455–469. Plenum, New York.

Johansen, R. (1977). Social evaluations of teleconferencing. *Telecommunications Policy 1,* 395–419.

Johansen, R., Miller, R. H., and Vallee, J. (1975). Group communication through electronic media: Fundamental choices and social effects. *In* "The Delphi Method: Techniques and Applications" (H. A. Linstone and M. Turoff, Eds.), pp. 517–534. Addison–Wesley, Reading, Massachusetts.

Johansen, R., Vallee, J., Spangler, K., and Shirts, R. G. (1977). "The Camelia Report: A Study of Technical Alternatives and Social Choices in Teleconferencing." Institute for the Future, Menlo Park, California. Also: (1979) "Electronic Meetings" Addison-Wesley, Reading, MA.

Johansen, R., De Grasse, R., Jr., and Wilson, T. (1978). "Group Communication through Computers: Vol. 5—Effects on Working Patterns." Institute for the Future, Menlo Park, California.

Kaplan, M. F. and Miller, C. E. (1977). Judgments and group discussion: Effect of presentation and memory factor on polarization. *Sociometry 40,* 337–343.

Keen, P. G. W. and Morton, M. S. S. (1978). "Decision Support Systems: An Organizational Perspective." Addison-Wesley, Reading, Massachusetts.

Koomen, W., and Sagel, P. K. (1977). The prediction of participation in two-person groups. *Sociometry 40,* 369–373.

Leduc, N. F. (1979). Communicating through computers: Impact on a small business corporation. *Telecommunications Policy 3,* 235–244.

Leduc, N. F., Shepard, C. D., Simpson, F., and Costa, J. (1979). "The Development of Telecommunications Services: A Review of Projects." Bell Canada and Canadian Department of Communications, Hull, Quebec. Volumes Two and Three.

Linstone, H. A., and Turoff, M., Eds. (1975). "The Delphi Method: Techniques and Applications." Addison-Wesley, Reading, Massachusetts.

Lipinski, H. M., and Miller, R. H. (1974). "Forum: A Computer-Assisted Communications Medium." (Paper presented at Second International Conference on Computer Communications, Stockholm, Sweden.)

Lipinski, H. M., Vian, K., Plummer, R., Spang, S., Tydeman, J., and McNeal, B. (1979). "Interactive Group Modelling and Hub User's Guide." 5 vols. Institute for the Future, Menlo Park, California.

McNurlin, B. (1978). The automated office. *EDP Analyzer 16* (No. 9), 1–13; (No. 10), 1–13.

Miller, R. H. (1978). "Computer Conferencing and Computer Mail; Impacts on Today's and Tomorrow's Office." Infomedia Corporation, Palo Alto, California.

Miller, R. H. (1980). (Vice-President of Infomedia, Inc.) Personal interview, January 9, 1980.

Mintzberg, H. (1973). "The Nature of Managerial Work." Harper and Row, New York.

Panko, R. R. (1977). The Outlook for Computer Mail. *Telecommunications Policy,* 242–253.

Panko, R. R. (1978). "The Costs of Computer Mail and Other Media." Stanford Research Institute International, Menlo Park, California (Project 6859 Report 1.)

Pford, W., Peralta, L., Prendergast, F., and Carey, D. (1978). TOPES: Timeshared office planning and engineering system. *Computer-Aided Design 10,* 363–370.

Price, C. R. (1975). Conferencing via computer: Cost effective communication for the era of forced choice. *In* "The Delphi Method: Techniques and Applications" (H. A. Linstone and M. Turoff, eds.), pp. 497–516. Addison-Wesley, Reading, Massachusetts.

Price, C. R., Turoff, M., and Hiltz, S. R. (1980). "Teleconferencing and Electronic Mail: Information or Communication?" (Paper presented to ASLIB Convention, Brussels.)

Rice, R. E. (1980). Impacts of computer-mediated organizational and interpersonal communication. *In* "Annual Review of Information Science and Technology," C. M. Williams, Ed.), (in press). Volume 15. Knowledge and Industry Publications, White Plains, N.Y.

Rice, R. E., and Richards, W. D., Jr. (1980). "Quantitative Network Analysis Methods." (Manual presented in Workshop on Communication Network Analysis, International Communication Association Conference, Acapulco, Mexico.) Also *in* "Research Methods in Social Network Analysis" (L. Freeman and D. White, Eds.), (to appear). University of California Press, Berkeley.

Roberts, L. G. (1978). The evolution of packet switching. *IEEE Proceedings 66,* 1307–1314.

Schuyler, J., and Johansen, R. (1972). ORACLE, Computerized conferencing in a computer-assisted instruction system. *In* "Computer Communications: Impacts and Implications" (S. Winkler, Ed.), pp. 155–160. ACM, New York.

Schwartz, B. (1978). Queues, priorities, and social process. *Social Psychology 41,* 3–12.

Short, J., Williams, E., and Christie, B. (1976). "The Social Psychology of Telecommunications." Wiley, New York.

Shulman, A. D., and Steinman, J. I. (1978). Interpersonal teleconferencing in an organizational context. *In* "Evaluating New Telecommunications Services" (M. C. J. Elton, W. A. Lucas, and D. W. Conrath, Eds.), pp. 399–424. Plenum, New York.

Stanford University. Task force on the Future of Computing at Stanford (1980). "Interim Status Report." Task Force on the Future of Computing at Stanford, Stanford Center for Information Technology, Stanford University, Stanford, California.

Stewart, R. (1967). "Managers and Their Jobs." MacMillan, London.

Stewart, R. (1976). "Contrasts in Management." McGraw–Hill, London.

Turoff, M. (1972). "Party-line" and "Discussion" computerized conference systems. *In* "Computer Communications: Impacts and Implications," (S. Winkler, Ed.), pp. 161–171. ACM, New York.

Turoff, M. (1978). The EIES Experience: Electronic Information Exchange System. *Bulletin of the American Society for Information Science 4* (No. 5), 9–10.

Turoff, M., and Hiltz, S. R. (1977a). "Computerized Conferencing: A Review and Statement of the Issues." (Paper presented at NATO Telecommunications Symposium.)

Turoff, M., and Hiltz, S. R. (1977b). Meeting through your computer. *IEEE Spectrum 14* (May), 58–64.

Turoff, M., and Hiltz, S. R. (1978). "Information and Communications in International Affairs." (Paper presented to International Studies Association, Toronto, Canada.)

Uhlig, R. P. (1977). Human factors in computer message systems. *Datamation 23* (May), 121–126.

Uhlig, R. P., Farber, D. J., and Bair, J. H. (1979). "The Office of the Future: Communications and Computers." North-Holland Publishers, Amsterdam.

Vallee, J. (1976). The Forum Project: Network conferencing and its future applications. *Computer Networks 1* (No. 1), 39–52.

White, R. B. (1977). A prototype for the automated office. *Datamation 23* (April), 83–90.

Williams, E. (1978). Teleconferencing: Social and psychological factors. *Journal of Communication 28* (No. 3), 125–131.

Zinn, K. L. (1977). Computer facilitation of communication in the Professional Communities. *Behavioral Research Methods and Instrumentation 9* (No. 2), 96–107.

7

Applying a Holistic Framework to Synthesize Information Science Research*

Karen B. Levitan
Division of Information Science and Technology
National Science Foundation

---

*A major share of the work was conducted under National Science Foundation Grant IST-7821078, while the author was on the technical staff of the MITRE Corporation, Metrek Division, McLean, Virginia.

241

I. INTRODUCTION

This paper is an attempt to deal with the problem of evaluating and synthesizing information science research by developing a holistic framework to integrate diverse, multidisciplinary studies about information phenomena. The framework is applied to a broad review of the research conducted by the constituencies of the American Society for Information Science and the Office (and later Division) of Science Information of the National Science Foundation from the later 1950s to the middle of 1970.

Information units, processes and systems are studied in virtually all of the sciences. However, there has been no obvious agreement as to the nature of information or the focus and methodology of information science research. The apparent universality of information concepts found throughout the sciences stimulated a search for an approach that could be used to synthesize the wide variety of research about the phenomenon of information across the sciences. Such a framework is proposed in this paper. It is developed by analyzing how information is observed and incorporating the elements of the observation into a framework to unify information science research.

The presentation begins with a background discussion of definitional and methodological problems and a description of how information is commonly observed. A holistic approach to information is developed in section 3. This section can be viewed as a "position paper," integrating much well-known literature on information and system theory. In section 4, a holistic framework is applied to a chunk of research whose authors identify themselves as "information scientists." The paper concludes with suggestions for applying the approach across the spectrum of science.

II. BACKGROUND

A. Problems in Communicating about Information Science Research

Information science is an emerging field of research dating back to the 1920s and 1930s. Fairthorne reports that the word "information" was rarely used prior to 1948. As yet, there is no consensus regarding its definition, methodology or community of researchers (Belkin, 1978; Debons, 1974; Harmon, 1971; Heilprin, prepublication draft; Otten, 1975; Shera and Cleveland, 1977).

1. Defining Information. Information has been analyzed from many perspectives and has been broken into many aspects. The following list of concepts, for example, reflects many authors' attempts to deal with the nature of information:

- **organization** (Thompson, 1968)
- **variety** (Belkin, 1975; Heilprin, 1973)
- **semiotics** (Artandi, 1975; Pearson and Slamecka, prepublication draft)
- **changed behavior** (Ackoff, 1958; Brookes, 1973; Mackay, 1969; Wersig and Neveling, 1975; Whittemore and Yovits, 1973)
- **learning** (Bruner et al., 1956; Donaldson, 1979; Heilprin and Goodman, 1965; Smith, prepublication draft)
- **subjective knowledge** (Ackoff, 1958; Wersig and Neveling, 1975; Whittemore and Yovits, 1973)
- **recorded knowledge** (Taylor, 1966; *Webster's New Collegiate Dictionary,* 1977)
- **problem solving** (Simon, 1969; Simon and Newell, 1977)
- **libraries** (Foskett, 1969)
- **goal seeking** (Simon, 1969; von Foerster, 1968)
- **decision making** (Simon, 1969; von Foerster, 1968)
- **information transfer** (Murdock and Liston, 1967; Weisman, 1972; Wellisch, 1972)
- **information flow** (Fairthorne, 1967)
- **information storage and retrieval systems** (Paisley and Parker, 1965; Vickery, 1965)
- **relevance** (Saracevic, 1975)
- **subject matter specialities,** such as information about chemistry, biology, physics, etc.
- **information processing** (Becker and Hayes, 1963; Lancaster, 1968; Meadow, 1973)
- **electronic information process and computers** (Artandi, 1968; Bourne, 1961; *Scientific American,* 1966)
- **message** (Herner and Herner, 1967)
- **medium** (McLuhan, 1964)
- **documents** (Vickery, 1971; Wersig and Neveling, 1975)
- **channel capacity** (Shannon and Weaver, 1949)
- **communication** (Artandi, 1973; Otten, 1975; Shannon and Weaver, 1949)
- **selective information** (Shannon and Weaver, 1949)
- **uncertainty** (Brillouin, 1962; Miller, 1978; Whittemore and Yovits, 1973)
- **stimuli** (Miller, 1956)
- **word frequencies** (Jolley, 1973)
- **representation** (Kochen, 1974; Smith, prepublication draft; Vickery, 1971)
- **entropy and negative entropy** (Boulding, 1978; Brillouin, 1962; Heilprin, 1973; Miller, 1978)

These concepts appear consistently throughout the literature and remain relatively undisputed (see Auerbach's comments, 1974). While they generate a tremendous range of possible directions for information science research, they provide no synthesis. The lack of a common thread in this list of concepts reflects that the field has been dominated by the question, "What is information?"

The problem which arises in asking "What is information?" is that the interrogative "what" inherently fosters description through reductionist thinking; i.e., whatever is being identified is reduced to its parts; the parts, in turn, are individually examined. As the above list demonstrates, instead of synthesizing, this question leads to fragmentation.

Moreover, although these concepts all characterize some aspect of information, they are by no means synonymous with information. Information is not a simple object that can be described in simple terms. It is complex and unusual. It is infinitely variable in that it characterizes every different subject one is able to recognize; it is ubiquitous in that it pertains to everything; it is evolutionary and can only be made from previous information; it can be transferred without being moved from its origin; it is not consumable in that it is not depleted after use; it is synergetic in that it is a whole which differs from its parts; its worth can only be determined by more information.

Just as physics, biology, psychology, sociology, and anthropology, etc., represent the study of their own respective phenomena, information science involves the study of the phenomenon of information. This phenomenon appears to be inherent to all systems—human and nonhuman, living and artificial (Haken, 1977; Haken and Wagner, 1973; Miller, 1978; Simon, 1969). Previous analyses indicate that research about information simultaneously cuts across, employs and develops many diverse fields, such as: communications, engineering, psychology, sociology of science, biology, neurophysiology, computer science, management sciences, library science, linguistics, logic, mathematics and statistics, and cybernetics (Kochen, 1974; Otten and Debons, 1970; Samuelson, 1976; Taylor, 1963). Many other fields are discussed later in this paper.

2. Identifying the Research Community. Because information concepts appear ubiquitously across the sciences, it is difficult to identify and establish a cohesive community of researchers. Although information content, form, processes and systems are part of the research in numerous scientific fields, most scientists do not focus on information *per se.* Among the most prominent research communities who have shown an interest in developing information science as a unique field of study are those affiliated with the American Society for Information Science (ASIS) and the heritage of research which evolved with the Office of Information Services (OSIS) in the National Science Foundation (NSF).

The establishment of information science as a field of study in its own right did not occur until 1968 when the American Documentation Institute became the American Society for Information Science. The small research community of ASIS was also the primary constituency of the Office of Science Information Service in the National Science Foundation. When NSF was founded in 1950, the OSIS was created to study and improve science information and communications. It became the focal point for a variety of information studies to support national science needs as well as a nationally recognized institution supporting information science research. The OSIS later became the Division of Science Information (DSI) and in 1978, the Division of Information Science and Technology (DIST). In spite of the fact that information science research and its community of researchers cannot be clearly defined, the membership of ASIS and the constituencies of the NSF science information programs represent a core from which to build a cohesive field. A review of their research is presented in section IV of this paper.

3. Evaluating Information Science Research.   The current lack of a unified perspective on information concepts also makes it difficult to evaluate information science research. While it is possible to study and evaluate a science by using bibliometrics (Brookes, 1973; Donohue, 1973; Narin, 1976) sociometrics (Crane, 1972; Crawford, 1971; Mulkay, 1977), other survey techniques (Herner and Herner 1967; Menzel 1976), and various models from the history and philosophy of science (Bohme, 1977), such techniques essentially describe the *status quo*. They are not directly applicable to a "formative" evaluation, which can integrate diverse fields. Bibliometrics, for example, can define the quantitative dependence of a field upon other fields, e.g., the degree to which cancer research cites the literature of virology, and whether that relationship changes over time. However, it cannot define the intellectual nature of the relationship, which is what this paper intends to address.

Moreover, these techniques rely on a set of core journals, core investigators and core problems which, when used in an evaluation, inherently result in describing the field as practiced. In several citation studies which have been conducted in the field of information science, the core journals reflected library science, documentation and various information systems journals, Predictably, the results of these studies emphasized the library and documentation aspects of information science research (Dansey, 1973; Gilchrist and Presanis, 1971; Goldstein, 1973; Pope, 1975; Saracevic and Perk, 1973). Since the objective of this study is to break from current practices and formulate a new, synthesizing approach for research, these techniques are not applicable to the objectives of this paper.

4. Need for a Holistic Approach.   A holistic approach is needed to synthesize the properties and dynamics of information. It must be broad in scope and rigorous in execution in order to accommodate the interdisciplinary character of information studies. As Otten and Debons (1970, p. 89) recognized, it must be capable of providing:

- ...a common basis upon which all information-oriented, specialized sciences and technologies can be understood and studied
- ...a common framework and language for all scientists and technologists concerned in some form or other with information
- ...integration for various theories that concern themselves with the phenomena of information on one side and man's relationship to the phenomena on the other side

The previous years of reductionist thinking about information have revealed its unique attributes. These attributes must serve as a foundation for information science so that scientific methods will be developed which will truly explain the observations made of information and, at the same time, preserve its integrity.

B. How Information is Observed

All of the sciences are based on human observation. The act of observing makes science "empirical." In order to understand information science, it is necessary to consider how information is commonly observed.

1. In the Context of a User-Producer.   To observe information requires perceiving the whole context of information and a user-producer. Information can exist only with a user-producer. Without a user there is only potential information. For human users, potential information takes the form of books, journals, articles, values, subject matter, etc. Information is not recognized unless it is transformed or generated by a user to suit his or her own needs. Therefore, every user of information is also a producer of information. This viewpoint is expressed by those who define information as "subjective knowledge" (Wersig and Neveling, 1975; Whittemore and Yovits, 1973), or "receiver effect" (Mackay, 1969; Paisley and Parker, 1965; Shannon and Weaver, 1949), or "changed behavior" (Brookes, 1973; Mackay, 1969; Wersig and Neveling, 1975; Whittemore and Yovits, 1973).

2. As a Unit of Content and Form.   For every user, information is grasped only as a whole unit of content and form, e.g., medium and message are inseparable and become information when used. Information content and form are meaningless out of context. Thus, any and every unit of information must be considered in the context of its corresponding user. In the field of semiotics, for example, signs are studied by mapping units of content and form (semantics and syntactics) to practice (pragmatics) or use (Pearson and Slamecka, prepublication draft).

3. In Time, as A Cycle of Events.   To observe information as a cycle or process requires recognizing all the events that occur during the time that it takes a user to acquire potential information (content and form) and produce or generate new information which is applicable to a user's development. Thus, an information process consists of a whole set of interrelated events over time, such as: searching, sorting, selecting, evaluating, organizing, directing, storing, retrieving, displaying, transferring and using. In order to observe information relative to a user, it is necessary to deal with all of these activities together in time, for one activity alone cannot produce information for a user.

4. In Space, as a System of Agents.   Information as a system includes the entire set of procedures, operations and functions involved in the collection, evaluation, storage, retrieval, dissemination and generation of information by a user (see Weik, 1969, pp. 285–286 for a similar set of information system functions).

Depending on the technology of the information system, i.e., its materials, energy and know-how (Boulding, 1978), these activities may reflect the organization of many or few subsystems. Regardless of the number of subsystems, all agents acting on the same information input are agents of the whole information system, and all actions are functions of the total information system. The inherent interdependence of functions characterizes it as a **cooperative** process. The resultant pattern is a network or system of interconnected actions (Figure 1), not a linear structure as customarily pictured.

No matter how one chooses to view information, it exists as a whole experience for a user. Because information requires a whole evolutionary or developmental cycle in order to exist for a user, it can only be perceived as a whole system after generation.

5. The Scientist's Perspective.   The nature of information imposes very strict requirements on the observer/scientist who must be able to view the entire set of events that occurs during the time it takes to use potential information and produce new information. Such an observation is often difficult because a user may employ many different and physically dispersed information systems.

A scientist whose goal is to understand information relative to a user-producer will identify with the user system. When a scientist has established a user's information system, it is then possible to reconstruct the total flow of information of the user-producer and observe the continuous transformations of content and form as well as the processes involved in these transformations. The observer thereby becomes an essential part of the observation (Bertalanffy, 1968; Churchman, 1971; Weinberg, 1975).

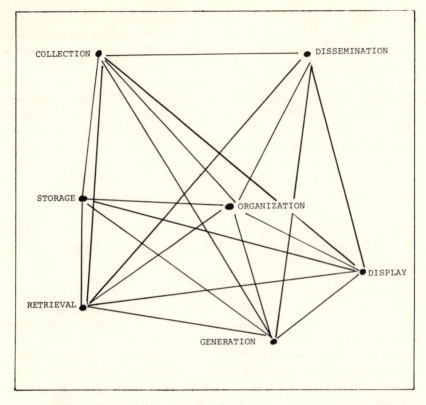

FIG. 1. Network of interdependent functions in a system of information at one point in time.

6. Summary. In sum, it has been shown that information is always observed in the context of a user-producer and appears as a whole unit, whole cycle, or whole system. The observer is a significant part of the observation. In order to be true to information, it is necessary to develop an approach which can incorporate what is observed with the way information is observed.

III. A HOLISTIC APPROACH TO INFORMATION SCIENCE

Such integration can be provided by developing a holistic approach to information science. This section will discuss holistic thinking in general, the concept of a user system, system survival in general, and the requirements of an information scientist.

A. Holistic Thinking

Holistic thinking emphasizes wholes rather than parts; it sets up a hierarchy of systems from which to view a whole system, and requires the observer to be a part of the observation.

The term "holistic" comes from the ideas of holism and system analysis. While holism describes the universe in terms of interacting wholes which are more than the mere sum of their parts, system analysis emphasizes the functional relations between parts and whole, as well as among the parts.

Viewing the system as a collective whole is commonly called holistic thinking (Kuhn 1974, p. 12). Examining the role that a system plays in relation to a larger supersystem is functionalist thinking; looking at its parts or subsystems is reductionist thinking; analyzing how it works is system analysis (see Figure 2). All three perspectives are obviously required to grasp the whole system, which is the essence of holistic thinking.

Only by establishing a fixed perspective is it possible to unambiguously identify a system and describe its relationship to other systems. The system under observation provides the required focal point and establishes a hierarchy in which to position the system and determine its function, its operation, organization, and its components. Holistic thinking provides an observer with a perspective on a whole system.

A system has been described as a way of looking at the world (Weinberg 1975). This explanation underscores that what one sees in the universe depends on the way one looks at the universe. A system is a way of thinking about entities as a set of components which are interrelated in working for a common goal. It allows one to grasp whole sets of entities changing over time (See Laszlo, 1969, 1972a,b).

A system need not be physically integrated and its parts are often widely dispersed. In order to view it as a whole, it is necessary to assemble its information system, study the information units which it uses and produces, and track its flow of information to and from the systems with which it interacts. This reveals the structure of the total system, its function and its effect as a whole.

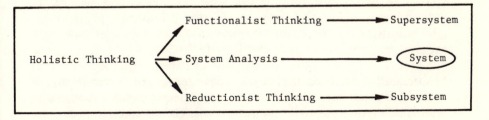

FIG. 2.   Holistic Thinking, adapted from Kuhn, p. 13 (Printed with permission from the publisher).

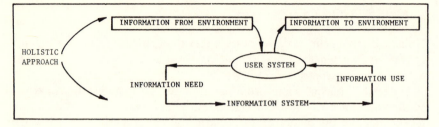

FIG. 3.   Holistic Approach to Information.

B. The Concept of a User System

A whole system can be observed by focusing on an information user-producer, hereafter called "user system." The focus on a user system provides a holistic approach to information which, in turn, provides a way to study information as it exists in concrete situations. As depicted in Figure 3, a system functions as a user system by acquiring and using potential information from its environment.

As a result of its constant interaction with the environment, a user system is depicted as a system which inherently needs information. Every interaction involves a choice, and every choice depends upon information, so that a continuing need for information is established. The need is directly related to use (how the user system functions in relation to its environment). Need, then, is essentially a surrogate for use. Hence, all user systems require information systems to accomplish their function. This function is a difficult process involving continuous communication, direction and control from the user system to its information system and back to its environment (Arbib, 1972; Ashby, 1956; Parkman, 1972). The total steering activity is expressed as information needs and uses which provide overall direction for a user system and its information system.

A user system is a dynamic system, constantly evolving. It is conceived as a whole system which orders or organizes itself into an information system so that it can transform information from its environment (see Figure 4). This appears to be the case regardless of what the user system may be: an individual, collectives of people, scientific disciplines, professions, governments, other human entities, animals and animal societies, biological, chemical and physical systems (Buckley, 1968; Gatlin, 1972; Kuhn, 1974; Sampson, 1976). The function or "purpose" of a user system may or may not be specifically articulated, may or may not be recognized. Nevertheless, it is understood as the force which drives the user system to organize itself into an information system and to function as a whole. The transition from disorder to order comes via information and requires a memory, processing and communication capabilities and the cooperative effort of all the diverse

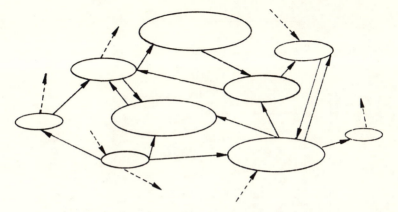

A. RANDOM INTERACTION OF DYNAMIC SYSTEMS

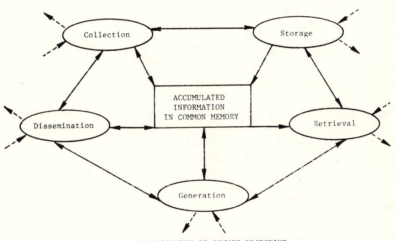

B.   ESTABLISHMENT OF COMMON OBJECTIVE

FIG. 4.   Formation of a User System.

agents involved in the information system or processing event. The effect of the whole system is that it functions in a way which seems "purposeful."

Dynamic systems are observed constantly interacting with their environments, acquiring and generating information. Over time the study of these interactions results in an accumulation of information which is common to all of the interacting systems. This accumulation may be called a common "memory" or knowledge base. The knowledge base contains information about how systems adapt, reproduce and survive over time in a common environment. In order to tap and maintain the knowledge base, it is understood that the different systems must cooperate with each other. The

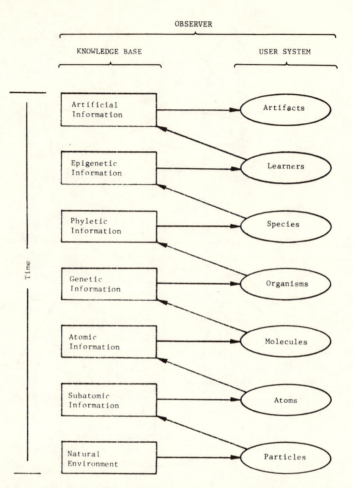

FIG. 5. Hierarchy of systems related to the evolution of knowledge bases.

cooperation of systems over time for the use of the same information provides a function (goal or purpose) which is common to all the interacting systems (and to the observer). These systems are formed into a new system—a user system.

From an observer's point of view, systems evolve by using and producing a common knowledge base. Figure 5, for example, depicts an important hierarchy in the evolution of systems and shows the formation of new levels of systems based on previously established and tested information. Systems of particles are understood through information from the natural environment, resulting in subatomic information, which, in turn, is used to conceptualize atoms; systems of atoms are understood through atomic information which is used to conceptualize molecules; systems of molecules are understood through epigenetic information which is used to conceptualize learners; systems of learners are understood through artificial information which is used to conceptualize artifacts.

Although each user system (or knowledge base) can provide a foundation for creating different hierarchies of systems, the model of relationships remains the same—user systems are understood as whole systems which form a knowledge base during continuous interaction with the environment and organize an information system to maintain and employ the knowledge base. The information system is seen as establishing a common objective for interacting systems, thereby creating a user system: a new level on a hierarchy of systems.

Over the years dynamic systems have been studied by focusing on adaptation (Sampson, 1976); self-organization (Buckley, 1978; Haken, 1977), reproduction and life (Gatlin, 1972), change (Havelock, 1969, 1972), regulation and control (Ashby, 1956). The concept of a user system reflects all of these aproaches, yet is different from them. A user system is a system which survives over time through the records of an observer.

A user system is understood as a whole system which must adapt, change, self-organize, steer itself and reproduce. It does this by continuously using and producing information. A user system enables a scientist to match internal information with information about objects and experiences external to the scientist.

C. System Survival

1. Identification. The concept of a user system essentially describes the evolution of all systems which survive. System survival is not simply a question of system endurance over time and space. The question of system survival depends on system identification—and that brings the observer into the observation. A system must be identified by an observer in order to exist and survive.

As Weinberg noted:

> To have identity is to have an identifier and hence, comes the difficulty of saying when a system exists or ceases to exist (Weinberg, 1975, p. 239).

Therefore, the identification of every system requires matching an observer's program and data base (information system) with that of the user system under observation. As Weinberg explained, from the perspective of general system theory, the question of system survival depends on:

- what the environment does
- how the system's program transforms the environment

- what variables are involved in its identity
- how the observer's program operates on those variables (Weinberg, 1975, p. 245)

A holistic perspective establishes the interface between a scientist/observer and a user system (see Figure 6). From this perspective, an information system is observed organizing collected information, processing it through its memory and disseminating the transformed information to the user system. An information system represents a level of order to the user system and to the observer by organizing information from the environment in order to be useful ("meaningful") to the user and to the observer.

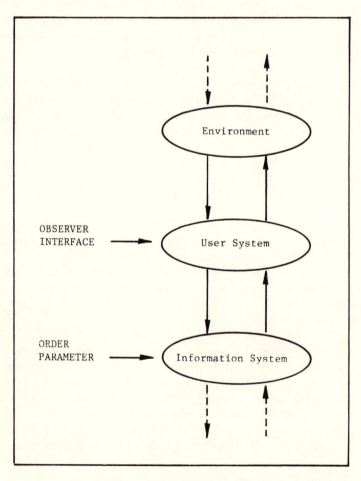

FIG. 6.   Observer's Point of View.

In human, societal contexts, information systems are generally designed, evaluated and operated on the basis of users' information needs and uses. Activities performed by an information system are linked to a user system through needs and uses. Consider, for example, the following basic set of information system functions:

- collection (selection and evaluation of information)
- organization (classification and indexing of information)
- storage (filing and shelving of information)
- retrieval (query formulation and searching for information)
- dissemination (display and transfer of information)
- generation (creation of new information, learning)

Every one of these functions involves the specification of information needs and uses. The ubiquity of information needs and uses in an information system explains why, in a computerized system, indexing and query formulation are seen as mirror images of each other (Ide and Salton, 1969; Lancaster, 1968). In a traditional library, cataloging and reference work complement each other the same way (Mooers and Brenner, 1958; Taylor, 1968), just as do dissemination and market (user) analyses for information systems of all sorts.

2. The Time Element.   Moreover, each of these functions requires agents to perform them and has information inputs and outputs of its own. Each aggregate of information agents, actions, inputs and outputs is a subsystem of the information system. Each subsystem is itself a user system and, therefore, must have an information system of its own. Although each subsystem must have a full set of information processing capabilities so as to use and produce information, it is seen performing one processing activity at a time in relation to the component subsystems of the information system. This point is critical and requires explanation.

In order to progress from the input to the output stage, all processing activities must be performed even though all may not be visible to the observer. The subsystem gets its identity from the activity that is visible. Thus, the function of each subsystem within the total information system appears to be time dependent. The time is determined by the observer of the information system. The difficulty for the observer/scientist is to match the time of observation with the exact time the system performs its function. When this match occurs, the observer achieves a synthesis. The synthesis occurs by understanding the structure and function of information at the time of the observation. Without such a synthesis, the observer/scientist cannot properly identify the system, clarify information concepts, or provide conditions for system survival. These points place significant requirements on the role of the information scientist.

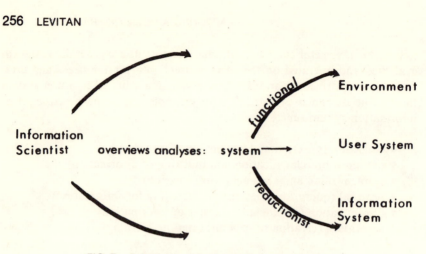

FIG. 7. Information Scientist as "Super Observer"

D. Requirements of an Information Scientist

The conduct of information science research requires a "super observer" who can transcend and synthesize the results of functional analysis, system analysis and reductionist thinking to provide an integrated perspective on the information units, processes and components of a user system.

According to general systems theory, system survival not only includes observing how a system adapts, organizes and reproduces in its environment, but also involves mapping information units, processes and systems of the scientist to those of the user system under observation. Most scientists are not aware of how they match their own "programs" and "memories" to the systems they observe. They do not put themselves into the observation. Such an activity requires transcending the whole observation so that the scientist becomes a "super observer." (Figure 7)

What methods are involved in analyzing the functions, operations, and components of the user system? Were these methods appropriate? In order to answer these questions, an information scientist must be able to integrate *what* is observed, a system surviving over time, with *how* the system is observed, through appropriate information technologies. Such integration requires the application and synthesis of the state-of-the-art of all the sciences relevant to depicting the user system in question.

IV. APPLYING THE HOLISTIC APPROACH TO PAST RESEARCH

Using a very broad brush stroke, this section presents a general picture of the information science research literature over the past 25 years. Given the ubiquity of the topic, this review is not intended to be exhaustive. It has been limited to the research cited in the *Annual Review of Information Science and Technology,* the *Journal for the American Society for Information Science* and various NSF reports (Mathtech, 1977; National Science Foundation, 1979). The examples of research in this review are included particularly because they reflect the framework of a user system interacting with its environment and with its components.

The holistic approach to information science research discussed in Section III emphasized the integration of the subject and methodology of research. The significance of such integration can be seen by applying the holistic approach to the research conducted in the 1950s, 1960s and early 1970s by the constituency associated within the science information programs at NSF. The main objective of these programs was to understand information within the context of science. On the whole, the research they supported involved studies about the use and production of information by a variety of user systems. The research required an interdisciplinary and eclectic methodology in order to characterize the different user systems under observation.

These user systems, their supporting information systems, their environments and the information technologies employed to observe them may be divided into two major themes: the development of science as a user system (the focus on what is studied); and the development of information science (the interdisciplinary methodology for studying user systems). Efforts in this area during the last quarter century provided a knowledge base for two areas of research. One area involves the study of science as a synergetic whole system and is reflected in the estabilshment of two NSF divisions; Science and Society; and Science Resources Studies. The other focuses on information science and technology as seen in the newly created division bearing that name.

A. Science as a User System

Traditionally, science has been viewed either as a body of knowledge concerning scientific methods (through studies in philosophy and history) or as a social system (through sociology). Information science research converged both perspectives in an effort to study how science as a collective whole uses and produces information. Science evolved as a user system by:

- establishing science information systems
- developing processing and communication capabilities
- maintaining, updating and reproducing the scientists' knowledge base
- steering information system agents towards cooperative interactions
- seeking direction and control from the appropriate authorities
- developing indicators of information needs and uses
- studying the above

The study of science as a user system began with a focus on the scientist as a user system. The initial efforts in the 1950s and early 1960s involved analyses of a scientists's information needs and uses as related to scientific research objectives (Allen, 1969; Allen and Gerstberger, 1967; Cuadra and Katter, 1967; Menzel, 1966; Paisley, 1968). These studies examined: a scientist's search for relevant information through informal channels (gatekeepers, colleagues) and formal channels (libraries, publications and meetings) (Allen, 1969; Crane 1972; Paisley, 1968; Utterback, 1969); collection and organization of information; application of information during the solution of a problem (Allen and Gerstberger, 1967); generation and publication of information at meetings and in journals (Garvey et al., 1970, 1972a,b; Johns Hopkins University, 1970). This type of analysis was conducted in many scientific fields and resulted in a universal pattern of information flow characteristic of the American scientist in general. (See Figure 8, steps 1-11).

Since the reviewed and tested research results were needed by all scientists, it was important to determine efficient and effective means of collecting, organizing, storing, retrieving and disseminating the information. This objective led to a focus on libraries, journals, abstracting and indexing services and computers as well as on information systems and processing. (See Figure 8, steps 12-19). The work of information system designers and implementors brought together various societal information agents into larger and more complex information systems. Efforts toward cooperation in information activities occurred repeatedly in the library field (Palmour and Roderer, 1978; Reynolds, 1972), in the publishing field (Doebler, 1970), in scientific societites (Gannett, 1973; Terrant, 1975), and across many societal sectors previously considered as unrelated, competitive or mutually exclusive (Berninger and Adkinson, 1978).

As indicated in the early attempts at networking (Miller and Tighe, 1974) and in the experiments to establish electronic editorial processing centers (Bamford, 1973a, b; Berul et al., 1974), cooperation by itself is not sufficient to make an information system work effectively. Planning, communication, direction and control must be exerted through techniques which can coordinate activities into a unified system.

The coordination of various science information agents, technologies and organizations which store, process and disseminate science information requires steering capabilities which are extremely sensitive and flexible. Such a capability is continuously evolving through the participation of numerous governments, industries and universities functioning at the administrative and managerial levels of their respective associations. Together they constitute what might be called the cybernetic system of science. While these steering capabilities have not yet been explicitly studied or clearly defined, they can be gleaned from research about information resource management (Buckland, 1974; Raffel and Shishko, 1969; Wasserman and Daniel, 1969) and from efforts to develop science information policies (see Whalen and Joyce, 1976, for a synopsis).

In spite of the emphasis on cooperation and coordination from many scientists, policy makers and societal information agents, the development of science information systems did not proceed without conflict and competition. On a much broader societal scale, research was required to understand such problems as copyright (Beard, 1974; Weil, 1975), privacy (Privacy Protection Study Commission, 1977; Westin, 1973), and accessibility (Wessel, 1976), as well as national information needs (Aines and Day, 1975). In retrospect, these studies were part of an emerging concern to develop national information policies (National Commission on Libraries and Information Services, 1976; Oettinger, 1976) as distinct from science information policies.

From studies of publications and citations, many methods were developed to characterize science as a user system. They involve the flow of scientific literature (Menard, 1971; Price, 1961, 1963), the quantification and organization of scientific literature (Garfield, 1972; King et al., 1976; Narin, 1976; Narin and Moll, 1977; Small, 1973), citation counts and patterns, publication counts and patterns, and communication networks as reflected in publications, citations and meeting attendance (Crane 1972; Crawford 1971; Johns Hopkins University, 1970). These techniques produced indicators which reflect the collective use and production of science information, and the productivity, growth and community of science.

Until the late 1960s, these indicators were used primarily to meet the internal needs of science as determined by studies of its knowledge base and social system. However, the perfection and diffusion of these methods also served to make "science" visible to its external environment. The widespread interests to apply scientific information to national objectives and various societal needs, to improve communication between scientists and citizens, and to exchange scientific information on an international basis represent science information needs and uses which are external to science; i.e., how science as a whole interacts with its environment. (See the following articles in Spiegel-Rösing and Price (1977): Lakoff (1977); McLeod (1977); Nelkin (1977); Sapolsky (1977); Sardar and Rosser–Owen (1977); Schroeder–Gudehas (1977); Skolnikoff (1977).)

Through the evolution of science as a user system, an enormous societal archive of science information has been produced with the processing and communication technologies which make these studies widely available. A new era of study is required, however, to develop information resources which can deliver scientific information to nonscientific user systems.

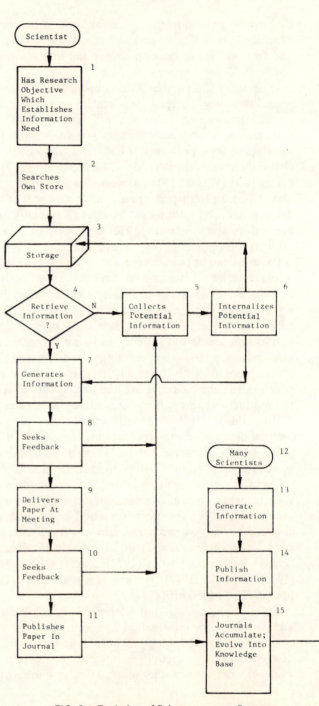

FIG. 8.   Evolution of Science as a user System

| Knowledge Base Needed By All Scientists | 16 | Social System Of Science Established | 17 | Use of Knowledge Base Becomes Common Objective For All Scientists | 18 | Synthesis of Knowledge Base And Social System Of Science Into New User System | 19 | Science | 20 |

261

B. The Eclectic, Interdisciplinary Methodology

In order to characterize science as a whole, it was necessary to create ways of "observing" science. In meeting this requirement, a holistic approach was employed to study many other systems. Figure 9 displays several prominent user systems analyzed during this period. In addition to science and the scientist, other major systems included: science as a body of knowledge, science as a social system, the library, the scientific discipline or field, the computer, the journal and professions. Each of these systems provided techniques for studying science as an information user, and together they indicate the interdisciplinary research. These systems are discussed below.

Science as a body of knowledge includes research about what is known and the methods of knowing. Historically, this area was the subject of the history and philosophy of science. In the past decade, however, studies have extended beyond epistemology, history and logic to include linguistics, semiotics, and many areas of psychology and sociology. Science as knowledge has evolved from the idea of pure "truth" to a complex system of ideas which have been tested by human societies and accumulated over time (see for example: Brown, 1977; Burks, 1963; MacLeod, 1977; Ziman, 1968).

Science a a social system involves a focus on the communication patterns of scientists, and draws upon a variety of social sciences, statistics, and applied mathematics. The main technique is to map into a network—scientists' use of formal and informal channels of information, including scientific meetings, publications, citations and even telephone calls. The network serves in understanding the reward system, the norms and behaviors of scientists (see Mulkay, 1977 for an overview). This area of study is evolving as a field which calls itself the Social Studies of Science (Society for Social Studies of Science *Newsletters* 1976 to present).

Understanding how a scientist searches, acquires, stores, processes and retrieves information evolved from a focus on user studies (see the *Annual Review of information Science & Technology* chapters on "Information Needs and Uses;" Menzel, 1966; Herner and Herner, 1967; Paisley, 1968; Allen, 1969; Lipetz, 1970; Crane, 1971; Lin and Garvey, 1972; Martyn, 1974; Crawford, 1978) to research on libraries, publications (particularly journals) and computers as users and producers of information. For example, many of the information units and processes involved in the technical and managerial functions of libraries became understood well enough to be automated, producing options for electronic library systems and interlibrary networking (see Palmour and Roderer, 1978; Reed and Vrooman, 1979). The evolution of the Institute for Scientific Communication and the publication of *Current Contents* plus the application of computer technology to publishing indicate a clear understanding of the operations and components of the journal and its

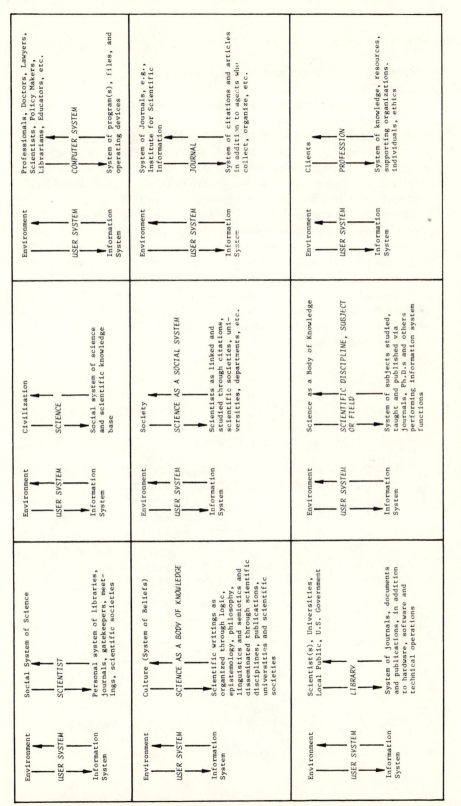

FIG. 9. Major User Systems addressed in science information studies.

relationship to its environments (see Bamford, 1973a, b; Garfield, 1977; Terrant, 1975).

Research on the subjects studied and taught at universities, discussed at scientific societies and published in journals evolved through a focus on *scientific disciplines* as user systems. This included the research objectives, results and organization of such fields as physics, chemistry, psychology, biology, biomedicine, the humanities and the behavioral sciences. In each of these areas, studies of information content, form, and flow produced insight and new techniques for handling information (Rush, 1978).

The study of science was also conducted from a perspective which concentrated on understanding various *professions*. Analyses were made of the knowledge base, resources, supporting organizations, ethics and beliefs of such professions as: medicine, education, law, engineering and management. Since its initial publication in 1966, these studies are reflected in every volume of the *Annual Review of Information Science and Technology*. This focus of research not only strengthened the individual professions but also provided many new techniques for studying information in general. Management science and operations research, for example, are prime generators of these methods.

V. CURRENT AND FUTURE RESEARCH

A. Examples of the User Systems Concept

Just as information scientists over the past 30 years have studied information in the context of the user system of science, so are other scientists studying information in the context of a wide variety of biological, chemical, physical, societal and artificial user systems. Although at the present time research on information units (content and form), systems and processes is being conducted across many sciences, this research is not consciously organized through a focus on information user systems. Examples of concepts which would easily be developed as user systems are listed below:

Administrator	Gene	Robot
Animal	Government	Satellite
Animal Society	Human Society	Science
Body	Journal	Scientific Field
Brain	Learner	Scientist
Business	Library	Species
City	Manager	State Government
Company	Nervous System	Supreme Court
Computer	Office	Treaty Nations
Congress	Organism	United Nations

Consumer	Organization	U.S. Government
Corporation	Policy-maker	Universe
Decision-maker	Profession	World
Executive Branch	Region	

Many study areas currently provide perspectives which lend themselves to the beginnings of a user system concept (see Levitan 1979, pp. 46–53 for additional areas). Some primary examples are listed below.

Animal as User System: Studies in ethology, evolutionary biology, and the behavioral sciences indicate how animals obtain and select information from their surroundings and from other animals. This work emphasizes the display of information, including mechanisms and messages of display, and characterizes behavioral and nonbehavioral information sources and properties of formalized interaction (Baerands et al., 1975; Sebeok, 1968; Smith, 1977).

Animal Society as User System: The fields of sociology and animal communications explain how animals and insects live as a society, through information and communication. Information transfer through chemical, acoustical and visual signals are analyzed with respect to the cooperative organization and functioning of the insect colony or animal society over time (Sebeok, 1968; Wilson, 1975).

Human Society as User Systems: From a focus on change had developed an eclectic field of social science which describes how societal information is produced, disseminated and used in the development of human society (Bennis et al., 1976; Havelock, 1972, 1969; Rogers and Shoemaker, 1971). These studies relate societal information needs to the generation of new products, services, and R&D, and examine the impact of information products and services on decision making.

Organism as User System: Research in the fields of developmental biology, theoretical and evolutionary biology, genetics, and morphology indicate how genetic information is translated into shapes and patterns during the developmental history of an organism. These studies link DNA and RNA to information about the position and composition of parts of the organism and describe the nature of interactions during development, as well as the information acquired during such interaction (Bryant et al., 1977; Waddington, 1968, 1972; Wolpert, 19–72).

Species as User Systems: Gould (1977) describes how phyletic information is created during the course of development of an organism, and used by the species to adapt and survive in a different environment.

Organization as User Systems: From the management sciences, business, economics and the field of organization development has come a focus on the organization and how it selects, evaluates and communicates information to learn and grow internally as a cooperative effort and to succeed externally in its interactions (Argyris, 1960; Cleland and King, 1969; Cyert and March, 1963; McGregor, 1960).

B. Requirements for Integration

In each of these interdisciplinary study areas information concepts are studied as part of a set of phenomena which also include:

- evolution—or development or irreversible time (Boulding's synthesis, 1978; Piaget, 1952; Waddington, 1969)
- systems and hierarchy—relationships among systems, open systems, cybernetic systems, general system theory (Bertalanffy, 1968; Buckley, 1978; Laszlo, 1972a; Von Foerster, 1968)
- dynamics and change—variation and variability over time (Prigogine, 1955)
- innovation—the development of new structures, systems, phenomena and their impact on a given environment (Havelock, 1969, 1972; Rogers and Shoemaker, 1971)
- "wholes"—a macro-perspective on whole systems, their collectivity, cooperative arrangements of subsystems or subelements, and the synergetic effect of the whole (Haken, 1977)

The capacity to clarify and explain these factors does not reside in any one person or any one field of science. It requires interdisciplinary research characterized by the following:

- state-of-the-art studies on particular user systems in their appropriate biological, physical, societal or artificial contexts; such work is currently in progress and needs to be identified and synthesized
- research which focuses on information units and processes across user systems; this type of research is not yet supported, but it is this type of effort that would provide an understanding of information *per se*
- studies which integrate the above

The future development of information science as an integrator of the sciences depends on the ability of its leaders and researchers to foster interdisciplinary research teams which could expand, test, refine and provide a holistic approach to information science research.

REFERENCES

Ackoff, R. L. (1958). Towards a behavioral theory of communication. *Management Science 4,* 218–234.

Aines, A. A., and Day, M. S. (1975). National planning of information services. *Annual Review of Information Science and Technology 10,* 3–42.

Allen, T. J. (1969). Information needs and uses. *Annual Review of Information Science and Technology 4,* 3–29.

Allen, T. J., and Gerstberger, P. G. (1967). "Criteria for Selection of an Information Source." Alfred P. Sloan School of Management, Massachusetts Institute of Technology, Cambridge, Massachusetts. (Working Paper No. 284–67.)

Arbib, M. A. (1972). "The Metaphorical Brian." John Wiley and Sons, New York.

Argyris, C. (1960). "Understanding Organizational Behavior." Dorsey, Homewood, Illinois.

Artandi, S. (1968). "Computers in Information Science: An Introduction." Scarecrow Press, Metuchen, New Jersey.

Artandi, S. (1975). Theories of information. In "Essays for Ralph Shaw" (N. R. Stevens, Ed.), pp. 157–169. Scarecrow Press, Metuchen, New Jersey.

Ashby, W. R. (1956). "An Introduction to Cybernetics." Chapman and Hall, London.

Auerbach, I. D. (1974). Future development in data processing. In "Information Science: Search for Identity" (A. Debons, Ed.) (Proceedings of the NATO Advanced Study Institute in Information Science, August 12–20, 1972, Champion, Pennsylvania.), pp. 371–378. Marcel Dekker, New York.

Baerends, G., Beer, C., and Manning, A. Eds. (1975). "Function and Evolution in Behaviour." Clarendon Press, Oxford, England.

Bamford, H. E., Jr. (1973a). A concept for applying computer technology to the publication of scientific journals. *Journal of the Washington Academy of Sciences 62,* 306–314.

Bamford, H. E., Jr. (1973b). The editorial processing center. *IEEE Transactions on Professional Communication PC-16* (No. 3), 82–83.

Beard, J. L. (1974). The copyright issue. *Annual Review of Information Science and Technology 9,* 381–411.

Becker, J., and Hayes, R. M. (1963). "Information Storage and Retrieval: Tools, Elements, Theories," Wiley, New York.

Belkin, N. J. (1975). Some Soviet concepts of information for information science. *Journal of the American Society for Information Science 26,* 56–64.

Belkin, N.J. (1978). Progress in documentation: Information concepts for information science. *Journal of Documentation 34,* 55–85.

Bennis, W. G., Benne, K. D., Chin, R., and Correy, K. E. (1976). "The Planning of Change." Third ed. Holt, Rinehart and Winston, New York.

Berninger, D., and Adkinson, B. W. (1978). Interaction between the public and private sectors in national information programs. *Annual Review of Information Science and Technology 13,* 3–36.

Bertalanffy, L. Von (1968). "General System Theory." George Braziller, New York.

Berul, L. H., King, D. W., and Yates, J. G. (1974). "Editorial Processing Centers: A Study to Determine Economic and Technical Feasibility." Report to the National Science Foundation, Office of Science Information Service, Washington, D.C.

Bohme, G. (1977). Models for the development of science. In "Science, Technology and Society" (I. Spiegel-Rösing and D. de S. Price, Eds.), pp. 312–351. Sage Publications, London.

Boulding, K. (1978). "Ecodynamics." Sage Publications, Beverly Hills, California.

Bourne, C. P. (1961). The historical development and present state of mechanized information retrieval systems. *American Documentaion 12* 108–110.

Brillouin, L. (1962). "Science and Information Theory." Second ed. Academic Press, New York.

Brookes, B. C. (1973). Numerical methods of bibliographic analysis. *Library Trends 22,* 18–43.

Brown, H. I. (1977). "Perception, Theory and Commitment." University of Chicago Press, Chicago, Illinois.

Bruner, J. S., Goodnow, J. J., and Austin, G. A. (1956). "A Study of Thinking." Wiley, New York.

Bryant, P. J., Bryant, S. V., and French, V. (1977). Biological regeneration and pattern formation. *Scientific American 237* (No. 1). 66–81.

Buckland, M. K. (1974). Management of libraries and information centers. *Annual Review of Information Science and Tehcnology 9,* 335–356.

Buckley, W. F., ed. (1968). "Modern Systems Research for the Behavioral Scientist." Aldine Publishing Company, Chicago, Illinois.

Burks, A. W. (1977). "Chance, Cause and Reason." University of Chicago Press, Chicago, Illinois.

Churchman, C. W. (1971). "The Design of Inquiring Systems." Basic Books, New York.

Cleland, D. I., and King, W. R. (1969). "Systems, Organizations, Analysis, Management: A Book of Readings." McGraw Hill, New York.

Crane, D. (1971). Information needs and uses. *Annual Review of information Science and Technology 6,* 3–39.

Crane, D. (1972). "Invisible Colleges: Diffusion of Knowledge in Scientific Communities." University of Chicago Press, Chicago, Illinois.

Crawford, S. (1971). Informal communication among scientists in sleep research. *Journal of the American Society for Information Science 22,* 301–310.

Crawford, S. (1978). Information needs and uses. *Annual Review of Information Science and Technology 13,* 61–81.

Cuadra, C. A., and Katter, R. V. (1967). The relevance of relevance assessment. *Proceedings of the American Documentation Institute 4,* 95–99.

Cyert, R. M., and March, J. G. (1963). "A Behavioural Theory of the Firm." Prentice Hall, Englewood Cliffs, New Jersey.

Dansey, P. (1973). A bibliometric survey of primary and secondary information science literature. *Aslib Proceedings 25,* 252–263.

Debons, A., and Montgomery, K. L. (1974). Design and evaluation of information systems. *Annual Review of Information Science and technology 9,* 25–55.

Doebler, P. D. (1970). Publication and distribution of information. *Annual Review of Information Science and Technology 5,* 223–257.

Donaldson, M. (1979). The mismatch between school and children's minds. *Human Nature 2* (No. 3), 60–67.

Donohue, J. C. (1973). "Understanding Scientific Literatures: A Bibliometric Approach." MIT Press, Cambridge, Massachusetts.

Fairthorne, R. A. (1967). The morphology of information flow. *Journal of the Association for Computing Machinery 14,* 710–719.

Foskett, A. C. (1969). "The Subject Approach to Information." Clive Bingley, London.

Gannett, E. K. (1973). Primary publications systems and services. *Annual Review of Information Science and Technology 8,* 243–275.

Garfield, E. (1972). Citation analysis as a tool in journal evaluation. *Science 178,* 471–479.

Garfield, E. (1977). "Essays of an Information Scientist." Institute for Scientific Information, Philadelphia, Pennsylvania.

Garvey, W. D., Lin, N., and Nelson, C. E. (1970). Communication in the physical and the social sciences. *Science 170,* 1166–1173.

Garvey, W. D., Lin, N., and Tomita, K. (1972a). Research studies in patterns of scientific communication: III. Information-exchange processes associated with the production of journal articles. *Information Storage and Retrieval 8,* 207–221.

Garvey, W. D., Lin, N., and Tomita, K. (1972b). Research studies in scientific communication: IV. The continuity of dissemination of information by "Productive Scientists." *Information Storage and Retrieval 8,* 265–276.

Gatlin, L. L. (1972). "Information Theory and the Living System." Columbia University Press, New York.

Gilchrest, A., and Presanis, A. (1971). Library and Information Science Abstracts: The first two years. *Aslib Proceedings 23,* 251–256.

Goldstein, S. (1973). CALL survey of library and information science periodicals. *CALL* (Current Awareness-Library Literature) *2* (No. 4). 3–13.

Gould, S. J. (1977). "Ontogeny and Phylogeny." Belknap Press, Cambridge, Massachusetts.

Haken, H. (1977). "Synergetics: An Introduction-Nonequilibrium Phase Transitions and Self-Organization in Physics, Chemistry and Biology." Springer-Verlag, Berlin.

Haken, H., and Wagner, M., eds. (1973). "Cooperative Phenomena." Springer-Verlag, New York.

Harmon, G. (1971). On the evolution of information science. *Journal of the American Society for Information Science 22*, 235–241.

Havelock, R. G. (1969). "Planning for Innovation through the Dissemination and Utilization of Knowledge." Institute for Social Research, Ann Arbor, Michigan.

Havelock, R. G. (1972). "Bibliography on Knowledge Utilization and Dissemination." Revised ed. Center for Research on Utilization of Scientific Knowledge, Ann Arbor, Michigan.

Heilprin, L. B. (Pre-publication draft). "Long Range Planning for Basic Research in Information Science: A Paradox." American Society for Information Science, Washington, D.C. (SIG Technical Publication Series.)

Heilprin, L. B. (1973). "Impact of the Cybernetic Law of Requisite Variety on a Theory of Information Science." University of Maryland Computer Science Center, College Park, Maryland (Report No. TR 236.) (ED 073 777.)

Heilprin, L. B., and Goodman, F. L. (1965). Analogy between information retrieval and education. *American Documentation 16*, 163–169.

Herner, S., and Herner, M. (1967). Information needs and uses in science and technology. *Annual Review of Information Science and Technology 2*, 1–34.

Ide, E., and Salton, G. (1969). User-controlled file organization and search. *Proceedings of the ASIS Annual Meeting 6*, 183–191.

Johns Hopkins University (1970). "The Role of the National Meeting in Scientific and Technical Communication." Vol. 1. Johns Hopkins University, Baltimore, Maryland.

Jolley, L. (1973). "The Fabric of Knowledge." Harper and Row, New York.

King, D. W., McDonald, D. D., Roderer, N. K., and Wood, B. L. (1976). "Statistical Indicators of Scientific and Technical Communication 1960–1980, Volume 1: A Summary Report." King Research, Rockville, Maryland.

Kochen, M. (1974). Views of the foundations of information science *In* "Information Science, Search for Identity" (A. Debons, Ed.), pp. 171–187. Marcel Dekker, New York.

Kuhn, A. (1974). "The Logic of Social Systems." Jossey-Bass, Washington, D.C.

Kuhn, T. S. (1977). "The Essential Tension." University of Chicago Press, Chicago, Illinois.

Lakoff, S. A. (1977). Scientists, technologists and political power. *In* "Science, Technology and Society" (I. Spiegel-Rösing and D. deS. Price, Eds.), pp. 355–391. Sage Publications, London.

Lancaster, F. W. (1968). "Information Retrieval Systems." Wiley, New York.

Laszlo, E. (1969). "System, Structure, and Experience." Gordon and Breach Science Publishers, New York.

Laszlo, E. (1972a). "The Relevance of General Systems Theory." George Braziller, New York.

Laszlo, E. (1972b). "The Systems Veiw of the World." George Braziller, New York.

Levitan, K. (1979). "A Holistic Approach for Integrating Information Science Research: A Formative Evaluation." The MITRE Corporation, McLean, Virginia.

Lin, N., and Garvey, W. D. (1972). Information needs and uses. *Annual Review of Information Science and Technology 6*, 5–37.

Lipetz, B. A. (1970). Information needs and uses. *Annual Review of Information Science and Technology 5*, 3–32.

McGregor, D. (1960). "The Human Side of Enterprise." McGraw Hill, New York.

Mackay, D. M. (1969). "Information, Mechanism and Meaning." MIT Press, Cambridge, Massachusetts.

MacLeod, R. (1977). Changing perspectives in the social history of science. *In* "Science, Technology and Society" (I. Spiegel-Rösing and D. deS.Price, Eds.), pp. 149–195. Sage Publications, London.

McLuhan, M. (1964). "Understanding Media: The Extensions of Man." McGraw-Hill, New York.

Martyn, J. (1974). Information needs and uses. *Annual Review of Information Science and Technology 8*, 3–23.

Mathtech (1977). "An Evaluation of the Science Information Activities of the National Science Foundation, 1950–1973." Report prepared under Contract No. NSF-C1023. Mathtech, Princeton, New Jersey; National Science Foundation, Washington, D.C. (PB 271 523.)

Meadow, C. T. (1973). "The Analysis of Information Systems." Second ed. Melville Publishing Company, Los Angeles, California.

Menard, H. W. (1971). "Science Growth and Change." Harvard University Press, Cambridge, Massachusetts.

Menzel, H. (1966). Information needs and uses in science and technology. *Annual Review of Information Science and Technology 1*, 41–69.

Miller, G. A. (1956). The magical number seven, plus or minus two: Some limits on our capacity for processing information. *Psychological Review 63*, 81–97.

Miller, J. G. (1978). "Living Systems." McGraw Hill, New York.

Miller, R. F., and Tighe, R. L. (1974). Library and information networks. *Annual Review of*

Mooers, C. N., and Brenner, C. W. (1958). A case history of a zatocoding information retrieval system. *In* "Punched Cards" (R. S. Casey, Ed.) Second ed., pp. 340–356. Reinhold, New York.

Mulkay, M. J. (1977). Sociology of the scientific research community. *In* "Science, Technology and Society" (I. Spiegel-Rösing and D. deS. Price, Eds.), pp. 93–148. Sage Publications, London.

Murdock, J. W., and Liston, D. M., Jr. (1967). A general model of information transfer: Theme paper 1968 Annual Convention. *American Documentation 18*, 197–208.

Narin, F. (1976). "Evaluative Bibliometrics: The Use of Publication and Citation Analysis in the Evaluation of Scientific Activity." NTIS, Springfield, Virginia. (PB 252 339.)

Narin, F., and Moll, J. K. (1977). Bibliometrics. *Annual Review of Information Science and Technology 12*, 35–58.

National Commission on Libraries and information Services. (1976). "National Information Policy." National Commission on Libraries and Information Services Washington, D.C.

National Science Foundation. Directorate for Scientific, Technological, and International Affairs. Division of Science Information. (1979). "Annotated Bibliography 1973–1977." National Science Foundation, Washington, D.C.

Nelkin, D. (1977). Technology and public policy. *In* "Science, Technology and Society" (I. Spiegel-Rösing and D. deS. Price, Eds.), pp. 393–441. Sage Publications, London.

Oettinger, A. G. (1976). "Elements of Information Resources Policy: Library and Other Information Services." Revised ed. NTIS, Springfield, Virginia. (PB 248 309.)

Otten, K. (1975). Information and communication: A conceptual model as framework for development of theories of information. *In* "Perspectives in Information" (A. Debons and W. J. Cameron, Eds.), pp. 127–148. Nordhof, Leyden, Netherlands.

Otten, K., and Debons, A. (1970). Toward a metascience of information: Informatology. *Journal of the American Association for Information Science 21*, 89–94.

Paisley, W. J. (1968). Information needs and uses. *Annual Review of Information Science and Technology 3*, 1–30.

Paisley, W. J., and Parker, E. B. (1965). Information retrieval as a receiver-controlled communication system. *In* "Proceedings of the Symposium on Education for Information Science" (L. B. Heilprin, B. E. Markuson, and F. L. Goodman, Eds.), pp. 23–31. Spartan Books, Washington, D.C.

Palmour, V. E., and Roderer, N. K. (1978). Library resource sharing through networks. *Annual Review of Information Science and Technology 13*, 147–177.

Parkman, R. (1972). "The Cybernetic Society." Pergamon Press, New York.

Pearson, C., and Slamecka, V. (Pre-publication draft). "Semiotic Foundations of Information Science: 1. A Theory of Sign Structure." American Society for Information Science, Washington, D.C. (SIG Technical Publication Series.)

Piaget, J. (1952). "The Origins of Intelligence in Children." W. W. Norton, New York.

Pope, A. (1975). Bradford's Law and the periodical literature of information science. *Journal of the American Society for Information Science 26,* 207–213.

Price, D. DeS. (1961). "Science Since Babylon." Yale University Press, New Haven, Connecticut.

Price, D. DeS. (1963). "Little Science, Big Science." Columbia University Press, New York.

Prigogine, I. (1955). "Introduction to Thermodynamics of Irreversible Processes." Charles C. Thomas, Springfield, Illinois.

Privacy Protection Study Commission (1977). "Personal Privacy in an Information Society." Government Printing Office, Washington, D.C.

Raffel, J. A., and Shishko, R. (1969). "Systematic Analysis of University Libraries: An Application of Cost-Benefit Analysis." MIT Press, Cambridge, Massachusetts.

Reed, M. J. P. and Vrooman, H. T. (1979). Library automation. *Annual Review of Information Science and Technology 14,* 193–216.

Reynolds, M. M., ed. (1972). "Reader in Library Cooperation." NCR Microcard Editions, Washington, D.C.

Rogers, E. M., and Shoemaker, F. F. (1971). "The Communication of Innovations: A Cross-Cultural Approach." Second ed. Free Press, New York.

Rush, J. E. (1978). Handling chemical structure information. *Annual Review of Information Science and Technology 13,* 209–262.

Sampson, J. R. (1976). "Adaptive Information Processing, An Introductory Survey." Springer-Verlag, New York.

Samuelson, K. (1976). General systems, cybernetics and informatics as an interdisciplinary breed. *In* "General Systems Theorizing: An Assessment and Prospects for the Future. Proceedings of the Annual North American Meeting, Boston, Massachusetts, February 18–21," pp. 2–8. Society for General Systems Research, Washington, D.C.

Sapolsky, H. M. (1977). Science, technology and military policy. *In* "Science, Technology and Society" (I. Spiegel-Rösing and D. deS. Price, Eds.), pp. 443–471. Sage Publications, London.

Saracevic, T. (1975). Relevance: A review of and a framework for the thinking on the notion in information science. *Journal of the American Society for Information Science 26,* 321–343.

Saracevic, T., and Perk, L. (1973). Ascertaining activities in a subject area through bibliometric analysis. *Journal of the American Society for Information Science 24,* 120–134.

Sardar, Z., and Rosser-Owen, D. G. (1977). Science policy and developing countries. *In* "Science, Technology and Society" (I. Spiegel-Rösing and D. deS. Price, Eds.), pp. 535–575. Sage Publications, London.

Schroeder-Gudehus, B. (1977). Science, technology and foreign policy. *In* "Science, Technology and Society" (I. Spiegel-Rösing and D. deS. Price, Eds.), pp. 473–506. Sage Publications, London.

Scientific American. (1966). (Special issue on computer processing of information.) *Scientific American 215* (No. 3), 65–260.

Sebeok, T. A., ed. (1968). "Animal Communication." Indiana University Press, Bloomington, Indiana.

Shannon, C. E., and Weaver, W. (1949). "The Mathematical Theory of Communication." University of Illinois Press, Urbana, Illinois.

Shera, J. H., and Cleveland, D. B. (1977). History and foundations of information science. *Annual Review of Information Science and Technology 12,* 249–267.

Simon, H. A. (1969). "The Sciences of the Artificial." MIT Press, Cambridge, Massachusetts.

Simon, H. A., and Newell, A. (1977). "Human Problem-Solving." Prentice Hall, Englewood Cliffs, New Jersey.

Skolnikoff, E. B. (1977). Science, technology and the international system. *In* "Science, Technology and Society" (I. Spiegel-Rösing and D. deS. Price, Eds.), pp. 507–533. Sage Publications, London.

Small, H. (1973). Co-citation in the scientific literature: A new measure of the relationship between two documents. *Journal of American Society for Information Science 24*, 265–269.

Smith, L. C. (Pre-publication draft). "Artificial Intelligence in Information Retrieval: An Overview Introduction." American Society for Information Science, Washington, D.C. (SIG Technical Publication Series.)

Smith, W., J. (1977). "The Behavior of Communicating." Harvard University Press, Cambridge, Massachusetts.

Spiegel-Rösing, I., and Price, D. deS., Eds. (1977). "Science, Technology and Society." Sage Publications, London.

Taylor, R. S. (1963). The information sciences. *Library Journal 88*, 4161–4163.

Taylor, R. S. (1966). Professional aspects of information science and technology. *Annual Review of Information Science and Technology 1*, 15–40.

Taylor, R. S. (1968). Question-negotiation and information seeking in libraries. *College & Research Libraries 29*, 178–194.

Terrant, S. W. (1975). The computer and publishing. *Annual Review of Information Science and Technology 10*, 273–302.

Thompson, F. B. (1968). The organization is the information. *American Documentation 19*, 305–308.

Utterback, J. M. (1969). "The Process of Technical Innovation in Industrial Firms." Unpublished dissertation, Massachusetts Institute of Technology.

Vickery, B. C. (1965). "On Retrieval System Theory." Second ed. Anchor Books, Hamden, Connecticut.

Vickery, B. C. (1971). Documentation description and representation. *Annual Review of Information Science and Technology 6*, 113–140.

Von Foerster, H., ed. (1968). "Purposive Systems." (Proceedings of the First Annual Symposium of the American Society for Cybernetics.) Spartan Books, New York.

Waddington, C. H., ed. (1968–1972). "Towards a Theoretical Biology." Vols. 1–4. Aldine Publishing Company, Chicago, Illinois; Edinburgh University Press, Edinburgh, Scotland.

Wasserman, P., and Daniel, E. (1969). Library and information center management. *Annual Review of Information Science and Technology 4*, 405–438.

Weik, M. H. (1969). "Standard Dictionary of Computers and Information Processing." Hayden Book Company, New York.

Weil, B. H. (1975). Copyright developments. *Annual Review of Information Science and Technology 10*, 359–382.

Weinberg, G. M. (1975). "An Introduction to General Systems Thinking." John Wiley and Sons, New York.

Weisman, H. M. (1972). "Information Systems, Services, and Centers." Becker and Hayes, New York.

Wellisch, H. (1972). From information science to informatics: A terminological investigation. *Journal of Librarianship 4*, 157–187.

Wersig, G., and Neveling, U. (1975). The phenomena of interest to information science. *Information Scientist 9*, 127–140.

Wessel, A. E. (1976). "The Social Use of Information: Ownership and Access." John Wiley and Sons, New York.

Westin, A. F. (1973). "Databanks in a Free Society." New York Times Book Company, New York.

Whalen, B. G., and Joyce, C.C., Jr. (1976). "Scientific and Technical Information: Options for National Action." The MITRE Corporation, McLean, Virginia.

Whittemore, B. J., and Yovits, M. C. (1973). A generalized conceptual development for the analysis and flow of information. *Journal of the American Society for Information Science 24*, 221–231.

Wilson, E. O. (1975). "Sociobiology." Harvard University Press, Cambridge, Massachusetts.
Wolpert, L. (1972). The concept of positional information and pattern formation. *In* "Towards a Theoretical Biology" (C. H. Waddington, Ed.), Vol. 4, pp., 83–94. Edinburgh University Press, Edinburgh, Scotland.
Ziman, J. (1968). "Public Knowledge: The Social Dimension of Science." Cambridge University Press, Cambridge, England.

8

Formative Evaluation of Children's Television as Mass Communication Research

Robert LaRose
Applied Communications Networks, Inc.
Santa Monica, California

Following the example of *Sesame Street,* formative evaluation, or decision-oriented audience research intended to improve media presentations under development (after Scriven, 1967) is becoming common in children's television programming.Now that millions of dollars have been spent for formative evaluation, it has achieved the status of one of the most active areas of research involving the mass media over the last decade. Yet the fruits of these efforts seldom find their way into the communications research literature. Conversely, theories and methods of mass communications research are perhaps too seldom incorporated in formative evaluation studies. The purpose of this review is to characterize the state of the art of formative evaluation for children's television from the perspective of mass communications theory and research. It is hoped that this will better acquaint mass media researchers with the methods and findings of formative evaluation and with some important theoretical issues implicit in such efforts. Practitioners of formative evaluation may benefit from a new perspective, hopefully one which will inspire further development of their craft.

I.   FORMATIVE EVALUATION AS MASS COMMUNICATIONS RESEARCH

In practice, formative evaluation is much more than "evaluation" in the limited sense of an assessment of the merit of educational materials against a set of objectives. The formative evaluator/researcher is invariably asked to advance hypotheses about "what works" to guide future production. While such questions can sometimes be answered—albeit at considerable expense— with a brute-force evaluative approach, the formative evaluator soon begins to search for lawful relationships that transcend specific content and which can inform creative decisions. By forming hypotheses about the appeal or likely effects of program content the formative evaluator becomes a mass communications theorist, if only at the level of theories of the "middle range."

A brief overview of the formative evaluation cycle for television will help to identify the points of contact with mainstream mass communications research. Formative evaluation often begins even before there is media to evaluate. Formative evaluators frequently participate in the conceptualization of series goals and objectives by offering their view of what is achievable through television with a particular target audience. They may also conduct needs assessments with the target audience to determine its "entry level" with respect to series objectives. Types of media content which appeal to the target audience may also be identified through consultation with television ratings or by surveying media preferences. These activities take place before the initiation of production and so fall outside the scope of this review. However, it is evident that even from the early states of program development, formative evaluators act in some respects as mass communications "theorists" by conceptualizing how television can be used to reach a specific audience with a purposive message.

Formative evaluation proper begins with the first evaluations of prototype media in the form of scripts, story outlines, story boards, or sample video segments. At this stage formative evlauation is usually most concerned with the decision to select an appealing and potentially effective format for the series as a whole. The major "ingredients" of a series—setting, characters, story premise, music, etc.—are of interest. Small samples and observational or open-ended assessment procedures are the rule here. Reactions of knowledgeable adults (e.g., teachers, parents) may also be solicited. This is very much an interative process in which a succession of creative ideas are developed, evaluated, and modified. Later, an evaluation of one of more pilots usually takes place, typically with more formal assessment procedures and including a much larger sample, often with some degree of national representation. Here, the relative appeal of alternate formats may still be of concern, but the emphasis shifts to assessing whether the intended message is understood by the target audience and whether the series may have its desired effects. Changes in the ingredients of the series and/or in specific sequences of the programs tested may be made, although they are usually on the order of fine tuning rather than sweeping revisions. As the final series comes to be, formative evaluators continue to consult with producers and writers to apply the lessons learned to the remaining episodes.

Throughout the process, the overriding goal of formative evaluation is to satisfy the practical needs of program decision makers. All research must be understandable to them and answer important questions that they have. Entire research projects must be completed in a matter of days or weeks. In the heat of the fray, the methods and theories of social science research are often put aside in deference to the pressing needs of the project. However, it is clear even from the above brief characterization that formative researchers still share the basic goals of social science: prediction and theory construction. They are repeatedly called upon to make recommendations about the likely appeal and effectiveness of television material from limited samples of people and media content and to project "real life" reactions from methods and measures in contrived viewing situations. Within their constraints, formative evaluators strive to follow careful social science research methods so as to maximize the validity of their inferences about the programs they test.

The research problems commonly addressed by formative evaluators fall roughly into three categories which parallel problems in mass communications research: testing the appeal, comprehensibility, and effects of program material. The goal of appeal testing is to select program ingredients that are attractive to the audience and which will keep them watching both within and between episodes. This goal is shared by mass communications research on attendance to the media, including the phenomena of selective exposure (Sears and Freedman, 1972) and selective attention, and by so-called "uses and gratifications research" (Blumler and Katz, 1974). The study of comprehensibility relates to information processing and hierarchy of effects notions (e.g., Lindsay and Norman, 1977; McGuire, 1973). Effects testing, including effects on knowledge, attitudes, and behavior of the audience, is also the central enterprise of "traditional" mass media effects research (e.g., Klapper, 1960; Roberts, 1972).

Given the commonalities in goals and research questions between formative evaluation and mass communications research, our point of departure will be that it behooves formative evaluators to subject their efforts to the methodological and conceptual standards of mass communications research whenever possible. At the same time, mass communications researchers would do well to look to formative evaluation for new findings and conceptual models which may challenge their assumptions. In applying a mass communications research perspective to formative evaluation, we may ask whether formative evaluators treat their research problems adequately in that light. Are the measures of key variables reliable and valid ones? Are the research problems conceptualized adequately? Given that formative evaluation strives to predict the merit of material it evaluates, the issues of concurrent, predictive and external validity of the procedures and measures used take on special importance.

In the sections that follow, each of the formative evaluation research problem areas (i.e., appeal, comprehensibility, and effects testing) will be considered in turn. An attempt will be made to characterize the goals and dominant approaches in the three areas. However, there will be no effort to catalog the methods used in every formative evaluation ever conducted for children's television. Rather, approaches that, in the opinion of the author, are the most common in each area will be referred to by their earliest or best developed examples, with reference also made to significant variations. The projects reviewed include *Sesame Street* (Palmer, 1974; Reeves, 1970; Shapiro, 1975), *Electric Company* (O'Bryan and Silverman, 1974; Rust, 1971; 1974), *Carrascolendas* (Laosa, 1974), *Rebop II* (Nelson, 1976), *Bread and Butterflies* (Flaugher and Knapp, 1974), *Self, Incorporated* (Rockman and Auh, 1976), *The Big Blue Marble* (undated), *Villa Allegre* (Bicultural Children's Television, 1973; Klein, 1975), *Vegetable Soup* (Graves and Shapiro, 1975), and *Freestyle* (LaRose, 1978; 1979; Williams, 1978). The adequacy of approaches to each problem area will be assessed, followed by suggestions for new approaches to formative evalution in each. Select issues raised by formative evaluation studies which are not found in the mass communications research literature will also be noted. Finally, the matter of the cost effectiveness of formative evaluation will be discussed.

II.   APPEAL TESTING

The purpose of appeal testing in formative evaluation is to assess whether a program can capture and maintain an audience, both within and between episodes. As described by Palmer (1974), appeal includes such viewer outcomes as visual orientation, attention, attitude (toward program content), and channel selection. Program ingredients such as characters, technical effects, music, etc. are treated as independent variables and the appeal measures are regarded as dependent variables. As a practical matter, program ingredients which consistently test out poorly on appeal measures may be dropped or modified. Those which succeed are retained or alotted greater exposure.

By far the most commonly used techniques to assess appeal are observational measures, most of which are derived from the so-called "distractor method" pioneered by the Children's Television Workshop (CTW, 1974; (Reeves, 1970). These procedures assume that when observers have their eyes on the television screen in the presence of a distracting stimulus this indicates that the program content is appealing. In the CTW version, the distraction is provided by a series of slides projected on a screen off to one side of a television set positioned in front of a single viewer. Alternatively, larger groups may be tested using the natural distractions of the classroom (Rockman and Auh, 1976). In all variations, coders observe viewers and rate the level of attention, using various ordinal coding schemes (e.g., "eyes on" vs "eyes off," "highly attentive, attentive, inattentive, distracted"). Observations are typically taken at 7.5 to 30 second intervals and then averaged across subjects to yield a "distractor curve" for the entire test program. The curves are then labelled with descriptions of program content. In more sophisticated approaches program attributes (e.g., the presence or absence of certain characters or types of action) are also coded and then related to the attention data via chi-square analysis (Rust, 1971, 1974). Reliability data available on the CTW version of this measure show it to be a reliable one, with intercoder reliabilities of 90 to 100 per cent. Laosa (1974) used a battery of observational measures, including ratings of facial expressions of mirth, verbalizations while viewing, verbal modelling, and physical modelling as well as visual attention (median intercoder reliability = 87 percent). These results were also processed into time-varying appeal curves. Eye movements within frames of a television program have also been measured using the corneal reflection method (O'Bryan & Silverman, 1974).

LaRose (1979) reported a variation of the program analyzer technique to obtain another kind of continuous rating of appeal. Groups of 100 subjects viewed test shows in an auditorium equipped with individual digital audience response stations. By moving their dials between a "happy face" (indicating interest) and a "sad face" (indicating dull program content), children were able to indicate their interest on a 100 point scale as they watched. This procedure provided a continuous interest curve similar to that resulting from the distractor method.

Others (LaRose, 1978; Nelson, 1976) used more molar measures of appeal, applied to entire program sequences or to program ingredients across sequences. Interval or ordinal level evaluative scales (e.g., ranging from "like" to "dislike," or "interesting" to "boring") were used. Williams (1978) and Nelson (1976) also employed measures of viewing intentions (e.g., "would you watch every week—yes, no, maybe, don't know"). LaRose (1979) reported choice measures in which children were asked to make hypothetical viewing decisions between the test show and popular television shows using paired comparisons. Broadcast ratings have also been used to evaluate the appeal of pilots shown on commercial television (Big Blue Marble, undated).

Open-ended interview techniques are frequently used to obtain information about aspects of the program that are especially liked or disliked. Children are asked open-ended questions in the course of individual or (focus) group interviews and their responses are then reported verbatim or coded into categories (e.g., Nelson, 1976).

All of the above techniques employ representative members of the target audience as subjects. However, the judgments of "experts" on the media preferences of the target audience (e.g., parents and teachers) are sometimes used in an effort to predict overall responses (e.g., Bicultural Children's Television, 1973; Smith, 1979) or continuous interest ratings (Becker and Wolfe, 1960).

A. On the Validity of Appeal Testing

The validity of appeal measures is most often examined in terms of concurrent validity; that is, their ability to differentiate popular and unpopular television programs already on the air. Reeves (1970) carried out validation studies of this nature for CTW's distractor method using popular television programs. Similar attempts have been made to validate program analyzer (LaRose, 1979) and global evaluation measures (LaRose, 1978) by obtaining the test measures on content assumed to be especially popular (e.g., a Bugs Bunny cartoon) or unpopular (e.g., an adult soap opera or a stock market report) with children. On their face, these results do offer some evidence of the validity of appeal measures. The Bugs Bunny cartoon soundly beat the stock market report, as expected. The distractor results seemed to compare favorably with the hierarchy of popularity obtained from perusing broadcast ratings.

However, these efforts fall far short of making definitive statements about concurrent validity. None have yielded correlational validity coefficients relating appeal measures to external criteria such as broadcast ratings or self-reports of viewing behavior. The samples of viewers and program content used were small and unrepresentative and there are undoubtedly considerable differences between both individual viewers and individual episodes. The broadcast ratings commonly available as criterion measures do not offer satisfactory breakdowns by ethnicity or age. Thus, neither the comparison data, the criterion measures, nor the methods of comparison have been at all adequate to establish concurrent validity.

The predictive validity of appeal measures, or their ability to predict viewing behaviors of ultimate interest, such as active participation while viewing or continued weekly viewing, is an important matter for formative evaluation. Without this property, appeal measures are a poor basis for making recommendations about changes in program content. Some of the observational measures of appeal may be outcomes of ultimate interest to program designers and, as such, be valid ones. For example, visual attendance during a program may be desirable in itself. It may be argued that such measures do not "need" to have their predictive validity established, particularly when they are performed in natural viewing situations (e.g., the classroom for series intended for use in school settings). The issue of predictive validity is still very much open for more obtrusive measures (e.g., the program analyzer, evaluation scales, and the like), those made in artificial viewing situations (e.g., the distractor method) or for observational measures which are meant to predict other outcomes (e.g., viewership between episodes). Unfortunately, formative evaluators have usually failed to address these issues in a rigorous manner and the results that do exist are far from persuasive.

Evidence of predictive validity was offered by Rust (1974). He attempted to predict attention scores for segments of episodes of *Electric Company* from the attention scores of a different sample of children who watched them in pilot form. Using a dichotomous rating scheme ("above average" vs. "below average"), the appeal of the segments in their final form was predictable from the pretest results 65 percent of the time. However, this was done for only 23 segments common to the final episodes and the pretest, so that this proportion is not significantly different from the chance level of 50 percent (using the standard error of the proportion).

The predictive validity of expert judgments of appeal can be assessed by comparing expert ratings with those subsequently obtained from the target audience. Teachers' estimates of children's interest in segments in script form correlated as high as .73 (Pearson r) with the "likability" ratings of a sample of children from different classrooms who viewed the same segments after they were produced (Smith, 1979). Past research (Becker and Wolfe, 1960) suggests that this success does not carry over to continuous ratings of audience interest, however.

Formative evaluation studies are also largely devoid of reference to the convergent and discriminant validity of appeal measures. Here, we expect that alternate measures of appeal will correlate highly with each other and correlate poorly with measures of other variables. For example, visual attention scores should correlate with observations of verbal or psychomotor activity, facial expressions of mirth or evaluation scales applied to the same content. Laosa (1974) calculated correlation coefficients on his battery of observational measures by collapsing across segments and using 360 individual viewers as cases. The correlations between facial expressions of mirth (i.e., observed smiling behavior) and physical modelling (.57), verbal modelling (.63) and other program-related verbalizations (.55) were high, as were the intercorrelations among the latter three. However, facial mirth did not correlate significantly with visual attention ($r = -.03$). Visual attention had significant *negative* correlations with verbal and physical modelling and other program-related verbalizations. Palmer (1978) reported that visual attention correlated .49 with learning. Palmer found in this data evidence of the validity of the visual attention method. However, since visual attention is intended to be a measure of appeal rather than of learning, this is in fact evidence to the contrary. The fact that Laosa's observations of smiling behavior correlated so poorly with visual attention also raises the question of whether the latter is a valid measure of "appeal," if we in any way mean by this an evaluative response to program content.

At this point we must begin to question whether formative evaluators have conceptualized the appeal problem satisfactorily. Perhaps their greatest failing is a tendency to lump quite distinct concepts and operational procedures together under the rubric of "appeal." For example, Palmer's (1974) model of presentational learning includes both attitudes and attention in the notion of appeal. Attempts to establish the concurrent validity of such measures further assume a relationship between an appeal measure—whether attention, attitude, or interest—and viewing behavior, as reflected in a program's popularity—broadcast ratings, in the final analysis.

However, the above are not equivalent concepts. They include psychological determinants of behavior (e.g., attitudes), information processing constructs (arousal, attention, and interest) and behavior. Mueller (1970) pointed out the fallacy of equating arousal, of which visual orientation is an indicator, and attitude. While arousal and/or visual orientation takes place in the presence of a strong attitude-arousing stimulus, the presence of a strong attitude cannot be inferred form the measurement of arousal/visual orientation. Moreover, there is no way of telling from the orientation response itself whether the related attitude is positive or negative. This means that an especially *un*appealing sequence—in the sense of "negatively evaluated" or "disliked"—may produce as much orientation/attention as an appealing one—one that is "positively evaluated" or "well-liked." Relatively strong attitude objects may also produce no visual orientation response. Although there is evidence that attitudes may predict behavior toward an attitude object (Fishbein and Ajzen, 1975)—television viewing behavior in this instance—there is no evidence that information processing variables do so. The fact that viewers consistently attend to isolated components of a show, or even that they exhibit high average attention throughout it simply does not guarantee that they will look forward to viewing future episodes. In mass communications terms, what is missing is the distinction between the phenomena of selective attention and selective exposure. By underemphasizing the latter, formative evaluation has overlooked a key outcome—the size of the audience that a program is likely to attract.

There is also some doubt that visual orientation adequately measures attention if the ultimate concern is to assure the processing of media content. Gross eye and head movements only guarantee that sensory information reaches the sense receptors. Unfortunately, the nervous system has ways of filtering sensory information (e.g., the reticular formation, cf., Lindsay and Norman, 1977) before it reaches higher brain centers where learning presumably takes place. Thus, visual orientation may be a measure of attention, but only of peripheral attention that is a poor indicator of higher-level information processing. Krugman's (1971) finding that the brain emits alpha waves, usually taken to be a sign of a relaxed nervous system, even when there is rapt attention to television leads us to question whether visual orientation is a valid criterion measure of higher order processing. It is easy to conceive of how the *lack* of visual orientation might sometimes be directly related to "attention" at higher brain centers, as when someone closes their eyes to concentrate on a vexing problem or almost-forgotten fact. The physiological basis for human information processing is not as yet completely understood, but it is evident that any single arousal measure is unlikely to be a valid measure of it, whether visual orientation, galvanic skin response, or brain waves. In short, formative evaluation has probably focused on an attention phenomenon which is too peripheral to be a useful measure of information processing.

B. Recommendations for Improving Appeal Testing

The most needed improvement in appeal testing for formative evaluation is perhaps a fundamental redefinition of the problem. What is commonly referred to simply as "appeal" in fact has at least two quite distinct components. One is the problem of assessing whether the audience is likely to tune in a program or, where there is a captive audience in the classroom, whether it will respond positively to the viewing experience. The second is the problem of evaluating whether viewers will attend to media content once they are exposed and/or become receptive to it. Formative evaluations typically dwell upon the latter problem at the expense of the former. The distractor method and other observational procedures for measuring attention are probably inadequate as measures of "appeal" of the first kind. Other methods for assessing the potential viewership of television programs must be developed. Evaluations of entire episodes or specific program ingredients now in use may help to predict viewing behavior and are first steps in the right direction. Formative evaluators already tend to conceptualize programs as "bundles of attributes." A logical next step would be to call upon so-called "additive" attitude models (e.g., Carlson, 1956; Fishbein and Ajzen, 1975; Nielsen, 1974) to better define attitudes toward media content which may predict viewing behavior.

Attitudes in themselves do not always predict behavior and viewing behavior is probably no exception. However, Fishbein and Ajzen (1975) have found that by also assessing perceived social norms relative to a behavior (in this case, significant others' likely reactions to program content as anticipated by viewers), such predictions can be greatly improved. Williams et al. (1979) provided a limited demonstration of the utility of this variable. They found that children's perceptions of the likely reactions of important others to a character were important predictors of the children's own reactions. This approach could also solve a major methodological problem in establishing the predictive validity of appeal measures: that of measuring actual viewing behavior. Fishbein and Ajzen argue that behavioral intentions are satisfactory criterion measures in lieu of actual observations of behavior.

Individual variables already identified as possible determinants of selective exposure—education and social class, utility of information and prior exposure history (Sears and Freedman, 1972)—also merit attention in the development of a model of viewing behavior. The "uses and gratifications" approach (e.g., Blumler and Katz, 1974) is another fertile source of ideas. It might be useful to test (and program selectively to) segments of the audience that come to television to satisfy differing needs or which use the medium for different purposes.

While visual orientation observations have some face validity as attention measures, further evolution may be needed. It would be useful to know how different attention measures relate to each other and to other variables of ultimate interest, such as higher level information processing or learning. Given the peripheral nature of the visual orientation phenomenon, attention measures which involve overt responses (and, likely, higher brain centers), such as the program analyzer or observed verbal and motoric responses while viewing, may be more satisfactory.

There are also the practical problems of interpreting individual and absolute differences in visual attention. Laosa (1974), for example, found inexplicable significant differences between the attention scores of different ethnic groups. At a minimum, the creation of norms for visual attention scores pertaining to different groups of viewers and types of content is imperative. Better, such scores should be compared with other criteria for information processing, such as higher brain activity.

While observing certain conceptual difficulties in appeal measurement from the perspective of mass communications research, we should also note at least one major contribution of formative evaluators: concern with message variables as determinants of viewing behavior. In contrast, communications researchers have lately tended to dwell upon receiver (e.g, uses and gratifications) and channel variables. The program attribute model implicit in most appeal testing reopens a relatively neglected approach to investigating attendance to the media. Moreover, this is an avenue of exploration which can lead mass communications research back into contact with producers and policy makes in mass media institutions instead of away from them, as is now too often the case.

III.   COMPREHENSIBILITY TESTING

Returning to Palmer's (1974) model of presentational learning, comprehensibility testing entails assessing whether viewers extract and interpret information as intended. From our perspective we can already see an overlap between this endeavor and attention testing as described above. Both may be regarded as checks on whether information processing is taking place, with "comprehensibility" perhaps referring to the higher level processing than "appeal," at least when the latter is assessed by visual attention measures.

Procedures for assessing comprehensibility range from highly structured, closed-ended questions to open-ended elicitations of recall of plot points or interpretations of their meaning. Multiple choice questions probing understanding of key story points are perhaps most common (e.g., Flaugher and Knapp, 1974; Nelson, 1976). Questions may test the ability of the audience to make simple identifications, recall of the sequence of events, or interpret the motivations of characters or events. In so-called "objective comprehension" items (LaRose, 1978), children were asked to interpret he "point" of a sequence by selecting the desired objective from statements of other (untreated) project goals. Questions are typically asked after the show is over, but in one variation (Palmer, 1974) the action is stopped at the crucial point and the question is posed immediately. Other approaches (e.g., Rockman and Auh, 1976) do not offer structured alternatives; open-ended answers are content analyzed or reported verbatim. Other methods include having viewers give a running account of the action during a second or third showing in which the sound track is removed, having them role-play the scenes (Palmer, 1974) or observing their spontaneous verbal and behavioral responses during (Laosa, 1974) or after (Rockman and Auh, 1976) viewing. Ratings of character perceptions using semantic differential-type (Rockman and Auh, 1976) or unipolar (LaRose, 1979) scales may also be viewed as comprehensibility measures testing understanding of the motivations and personal qualities of television characters.

A. On the Validity of Comprehensibility Testing

To the extent that an understanding of the events in a program and the reasons behind them are themselves desirable outcomes, the above all have some degree of face validity as comprehensibility measures. However, if the goal is to predict the relative or absolute comprehensibility of program materials so that judgments about whether to cut, retain, or change program sequences can be made, then many of the measures currently in use are seriously flawed. Closed-ended comprehension questions that are specific to program content do not allow a relative comparison between materials unless the items are carefully constructed to be of equal difficulty. Even when attempts are made to equilibrate item difficulty, as by removing alternatives that draw off excessive numbers of wrong answers (Williams, 1978), there is no assurance that the items adequately sample media content—particularly when only one item is used. Thus, we cannot be sure that they provide an absolute measure of a child's comprehension of a sequence. If care is taken via pretesting or the use of expert judgment to identify the most salient points in each program *as they are likely to be perceived by children* then this objection may be overcome. Open-ended procedures are free of these problems, but such results are seldom treated in a way that yield statistics for making comparisons between sequences.

Other issues relating to the validity of comprehensibility measures have not been addressed in formative evaluations and will only be raised here. Do verbal measures "really" measure understanding of a visual medium? How do measures of different aspects of comprehensibility (e.g., recall, comprehension, character perception) relate to one another? Do comprehensibility measures have predictive validity for other information processing variables such as learning? Do character perceptions predict overall responses to characters?

B. Recommendations on Comprehensibility Testing

A conceptual framework borrowed from mass communications research may be of some value in re-directing formative evaluation testing of comprehensibility; namely, the concept of hierarchy of effect. McGuire

(1973), describes six steps in achieving a change in behavior: presentation, attention, comprehension, yielding, retention, and action. Attention, comprehension, and retention can all be encompassed by the notion of comprehensibility; yielding and action are subsumed by effects testing and presentation is included in the selective exposure problem.

The various observational measures of attention along with simple identification items may be categorized as attention measures. Multiple-choice and open-ended questions assessing the recall of key plot points or interpretations of the reasons behind events correspond to comprehension measures. Retention measures, or efforts to determine whether viewers remember important parts of the message over time, are not to be found in short-term formative research studies. We have already seen that presentation is inadequately measured in formative evaluation. We will shortly raise similar challenges to measures of yielding and action as well. Thus, no formative evaluation to date has considered all of the steps in the hierarchy in depth. While each step is a prerequisite for the succeeding step, there need be no relationship between steps in the hierarchy. Attention does not "guarantee" comprehension, comprehension does not always entail yielding and so on. Indeed, McGuire (1973) describes circumstances under which inverse relationships may exist between steps in the hierarchy. Thus, by leaving stages in the hierarchy of effect unsampled, formative evaluators run the risk of reaching erroneous conclusions about the value of the materials they test. In practice, it would probably be impractical to evaluate all steps in the hierarchy for each and every television sequence. However, some attempt should be made to sample each of the steps for the most important goals of a series.

Development of unaided or aided recall measures which yield numerical results is desirable as a potential means of providing relative assessments of merit between sequences. In commercial advertising, such measures (e.g., the Burke Advertising Day After Recall measure) have proved to be quite useful means of comparing media content once a systematic procedure and norms are established.

Due to their ease of administration and familiarity to children, multiple choice comprehension measures will undoubtedly continue to be a favored mode of assessing comprehensibility. However, it would be wise to submit the items to pretesting to remove alternatives which draw off disproportional shares of "wrong" answers. Better, it might be advisable to pretest the *programs* so that key points of understanding in the eyes of the target audience could be identified for inclusion in closed-ended multiple choice items.

Once again, we should also recognize some potential contributions of formative evaluation to mass communications research. Although imperfect, efforts to assess outcomes within a variety of steps in the hierarchy of effect have been quite extensive. Here is a body of findings which may shed light on relatively poorly understood relationships between steps in the hierarchy of effect and in human information processing.

IV. EFFECTS TESTING

A third problem area often addressed by formative evaluations is one which receives wide attention in the mass communications literature—the problem of inducing mass media effects among audience members. In formative evaluation studies, effects testing simply establishes whether the program material in question is having the prosocial effects intended by program developers. Thus, the effectiveness of program content is commonly tested against the stated goals and objectives of the series in question, which are sometimes written as proper (i.e., specific and measurable) educational objectives. Other common concerns of mass media effects researchers such as incidental learning, unintended or antisocial effects receive little attention. However, a broad range of behavioral outcomes which may support the ultimate series goals, described by Palmer (1974) as the activity-eliciting potential of television, are of interest. These include attitude change in support of changes in behavior, active viewer participation in support of cognitive outcomes, and so on.

The measures used in effects testing are as diverse as the objectives of the series themselves. They range in complexity from short-term cognitive outcomes such as the basic reading and numerical skills of *Sesame Street* to long-range affective and behavioral outcomes like reducing the effects of sex-role stereotyping on career awareness in *Freestyle*. A full assessment of the adequacy of these measures would require a review of the many literatures from which they are drawn and is beyond our scope. We can only characterize the measures and procedures commonly in use.

Effects studies commonly rely on familiar verbal measures such as attitude scales and achievement tests. However, the severe time pressures of formative research do not usually permit careful construction of these measures. Cognitive measures seldom meet the requirements of criterion-referenced tests, thus offering a tenuous basis for assessing the absolute or relative effectiveness of program content. At best, formative evaluators try to imbue cognitive measures with face validity in terms of the educational goals of the series (Reeves, 1970). However, with the possible exception of the Educational Testing Service battery used by Klein (1975) there is little evidence of careful pretesting or item analysis.

Much the same criticism holds for attitude measures. There is no example of attitude scaling as it is idealized in communications research. Attitude measures are often single items or at best unrefined multiple-item scales.

Approximations of Likert-type, semantic differential-type, and Gutman scales (LaRose, 1978, 1979) can be found, but with corrupted item formats and no effort to carry out recommended statistical refinements on the items. Williams (1978) treated a set of attitudinal measures to factor analysis but failed to create a composite scale from them in reporting his results. Thus, the reliability and validity of attitudes measures used in the formative evaluations of children's television are suspect.

There are a few noteworthy instances of unobtrusive behavioral measures such as counting pen-pal applications sent into the *Big Blue Marble* (undated). Structured observations of verbalizations and psychomotor activities while viewing (e.g., Laosa, 1974) or in discussions immediately following (Rockman and Auh, 1976) also qualify as valid behavioral measures to the extent that such behaviors are themselves deemed desirable effects of the series. Modelling of activities portrayed on screen has also been measured via structured observation (Laosa, 1974). An intersting behavioral measure was reported by LaRose (1979). This was a verbal measure, dubbed a "modelling intention" in which viewers were asked to indicate on a five-point agree-disagree scale whether they would like to perform an activity in the same way as the on-screen model. Another measure of behavioral intentions is Nelson's (1975) social distance scale, consisting of stated intentions to engage in various social behaviors toward the show's characters and other children like them (e.g., "Would you like to go to school with [the character or other children from the same ethnic group]; be on a team with X; invite X to your home?"). Observational measures of behavior win high marks for being unobtrusive and hence unreactive experimental procedures. However, as Fishbein and Ajzen (1975) point out, valid behavioral measures should be scaled just as attitude measures are. Observational measures are suspect because they are, by analogy, single item measures which are probably unreliable and do not sample the domain of the target behaviors. Multiple item behavioral measures can overcome this objection if treated by acceptable scaling procedures like factor analysis.

Turning to the experimental designs used in formative evaluation effects studies, the one-group pretest-posttest (LaRose, 1978; Reeves, 1970; Shapiro, 1975) and pretest-posttest control group designs (Flaugher and Knapp, 1974; Reeves, 1970) are adequate protection for internal validity, at least in the situations in which they are most often used. The one-group pretest-posttest design commonly used in the early stages of formative evaluation are vulnerable to the time-related effects of history and maturation. However, the interval between pretest and posttest is frequently short and the environment is controlled so that these are not major threats. For the same reason, testing effects, or the effect on the posttest score of taking the pretest, are a potential threat. This is particularly true when the same measures are repeated (as in Shapiro, 1975). In later stages of formative evaluation, which may have longer latencies between pretest and posttests to allow for the viewing of multiple pilots (e.g., Reeves, 1970), time related effects are of concern. The addition of a control group (Flaugher and Knapp, 1974; Reeves, 1970) eliminates this threat and those of testing and instrumentation as well. Attitudinal (Williams, 1978) or behavioral measures (Big Blue Marble, undated; Nelson, 1976) incorporated in a one-group, posttest only design serve no purpose since it is impossible to trace effects to the experimental treatment with such designs.

The picture for external validity, or generalizabiity, of formative research of effects is not as rosy. When pretests are administered in a school setting and identified with the program in question, they may sensitize respondents to the kinds of content to "watch out for" as they view. Multiple treatment interference poses a problem to those studies whch evaluate multiple pilots (e.g., Reeves, 1970) or multiple bits within a program. Only Williams, (1978) addressed this difficulty by counterbalancing presentation order between evaluation sites. The fact that formative research frequently takes place in laboratory (e.g., Reeves, 1970) or classroom settings (e.g., Rockman and Auh, 1976) poses problems of generalizability to other settings, notably viewing in the home. Repeated attempts to include home viewing conditions in formative evaluation studies (e.g., Reeves, 1970; Williams, 1978) have met with failure.

A. Toward a Revised Media Effects Model

We can see that on a conceptual level formative evaluators are concerned with the induction of what are known are primary media effects—direct effects of mass media interventions on audience cognition, attitude, and behavior. As such they "throw down the gauntlet" before the most hallowed precept of mass media effects research; namely, that the mass media have no—or, at best, very limited—effects (cf., Klapper, 1960; Roberts, 1972). At first glance, this may seem a naive challenge. After all, mass communications research has long since been able to "explain away" the occurrence of mass media effects found in experiments such as the ones formative evaluators typically conduct, effects which inevitably disappear in survey studies in the "real world" (Hovland, 1972). The reasons are well known: Experimental studies do not have to contend with the selective viewing processes—selective exposure, selective attention, selective perception, selective retention. Experimental research uses highly credible sources employing specially contrived arguments to bring about immediate effects on attitudes about issues that have low involvement for their audiences. In contrast, real world persuasion campaigns (such as political campaigns) include a mix of information sources with varying levels of credibility and conflicting messages about topics of high salience to the audience, all of which retard the kind of effects that are so easily produced experimentally. Perhaps most importantly, experimental subjects are removed from the web of everyday experiences, social relationships, and behavioral norms which seem to sharply attentuate primary media effects.

In response, it should be noted that projects employing formative research are deliberate attempts to "engineer" television to extend the successes of the laboratory to the real world. We have already seen how the goal of appeal testing is to overcome the problems of selective attention and selective exposure. Comprehensibility and effects testing seeks to uncover presentation strategies which have maximum audience impact. The strategies are then incorporated into continuing and internally consistent message "campaigns" ranging anywhere from several months to several years in length. Social networks in the audience are actively enlisted in the cause of change. This is done through the creation of support materials like parent and teacher guides (Filep et al., 1971; LaRose, 1978). One project (LaRose, 1979) even tackled behavioral norms by attempting to alter them through message content, rather than adopting the common view that such norms only act as barriers to media effects.

Implicit in these projects is a model of powerful mass media which, when wedded to multifaceted intervention strategies which tap nonmediated sources of social influence, are capable of causing changes in the cognitions, attitudes, and behavior of the audience. This implicit model is akin to diffusion of innovation research in its assumptions (Rogers and Shoemaker, 1971). It goes beyond the latter paradigm by according the mass media a central, rather than a peripheral, role in initiating, coordinating, and maintaining social change. In the formative evaluation "model" the media are treated as a hub around which support activities are focused. To date, the success of programs subjected to formative evaluation is not well established nor, as we have seen, even adequately measured or conceptualized. In fact, most formative evaluators stop short of testing effects, perhaps mindful of the pessimism of mass communications research in this matter. Still, formative research offers the following challenge to twenty years of communications research which as led the field away from the consideration of primary media effects: *The reason the mass media have little effect is because their messages are poorly designed. Careful engineering of mass media content, coupled with multifaceted intervention strategies which enlist other sources of social infuence, can produce primary media effects.* Lest this be dismissed as wishful thinking, we note in passing that it parallels the challenge to the conventional wisdom about media effects made by Fishbein and Ajzen (1975). These authors assert that a great many of the inconsistencies and null findings in persuasion studies are attributable to the failure to manipulate important message variables which may impact attitudes and social norms.

B. Recommendations for Improving Effects Testing

Before this claim can be evaluated, some changes in effects testing are in order. Overall, formative evaluators should devote more effort to effects testing. Recalling that the measurement of one step in the hierarchy of effect may not predict success at succeeding steps, assessment of "enroute" outcomes such as attention and comprehension are wholly inadequate tests of whether a television series is capable of achieving its ultimate goals. Testing for immediate effects on attitudes and behaviors will not assure long-term success in achieving such outcomes, but would likely be a better predictor of success than "stopping short" after proceeding to the comprehension step in the hierarchy of effect. Better item development procedures, including attitude and behavior scaling, are needed. Scaling, even if done after results are rushed to creative decision makers, would help to adapt formative evaluation data bases to explore media effects. When multiple shows are tested, presentation order should be counterbalanced between subsets of the sample. Evaluations in which there are long latencies between pretest and posttest should include an unexposed control group. Closer liason between so-called "summative" and formative evaluation would help to answer questions about cumulative effects and the retention of short-term outcomes found in laboratory settings.

Above all, formative evaluators should now begin to explicate their hitherto implicit media effects model describing the transmission of social influence through television-centered interventions. As a first step, attention should be given to classes of mass communications concepts which have proven to be important determinants of media effects. These include source credibility, source attractiveness, counterarguing, source-receiver discrepancy, and presentation order (cf., McGuire, 1973). Ultimately, a fresh conceptualization of the persuasion process is needed, describing the transmission of parallel influence through mass media and interpersonal channels in dynamic social systems.

V.   COST EFFECTIVENESS OF FORMATIVE EVALUATION

At the outset we noted that millions have been spent on formative evaluation in the last decade, an amount which may approach or even exceed the amount invested in "theoretical" mass communications research in that period. We can now ask whether this investment has been worthwhile; is formative evaluation "cost effective?" Despite its applied nature and the conceptual and methodological shortcomings alluded to above, formative evaluation may have considerable value as mass communications research in its own right. As we have seen, it sheds new light on some of the seminal problems in the field. The efforts of formative evaluators have been at the forefront of applying mass communications research to achieving such pressing social goals as reducing racial, economic, and sexual inequality. From the point of view of society, formative evaluation might even be regarded to be what makes mass communications research a worthwhile social investment.

The cost effectiveness, or average cost per unit output (Levin, 1975), of formative evaluations may be assessed more formally as a component of the overall cost-effectiveness of the educational programs of which they are part. For these purposes, formative evaluation may be included in production costs (Jamison et al., 1978). However, it is extremely difficult to quantify educational outcomes and to parcel them out to isolated aspects of the production process. For example, a likely outcome of an evaluation of a television series using formative evaluation might be that there was a (statistically) significant treatment difference between an experimental and a control group. This is no help at all in cost-effectiveness calculations since we need to estimate, at a minimum, how many used the series and, hopefully, how many were affected by it. A large-scale field experiment or survey study employing a national random sample would be needed to help answer the "how many" question. We would attempt to estimate cost effectiveness on a "per exposure" basis and compare this with other modes of delivery, setting aside for a moment the matter of how many receiving the message were actually affected by it. In such an analysis formative evaluation would invariably be an extra production cost that would always detract from the cost effectiveness of the overall television approach. We would need additional experimentation to tease out the cost-effectiveness of formative evaluation apart from that of the larger project. The problems of evaluating formative evaluation in this manner are discussed by Baker and Alkin (1973). To answer this question, one would need parallel television series, some with formative evaluation, some without, some using one set of measures, some using other sets. The cost of such an evaluation would obviously be prohibitive. Even then, there would still be the problem of tracing measurable effects to quantifiable and economically meaningful behavioral outcomes. This last is a problem that is perhaps beyond the grasp of behavioral science at present. To this state of ambiguity we must add a note of pessimism: it appears that educational television is not in itself a cost effective proposition when compared with other modes of instruction (Carnoy, 1975)—whether or not formative evaluation is carried out. Still, we may wonder if formative evaluation is worthwhile once an initial decision is made to "go with" television.

Lacking credible measures of program outcomes, it would still be possible to estimate the cost effectiveness for formative evaluation using Bayesian techniques. Myers and Samli (1969) reported a model of this kind to estimate the cost utility of marketing research. At the core of the model is the notion of opportunity loss—either the loss from failing to reach the break even point on the introduction of a new product or the potential loss from failing to introduce it. The opportunity loss is calculated from decision-makers' subjective probability estimates of different outcomes of a marketing campaign multiplied by their monetary value (e.g., "I have a 10 percent probability of losing one million dollars, a 50 percent chance of breaking even, a ten percent chance of making two million"). The cost of various research projects is then balanced against the product of the conditional probability that each project will yield accurate predictions at each level of loss or gain times the maximum reasearch benefit (equal to the sum of all of the opportunity losses). In this way, the cost utility of different levels of research effort can be assessed. It might also be possible to estimate monetary benefits of purposive television series to society in such terms as lifetime earnings of viewers (cf. Yin, 1973). However, such estimates perforce rely on the knowledge of an unknown; namely, how much effect can television have on behavior compared to other media and all the other influences on behavior? As Comstock (1979) points out, this matter of "how much effect," as opposed to the simpler question of "is there an efffect," is one of the unresovled issues of mass communications research. Thus, only after more experience is gained with television-based interventions of the type reviewed here will it become possible to make some educated guesses about the cost effectiveness of formative evaluation.

VI. CONCLUSION

Children's television projects using formative evaluation offer a worthy challenge to the limited effects model that dominates thinking about mass media impact. Formative evaluation suggests new content variables and message strategies which take advantage of social influence in mass media audiences and which deserve attention from mass communications theorists. The attribute model of appeal implicit in formative evaluation constitutes a fresh departure from the uses and gratifications paradigm that dominates thinking about why people attend to the mass media.

In turn, greater contact with mass communications research paradigms can improve formative evaluation. Formative evaluators could especially benefit from making clearer distinctions between levels in the hierarchy of effect, especially by separating the problem of selective exposure from that of selective attention. Better conceptualizations of the attention phenomenon which include higher-order information processing variables are also needed. Beyond question, the continued use of visual orientation as a primary means of assessing program appeal deserves careful review. Procedures for scaling attitudes and other outcome measures which are recommended practices in communications research should also become the standard for formative research. There should also be better utilization of the various conceptual frameworks of media effects that are available from mass communications research.

In sum, formative evaluation studies deserve recognition as an addition to the corpus of mass communications research. Far from being "merely" applied research, formative evaluation on children's television programing poses some far-reaching alternatives to models which have held sway in mass communications research for many years. At the same time, it is clear that mass communications research paradigms suggest some methodological and conceptual changes that could vastly improve formative research. It is hoped that contact between the two will increase and that this article will play some small role in bringing that to pass.

REFERENCES

Baker, E. L., and Aikin, M. C. (1973). Formative evaluation of instructional development. *Audio-Visual Communication Review 21,* 389–418.

Becker, S. L., and Wolfe, G. J. (1960). Can adults predict children's interest in a television program. *In* "The Impact of Educational Television" (W. Schramm, Ed.), pp. 214–226. University of Illinois Press, Urbana, Illinois.

Bicultural Children's Television (1973). "A Summary of the Formative Research on Pilot Shows 02 and 03." Bicultural Children's Television, Oakland, California.

"Big Blue Marble. A Summary of Research Background of the New Television Series 'Big Blue Marble'" (Undated). Big Blue Marble Information Center, New York.

Blumler, J. G., and Katz, E. (1974). "Uses of Mass Communications." Sage Publications, Beverly Hills, California.

Carlson, E. R. (1956). Psychological satisfaction and interest in news. *Journalism Quarterly 37,* 547–551.

Carnoy, M. (1975). The economic costs and returns to educational television. *Economic Development and Cultural Change 23,* 207–248.

Children's Television Workshop (1974). "Reviews of In-House Research on Sesame Street Target Children's Attention to Four Categories of Affect Segments." Children's Television Workshop, New York.

Filep, R., Millar, G., and Gillette, P. (1971). "The Sesame Mother Project." Institute for Educational Development, El Segundo, California. (ERIC No. PS 005 198.)

Fishbein, M., and Ajzen, I. (1975). "Belief, Attitude, Intention and Behavior." Addison–Wesley, Reading, Massachusetts.

Flaugher, R. I., and Knapp, J. (1974). "Report on Evaluation Activities of the Bread and Butterflies Project." Educational Testing Services, Princeton, New Jersey.

Graves, S., and Nelson–Shapiro, B. (1975). "Formative Research on Vegetable Soup." University of Massachusetts, Amherst, Massachusetts.

Hovland, C. I. (1972). Reconciling conflicting results derived from experimental and survey studies of attitude change. *In* "The Process and Effects of Mass Communications" (W. Schramm and D. F. Roberts, Eds.), pp. 495–515. University of Illinois Press, Urbana, Illinois.

Jamison, D. T., Klees, S. J., and Wells, S. J. (1978). "The Costs of Educational Media." Sage Publications, Beverly Hills, California.

Klapper, J. T. (1960). "The Effects of Mass Communication." The Free Press, Glencoe, Illinois.

Klein, S. P. (1975). "A Program Evaluation of Four Bilingual Children's Television Shows." (Paper read for the American Educational Research Association.) (ED 109 260.)

Krugmen, H. E. (1971). Brain wave measures of media involvement. *Journal of Advertising Research 11*, 3–9.

Laosa, L. B. (1974). "Carrascolendas: A Formative Evaluation." University of California, Los Angeles, Los Angeles, California. (ED 090 968.)

LaRose, R. (1978). "Project Freestyle: Baseline Studies." University of Southern California, Los Angeles, California. (ED 157 107.)

LaRose, R. (1979). "Final Report on Formative Evaluation of Freestyle." University of Southern California, Los Angeles, California.

Levin, H. M. (1975). Cost effectiveness analysis in evaluation research. *In* "Handbook of Evaluation Research" (M. Guttentag and E. L. Struening, Eds.), pp. 89–122. Sage Publications, Beverly Hills, California.

Lindsay, P. H., and Norman, D. A. (1977). "Human Information Processing." Academic Press, New York.

McGuire, W. J. (1973). Persuasion, resistance, and attitude change. *In* "Handbook of Communication" (I. De Sola Pool, Ed.), pp. 216–252. Rand McNally, Chicago, Illinois.

Mueller, D. J. (1970). Physiological techniques of attitude measurement. *In* "Attitude Measurement" (G. Summers, Ed.), pp. 534–554. Rand McNally, Chicago, Illinois.

Myers, J. H., and Samli, A. C. (1969). Management control of marketing research. *Journal of Marketing Research 6*, 267–277.

Nelson, B. (1976). "Formative Evaluation of the Rebop II Pilot." Abt Associates, Cambridge, Massachusetts.

Nielsen, R. P. (1974). A generalized attitude model for TV programs. *Journal of Broadcasting 18*, 153–160.

O'Bryan, K., and Silverman, H. (1974). "Experimental Program Eye Movement Study." Children's Television Workshop. New York. (ED 126 870.)

Palmer, E. L. (1974). Formative research in the production of television for children. *In* "Media and Symbols: The Forms of Expression, Communication and Education" (D. R. Olson, Ed.), pp. 303–329. University of Chicago Press, Chicago, Illinois.

Palmer, E. L. (1978). International adaptations of 'Sesame Street.' *Intermedia 6* (No. 6), 19–23.

Reeves, B. F. (1970). "The First Year of Sesame Street: The Formative Research." Children's Television Workshop, New York. (ED 122 823.)

Roberts, D. F. (1972). The nature of communications effects. *In* "The Process and Effects of Mass Communications" (W. Schramm and D. F. Roberts, Eds.), pp. 347–388. University of Illinois Press, Urbana, Illinois.

Rockman, S., and Auh, T. (1976). "Formative Evaluation of Self Incorporated Programs." Agency for Instructional Television, Bloomington, Indiana. (ED 119 712.)

Rogers, E., and Shoemaker, F. (1971). "Communication of Innovations.' Free Press, New York.

Rust, L. W. (1971). "Attributes of the Electric Company Pilot Shows that Produced High and Low Attention in 2nd and 3rd Graders." Children's Television Workshop, New York. (ED 126 872.)

Rust, L. W. (1974). "Visual Attention to Material in the Electric Company: Summary of Attribute Research." Children's Television Workshop, New York. (ED 122 813.)

Scriven, M. (1967). The methodology of evaluation. *In* "Perspectives of Curriculum Evaluation" (R. W. Tyler, R. M. Gagne, and M. Scriven, Eds.), pp. 39–83. Rand McNally, Chicago, Illinois.

Sears, D. O., and Freedman, M. (1972). Selective exposure to information: A critical review. *In* "The Process and Effects of Mass Communications" (W. Schramm and D. F. Roberts, eds.), pp. 209–234. University of Illinois Press, Urbana, Illinois.

Shapiro, B. N. (1975). "Comprehension of Television Programming Designed to Encourage Socially Valued Behavior in Children: Formative Evaluation Research on Sesame Street Programming with Social and Affective Goals." Children's Television Workshop. (ED 122 863.)

Smith, K. (1978). The utilization of teacher feedback in ETV development. *Educational Technology 18,* (Oct.), 49–51.

Williams, F. (1978). "Project Freestyle: National Sites Results." University of Southern California. (ED 157 104.)

Williams, F., LaRose, R., and Frost, F. (1979). "Children, Television and Sex-Role Stereotyping." University of California, Los Angeles, California (in press).

Yin, R. K. (1973). "The Workshop and the World: Toward an Assessment of the Children's Television Workshop." RAND Corporation, Santa Monica, California. (ED 086 722.)

9

American Television Drama—
Men, Women, Sex, and Love

Mildred H. Downing
School of Library Science
University of North Carolina at Chapel Hill

I. INTRODUCTION

The symbolic world of television drama in the late 1970's depicted a society of powerful, unmarried white males, leading a constituency of provocative women, subordinate black men, and ineffective aging persons. It was a society wherein sex had replaced violence as a dramatic vehicle for demonstrating the exercise of power. It will be the purpose of this review to examine the nature of the reality that television, an ubiquitous educator, presented to the American public as the eighth decade of the twentieth century drew to a close.

"Television drama," as defined in this paper, includes all daytime and prime time drama written specifically for television broadcasting, but excludes motion pictures originally produced for theatre audiences, and later telecast.[1] Situation comedy will be dealt with, as will those full-length feature films which were produced especially for television broadcasting. Excluded are advertisements and game shows, not because their messages are insignificant, but because they are outside the scope of this paper and deserve separate consideration. Emphasis will be on the portrayals of men, women, love, and sex. Findings from such diverse fields as medicine, sociology, communications, education, and popular news will be examined, with some emphasis on recency of publication. The image of men, women, and love being purveyed on American television drama has implications for the psychiatrist as well as for the educator. Further, the investigator cannot divorce a study of fictional representation of men, women, and love from an examination of many of the themes also portrayed in television drama. Such variables as race, aging, occupation, power, solving of problems, and even humor, all bear upon and interact with depiction of men, women, sex roles, and love.

Substantial differences exist between daytime television serial drama and prime time drama. They will therefore be examined separately as well as together.

For example, daytime serials all take place in the present and in a domestic in-door setting, whereas prime time dramas display a range of locale. Soap operas are open-ended, intended to last indefinitely, and employ writers who are responsible for the story line on a continuing basis. The individual episodes of a soap opera are imcomprehensible in themselves, having neither a beginning or an end. Considerable diversity exists in the demography and social world of prime time drama, while that of daytime drama is uniform. The first section of this review, therefore, will point out some of the major characteristics of the exceedingly popular daytime serial dramas, in order to illuminate the differences between prime time and daytime television drama.

---

[1]Such dramas represent a different era.

II. THE WORLD OF DAYTIME TELEVISION
SERIAL DRAMA

Plays presented in serial form have a long history. Some of the daytime television dramas now being broadcast are continuations of radio serials extending back to the 1930's (Stedman, 1977). These radio plays are themselves one variation of a form of mass entertainment that has existed since the first decade of the 20th century. Before that, novelists, such as Dickens, published their works in installments for eagerly waiting publics. Daytime serial drama differs from prime time drama in settings, demography, thematic content, and, to some extent, in the images of men, women, love, and sex portrayed. The purpose of this section is to discuss the research that has examined the "soap opera" and its attributes.

A. Settings

Downing (1974), Lopate (1977), and Ramsdell (1973) all found that American daytime serials take place in a small town in the continental United States, and that the time coincides with the actual date. Time is subject to distortion, however, so that dramatization of events requiring only hours to occur, can be extended over a period of two weeks. The indoor scenes take place among surroundings of comfort, conservative decor, and perfect order. Ross (1976), in a study of the Quebec soap opera, found that characters represent a privileged class, only 13 percent of which has residences which could be called "unsatisfactory." Maykovich (1976, p. 139), in contrast, found a time span for Japanese soap opera extending backward to World War II, or even to the previous century, and states that "geographically, Japanese drama settings extend from the north to the south, from a little fishing village to a big metropolis." However, Maykovich also states that the Japanese serial dramas are not written as open-ended, continuing serials in the American sense, but are, instead, adaptations of existing long novels, wherein themes develop quickly and have definite endings. Japanese soap operas may resemble prime time American series drama more closely than the daytime serial genre. In general, however settings of American soap are static, and vary little from one drama to another. One reason for this uniformity is economic; serials are the "bread and butter" of TV. They are produced at the lowest possible cost (Mathewson, 1979), are profitable, and may be thought of as subsidizing some of the costly prime time productions. In daytime serials elaborate settings are not needed to carry forward dramatic development and would reduce the cost effectiveness of daytime drama.

B. Demography

As Gerbner and Gross (1976) comment, "Representation in.the fictional world signifies social existence; absence means symbolic annihilation." Such factors as sex, age, race, marital status, social class, physical attributes, and occupational level of drama characters, convey messages to the audience, not only by their existence, but by their selectve proportion and attribution. Downing (1974), for example, found that half of the daytime serial characters were women, in contrast to prime-time's representation of women as constituting no more than one-fourth of prime-time characters (Gerbner, 1972; Seggar and Wheeler, 1973; Tedesco, 1974).

Nonwhite persons are similarly under-represented in daytime serial drama, 97.3 percent of the characters being white (Downing, 1974). Nonwhite persons are idealized characters, young, beautiful, professional, upper-middle class, and without flaws. As Ramsdell (1973, p. 301) puts it "No black on the programs is either unemployed or on welfare." Nonwhite players appear as adjuncts to their white associates, and are not shown as pursuing objectives of their own. No black character, for example, is portrayed as a leader of the black community, with interests in opposition to those of the white community.

Harris and Feinberg (1977) found that only 6 percent of all characters in daytime drama were over 60, and Downing (1974) found a clustering of characters in the middle-range, with few players under fourteen and over sixty-five. There is, in addition, a sex-aging interaction, with male characters maintaining effectiveness in old age unless struck by misfortune, while female players deteriorate because of aging alone.

The family and family relationships are the essence of domestic drama. Few characters, therefore, either male or female, remain unmarried. Those who appear single do so because of divorce, separation, or death—and speedily remarry to form a romantic attachment. There is a good deal of quasi-inbreeding among daytime serial characters, because of the smallness of the cast.

Everyone who has examined the American daytime serial drama (Downing, 1974; Katzman, 1972; Lopate, 1977; Mariani, 1978; Maykovich, 1975; Ramsdell, 1973; Ross, 1976) comments upon the unrealistically high level of social class and occupational status. Most of the characters are professionals of the upper middle class, with the blue-collar worker (who is actually the largest segment of the real-world class) almost absent. Further, serial players tend to be young, slender, beautiful, and handsomely clothed.

Other characteristics of the daytime serial are unique. Individual episodes are incomprehensible; it takes about four weeks of viewing before the viewer perceives what is going on or who the characters are. Katzman (1972), whose teams of observers limited their viewing to a single week, found that from such a brief sample "minimal inferences could be made." Episodes open abruptly with a conversation already in progress among persons not identified to the audience. Then comes an "organ break," succeeded by a series of commercials. A series of short scenes, each separated by several advertisements, follows, during which the characters address each other as "dear," "darling," or no appellation at all. Conversation is the business of the soap opera, with little action taking place on camera. There is not a single story line, but several subplots, all running at once. With the expansion of daily episodes into an hour's length, the leisurely pace and the multiplicity of substories has increased. The television serial lacks the expository announcer of its predecessor, the radio daytime serial. Thus, there is no longer a mellifluous male voice to tell us that "we now take you to the office of Dr. Bill Harwood, Sunny Valley's leading obstetrician..."

One reason for this absence of identification or review of story line is the fierce loyalty and unquestioning acceptance of the viewing audience, many of whom have been watching the same serial for years and consider "my story" time to be inviolate. Viewers write letters addressed to the actors by their fictional names (Mariani, 1978), and build their days around the times of a serial telecast. Another reason for the peculiar dramatic structure of the daytime serial is that it allows the viewer to miss episodes without losing the thread of any of the ministories.

C. Thematic Content

1. Forms of Love and Friendship. The world of the daytime serial is one in which romantic love, intense interpersonal relationships, and preoccupation with personal problems dominate—in fact, dictate—the action. Romantic love, Downing (1974) found, was a theme of 253 (84%) out of the 300 episodes monitored; interpersonal relationships, 294 (98%); and personal problems, 295 (98%). Only five out of 300 episodes monitored failed to deal with personal problems (each consisting of a courtroom scene involving a murder trial). These findings agree with those of Katzman (1972), Lopate (1977), and Ramsdell (1973). Investigators of nonAmerican serial drama have found somewhat different emphases. Ross (1976) perceived, in his study of Quebec soap opera, a preoccupation with upward social mobility, and Maykovich (1975), comparing American and Japanese soap operas, found an emphasis on family continuity, in Japan, rather than romantic love. (In the traditional Japanese family, Maykovich (1975, p. 136) points out, "romantic love was considered irrelevant.")

Not only are the themes of romantic love, interpersonal relationships and personal problems intertwined, but the intensity of interpersonal relationships is in itself an important thematic element of American daytime television serial drama. Serial casts are restricted to fourteen to twenty persons, producing a somewhat artifactual complexity of involvement among serial personnel. As noted above, at least three subplots run concurrently in each of the serial dramas, requiring tie-ins among the ministories to give an appearance of coherence to the whole. Each actor is therefore maximally utilized. Roles assigned permit the incumbency of several subroles (worker, father, husband, colleague, etc.) This overlapping leads to complications of personal interaction in a seemingly inevitable manner. Pairs of individuals are involved in more than one relationship with each other, examples being brother-in-law/sister-in-law + lovers; father/son + professional colleagues; doctor/patient + friendly acquaintances. Downing (1974) and Lopate (1977) found that "friendly acquaintances" account for a large share of total pairs. "Friendly acquaintances" are persons who share portions of their private lives, but are not close, intimate friends. Since forward movement of serial drama is carried out by conversation, not action, many "friendly acquaintance" interactions are required. Thus, professional colleagues visit at one another's homes, or select secluded working areas in which they can exchange nonwork-related information. Married women drop in on each other for coffee. The two most commonly-occurring overlaps of interpersonal relationships are "friendly acquaintances" with "colleagues" and "professional/client" respectively. Work relationships are emotionally toned; work-related interactions do not necessarily reflect a high commitment of serial episodes to the problems of the working world, since they often occur in tandem with other, closer relationships.

So important is the motif of romantic love to the American daytime television serial that the dramas would have little substance without it. All characters—with one or two exceptions of widowed persons over fifty years of age—are members or of one or more romantic pairs. Love is always heterosexual. No investigator of the genre has discovered an instance of homosexual love on daytime and serial drama. Heterosexual love takes several forms, from the sentimental marital attachments of the grandparent generation, couples married or living together in quasi-permanent arrangements, through rape of innocent females by leading males, down to the infatuation of adolescents.

Certain conventions are observed in the depiction of love. Romantic love pairs involve individuals of the same age, or older-man, younger-woman combinations. The male perpertrators of rape are not strangers to their victims; the rapist tends to be a relative or colleague of the woman's husband or lover. Extra-marital relationships tend likewise to involve relatives of the spouse. Because of the closeness of family ties and the tendency for the serial players to be all related to each other either by blood or marriage, love relationships also acquire an incestuous tinge.

Love is portrayed as both eternal and constantly changing. The principal business of the daytime serial is conversation, and the major topic is love. This is true of both men and women; members of both sexes are preoccupied with seeking, or maintaining, a positive response from those they love. Also, each player talks about his or her feelings and speculates on the emotions of the other players. Love liaisons entered into require secrecy, complications of attitude and behavior, deceit, and above all, suffering. The self-defeating actions of the players ensure continuance of the plan.

Despite the handling, in the daytime serial, of such themes as rape, abortion, illegitimacy, contraception, vasectomy, sexual freedom, and female liberation, the portrayal of sex is conservative, in that nudity or explicit sexual behavior is suggested rather than demonstrated. The "sultry sirens of the daytime soaps" (Mariani, 1978) have become multidimensional in character. They are portrayed as motivated by other impulses than sexual desire, such as greed, revenge, insecurity. Appeal to prurient interest, in the daytime serial, is subtle, with overtones of judgmental attitudes.

At the same time, sexual behavior on daytime television is portrayed in a relatively straightforward manner, as compared to prime time television. Absent is the innuendo noted by many researchers of sex motifs in prime time television (Feldman and Tickton, 1976; Fernandez–Collado et al., 1978; Fischer, 1978; Franzblau et al., 1977; Kitman, 1978; Rosen, 1977; Waters, 1978b). Sexual interaction, while implied rather than displayed, is taken seriously, shown as involving personal commitment, and reacted to, and discussed without any of the humourously-toned comment pervading prime time telecasting.

2. *Other Motifs of Daytime Drama.*   That the daytime television serial is preoccupied with themes of romantic love, interpersonal relationships, and personal problems does not mean that other motifs do not exist—although Ross' study of Quebec soap opera revealed that the players' concern with their private lives led them to ignore the outside world altogether.[2] American investigators (Downing, 1974; Lopate, 1977; Ramsdell, 1973; Stedman, 1977) have found themes of physical disability, drug addiction, abortion, alcoholism, juvenile delinquency, ecology, religious apostacy, artificial insemination, abuses of legal procedure, sex roles, women's liberation, irresonsible newspaper sensationalism, divorce, and death dealt with, in many cases effectively. As Ramsdell (1973, p. 302) says, "death is presented openly and realistically, and many of the psychological factors of grief are

---

[2]"Les problemes sociaux n'existent pas puisque, a la limité, la societé elle-même n'existé pas" (Ross, 1976).

handled with validity." Further, while far more thematic content in daytime serials deals with personal rather than social and community issues, it does not follow that nonpersonal issues raised are perceived as insignificant by the audience. What appears to be brief and cursory mention of nonpersonal thematic material may over the long run have considerable impact on viewers, because of the tendency for regular viewers to keep watching the same serial over long periods of time. Subjects of particular interest to members of the audience will engage attention even if dealt with in passing. For example, "One Life to Live" received 9,000 requests for an article on veneral disease offered to serial viewers (Pierce, 1973).

Two soap opera themes deserve special consideration—those of attitudes toward work and of social class. Both the Canadian and the American investigators found that, on the one hand, the occupational status depicted for the serial characters was spuriously high, and, on the other, that no one in the dramas did any real work nor gave any evidence of real interest in his/her occupation. For serial characters taken as a whole, "professionals" (doctors, lawyers, judges) lead all other daytime serial employment categories, including "housewives," with blue collar workers being almost absent.[3]

Offices of daytime's professional characters are identical from serial to serial, featuring bookshelves and walnut desks of conservative design. No papers or professional journals clutter up the neat tops of the desks and tables in the professional office. Neither at home or in the office do any of the by-products of work (clutter, unfinished tasks, trash, disarray) ever appear. Work situations do not depict the execution of tasks, but rather serve as settings for emotional involvement. Everyone has time for conversation. Hospital chiefs of staff, who might reasonably be assumed to be pressured by shortages of money, labor unions, difficulties in finding qualified personnel, coping with advancing technology, allowing themselves to be interrupted by visitors, with whom they discuss, not work, but personal problems. Housewives—always immaculately dressed and becomingly groomed—never express dismay, but only pleasure when a friend drops in for a chat. As Ross (176, p. 228) puts it, "Que fait-on donc dans les teleromans? On cause."

Sex differences exist in the daytime serial drama's portrayal of the professional man and woman. First of all, men are overwhelmingly depicted as professionals, managers, proprietors, or law enforcement personnel; while,

---

[3]Maykovich (1975, pp. 138–139) points out that this is not true of Japanese soap opera, where 31 percent of the characters belonged to a "middle status group" and 24 percent of the male characters occupied low status. However, Maykovich's definition of "low status," included such occupations as carpenters (American blue collar). Also, Maykovich's occupational table, headed "Husband's occupation," together with his comment "As for female occupations, Americans programs provide more variety than the Japanese," reflects not only considerable difference in American and Japanese societal attitudes toward women, but also the differing origin and character of the Japanese soap opera, as serialized dramatizations of existing novels.

with women, the profession of "full-time housewife" ranks first, with "professionals" second. Second, the female professionals tend to be nurses, doctors, and lawyers—but never judges or chiefs of medical staff. Third, the ideal of romantic love as the be-all and end-all of life is stressed for both men and women, but seems almost mandatory for the latter. More than one woman has given up or changed a career for love. Lastly, older men retain their professional status, but older women do not. At the age of fifty, occupational level for women declines, while men are shown to continue in positions of power and prestige beyond the age of sixty-five.

Since the world of daytime serial drama is a symbolic universe, aimed primarily at the advertiser's market of women who are home in the daytime, the serials' purpose might reasonably be assumed to be that of entertaining and holding captive such an audience. There is no reason, therefore, why in this case fiction should reflect fact, since the truths conveyed by the dramas may have more honesty than the facts they overlook. At the same time, it may help to define the parameters of the daytime serial world by contrasting occupational level depicted in that universe with "reality" as defined by the U.S. Bureau of the Census.

Of women in the United States over twenty years of age, gainfully employed in September, 1978, 32 percent fell into the 45-64 age group and 1,060,000 of all women employed at that age were over the age of 65. (U.S. Bureau of Labor Statistics, 1978, p. 48). Since 1950, women over the age of sixty-five have formed from 3.2 percent to 3.9 percent of the female (wage-earing) labor force. (The U.S. Bureau of Labor does not recognize the "housewife" as part of the labor force)

A projection of male–female participation in the labor force, for persons over the age of 65, made by the United States Bureau of the Census for the years 1980 and 1985, shows that, while the number of employed over-sixty-five men will *decrease* from 1980-1985, the number of employed over-sixty-five women will increase. The statistics suggest that increasing age, per se, does not, in reality, work to the disadvantage of women. However, the mere fact that women live longer than men and that older women are contained in the work force to a much greater extent than indicated by television drama says nothing of the quality of either their lives or occupations.

Occupational status is related to social class, which, in the American soap opera, is confined to a well-to-do middle class. Households are servantless, but beautifully furnished and immaculately appointed—no dust, no fingerprints on the wallpaper, no chips in the paint, no handles missing from drawers; with neither snow to shovel in winter nor grass to mow in the summer. No one mentions money or old-age pensions. The boundaries of the daytime serial middle class ae amorphous. For example: women doctors talked, dressed, and behaved no differently than did women clerical workers. Male law enforcement personnel were identical to professors in speech and demeaner. Hair style, dress, and speech of all characters are impeccable; the serial writer, when wishing to depict a "lower class" player, writes a pseudo-style of speech and manner which is unconvincing. Furthermore, the preoccupations of those few members of the "lower class" who do appear in the plays are the same as those of all members of the cast—romantic love, interpersonal relations, and personal problems, rather than inflation, unemployment, or future prospects. At the same time, upward social mobility is shown on both American and Canadian soap opera as obtainable, and as a worthy objective.

D. The Image of Men and Women on Daytime Television Serial Drama

From the foregoing discussion it might be inferred that the image of men on the soap opera is much better than the image of women, and that women are portrayed negatively. This is not necessarily true.

To begin with, the fifty–fifty representation of men and women, which resembles population sex proportions much more realistically than prime time drama character proportions, means that women are at least as visible as men. More important, the portrayal of men on daytime television is unidimensional. Both black and white men are portrayed as too good to be true—except for a scattering of obvious villains. The men are all-wise, all-powerful, all-good, always at the disposal of women and children. Every woman has a man to herself. Turow (1974) found that it was men who gave the orders; that when female opinion prevailed, it was on "feminine" matters.

In prime time, sexuality, or "femaleness" is emphasized among women. The woman is seen as a sexual partner or underling, rather than as a friend or an intellectual equal. A provocative appearance and demeanor is mandatory even for females ostensibly playing professional roles. Only in situation comedies, particularly those showing a black household, does the woman exercise real leadership. In daytime drama, on the other hand, women "tent-pole" characters form a focus for the action in each of the serials. Not only do men and women converse with each other, but women are portrayed as being real friends to each other. While neither men nor women in the daytime drama are portrayed as unmarried, unattached individuals having no antecedents—as often happens in prime time—women, on the whole, are shown on daytime drama as more fully faceted and multidimensional than men. The same woman is mother, wife, friend, colleague—performing effectively in each role. She is sympathetically handled by the script writers, and is portrayed as a motivated individual with good and bad characteristics. She comes across as real; and is, at her best, worthy of emulation (Downing, 1974).

E. The Audience of the Daytime Television Serial Drama

Studies of daytime audiences, comparable to that of Herzog (1944) on the audience of the earlier radio serial, have not been done. Some clues are suggested by Nielson ratings, which, at intervals, published demographic breakdowns of the audiences for particular time periods and types of shows. Nielson rating comparisons among the three major daytime television categories—daytime drama, situation comedy, and quiz and audience participation shows—indicate that daytime drama draws a larger audience than either of the other two entertainment forms. Women daytime viewers outnumber men by about seven to one. Women prefer the dramas while men prefer the quiz shows; for both men and women, preference for daytime drama is greatest for persons over fifty years of age. If the Nielson ratings accurately measure audiences, one might think of the typical daytime drama viewer as a woman over fifty who is not gainfully employed during the hours of 10:00 a.m. and 5:00 p.m. However, Herzog (1944), Kaufman (1944), and Lang (1957), in discussing the appeal of the daytime serial to its audience, challenge the assumption that the latter is a homogeneous group of captive housewives; a point supported by an article in Media/Scope ("Daytime television's male call," 1965); demonstrating that 30 percent of the viewers of daytime serials are male.

It is probable that there exists, in addition, an unmeasured and unmeasurable group of viewers who will not admit to watching soap operas. These include university students who congregate in student lounges, retired husbands of serial devotees, and individuals who, for any of a number of reasons, find themselves immured at home for an extended period of time. In any case, the soap opera—critized, mocked, analyzed, denigrated—goes on year after year, maintaining an audience sufficiently interesting to advertisers to spend money to support the genre. As of the beginning of 1979, 11 serials were being broadcast, of which five had been telecast for twenty years or more, and only two for less than ten years.

What is the appeal of the soap opera which inspires such fanatic loyalty? Why do the viewers so believe in the reality of the portrayals that they send gifts to the fictional characters upon such serial events as weddings and births? Surely the typical viewer, housebound, is not likely to be a member of the comfortable, articulate, well-dressed, handsome, professional upper middle class she sees on the screen, but rather "a southern or midwestern woman from a large household with relatively low educational and income levels" (Katzman 1972). One might speculate, in fact, that to accept as real a serial world in which men and women are all paired with an understanding mate, where everybody is slim and good-looking, where doctors and lawyers will not only remember clients' names but have plenty of time to sit and talk, where nobody has to be concerned about job security, and where households magically clean themselves, might be dysfunctional to the well-being of the viewer. In addition, the viewer absorbs a moral atmosphere in which deceit, keeping secrets, and maladaptive behavior causes the characters to bring trouble upon themselves. Problems are not solved rationally, but emotionally. Yet the extent of the identity of viewer with player is such that afacionadoes not only refer to "my story," but come to talk about the daily actions of the players in terms of what "Bill," "Tom," or "Alice" did today.

Thornton (1976) found a negative relationship existing between television viewing and self-esteem, so that heavy television viewing and a favorable attitude toward television were associated with low education and low self-esteem. Horton and Wohl (1956) point out that mass media give the illusion of face to face relationships with the performer. One might reasonably speculate that the soap opera enthusiasts grow so intimately acquainted with the serial family that the latter become an essential of daily existence. In England, where radio has retained more popularity and offers a wider range of programming than radio in the United States, a daytime serial, "The Dales," was broadcast on British radio for over twenty-one years, ceasing in April, 1969. Blumler et al. (1970) studied the reaction of viewers to the serial's demise, and found that the program had become the focal point of the day for many women for whom the serial provided a para-social involvement; they described "The Dales" as "part of my life." "It was the programme's projection of a well-ordered fmaily life that was missed most keenly" (Blumer et al., 1970); the sheer existence of "The Dales" was reassuring to the viewers, who saw British family values and activities as threatened and on the wane.

Involvement with a continuing set of believable characters is not the only reason, although it may be a major one, for the popularity of the daytime serial. In the end, the soap opera supports highly conservative values. Societal myths of upward mobility, the indispensability and rigid definition of romantic love, the over-riding importance of the extended family, and woman as a sustainer rather than innovator, still serve as dominant themes in serial drama, despite the introduction of forward-looking and important issues. Such issues are selectively chosen and presented; the soap opera is not yet ready for that growing segment of the American population, the self-sustaining individual who remains unmarried by choice and devotes himself/herself to work, constructive leisure, and the pursuance of idiosyncratically selected goals. Soap operas, designed as show cases for the display of advertised products, must sustain the ideals and goals of individuals, predominately women, confined at home during daylight hours.

These goals and ideals might reasonably be assumed to center about the home, children, and family, with the woman of the household playing a nurturing, supporting, somewhat self-effacing role. It may be that daytime television serial drama gives such women a comforting sense of order, coherence, and identification—or aspiration to an ideal.

III.   PRIME TIME TELEVISION DRAMA

Prime time television drama lacks the homogeneity of daytime television serial drama. Time, place, habitat, and setting for prime time drama vary, with time extending from the long past to the distant future, and place including habitats which are imaginary. Themes, demography, and point of view also exhibit heterogeneity. From the provocative ectomorphic female trio of "Charlie's Angles" to the authoritarian aging male professor of "Paper Chase," characters of prime time television drama interact in situations ranging from ludicrous to compelling. In fact, the present writer suggests that a degree of polarization of dramatic offerings on prime time television has taken place which presents, for the viewer's choice, two co-existing symbolic worlds, the one to some extent the antithesis of the other.

Over the past ten years of communication research in prime time drama this has not been. The position taken by investigators, have treated the form as if it were one entity. And, indeed, examination of the dramatic offerings of prime time television reveal characteristics which certainly appear common to all prime time drama. This section of the review reflects the findings of researchers of prime time drama, in an effort to determine what generalizations can be made about the image of men, women, sex, and love; and about the factors, such as aging, which bear upon such images.

Prime time drama[4] written for commercial television at the end of the 1970s, might be grouped into three categories: (1) the once-a-week series; (2) the situation comedy; and (3) the "specials," the latter being dramas of one to two hours in length, presented occasionally, and superseding regular programming. The series and the situation comedy are not mutually exclusive, in that each has a set of continuing characters and appears at a regular time slot once a week during the hours of 7:00 p.m. to 11:00 p.m.

In addition, on public television, dramatizations of plays and novels were broadcast in a finite number of episodes and resemble serial drama—especially Japanese serial drama—in that the individual episodes, though not necessarily self-contained, were part of a predictable whole. However, consideration of nonprofit public television drama has been excluded from this review for several reasons. First, public television programming varies from one section of the country to another. Second, public television is under

---

[4]As stated before, movies produced for theatre viewing and later telecast are not being examined, since they often represent a past era.

no pressure to make a profit, and hence need not appeal to the largest possible audience. Third, daytime television serial drama has no real coutnerpart in public television drama. Fourth, public television has, to a great extent, objectives which are different from those of commercial television, and can therefore include a wide latitude of content, format, and special interest.

In any case, prime time commercial television drama differs from daytime drama in the several ways which will be outlined below, but chiefly in that individual episodes of prime time drama are intelligible in themselves, not requiring the same quality of dedicated consistency of viewing needed to comprehend portions of a daytime serial.

A. Demography of Prime Time Drama

1. Review of Prior Research. Investigators have found certain demographic attributes common to all prime time drama players. Under-representation of women in prime time, Tedesco (1974) found, had existed for the past thirty years of telecasting, with women still comprising only about one-fourth of all players. Aronoff (1974) found a similar under-representation of aged persons, with some differences in treatment of older men and women.

A generation of consciousness-raising among nonwhite persons has not resulted in significant improvements in nonwhite portrayals. Sklar (1978a) points out that black shows on television tend to be comedies, rather than serious drama. Also, the comparative lack of black writers, producers, and directors in television militates against the expression of an authentic black point of view. Seggar (1977), set out to discover whether the gains in proportionate representation and quality of imagery of women and nonwhites achieved at the end of the 1960s had persisted in the 1970s. Seggar found that, while gains had been made, women have tended to experience a 20-year cycle, with proportionate representation in 1975 about like that of 1953. Blacks have gained in numbers, but not other minorities, with fewer nonblack minority portrayals in 1975 than 1971.

Donagher et al. (1975) found that distinct patterns emerged in the portrayals of four racial-sex groups (male–white; male–black; female–white; female–black), with black males and white females being shown as similar to each other in several ways. Both of these subgroups were shown as engaged in altruistic acts of helping, sharing, and cooperating, and were not seen as forceful or powerful in traditional ways. The white male, "a powerful, rule-breaking, independent, and rather callous individual" contrasted with the black female who "used explanations of feelings and actions in the attempt to increase understanding in others, resolve strife, or reassure others" (Donagher et al., 1975, p. 1032).

This white female/black male correspondence echoes the finding of Nicholas et al. (1971) that, in a study of the effects of race and sex on the imitation of television models among children, white girls chose as models the white boy and black boy most frequently; and that, overall, girls imitated boys significantly more frequently than boys imitated girls.

Not only is there an interaction among race, sex, and age in prime time television drama, but both race and sex affect portrayals of marital status and occupational level. Men, in prime time drama, do not marry (Gerbner, 1972; Tedesco, 1974). They must remain free, without antecedents or dependents, in order to assume the variety of roles available to them. They must be able to come and go at will, undertaking any adventure which offers itself. Except for "family" shows, men in lead male roles tend to be loners, uncommitted to any continuing love or sexual relationship.

Women do not remain aloof from interpersonal relationships as do men. Statistically, about 50 percent of all female television prime time drama characters are portrayed as married (Gerbner, 1972), as opposed to 29 percent of the men. Aronoff (1974) reporting the age distribution of 2,125 male and 749 female dramatic (noncartoon) characters in a population of prime-time television programs, found that the percentage of women was highest in their twenties, the proportion of women dropping sharply when they no longer fit the conventional romantic roles.

In other words, women players are significantly more often younger than men, but, at the same time, more often shown as married.

Several points of divergence between men and women exist with respect to occupational level. Occupations depicted for men include lawyers, doctors, judges, law enforcement personnel, managers (Kaniuga et al., 1976; McNeil, 1975a, c; Manes, 1974, Marting, 1973; Rosen, 1977; Ross, 1976; Seggar and Wheeler, 1973; Tedesco, 1974), with a concentration in the "professional" categories and a disportionately low representation of blue-collar workers. In contrast, almost two-thirds of prime time female characters are not shown as gainfully employed (Tedesco, 1974), with 17 percent of those employed being professionals and 14 percent portrayed as managers or clerical workers. Housewives predominate, and the occupational, "cannot tell," category is much larger for women players than for men.

Occupation identifies men to a greater extent than it does women. For example, among prime time female "professionals," 54 percent of those so categorized were entertainers, while 63 percent of male professionals were in the work-related areas of health, government, education, and business (Tedesco, 1974).

There are also occupational differences between black and white male players. No drama that is not predominantly black in cast, point of view, and situation depicts a black man in a position of authority, although black men (and, indeed, white and black women) are shown as loyal, dedicated, one-dimensional "second-in-command" adjuncts to white leaders in several series.

In sum, a review of the literature concerning the demography of prime time drama depicts a society wherein men outnumber women; men tend to be older than women; they are less often married; they are portrayed in a greater variety of occupational categories than women; they exercise leadership and are more often cast in leading roles. For both sexes, occupational level was disclosed as spuriously high, with little representation of blue-collar workers. Aged persons seldom appear, and nonwhite persons are inadequately represented.

2. Demography of Prime Time Television Drama, March 1979. In order to evaluate the findings cited in previous paragraphs, the present investigator examined the prime time commercial television dramas broadcast in March 1979 (TV Guide, March 3–9, 1979) to determine what changes, if any, had taken place in the demography of prime time players. Results are displayed in Tables I, II, and III, representing summaries of network offerings of ABC, CBS, and NBC.

Study of Tables I, II and III indicates that, out of fifty-eight prime time commercial dramas broadcast in March, 1979, forty-seven shows contained lead players who were male. Of the nineteen chief protagonists who were female, eleven shared their leading roles with men, leaving only 8 female sole principal characters in prime time drama.

Nonwhite lead players occurred in 8 shows and, of the four shows containing sole black lead protagonists, three were situation comedies.

Of male leads, twenty-four were thirty years of age or over, while, of the eight female lead players, three were over thirty and five were younger. A single marital status is common to both men and women, with only eleven shows featuring married persons; of these eleven shows, the state of matrimony or family life was essential to the situation of the play.

Occupation varies, with greater representation of middle management and blue collar employment than had, according to the studies heretofore cited, been the case. At the same time, Tables I, II and III clearly indicate the superior occupational level of the men. None of the women are captains, chiefs, hosts, or editors. Mrs. Pynchon, the owner of the newspaper of which Lou Grant is the editor, is the exception rather than the rule.

Demographically speaking, then, white males of mature age had not, as of March 1979, relinquished their control of the symbolic world of television drama. Further, in each of the shows depicting a woman heading a household, such a woman tends to portrayed as people-oriented rather than career-oriented. There are no female counterparts of Starsky and Hutch, Steve McGarrett, or Quincy. The Western frontier mountain man of "How the West Was Won" is converted into the nurturing mother of "Little House on the Prairie."

B. Thematic Content

1. Love, Sex, and the Family in Prime Time Drama. Pressure from special interest groups concerned by the amount of violence shown on television during the 1960s and 1970s resulted, at the end of the eighth decade of the 20th century, to a shift of emphasis from overt violence to concentration on love and sex. Any drama is an artificial device, in which power roles must be shown and stories developed and resolved quickly. Violence is a sine qua non for the depiction of the relative significance and effectiveness of the players. (For example, Gerbner (1972) demonstrated that women were more often victims than perpetrators of violence.)

With violence no longer available as a quick and easy way of defining characterization, writers and producers have turned to love and sex as the next best motif. Not only television, but all of the American media in the latter part of the 20th century are permeated with a concern with romantic love and sexual emotion. The "entertainment" sections of the newspaper; the themes of best-seller novels; the "lyrics" of popular songs; advertising—all reflect the American obsession with romantic love and sexual emotion. One religious body is even using sexual provocation as a means of attracting new members (Wallis, 1978).

Media portrayals of love and sex can easily fulfill the same purpose as violence did in previous decades. Exercise of power and resolution of conflict can be shown by transforming love relationships in contests with "winners" and "losers." Who gets the girl? How old are the respective sexual partners? Who determines what decisions each shall make?

At its very best, television portrayals of love can be varied and multidimensional. Of continuing series, the family relationships shown on such regularly-appearing dramas as "Family," "Little House on the Prairie," and "The Waltons" may be idealized and more splendid than life, but they represent an attempt to convey some of the complexities of family affections and interactions. "Mother" and "father" are portrayed as strong, dignified, positively-oriented characters who have made life-long commitments to each other and to the members of their families.

From time to time, homosexual love has been portrayed, if not sympathetically, at least in depth, in such vehicles as "That Certain Summer," "In this House of Brede," and "The Collection," with players being given some dimension. In general, however, homosexual love is not treated seriously—more truly, it is not treated at all.

"Love," on prime time television, tends to be defined in terms of sexual relationships, and the treatment of love depicted in the dramas cited above is not the norm for TV as a whole. Interestingly, commercial advertisements, as, for example, for telephone service or soft drinks, more often depict the breadth of the expression of human love than the dramas in which they are embedded. Much of the published material which examines love and sex on television drama concerns itself with the shift from emphasis on violence to a focus on sex, and deals to a greater extent with television's portrayal of physical intimacy. (Cf. Baran, 1976a; English 1978a; Feldman and Tickton, 1976; Fernandez–Collado et al., 1976; Fischer, 1978; Franzblau et al., 1977;

TABLE I

Prime Time Television Drama: ABC—Characteristics of Leading Players

Name of Show	Type	Demography of Lead Player(s)						
		Sex		Race		Marital Status	Approximate Age	Occupation
		Male	Female	White	Non-White			
ANGIE	Comedy-Drama		X	X		Married	24	Philadelphia Waitress
BARNEY MILLER	Comedy-Drama	X		X		Separated	40	Policeman
BATTLESTAR GALACTICA	Science Fiction	X		X		Cannot Tell	60	Captain of Space Ship
CHARLIE'S ANGELS	Comedy-Detective		X	X		Single	24	Undercover investigators
DELTA HOUSE	Comedy	X		X		Single	19	College Students
EIGHT IS ENOUGH	Comedy-drama	X	X	X		Married	Varies among family members	Newspaper Editor, Teacher, Students
FAMILY	Drama	X	X	X		Married	Varies among family members	Attorney, Housewife, Students
FANTASY ISLAND	Comedy-Drama	X		X		Single	60	Host of Resort Island

Program	Genre					Marital Status	Age	Occupation
HAPPY DAYS	Comedy-Drama	X			X	Single	19	Students
HOW THE WEST WAS WON	Drama	X			X	Single	55	Western Frontier Mountain Man
LAVERNE AND SHIRLEY	Comedy-Drama	X	X		X	Single	24	Beer Brewery Workers
LOVE BOAT	Comedy-Drama	X		X	X	Divorced	50	Captain of Cruise Ship
MAKIN' IT	Comedy-Drama	X			X	Single	19	Student-Disco Dancer
MORK & MINDY	Comedy	X			X	Single	23	Alien Being
SALVAGE I	Adventure	X			X	Single	50	Large-Scale Salvage Dealer
SOAP	Comedy	X		X	X	Varies	Varies among family members	Various
STARSKY & HUTCH	Crime-Drama	X		X	X	Single	30	Undercover Police
TAXI	Comedy	X	X		X	Varies	40	Taxi Drivers
THREE'S COMPANY	Comedy	X	X		X	Single	23	Various
VEGA$	Crime-Drama	X		X	X	Single	34	Private Investigator
WELCOME BACK, KOTTER	Comedy-Drama	X			X	Varies	30 & 18	High School Teacher and Students
WHAT'S HAPPENING	Comedy	X			X	Single	18	Student

TABLE II

Prime Time Television Drama: CBS—Characteristics of Leading Players

| Name of Show | Type | Sex | | Race | | Demography of Lead Player(s) | | |
		Male	Female	White	Non-White	Marital Status	Approximate Age	Occupation
ALICE	Comedy-Drama		X		X	Widow	35	Waitress
ALL IN THE FAMILY	Comedy-Drama	X	X	X		Married	50	Foreman (Loading Dock) Housewife
BARNABY JONES	Crime-Drama	X		X		Single	65+	Detective
BILLY	Comedy	X		X		Single	19	Daydreamer
DALLAS	Drama	X		X		Married	60	Oil-Cattle Magnate
DUKES OF HAZZARD	Comedy-Drama	X		X		Single	30	Car Drivers
FLATBUSH	Comedy	X		X		Single	16–19	Male Gang Members
HAWAII 5-O	Crime-Drama	X		X		Single	45	Chief of Homicide
INCREDIBLE HULK	Drama	X		X		Widower	35	Doctor
								Businessman, Housewife,

Show	Type					Marital Status	Age	Occupation
JEFFERSONS	Comedy-Drama	X		X	X	Married	Varies	Student
JUST FRIENDS	Comedy	X	X			Divorced	24	Assistant to Body Builder
KAZ	Crime-Drama	X	X	X		Single	35	Ex-Con turned Lawyer
LOU GRANT	Drama	X	X	X		Divorced	50+	News Editor
MARRIED: THE FIRST YEAR	Drama	X	X	X		Married	17–19	Cannot Tell
M*A*S*H	Comedy-Drama	X	X			Varies	Varies	Army Physicians
MISTER DUGAN	Comedy-Drama	X			X	Cannot Tell	30	Newly Elected Member of Congress
ONE DAY AT A TIME	Comedy-Drama	X	X	X		Divorced	35	Public Relations
PAPER CHASE	Drama	X	X	X		Single	23 & 65	Students & Professor of Law
WALTONS	Drama	X	X	X		Married	45	Lumberman & Housewife
WHITE SHADOW	Comedy-Drama	X	X		X	Single	33 & 17	Teacher/Coach and Students
WKRP IN CINCINNATI	Comedy-Drama	X	X		X	Varies	Varies	Radio Station Employees

TABLE III

Prime Time Television Drama: NBC—Characteristics of Leading Players

Name of Show	Type	Sex Male	Female	Race White	Non-White	Marital Status	Approximate Age	Occupation
B. J. AND THE BEAR	Comedy	X		X		Single	25–30	Ex-Chopper Pilot turned Truck Driver
BROTHERS & SISTERS	Comedy	X			X	Single	19	College Students
CHIPS	Crime-Drama	X		X		Single	30	Highway Patrolman
CLIFFHANGERS	Suspense-Drama	(Show consists of three horror stories, varying each week)						
DIFF'RENT STROKES	Comedy	X			X	Single	10	Adopted Child of Millionaire
HELLO LARRY	Comedy	X		X		Divorced	50	Radio Talk Show Host
LITTLE HOUSE ON THE PRAIRIE	Drama	X		X		Married	40	Farmer & Housewife
LITTLE WOMEN	Comedy-Drama		X	X		Varies	Varies	Students & Housewives
MRS. COLUMBO	Crime-Drama		X	X		Married	30	Amateur Detective/Housewife
NBC NOVELS FOR TELEVISION		(Series of dramatizations of novels; started with "Studs Lonigan" by James T. Farrell)						
QUINCY	Drama	X		X		Single	50+	Coroner
ROCKFORD FILES	Crime-Drama	X		X		Single	45	Private Detective
SUPER TRAIN	Drama					(Information not available at time of report)		
SWEEPSTAKES	Comedy-Drama	X	X		X	Varies	Varies	Winners & Losers of Sweepstakes Lottery
TURNABOUT	Comedy	X	X	X		Married	35	Cosmetic Designer

Kitman, 1978; Mann, 1977; Rosen, 1977; Rubens, 1978; Waters, 1978b; Whitehead, 1970.)

Nessen (1978), commenting on the "gleeful press coverage" of Soviet defector Arkady Shevchenko's relationship with a "love-for-hire girlfriend," points that no legitimate public issue was involved, and that, had Shevchenko's preoccupation been in another area (basketball games, Nessen suggests), no expose would have been deemed necessary. "The conclusion has to be," states Nessen, "that the Shevchenko coverage, with its humorless and pious tone, demonstrated the media's deep streak of puritanism about other people's sex lives."

Rubens (1978, p. 171), commenting on sex on television, calls the medium "the most conservative of the media." The conventionality of television drama's depiction of sexual behavior may be related to confused, ambiguous attitudes toward sex and love in American Society, contend such researchers as Baran (1976b), Feldman and Tickton (1976), Fernandez-Collado et al. (1978), Franzblau et al. (1977), and Waters (1978b).

As in the daytime television serial drama, certain conventions have been observed to obtain in the portrayal of love and sex on prime time drama.

First, as suggested above, the love partners consist of either a young male and a young female, or a not-so-young male and a young female. "Love" between a man and a woman is defined as a sexual relationship. Friendship exists only in work-related situations, with the woman as second in command. Waters (1978) points out that even same-sex friendships are not often portrayed. He quotes Elizabeth Roberts, executive director of the Project on Human Sexual Development based in Cambridge, Massachusetts, as saying "You don't usually see women solve their own problems, or even be close friends. These are massive messages TV is putting out and they need to be questioned."

Male–male friendships do exist on prime television, usually in work related situations, and containing some underlying, but never overtly expressed, elements of homosexual love. One example is the association between Steve McGarrett and Danny Williams of "Hawaii 5-0" (Cf., Weibel's "superhero," 1975) Absolute trust exists between the two men, with no questioning of Steve's dominance or Danny's indispensability to Steve. This situation exists in many regularly scheduled series, wherein the leader male has a sidekick of undying loyalty and singleness of purpose—the purpose being to serve his mentor.

The present writer suggests that a certain amount of latent or quasi-homosexuality underlines many of the male–male relationships depicted on prime time television drama. Starsky and Hutch, for example, are obviously devoted to each other above all other considerations. Male bonding is evident in the "gangs"—the fraternity brothers of "Delta House" and "Brothers and Sisters," the friends of "Happy Days," the troubled teen-agers of "White

Company" and "Welcome Back, Kotter," the "Fungo" gang of "Flatbush." A number of shows depict groups of men who work together amicably, with a lone female present for the men to react to as male beings. Shows, such as "Chips," "Hawaii 5-0," "Lou Grant," M*A*S*H," "The Paper Chase," "WKRP in Cincinnati," "Battlestar Galactica," "Love Boat," "Salvage 1," and "Taxi" portray all predominatly male work situations in a manner not paralleled by a similar treatment of female workers.

Among "second leads" occur either close male mentors of the heroes-as in "Kaz," wherein a fiftiesh attorney smooths the way for the idiosyncratic behavior of the ex-con turned lawyer hero, aged about thirty—or dedicated followers, as in the crime dramas. Similar relationships do not occur among women. In fact, female–female friendships that are not treated as humorous (Cf., "Laverne and Shirley") tend to be a property of daytime serial drama, not prime time drama.

Second, love tends to be defined as physical attraction, with little subtlety or tender feeling involved. Television drama portrays love as adequately expressed by sexual intimacy, and sexual acts as gloriously positive, a depiction which Baran (1976b) finds potentially disturbing to the adolescent sexual self-image. The lack of correspondence between sex as portrayed on television and the facts of the real world have been commented upon by such observers as Rosen (1977), who finds that "every one of these ostensibly independent heroines exists merely as auxiliary to a thinking man."

A third, and very striking, characteristic of prime time television drama portrayals of love and sex lies in their adolescent quality. Waters (1978b) observes that "What is disturbing, however, is that so much of the sex on TV seems designed to pander to prurience in the most cheaply exploitative manner. With snigger and smirk, the new batch of sitcoms and miniseries flaunt their boldness like prepubescents mouthing dirty words around the schoolyard." The use of jokes and innuendo to avoid dealing with the difficulties of sensitive, realistic treatment of love and sex is pervasive, a point on which there appears to be no difference of opinion among investigators. (Cf., Feldman and Tickton, 1976; Fernandez–Collado et al., 1978; Fischer, 1978; Franzblau et al., 1977; Kitman, 1978; Rosen, 1977; and Waters, 1978).[5] Franzblau writes "The finding that physically intimate behaviors and references appear most frequently on situation comedies and variety shows supports the conventional notion that sex is a disturbing topic and is best handled humorously."

While love, in the sense of ultimate concern for the well-being of another human being, and a commitment to the self to the beloved, finds little

---

[5]With respect to humor generally, Cantor (1976) found that, while the amount of humor varies from genre to genre, humor is not entirely absent from any form of TV entertainment, including religious programs.

expression in the television drama of the eigth decade of the twentieth century, sexual behavior, however, poorly handled, is almost ubiquitous. Provocative titillating situations appear in many of the continuing shows of the later 1970s. "Soap," a satire on daytime serial drama, handles impotency, blackmail, transvestitism, homosexuality and murder as comedy. (Mann 1977). "Three's Company" depicts a household consisting of a young man, two young women, all unrelated. "Charlie's Angles" show three female ectomorphs solving crimes under the direction of a male voice, to whose owner they are never introduced.

Stein (1979, p. 5), remarking on the disparity between the television world and real life, describes his reaction to a scene from "Charlie's Angels":

> A while ago, I saw an episode of Charlie's Angels about massage parlors that were really houses of prostitution. The three beautiful "angels" of the show were compelled to pretend they worked at massage parlors in seamy areas. Anyone who has ever passed by a massage parlor knows that they are invariably dirty, shabby places, with pitiful and degraded denizens. On Charlie's Angels, the Paradise Massage Parlor compared favorably in terms of cleanliness with the surgical theatre at Massachusetts General Hospital. The girls were immaculate and well-groomed, soft of speech, and clear of eye and skin.

Depiction of the family has undergone considerable change since the 1950s. Sklar (1978b), recalling such family shows as "Trouble with Father," "Make Room for Daddy," and "Father Knows Best" calls attention to the fact that the family as presently portrayed on television drama is likely *not* to include a father, mother, and children. Rather, Sklar points out, menages consist of children with a single parent, unmarried adults living together in various combinations, or travesties of family life, as in "Soap." Hofeldt (1978) refers to the ensemble of M*A*S*H as a kind of family, similar to the work-related quasi-family groups of "Lou Grant," the former "Mary Tyler Moore Show," and several of the lawyer or policeman lead-player and followers groups. Posey (1978), asking viewers for reaction to "Three's Company," found that the "under-thirty-five crowd" considered the "family" situation believable, and states "this show is cunningly devised to reach the group advertisers lie awake at night scheming to attract. As of March, 1979, three shows—"Alice," "Hello, Larry," and "One Day at a Time"—were treating as comedy the situation of a single parent heading a family unit.

The television drama series concerning itself with family which had the greatest influence of any single television drama series at the end of the 1970s may have been Alex Haley's "Roots." The series awakened a whole new interest in geneology. Levine (1978), commenting on the phenomenon of "Roots" unpredicted success, stated that, while artistically, "Roots" left a great deal to be desired, it was "an undeniable powerful experience." It is not really a family drama at all. Says Levine (1978, p. 54)

Roots is no mere story but a full-blown myth, and myths can be told, or retold, in any number of art forms from the Great Novel to the Classic Comic (the level of Roots) to the inside of bubble gum wrappers without losing their essential appeal. In the case of Roots, what is being told is the extreme version yet of the preeminent television myth about the American family... Since any myth about a fast-changing social institution must be both timeless and perpetually out of date—that is, rooted in nostalgia—the TV family is a hopelessly rearguard attempt to preserve an ideal image at the expense of an unpleasant reality.

Levine (1978, p. 56) confirms the comment made previously about the work-related family: "The trend in sitcoms will continue to move away from block-related families to the work-related 'family' epitomized by The Mary Tyler Moore Show." Hofeldt (1978, pp. 97–98), discussing cultural bias in M*A*S*H, feels that the group of characters depicted represent a kind of family structure, with Colonel Sherman Potter as the elder statesman. "As chief arbiter of disputes and counselor for troubled souls, this surrogate father provides the moral leadership for all those around him." Hofeldt feels, however, that M*A*S*H actually emerges as a "microcosm of American society itself." He feels that the attitudes and values expressed in M*A*S*H are supportive to traditional American beliefs.

Traditionally the central unit of American society, the 'family' format is a common reference point for the audience and a natural arena for problem solving... Every series faces the task of audience reassurance by resolving issues or complications which in some way touch the lives of as many viewers as possible. These problems must be set in a framework familiar to the audience and resolved in a manner consistent with American cultural traditions.

2. Other Motifs of Prime Time Television

A. Images of Aging and the Aged

Alberta Hunter, described by Treaster (1978, p. 23) as the "freshest face in show biz," an eighty-three-year-old black woman, was, in the autumn of 1978, belting out the blues at a New York supper club. Ms. Hunter had interrupted her career as an entertainer in 1957 to become a practical nurse, lying about her age, which was then sixty-two. Alberta Hunter's counterpart is not found in prime time television, where the aged are not only invisible (Gerbner, 1972), but "associated with increasing evil, failure, and unhappiness" (Aronoff, 1974, p. 87). Further, Aronoff found that, while male characters fail because they are evil, female characters fail because they grow old. Harris and Feinberg (1977, p. 467) similarly found that "the portrait of the older person was essentially unflattering: unhealthy, unstylish, uninteresting... The television portrayal of older women was particularly harsh. In contrast to men, women experienced tragic declines in esteem as age increased. For women, youth seemed to be the *sine qua non* of success." Petersen (1977, p. 573) found a less negative image of old people, taken as a whole, but agrees that elderly women are under-represented, saying "It appears that television, is, indeed, a man's world for the elderly." Kubey (1977), commenting on the use of television by the aged, pointed out that, while TV watching constitutes a major daily activity for the aged, TV programming is directed toward a younger market. Wimmer (1976) does not necessarily agree. He found that older people do not use television to a greater extent than they use any of the mass media, and he reminds us that the present over-sixty-five population did not grow up with television, but rather relied on printed media as sources for information.

In any case, the image of the elderly on prime time TV is not only unflattering, but not in consonance with reality as defined by the U.S. Bureau of the Census (1977).

In 1976, Americans aged sixty-five and over comprised about 10.5 percent of the total population, and 8.2 increase over 1960. It has been estimated that by the year 2000, the elderly will comprise 11.2 percent of the total population. In 1970, of those sixty-five and older, there were 72.2 males for 100 females (94.8/100 in the general population). This is a decrease from 82.8/100 in 1960. The estimates for the year 2000 indicate that there will be sixty-seven males per 100 females, among the elderly. In 1974, the average life expectancy at birth was sixty-eight years for males and seventy-six for females. In 1900 those who reached age sixty-five could expect to live, on the average, 16 more years, only four years longer than at the turn of the century. A 1969–70 survey showed that 57.7 percent of the elderly have no activity limitation (compared to 88.3 percent in the general population), while 42.3 percent have some sort of activity limitation, with heart conditions and arthritis being most common causes of this limitation. Three percent of the total American labor force is over 65; 3.1 percent of males over sixty-five are gainfully employed and 2.7 percent of the women.

The negative image of the elderly on prime time television drama may reflect general American attitudes toward the aged; or, possibly, the fact that they are not a lucrative market for the products sold through television advertisement.

B. Nonpersonal issues in prime time drama

While prime time drama of the late 1970s appears to be primarily devoted to sex and modified violence, other themes do occur in the context of the plays. One episode of "Lou Grant" dealt with the inability of a middle-aged man to deal with his mother's coming death. Another motif which occurs with reasonable frequency is serious or mortal illness, a topic which Waters (1978a) feels is inadequately handled in television drama. Using the disease cancer as an example, Waters cites what he calls "guidelines" in TV presentations:

> Never portray the victim as anything but valiant.
> Never present the victim's family as anything but supportive.
> Never show the disease's physical ravages.

What Waters observes about cancer might apply to TV drama's presentation to any serious physical disability—blindness, deafness, incapacity of the limbs. The human being who is blind, deaf, or disabled is portrayed in terms of his disability—not as an individual, who among other attributes, is blind, deaf, or unable to walk without aid. One interesting exception occurred on the series "Paper Chase", in which one episode had as a principal character a wheel-chair victim who exploited his handicap.

Crime and the criminal formed a major motif for many of the dramatic shows shown at the end of the 1970s, despite public feeling about portrayals of violence. The semi magical heroes and heroines of such shows as "Bionic Woman" and "Wonder Woman" fought master criminals impervious to the regularly instituted police force. Superheroes McGarrett, Quincy, Dan Shay, Starsky and Hutch, Dan Tanna, Eddie Capra, and Kaz, all fought valiantly, and often in quasi-opposition to, ordinary law-enforcement personnel; exposing themselves to great personal danger from vicious, powerful, brutal criminals. When such men were not fighting crime they were opposing institutional leaders—such administrators portrayed as reactionary, lacking in understanding, fearful of taking action, etc., thus obliging the superhero to risk his career or his life (or both) to carry one alone. Dominick (1973, p. 244) who states "law-breaking is a common element in prime time network dramatic offerings", points out that the image of crime and law enforcement on prime-time television is not supported by the facts as revealed by F.B.I. reports. For example: on television, crime is almost always unsuccessful, while the F.B.I. report data indicate that in actuality, only 23 percent of major crimes are cleared. In real life, 35 percent of all criminals are under the age of twenty, while no one under twenty appeared in a criminal role on the dramatic shows Dominick studied. Ninety-three percent of television criminals are white, while F.B.I. reports indicate that 70 percent of actual criminals are white. Male–female proportions are about the same as reflected in F.B.I. data. Other aspects of crime as portrayed on television prime time drama are pointed out by Dominick (1973, p. 246) "A significant part of the legal process is invisible in the TV world. While track-down and capture are common, arrangements, indictments, pretrial hearings, jury selection, and plea-bargaining are rarely shown."

Dominick (1973, p. 246) also describes the television crimininal: "In terms of occupation, television criminals are seldom identified in any way other than as criminals.... almost two out of three criminals were portrayed as rootless individuals with most of their time free to be devoted to crime." As to type of crime, Dominick (1973, p. 249) found, "Television over-represents violent crimes directed at individuals. Real-world crime is usually nonviolent and directed as property... Violent crimes between family members are under represented."

Television crime tends to be a "cops and robbers" type of "good guys" vs. "bad guys" affair, or, as Dominick (1973, p. 249) puts it "Good versus bad is an important element in dramatic offerings; it is a classic theme, heavily used in TV drama."

Female crime-fighters tend to be jokes rather than pursuers of justice. As pointed out earlier, the ectomorphic group of three "Charlie's Angels" are not only constantly portrayed in situations which exploit their sexuality, but they take orders from a male voice, over a telephone. This subordination to a male—often ostensibly a "second lead"—prevails even in such shows as "Police Woman." It is not that women are never as heroic, as risking their lives, as effective—but such portrayals are the exception rather than the rule, and such heroines act in an otherwise male-dominated crime-fighting situation.

One final social issue might be mentioned in passing. Drug abuse and overuse of alcohol are serious problems in American society, but Fernandez–Collado et al. (1975, p. 36) found, in a study of sexual intimacy and drug use in television dramatic series, that "the use of alcohol in commercial television series is extensive and frequent, occurring more than twice each program hour.... Insofar as the drugs examined in this study are concerned, alcohol achieves a prominence and a frequency worthy of continuing investigation... in several different show types, taking a drink and offering a drink occur regularly." In other words, in prime time drama, the use of alcohol is portrayed as a customary act of social interaction.

C. Image of Men and Women on Prime Time Drama

On the whole, study of the image of women on television drama has received more direct attention than consideration of the depiction of men, the latter often derived as a result of male–female comparisons. A debate took place between John Seggar (1975 a, b, c) and Jean McNeil (1975 a, b, c) in the *Journal of Broadcasting*. Each studied the imagery of women in television drama, with somewhat different results. McNeil (1975a, p. 286) taking the position that TV does not reflect the feminist movement, states: "The results [of the study] indicate that the typical viewer is likely to learn several things: that they occupy a restricted sex-defined sphere; that they serve primarily as auxiliaries to men; and that all this is as it should be." She quotes historian Aileen Kraditor as asserting "Men... have always been human beings who happened to be male. Women, on the contrary... have been thought of as females who happened to be human." Seggar, on the other hand, concluded from his study of female roles that progress had been made in the imagery of the female, citing among other facts that the number of drama roles for females had increased, and that women were more often shown working in professional capacities than was true in 1971. He makes the comment (Seggar, 1975b, p. 281) "One of the major concerns of feminists is a belief that women are kept in subordinate roles in TV drama programs. However, in this study, of the 199 roles in which females were interacting with males, 67 (33%) females were found in the interaction pattern to be superordinate; that is, they were telling, commanding, giving orders, directing, or counseling males. Eighty-nine (43%) were shown equal to their male counter-parts and 43 (24%) were found to be subordinate." Seggar (1975b, p. 278) also asserted "As long as women are anatomically different and have distinguishable hair styles and clothes, their femininity is likely to keep them in a sexist category." Ensuing rebuttal from both investigators suggests that neither changed his/ her mind.

While television commercials have been excluded from the coverage of this review, four studies, those of Lull et al. (1977), Verna (1975) O'Donnell (1978), and Maracek et al., (1978) contrasting the presentation of men and women on commercials, make a pertinent point. They found that a *male* voice was used to sell products and that the male person was explicitly or implicitly the authority figure. English (1978a) and Northrop (1977) feel that the stereotype of male and authoritativeness will be modified in the future; English, because more and more women are moving into television power positions as writers, producers, directors, and executives, and Northrop, because of the increasing number of shows in which·women participate as human beings with a serious purpose. On the other hand, Harwood (1976) found that earnings of men in media occupations were, overall, about twice that of women. Harwood also found that, for authors and for radio and television announcers, the median age for women was *older* than for men; that, while 35 percent of the men and 33 percent of the women had completed at least 4 years of college, earnings *per school year completed* were more than twice as high for men than for women. Whittaker (1976) in a study of the relative effectiveness of male and female newscasters, found no difference reported in the believability of the news recounted by a male or female voice.

Observation of male "leads" at the beginning of 1979 indicates that, while "toughness" is still a primary requisite for male leadership, the female "second leads" often exercise a predominating action leadership. Mrs. Pynchon, owner of the newspaper which employs Lou Grant as editor, exercises real power over, and is respected by, her staff. (Mrs. Pynchon is also portrayed as an effectively aging female.) "Hot Lips," of M*A*S*H, retains her identity while interacting with an otherwise all-male cast. The black woman assistant principal of "White Shadow" is shown as giving advice to, and assisting in the solving of the problems of, Coach Reeves. The archetypal mothers of the prime time's full-membered family shows ("All in the Family," "Little House on the Prairie," "Happy Days," "Eight is Enough," "The Jeffersons," "The Waltons," and "Family") tend to be super-virtuous, but, still, they are portrayed as indispensable to the families of which they form an essential part, and as providing leadership.

Stocking et al. (1977) studied sex discrimination in prime time humor. They found males to be the butt of both male and female jokesters far more often than the female—but males were also more often the disparagers. Males disparaged males, but females did not disparge females. Only in sexual humor was the female disparaged as often as the male.

A summary statement of male–female imagery is that of Tedesco (1975, 4092-A) who says, "The image of femininity revealed in this analysis of characterizations is one of passivity; overall, females are married, portray comical roles, are unemployed, are young, and neither successful nor unsuccessful. They are attractive and warm, but also powerless and stupid. Females generally lack independence and are missing when adventures take place. Moreover, they are more likely to be victimized than commit violence, and are less likely to be bad.

"The image of masculinity in television drama is, in many respects, just the opposite of that of femininity. Males are active and independent; they are older, portray serious roles, are employed, have adventures, and are more likely to be involved in violence. Males are active, powerful, and smart while also fairly attractive and warm. However, their independence requires that they remain unattached (not married) and thus are able to take risks."

Underlying studies of the image of women and male–female comparisons is a concern for the reaction of the viewer to the media portryal. Kaniuga et al. (1976) examined the depiction of working women on evening television programs. Gainful employment, they found was not shown as a primary life style for women; TV women employed tended to be professionals, not complete artisans or factory workers. While Filoso (1974) found that adolescent females were able to perceive that television is different from the real world, Manes and Melnyk (1974), in a study of televised models of female achievement, found that all working women shown were portrayed as unsuccessfully married. The majority of Filoso's subjects' real world models were married, whereas their female television character models tended to be single and fall into a career work status. Marriage, on television drama, did not appear to be depicted nor perceived as compatible with employment effectiveness.

Wiebe (1970), in a study of psychological factors in media audience behavior, asks why programs with potentially dystonic material continue to attract huge followings. He finds two factors, one, a resistence to change except under conditions not characteristic of mass media; and, second, "reluctance to cope with 'the other.'" Gutman (1973) employed the latter concept in an examination of self-concepts and television viewing among women. Viewing television is a parasocial act, in which a response appears to have been evoked from the performer without the viewer having had to exert any effort to evoke one. Gutman found that heavy viewers identified themselves as more sociable and possessing lower self-esteem than light viewers, the latter perceiving themselves as less passive and more desirous of achievement through their own efforts.

One might be tempted to conclude that the female viewer who is most likely to place herself under the influence of the pejorative female image on prime time television is also the more easily encouraged not to break away from stereotyped behavior. However, Marting (1973) using "600 subjects of diverse demography" found that the images of male and female dramatic characters in prime time TV drama were perceived as different from the images of males and females in real life and that prime time drama does not reflect a mirror image of males and females in real life.

Dembo (1973) found, in a study of gratifications found in media by British teenage boys, that non-aggressive youngsters with a high dependence on peer culture tended to be media-oriented, talking more often to their friends about their media experience than aggressive boys. Dembo did *not* find a relationship between aggressive behavior and exposure to TV violence, and points out that effects of television are mediated by the social milieu through which mass media are experienced. Dembo (1973, p. 525) states "The thrust of the English research results argue it is vital to see agression and non-aggression as representing the youths' adjustments to their neighborhood as they perceive it." On the other hand, Gorney et al. (1977), studying the impact of dramatized television entertainment on adult males, conducted an investigation in which two groups of men were observed at home, one group having been instructed to watch a week of "helpful" programs and the other, seven days of "hurtful" dramas. A significant decrease in aggressive mood and lower levels of hurtful behavior was observed in viewers of helpful programs as compared with a control group, along with some evidence that emotional arousal in response to helpful programs is negatively correlated with aggressive mood. Rogers (1978) feels that the effects of what is seen on television drama is the result as much as what apperceptions the viewer brings to the medium, as it is a consequence of the material presented. As Busby (1975) points out, the sex of the viewer will influence what he or she selects to watch although Busby also reminds us that most media gatekeepers are male.

Busby's thorough overview and summary of sex-role research in the mass media underlines the comment made earlier that male roles, considered other than in relation to female roles, have not yet been examined in depth, particularly with respect to various aspects of males vis-a-vis other males. The many studies done on the image of women by necessity include the male image; but the male image is held up as a sort of "norm" against which the female image is compared. Whetmore (1976, p. 1283-A) cites an example of the use of the concept "androgny," rather than "masculinity" or "femininity" in the measurement of sex role perception in television situation comedies, explaining that the androgny rating model "evolved from a theoretical commitment to the belief that each person has a masculine and feminine set of personality traits, and that the capacity of one set need not necessarily limit the capacity of the other". Whetmore found, however, that popular male and female drama characters (Edith Bunker, Joe Gerrard) were judged to exhibit what the research participants labeled "sex-appropriate" behavior. It might be inferred that stereotype serves a useful function in defining fictional players.

Male leads listed in Tables I, II, and III tend to fall into four categories: the superheroes, the anti-heroes, the comedians, and the ostensibly real. Respective examples of each might be Adama of "Battlestar Galactica" Blotto of "Delta House," Fonzie of "Happy Days," and Doug of "Family." One quality they all share is the power to influence others, mainly by charisma. One can ony speculate on the perception of "Fonzie" by the lonely, inarticulate teen-age boy, who has trouble with authority figures and for whom girls do *not* jump at the snap of the fingers. At the same time, Coach Reeves, experiencing difficulties in dealing with the potential homosexuality of one of his team players (together with Reeves' seeking the help and advice of two female associates), conveyed a ring of authenticity.

Women characters on prime time television drama, who, as is evident from Table I, II, and III, usually do not play chief protagonist roles, may almost be divided into two categories: Lilith and Eve. Strong Louise of "The Jeffersons," Elizabeth of "The Waltons," Laura of "Little House on the Prairie," Hot Lips of "M*A*S*H," and Billie of "Lou Grant" are all essentially "good" women (Eve), shown as supporting and encouraging others, chiefly men. Lisa, Marcy, Pam, the three airline stewardesses of "Flying High," and Sabrina, Kelly and Kris of "Charlie's Angels" are all representative of the 1979 television drama's portrayal of a sexually provocative woman (Lilith): tall, thin, young, with pretty faces, bountiful hair, and apparently incapable of independent thought or independent action, since they defer to a man (or a man's voice) for decision. Not since "Mary" of the "Mary Tyler Moore" show has a continuing series portrayed a woman in a leading role who conveyed independence and individuality. Single parents and divorcees are shown as comic figures, getting into "scrapes," concerned with relatively parochial concerns, and, on the whole, devoted to interpersonal relationships and interested in being attractive to men. (This is not to say that the men are shown as *not* interested in being attractive to women. The assumption of the television drama is that they are, without having to concern themselves about the issue, that romance is secondary to their work and; that they have actual or potential women partners "on tap." As a matter of fact, the Steve McGarrett—Starsky and Hutch type of hero is almost never shown in sexually-toned interaction; they are somewhat like the "pure" Western heroes of another era.)

Scattered among prime time television drama programs are instances of interesting, individualistic women; but there is not the range of characterization shown as is the case for men. The male "loner," for example, has no female counterpart. Such portrayals as Dr. David Banner, of "The Incredible Hulk," Steve McGarrett, of "Hawaii 5-0," and, in past years, Paladin of "Have Gun-Will Travel" depict a man, without antecedents or living relatives, who floats in and out of people's lives, effecting permanent changes to such lives, but never committing himself to any of the potentially close relationships offered to him. These men, to whom Weibel (1975) refers to as "super-heroes," enjoy prestigious occupations, are passionately devoted to truth and justice, command fanatical loyalty from their followers, are themselves unimpeachable and invincible, yet not bound to any living human being.

D. The Two Worlds of Prime Time Television Drama

There appear to be some aspects of prime time drama which are, broadly speaking, common throughout all prime time drama. The most obvious pervading element is the great disparity of portrayal between men and women. Men outnumber women; they are the leaders; they are, in general, older than prime time women; they do not marry as often; they occupy more prestigious occupations; they are more often the criminals; they are not exploited as sexual provocateurs; they remain effective as they grow old; they are human beings.

Second, crime, its detection and resolution, forms a major motif of dramatic shows, with 12 hour-long shows (as of the beginning of 1979) being detective or mystery dramas. Violence, while ostensibly lessened in incidence because of public pressures, still occurs so often and is depicted in such a manner that Gerbner (1975) feels that the quality of its portrayal serves to produce a feeling of fear and helplessness in viewers—an apprehension of potential victimization.

Third, black individuals are not only under-represented, but tend to be found mainly in comedy, particularly black situation comedy, as "What's happening?" "Good Times," "The Jeffersons," "Diff'rent Strokes." The very names suggest a humorous point of view. Black writers, directors, and producers are few (Sklar, 1978), so that their effect on television programming is therefore minimal.

Fourth, mature, sensitive, realistic portrayals of sex and love on prime television drama are rare. Sex, since it is difficult to handle well, is treated facetiously. Explicit sexual behavior is not so often shown as hinted at; innuendo is common. Sex is at once depicted as a very amusing area of life—and at the same time as a primary preoccupation for all men and women. Love, with its complexities, is, as a whole handled minimally by commercial prime time drama.

Last, there appears to exist a range of quality among prime time television dramatic shows. Admittedly, this is a qualitative judgment on which opinion varies; but consideration of television drama at its best as contrasted with the same vehicle at its worst—together with the undisputable fact that most Americans are spending major portions of their waking life watching television and being exposed to its messages, explicit and implicit—is a factor worthy of concern. A medium which can produce "Little House on the Prairie," "Family," "Paper Chase," "Lou Grant," and which has, upon occasion, shown on one broadcast a play of Shakespeare to more viewers than had previously seen the drama in all the hundreds of years prior to the single broadcast, can also make available, to millions of viewers "The $1.98 Beauty Show," "Soap," and "Charlie's Angels." Since, however, quality is a matter of opinion, little can be asserted other than that what might be termed "better" and "worse" material shown on prime time ranges to a far greater extent than on daytime television serials.

The fact that prime television drama does not appear to have the coherence, homogeneity, clarity, and uniformity of daytime television serial drama leads the present reviewer to suggest that prime time drama is projecting, not one, but at least two, symbolic worlds.

The first might be an ideal world, a world to which the human being might aspire, a world which might be labelled the "adult's world." The choice of examples may vary according to the point of view of the chooser, since a drama which might seem "true to life" to one viewer may prove dystonic to another. However, the present investigator will risk the conjecture that "The Waltons," "Family," "Eight is Enough," "The Paper Chase," "Little House on the Prairie," and "Lou Grant" all represent shows which attempt to deal with real problems in a mature way, and contain characters which give some impression of depth and multidimensionality.[6]

The second, and larger, world of prime time drama is that into which the viewer can escape, which might be called the "adolescent's world. Here are the fantasies, the adventure stories, the comedies, and all of the good vs. evil morality tales. Here the viewer can become a macho hero of "Chips," a passenger assured of romance on "The Love Boat," a winner of

---

[6]Caution must be exercised in making subjective judgments of this sort. Years ago, the show "Father Knows Best" gave great distress to at least one teenager because of the idealistic father–son relationship depicted, a relationship which contrasted strongly with the adolescent viewer's own experience.

"Sweepstake," a powerful changeling like "The Incredible Hulk," an irresponsible, care-free adolescent of "Delta House," "Billy," "Flatbush," "Happy Days," or "Brothers and Sisters," or a female sexual provocateur a la "Charlie's Angels" or any of the beautiful women who serve as the only female figure in an otherwise all-male cast. The question of whether or not this second world of prime time drama provides catharsis, escape, or provocation is outside the scope of this report. The point to be made here is that prime time drama seems to range along a continuum of types, with some fairly distinct polarities at either end.

IV.   ATTRIBUTES COMMON TO DAYTIME AND PRIME TIME TELEVISION DRAMA

While the foregoing discussion reveals differences between daytime serial drama and prime time drama of so distinct a nature that each genre must be looked at separately, certain characteristics are common to all television drama.

The first is television drama's pervasive conservatism. Rubens (1978) has called television "the most conservative of the media," and few researchers fail to refer to television drama's "conventional morality." Television does reflect change—the family situation comedy of the 1950s has partially yielded to the single-parent "comedy" of the 1970s—but television follows changes in societal attitudes; it does not lead. Television drama is not innovative, but tends, rather, to lag behind trends of the larger society.

What is the function of commercial television? To sell products to consumers by inserting advertisements in entertainment offerings. Television dramas are vehicles for the display of products. It might be conjectured that the conservatism of television drama is in consonance with the attitudes of the greater part of the television audience—and therefore is serving the greatest possible number of potential buyers.

Another factor is the lack of consonance between television drama and reality, if census figures and F.B.I. reports can be cited as examples of "real life" data. Television drama overlooks large segments of the American population, such as the aged and nonwhite members of our society. Crime, which is alive and well in American society, does not pay on television drama. People in television drama are beautiful, slender, clean, healthy, and concerned with emotional rather than practical problems.

The exploitation of sexual attractiveness as a goal for everyone is so ubiquitous on television drama that it is difficult to imagine any player (other than the austere "superhero") repudiating romantic love as a major life goal. The word "love" has ceased to have meaning. (A Philadelphia bank used to run a commercial which sang "Put a little love away," meaning "Make regular deposits in a savings fund for an occasion when you'll need the money.")

Already referred to has been television drama's conventional morality. TV drama is also replete with conventional political and social attitudes, with "conservatives" being the bad guys and "liberals" being the good people. A 1979 drama referred to Anita Bryant's "crusade" against homosexual teachers as a movement which all "good" people would naturally oppose. Another assumption is that only reactionaries would oppose the ratification of the E.R.A. amendment. Obviously, the present investigator is not defending Anita Bryant nor attacking the E.R.A. amendment; only pointing out that such black/white thinking is inserted into television drama as the natural, obvious way all citizens *should,* or, in fact, do, believe. Difficult, complex social and political issues are presented as simple, as having once-for-all solutions, and as capable of being conceptualized in "right" or "wrong" terms.

V.   TELEVISION AS A MEDIUM OF COMMUNICATION

A factor common to all television is the power of the medium itself, and of the techniques which it employs. The television medium, *qua* medium, is able to make commentary in a way nonvisual media cannot. Greene and Hoats (1969) and Wurtzel and Dominick (1971), among others, call attention to the physical properties of television, and particularly to shot selection and camera focus. In the 1968 Democratic National Convention, the camera continually focussed on dissident participants, strife, and evidence of discord and disharmony. More recently, a drama ostensibly laid in Chapel Hill, North Carolina, showed chiefly the garbage cans of the back alleys and the city dump, ignoring the environs of the University of North Carolina entirely. Camera focus on breasts, hips and legs of women constitutes describing women in terms of physical characteristics. Close-ups immediately inform the viewer, "This is an object or person of total importance."

Dumont (1976, p. 457), a psychiatrist, calling attention to the "incessant changes of camera and focus" on television, suggested that the "constant shifting of visual frames in television shows is related to the hyperkinetic syndrome" of children. Dumont feels that these rapid changes of camera focus "literally program a short attention span and probably account for the almost hypnotic attraction television has for most of us."

While the motion picture film also employs a camera capable of selection, exaggeration, and distortion, there are crucial differences between viewing a film in a movie theatre and watching a drama on a television set. The former is at least a quasi-social act, while television can be viewed without any other human being present. The movie drama does not purport to be a news program, while the human interest dramas labelled, "Evening News," are presented as the truth of the day (cf., Epstein, 1974). But most important of all is the totalness of television for most of the American public. Haden-Guest (1977) describing a group interview of researchers on the show *Not for Women Only* quotes Marshall McLuhan quipping, "If you wish to retain the American Way of life, it (TV) should be turned off *totally.*" George Gerbner, long the leading investigator of violence on television, was asked how the importance of television compared with the family, or the president of the United States. Gerbner is quoted as saying "They are not competitive anymore. Television has won."

Gerbner further told Haden–Guest (1977, p. 34) "What we have to ask is this: Is television just another medium? I think it isn't. People are born into a television room. They absorb it before they can speak, let alone read. They use it nonselectively. It has become a collective responsibility, and should be handled not as books and films are handled but as religion is handled.

"It has become a centralized process, with its myths and rituals in a seamless whole. Separating news from drama or entertainment is like separating the sermon from the hymns you sing. The historic nexus of power, church, and state has been replaced by another; television and state."

A somewhat different point of view is taken by researchers who feel that the ubiquity and power of television must be considered in the the light of other social factors. To begin with, as Robinson (1975), among others, has found, the television audience is not a homogeneous mass of uncritical consumers. Robinson, (1975, p. 195) commenting on the point that "Audience research has consistently shown that highly educated, professional, urban, upper-middle income people are unenthusiastic, if not scornful, TV and film viewers," suggests that demographic data in themselves do not discriminate among types of people who may have different attitudes toward television, but exist within the specified demographically-described class. Robinson examined a group of upper-middle-class viewers, and found that television behavior differed for what she termed "Information Absorbers" and "Community Leaders" (cf. Dembo's (1973) groups of passive and active teenagers). The former watched twice as much television as the latter, although both groups preferred public television programs to the light entertainment programs on educational television. Individuals with a positive attitude toward viewing television were very careful about what they chose to watch and used selection sources other than just the local newspaper and film pages; in other words, they planned their viewing in advance and were more likely to analyze television content and technique than negatively-oriented peers. Robinson further states, "Occupation seemed to be an important variable in media behavior and attitude...This variable was probably compounded by time availability."

VI.   FINAL COMMENT

Since television drama serves as a showcase for commercial advertising, it is tempting to conclude that the distortions and inequities of the world of television drama result from the medium's preoccupation with selling products to those most able and likely to buy. Old people, one might insist, have little clout in the market place and are therefore not a lucrative audience toward which to aim dramatic content.

Certainly there are large segments of the American population who would appear to find little with which to identify on American television drama. Included among such groups might be middle-class black persons; single, older women; persons whose physical appearance does not fit the current mass media standard of beauty; anyone over sixty-five years of age; men who are neither powerful nor totally ineffectual; and a large amorphous body of men and women whose lives contain tragedy, some happiness, little distinction, and a minimum of excitement.

The addiction of Americans to television is almost total. Why? What do people find there? What are they looking for? Certainly, for the most part, not themselves.

Early in 1979, a pastiche was broadcast entitled, "Heroes of Rock and Roll." To the present investigator, the interest of the telecast lay not in the segments allotted to the various musical performers, but to the camera's study of the behavior of the audience. Weeping, screaming, fainting, attempts to lay hands on the performers, expressions of adulation ("He's just the greatest!, He's so gorgeously ugly!") suggest that the anonymous individuals who make up the mobs of admirers are looking for something, anything, anybody to believe in.

And so, as the relatively powerless, harrassed member of the audience turns on "The Incredible Hulk," to find out what concrete-and-steel structure the Creature will demolish this week, he (or, as a matter of fact, she) gains a sense of power by vicarious participation in the destruction. Each member of the audience has control over what he will watch; he can turn the set off or on, and he can direct his attention from channel to channel.

Were one to reduce all the characteristics of the players of television drama to a very few general traits, one might conjecture that all players fall into one of a limited number of categories:

The powerful male leader
The beautiful woman
The evil one
The buffoon
The followers

The present reviewer suggests that television drama of 1979, like all fiction, revolves about motifs that are as old as story-telling itself. Good vs. evil, with the God-like, all powerful make as the deliverer and protector of the weak and helpless; the struggle for power, and the maintenance of supremacy once attained; laughter, with its relief of tensions and hostilities; sexual emotion, providing confusion, torment, and delight; the fulfillment of daydreams; and, above all, answers (whether right or wrong) to the troubling question of the meaning of life itself.

REFERENCES

Aronoff, C. (1974). Old age in prime time. *Journal of Communication 24* (No. 4), 86–87.

Baran, S. J. (1976a). How TV and film portrayals affect sexual satisfaction in college students. *Journalism Quarterly 53*, 468–473.

Baran, S. J. (1976b). Sex on TV and adolescent sexual self-image. *Journal of Broadcasting 20*, 61–67.

Blumler, J. G., Brown, J. R., and McQuail, D. (1970). "The Social Origins of the Gratifications Associated with Television Viewing." Center for Television Research of the University of Leeds, Leeds, England. (Social Science Research Council Report.)

Busby, L. J. (1975). Sex-role research on the mass media. *Journal of Communication 25* (No. 4), 107–131.

Cantor, J. R. Humor on television: A content analysis. *Journal of Broadcasting 20*, 501–509.

Daytime television's male call—ARB (1965). *Media/Scope* (March), 76.

Dembo, R. (1973). Gratifications found in media by British teenage boys. *Journalism Quarterly 50*, 517–526.

Dominick, J. R. (1973). Crime and law enforcement on prime-time television. *Public Opinion Quarterly 37*, 241–250.

Donagher, P., Poulos, R. W., Liebert, R. M., and Davidson, E. (1975). Race, sex and social example: An analysis of character portrayals in interracial television entertainment. *Psychological Reports 37*, 1023–1034.

Downing, M. H. (1974). Heroine of the daytime serial. *Journal of Communication 24* (No. 2), 130–137.

Dumont, M. P. (1976). Focusing on television. *American Journal of Psychiatry 133*, 457.

English, D. (1978a). The sex that sells... *Vogue 168* (Jan.), 40.

English, D. (1978b). A woman's point of view. *Vogue 168* (Aug.), 48.

Epstein, E. (1974). "News from Nowhere: Television and the News." Random House, New York.

Feldman, C., and Tickton, S. (1976). Obscene/indecent programming: Regulation of ambiguity. *Journal of Broadcasting 20*, 273–281.

Fernandez-Collado, C., Greenberg, B. S., Korzenny, F., and Atkin, C. K. (1978). Sexual intimacy and drug use in TV series. *Journal of Communication 28* (No. 3), 30–37.

Filoso, K. (1974). "Female Adolescents' Perceptions of Self, of Their Television Fictional Role Models, and of Their Real World Role Models: An Exploratory Study." Unpublished dissertation, Ohio State University.

Fischer, R. L. (1978). Television drops the other shoe—sex replaces violence. *USA Today* (July), 48–50.

Franzblau, S., Sprafkin, J. N., and Rubinstein, E. A. (1977). Sex on TV: A content analysis. *Journal of Communication 27* (No. 2), 164–170.

Gerbner, G. (1972). Violence in television drama: Trends and symbolic functions. *In* "Television and Social Behaviour" (G. A. Comstock and E. A. Rubenstein, Eds.), Vol. 1, pp. 28–187. U.S. Department of Health, Education and Welfare, Washington, D.C.

Gerbner, G. (1975). Scenario for violence. *Human Behavior 4* (Oct.), 64.

Gerbner, G., and Gross, L. (1976). Living with television: The violence profile. *Journal of Communication 26* (No. 2), 172–199.

Gorney, R., Loye, D., and Steele, G. (1977). Impact of dramatized television entertainment on adult males. *American Journal of Psychiatry 134,* 170–174.

Greene, R. J., and Hoats, D. L. (1969). Reinforcing capabilities of television distortion. *Journal of Applied Behavior Analysis 2,* 139–141.

Gutman, J. (1973). Self-concepts and television viewing among women. *Public Opinion Quarterly 37,* 388–397.

Haden–Guest, A. (1977). The man who's selling TV violence. *New York 10* (No. 28), 33–36.

Harris, A. J., and Feinberg, J. F. (1977). Television and aging: Is what you see what you get? *Gerontologist 17,* 464–468.

Harwood, K. (1976). Earnings and education of men and women in selected media occupations. *Journals of Broadcasting 20,* 232–237.

Herzog, H. (1944). What do we really know about daytime serial listeners. *In* "Radio Research, 1942–43" (P. F. Lazarsfeld and F. Stanton, Eds.), pp. 3–33. Duell, Sloan and Pearce, New York.

Hofeldt, R. L. (1978). Cultural bias in M*A*S*H. *Society 15* (No. 5), 96–99.

Horton, D., and Wohl, R. (1956). Mass communication and parasocial interaction: Observations on intimacy at a distance. *Psychiatry 19,* 215–229.

Kaniuga, H., Scott, T., and Gade, E. (1976). Working women portrayed on evening television programs. *Vocational Guidance Quarterly 25,* 134–136.

Katzman, N. (1972). Television soap operas: What's been going on anyway? *Public Opinion Quarterly 36,* 200–212.

Kaufman, H. J. (1944). The appeal of specific daytime serials. In "Radio Research 1942–43" (P. F. Lazarsfeld and F. Stanton, Eds.), pp. 86–107. Duell, Sloan and Pearce, New York.

Kitman, M. (1978). TV's sex problem. *New Leader 61* (March 13), 25–26.

Kubey, R. W. (1977). Television and the elderly: A critical review. *Gerontologist 17,* 84.

Lang, K. (1957). Mass appeal and minority taste. *In* "Mass Culture" (B. Rosenberg and D. White, Eds.), pp. 379–387. Free Press of Glencoe, London.

Levine, R. M. (1978). Roots and branches. *New Times 11* (Sept. 4), 54–57.

Lopate, C. (1977). Daytime television: You'll never want to leave home. *Radical America 11* (No. 1), 33–51.

Lull, J. T., Hanson, C. A., and Marx, M. J. (1977). Recognition of female stereotypes in TV commercials. *Journalism Quarterly 54,* 153–157.

McNeil. J. C. (1975a). Feminism, femininity, and the television series: A content analysis. *Journal of Broadcasting 19,* 259–271.

McNeil, J. C. (1975b). Imagery of woman in TV drama: Some procedural and interpretive issues. *Journal of Broadcasting 19,* 283–288.

McNeil, J. C. (1975c). Whose values? *Journal of Broadcasting 19,* 295–296.

Manes, A. L., and Melnyk, P. (1974). Televised models of female achievement. *Journal of Applied Social Psychology 4,* 365–374.

Mann, J. (1977). More sex, less violence: TV's new pitch. *U.S. News and World Report* (Sept. 12), 20–23.

Marecek, J., and Piliavin, J. A., Fitzsimmons, E., Krogh, E. C., Leader, E., and Trudell, B. (1978). Women as TV experts: The voice of authority? *Journal of Communication 28* (No. 1), 159–168.

Mariani, J. (1978). Everybody loves to hate those sultry sirens of the daytime soaps. *Family Weekly* (Nov. 5), 4–5.

Marting, L. P. (1973). "An Empirical Study of the Images of Males and Females During Prime-Time Television Drama." Unpublished dissertation, Ohio State University.

Mathewson, W. (1979). When we left you all was in turmoil on "One Life to Live." *Wall Street Journal* (Feb. 23), 1.

Maykovich, M. K. (1975). Comparison of soap opera families in Japan and the United States. *International Journal of Sociology of the Family 5*, 135–149.

Nessen, R. (1978). Prudes in the press. *Newsweek* (Nov. 6), 25.

Nicholas, K., McCarter, E., and Heckel, R. V. (1971). The effects of race and sex on the imitation of television models. *Journals of Social Psychology 85*, 315–316.

Nielson, A. C. (1979). Viewers in profile. *Demographic Sweep Reports* (Feb.), 10.

Northrop, A. (1977). This may be the year to stay tuned. *MS 7* (Dec.), 44–45, 99.

O'Donnell, W. J., and O'Donnell, K. J. (1978). Update: Sex-role messages in TV commercials. *Journal of Communication 28* (No. 1), 156–158.

Petersen, M. (1973). The visibility and image of old people on television. *Journalism Quarterly 50*, 569–573.

Pierce, P. (1973). Souping up the soap operas. *McCall's 100* (June), 39.

Posey, G. (1978). Three's company: Why is this man smiling? *Saturday Evening Post 250* (No. 6), 62–63.

Ramsdell, M. L. (1973). The trauma of TV's troubled soap families. *The Family Coordinator 22*, 299–304.

Robinson, D. C. (1975). Television/film attitudes of upper-middle class professionals. *Journal of Broadcasting 19*, 195–209.

Rogers, F. (1978). What do you bring to TV? *Saturday Evening Post 250* (No. 6), 50–51.

Rosen, M. (1977). "Farrah Fawcett–Majors Makes Me Want to Scream?" A look at TV sex: Charlie's Angels, Police Woman—and now, Soap. *Redbook Magazine* 149 (Sept.), 102–109.

Ross, L. (1976). Les representations du social dans les teleromans Quebecois. *Communication et Information 1*, 215, 230.

Rubens, W. S. (1978). Sex on television, more or less. The most conservative of the media. *Vital Speeches of the Day 44*, 171–174.

Seggar, J. F. (1975a). Imagery as reflected through TV's cracked mirror. *Journal of Broadcasting 19*, 297–299.

Seggar, J. F. (1975b). Imagery of women in television drama: 1974. *Journal of Broadcasting 19*, 273–282.

Seggar, J. F. (1975c). Women's imagery on TV: Feminist, fair maiden, or maid?: Comments on McNeil. *Journal of Broadcasting 19*, 289–293.

Seggar, J. F. (1977). Television's portrayal of minorities and women, 1971–1975. *Journal of Broadcasting 21*, 435–445.

Seggar, J. F., and Wheeler, P. (1973). World of work on TV: Ethnic and sex representation in TV drama. *Journal of Broadcasting 17*, 201–214.

Sklar, R. (1978a). The family on TV. *Horizon 21* (Aug.), 77–79.

Sklar, R. (1978b). Is television taking blacks seriously. *American Film* (Sept.), 25–29.

Stedman, R. W. (1977). "The Serials: Suspense and Drama by Installment." University of Oklahoma Press, Norman, Oklahoma.

Stein, F. (1979). Here's why life on TV is so different from reality. *TV Guide 27* (No. 3), 4–10.

Stocking, S. H., Sapalsky, B. S., and Zillmann, D. (1977). Sex discrimination in prime time humor. *Journal of Broadcasting 21*, 447–457.

Tedesco, N. S. (1974). Patterns in prime time. *Journal of Communication 24* (No. 2), 119–124.

Tedesco, N. S. (1975). "Men and Women in Television Drama: The Use of Two Multivariate Techniques for Isolating Dimensions of Characterization." *Dissertation Abstracts International 36A* (No. 7), 4092–A.

Thornton, L. R. (1976). "A Correlation Study of the Relationship Between Human Values and Broadcast Television." Unpublished dissertation, Michigan State University.

Treaster, J. B. (1978). Belting out the blues at 83. *Quest/78 2* (No. 5), 23, 30.

Turow, J. (1974). Advising and ordering: Daytime, prime time. *Journal of Communication 24* (No. 2), 138–141.

U. S. Bureau of Labor Statistics (1974). *Employment and Earnings 20* (No. 7), 27, 29, 37.

U. S. Bureau of Labor Statistics (1978). *Employment and Earnings 25* (No. 10), 48.

U. S. Bureau of the Census. (1977). "Statistical Abstract of the United States." Government Printing Office, Washington, D.C.

Verna, M. E. (1975). The female image in children's TV commercials. *Journal of Broadcasting 19*, 301–309.

Wallis, R. (1978). Recruiting Christina Manpower: Sex as a lure. *Society 15* (No. 4), 72–74.

Waters, H. F. (1978a). How TV treats cancer. *Newsweek 92* (No. 20), 131–132.

Waters, H. F. (1978b). Sex and TV. *Newsweek 91* (No. 8), 54–61.

Weibel, K. P. (1975). "Life Styles and Ethical Values of Men and Women on Television, 1960–1974." Unpublished dissertation, Michigan State University.

Whetmore, E. J. (1976). Androgyny and sex role perception in television situation comedies. *Dissertation Abstracts International 37A* (No. 3), 1283A.

Whitehead, P. C. (1970). Sex, violence, and crime in the mass/media. *Canada's Mental Health 18* (No. 2), 20–23.

Whittaker, S., and Whittaker, R. (1976). Relative effectiveness of male and female newscasters. *Journal of Broadcasting 21*, 177–184.

Wiebe, G. D. (1970). Two psychological factors in media audience behavior. *Public Opinion Quarterly 33*, 523–536.

Wimmer, R. D. (1976). Mass media and the older voter: 1972. *Journal of Broadcasting 20*, 313–322.

Wurtzel, A. H., and Dominick, J. R. (1971). Evaluation of television drama: Interaction of acting styles and shot selection. *Journal of Broadcasting 16*, 103–111.

Author Index

Numbers in *italics* indicate where complete references are listed.

Subject Index